Severe Personality Disorders

Severe Personality Disorders:
Psychotherapeutic Strategies

OTTO KERNBERG

Yale University Press   *New Haven and London*

Gratitude for permission to reprint material
is expressed in the acknowledgments.

Published with assistance from the
Louis Stern Memorial Fund.

Designed by James J. Johnson
and set in Palatino Roman.
Printed in the United States of America by
Vail-Ballou Press, Binghamton, New York.

The paper in this book meets the guidelines for permanence
and durability of the Committee on Production Guidelines
for Book Longevity of the Council on Library Resources.

Library of Congress Cataloging in Publication Data

Kernberg, Otto F., 1928-
    Severe personality disorders.

    Bibliography: p.
    Includes index.
    1. Personality, Disorders of. 2. Borderline personality disorder. 3. Narcissism.
I. Title. [DNLM: 1. Narcissism. 2. Personality Disorders—diagnosis. 3. Personal-
ity Disorders—therapy. 4. Psychotherapy—methods. WM 190 K39s]
RC554.K47 1984   616.85'8   84-40197
ISBN 0-300-03273-0

10 9 8 7 6 5 4

Contents

Preface

My aims in this book are twofold. The first is to present extensions of the findings and formulations contained in my previous work, with special emphasis on the diagnostic and treatment aspects of severe cases of borderline and narcissistic pathology. The second is to explore other recent developments regarding these issues in the field of clinical psychiatry and psychoanalysis and to review them critically in the light of my present thinking. A major concern reflected throughout the book is the wish to make my theoretical formulations clinically relevant and, particularly, to provide the clinician with technical tools to diagnose and treat the difficult case.

To this end, I begin by trying to reduce confusion in a most difficult area by describing a specific mode of differential diagnosis and a technique for conducting what I call a structural diagnostic interview. I also establish links between that technique and the criteria for prognosis and type of treatment most appropriate for each case.

I then detail treatment strategies for borderline patients, giving particular attention to the severest cases. In this section of the book I include a systematic examination of expressive and supportive psychotherapy, both stemming from a psychoanalytic frame.

In several chapters on the treatment of narcissistic pathology I focus on developments in technique that I have found useful in dealing with severe and pervasive character resistances.

Another troublesome treatment area is the management of the unresponsive or otherwise difficult patient: how to cope with stalemates in treatment, how to handle patients who persistently threaten suicide, how to differentiate treatable from untreatable antisocial patients, how to respond to patients with paranoid regressions in the transference that seem to verge on the psychotic. These are some of the questions dealt with in part four.

Finally, I offer a model of hospital treatment, based on but somewhat different from earlier therapeutic-community models of treatment for patients requiring extended hospitalization.

This book, then, is largely clinical. My aim is to provide the psychotherapist and psychoanalyst with a broad armamentarium of specific psychotherapeutic techniques. At the same time, within the context of relevant clinical data, I elaborate on my previous theoretical contributions regarding the psychopathology of ego weakness and identity diffusion with new hypotheses concerning severe superego pathology. This volume, therefore, contains the latest developments in ego psychology and object relations theory.

Acknowledgments

The theoretical elaborations referred to in the preface rely heavily on the work of the late Edith Jacobson. Her formulations and Margaret Mahler's creative exploration and application of these formulations to studies of child development continue to inspire my thinking.

A small group of distinguished psychoanalysts and close friends have continued to provide me with challenging critical, yet supportive, feedback, which I have found invaluable. I wish to thank particularly Doctor Ernst Ticho, with whom I have worked collaboratively now for 22 years, and Doctors Martin Bergmann, Harold Blum, Arnold Cooper, William Grossman, Donald Kaplan, Paulina Kernberg, and Robert Michels, all of whom not only have given generously of their time but also have felt free to disagree sharply and point to problems in my formulations.

I also thank Doctors William Frosch and Richard Munich for their critical review of my thinking regarding hospital treatment and the therapeutic community, and Doctors Ann Appelbaum and Arthur Carr for their unending patience with my requests for their help in formulating my ideas more precisely. Finally, I thank Dr. Malcolm Pines for his encouragement of my critique of the therapeutic community and Dr. Robert Wallerstein for his thoughtful critique of my views regarding supportive psychotherapy.

Doctors Stephen Bauer, Arthur Carr, Harold Koenigsberg, John Oldham, Lawrence Rockland, Jessie Schomer, and Michael Selzer, at the Westchester Division of New York Hospital, contributed to the development of the clinical diagnostic methodologies involved in the differential diagnosis of borderline personality organization. More recently, they and Doctors Ann Appelbaum, John Clarkin, Gretchen Haas, Paulina Kernberg, and Andrew Lotterman have contributed to the operational definitions of the differences between expressive and supportive modalities of treatment as part of an ongoing psychotherapy research project on borderline conditions. To all of them I express my gratitude. As before, I need to absolve all these friends, teachers, and colleagues from any responsibility for my formulations.

I am deeply grateful to Mrs. Shirley Grunenthal, Miss Louise Taitt, and Mrs. Jane Carr for their endless patience in typing, revising, proofreading, and organizing the seemingly endless versions of the manuscript. Mrs. Jane Carr particularly, who joined our staff only recently, has displayed remarkable aptitude in carrying out these tasks. Miss Lillian Wahrow, librarian at the Westchester Division of New York Hospital, and her staff, Mrs. Marilyn Bottjer and Mrs. Marcia Miller, provided me with invaluable help in bibliographic research. Finally, Miss Anna-Mae Artim, my administrative assistant, has once again accomplished the impossible. She has coordinated the editorial work and the preparation of the manuscript; she has unerringly anticipated and prevented innumerable possible problems; and, in her cheerful yet unrelenting way, she has managed to meet deadlines and somehow assure completion of this book.

Working, for the first time, with the help of both my editor in recent years, Mrs. Natalie Altman, and the editor at Yale University Press, Ms. Gladys Topkis, I found myself in the highly privileged position of being watched and controlled at every step in my efforts to express my thoughts clearly and in acceptable English. In the process, I often came to suspect them of knowing much more about psychoanalysis, psychiatry, and psychotherapy than I did. I cannot say how extremely grateful I am to both of them.

Permission to reprint material in the following chapters is hereby acknowledged.
Chapter 1: Adapted from "The Structural Diagnosis of Borderline Personality Organization," in *Borderline Personality Disorders*, ed. P. Hartocollis, 1977, pp. 87–122. Published with permission of International Universities Press, Inc.
Chapter 2: Adapted from "Structural Interviewing," *Psychiatric Clinics of North America*, 4: 1, 169–95, 1981; with permission.
Chapter 3: Adapted from "The Diagnosis of Borderline Conditions in Adolescence," *Adolescent Psychiatry*, 6 (1978): 298–319. Copyright © 1978 by The University of Chicago. Published with permission of the University of Chicago Press.
Chapter 4: Adapted from "The Fate of Personality Disorders in Old Age," in *Psychodynamic Research Perspective on Development, Psychopathol-*

ogy, and Treatment in Later Life, ed. N. E. Miller and G. D. Cohen (in press). Published with permission of International Universities Press, Inc.

Chapter 6: Adapted from "The Psychotherapeutic Treatment of Borderline Personalities," in *Psychiatry Update: Volume I,* ed. L. Grinspoon. Washington, D.C.: American Psychiatric Association Press, Inc., 1982. Copyright 1982 American Psychiatric Association. Used with permission.

Chapter 7: Adapted from "Contrasting Approaches to the Psychiatry of Borderline Conditions," in *New Perspectives on Psychotherapy of the Borderline Adult,* ed. J. F. Masterson, 1978, pp. 77–104. Published with permission of Brunner/Mazel.

Chapter 8: Adapted from "Psychoanalytic Psychotherapy with Borderline Adolescents," *Adolescent Psychiatry,* 7 (1979): 294–321. Copyright 1979 by the University of Chicago. Published with permission of University of Chicago Press.

Chapter 9: Adapted from "Supportive Psychotherapy with Borderline Conditions," in *Critical Problems in Psychiatry,* ed. J. O. Cavenar and H. K. Brodie, 1982, pp. 180–202. Published with permission of J. B. Lippincott Company.

Chapter 12: Adapted from "An Ego Psychology and Object Relations Approach to the Narcissistic Personality," in *Psychiatry Update: Volume I,* ed. L. Grinspoon. Washington, D.C.: American Psychiatric Association Press, Inc.,1982. Copyright 1982 American Psychiatric Association. Used with permission.

Chapter 13: Adapted from "Object Relations Theory and Character Analysis," *Journal of the American Psychoanalytic Association,* in press. Published with permission of the Journal of the American Psychoanalytic Association.

Chapter 14: Adapted from "Self, Ego, Affects, and Drives," *Journal of the American Psychoanalytic Association,* 30 (1982): 893–917. Published with permission of the Journal of the American Psychoanalytic Association.

Chapter 15: Adapted from "Structural Change and Its Impediments," in *Borderline Personality Disorders,* ed. P. Hartocollis, 1977, pp. 275–306. Published with permission of International Universities Press, Inc.

Chapter 16: Adapted from "Diagnosis and Clinical Management of Suicide Potential in Borderline Patients," in *The Borderline Patient: Emerging Concepts, Diagnosis, Psychodynamics and Treatment,* ed. James Grotstein, Marion Solomon, and Joan Langs, in press. Published with permission of Lawrence Erlbaum Associates, Inc.

Chapter 20: Adapted from "Psychiatric Hospital Treatment in the United States," *Nordisk Psykiatrist Tidsskrift,* 35, no. 4 (1981): 293–298. Published with permission of Nordisk Psykiatrist Tidsskrift.

Chapter 21: Adapted from "Advantages and Liabilities of Therapeutic Community Models," in *The Individual and the Group*, ed. M. Pines and L. Rafaelson, vol. 1, 1982, pp. 543–565. Published with permission of Plenum Press.

Chapter 22: Adapted from "Some Issues in the Theory of Hospital Treatment," *Tidsskrift for Den Norske Loegeforening*, 14 (1981): 837–843. Published with permission.

PART ONE: *Diagnostic Considerations*

CHAPTER 1: *Structural Diagnosis*

One of the problems plaguing the field of psychiatry has been that of differential diagnosis, especially when the possibility of borderline character pathology exists. Borderline conditions must be differentiated from, on the one hand, the neuroses and neurotic character pathology and, on the other hand, the psychoses, particularly schizophrenia and the major affective disorders.

Both the descriptive approach to diagnosis, which focuses on symptoms and on observable behavior, and the genetic approach, which emphasizes mental disorder in the patient's biological relatives, are valuable, especially with major affective disorders and schizophrenia, but, whether used singly or together, neither has proved sufficiently precise when applied to personality disorders.

I believe that an understanding of the intrapsychic structural characteristics of patients with borderline personality organization, together with criteria stemming from descriptive diagnosis, can result in a vast improvement in diagnostic precision.

Although a structural diagnosis is more difficult to carry out, requires more practice and experience from the clinician, and presents certain methodological difficulties, it has definite advantages, particularly with patients who do not fall easily into one of the major categories of neurotic or psychotic illness.

A descriptive approach with borderline patients may be misleading. For example, several authors (Grinker et al., 1968; Gunderson and Kolb, 1978) have described intense affect, particularly anger and/or depression, as characteristic of borderline patients. However, patients with typical schizoid personalities and borderline personality organization may not present anger or depression at all. The same holds true for some narcissistic personalities who have a typical underlying borderline

3

personality organization. Impulsive behavior has also been described as a common characteristic of borderline patients, but many typical hysterical patients with a neurotic structure also show impulsive behavior. Clinically, therefore, a descriptive approach alone falls short with some borderline cases. These limitations also apply to efforts to arrive at a diagnosis using a purely genetic approach. The study of the possible genetic relations of severe personality disorders to the schizophrenic spectrum and to major affective disorders is still in an early stage, and it may be that important findings are awaiting us in this area. At present, however, the genetic history usually has very little to contribute to the clinical problem of differentiating neurotic, borderline, and psychotic symptomatology. It is possible that a structural approach will contribute to understanding the relation of genetic predisposition to overt symptomatology.

A structural approach may have the additional advantage of bringing into sharper focus the relation between the various symptoms of borderline disorders, particularly the constellations of pathological character traits one so typically finds in this group. As I have pointed out in earlier work (1975, 1976), the structural characteristics of borderline personality organization have important prognostic and therapeutic implications. The quality of object relations and the degree of superego integration are major prognostic criteria for intensive psychotherapy of borderline patients. The nature of the primitive transferences that these patients develop in psychoanalytic psychotherapy and the technique for dealing with them stem directly from the structural characteristics of their internalized object relations. In an even earlier study (Kernberg et al., 1972), we found that nonpsychotic patients with ego weakness responded well to expressive modalities of psychotherapy but poorly to nonmodified psychoanalysis and to supportive psychotherapy.

In short, the addition of the structural approach enriches psychiatric diagnosis, particularly of cases that resist easy classification, and contributes as well to determining prognosis and treatment.

Mental Structures and Personality Organization

The psychoanalytic concept of mental structure first formulated by Freud in 1923 has referred to the postulated division of the psyche into ego, superego, and id. Within psychoanalytic ego psychology, structural analysis has referred to the view (Hartmann et al., 1946; Rapaport and Gill, 1959) that the ego can be conceptualized as (1) slowly changing "structures," or configurations, which determine the channeling of mental processes, (2) the mental processes, or "functions," themselves, and (3) "thresholds" of activation of these functions and configurations. Structures, according to this concept, are relatively stable configurations of mental processes; superego, ego, and id are structures which dynamically integrate substructures, such as the cognitive and defensive configurations of the ego. More recently I have used the term *structural analysis* to describe the relation between the structural derivatives of internalized object relations (Kernberg, 1976) and the various levels of organization of mental functioning. In my view, internalized object relations constitute substructures of the ego, substructures that are, in turn, hierarchically organized (see chap. 14).

Finally, in recent psychoanalytic thinking, structural analysis also refers to the analysis of the permanent organization of the content of unconscious conflicts, particularly to the Oedipus complex as an organizational feature of the mind that has a developmental history, is dynamically organized in the sense that it is more than the sum of its parts and incorporates early experiences and phase-specific drive organizations into a new organization (Panel, 1977). This last conception of mental structures relates to the object relations approach with regard to the structuralization of internalized object relations: The predominant mental contents, such as the Oedipus complex, reflect an organization of internalized object relations. Both recent viewpoints imply hierarchically organized motivational sequences in contrast to purely linear development and a sequence of discontinuous hierarchical organizations rather than a simple genetic one (in a psychoanalytic sense).

I have applied all these structural concepts to the analysis of the predominant intrapsychic structures and instinctual conflicts of borderline patients. I propose the existence of three broad structural organizations corresponding to neurotic, borderline, and psychotic personality organization. In each instance the structural organization performs the function of stabilizing the mental apparatus, mediating between etiological factors and direct behavioral manifestations of illness. Regardless of the genetic, constitutional, biochemical, familial, psychodynamic, or psychosocial factors contributing to the etiology of the illness, the effects of all these factors are eventually reflected in the individual's psychic structure, which then becomes the underlying matrix from which behavioral symptoms develop.

These neurotic, borderline, and psychotic types of organization are reflected in the patient's overriding characteristics, particularly with regard to (1) his degree of identity integration, (2) the types of defensive operations he habitually employs, and (3) his capacity for reality testing. I propose that neurotic personality structure, in contrast to borderline and psychotic structures, implies an integrated identity. Neurotic personality structure presents a defensive organization centering on repression and other advanced or high-level defensive operations. In contrast, borderline and psychotic structures are found in patients showing a predominance of primitive defensive operations centering on the mechanism of splitting. Reality testing is maintained in neurotic and borderline organization but is severely impaired in psychotic organization. These structural criteria can supplement the ordinary behavioral or phenomenological descriptions of patients and sharpen the accuracy of the differential diagnosis of mental illness, especially in cases that are difficult to classify.

Additional structural criteria helpful in differentiating borderline personality organization from the neuroses include the presence or absence of nonspecific manifestations of ego weakness, lack of anxiety tolerance, impulse control, and the capacity for sublimation; and—for the purpose of differential diagnosis of schizophrenia—the presence or absence in the clinical situation of primary-process thinking. Because the nonspecific manifestations of ego weakness are clinically less essential in the differentiation of borderline and neurotic conditions, and because psychological testing rather than clinical interviews may be most helpful in the differentiation of borderline and psychotic cognitive functioning, I am not examining these criteria in detail here. The degree and quality of superego integration are additional prognostically important structural characteristics differentiating neurotic and borderline organization.[1]

The Structural Interview as a Diagnostic Method

The traditional psychiatric interview was modeled after the general medical interview, adapted largely for psychotic and organic patients (Gill et al., 1954). Under the influence of psychoanalytic theory and practice, the emphasis gradually shifted to the patient–interviewer interaction. A more or less standard sequence of questions was replaced with a more flexible evaluation of the predominant problems, focused on the patient's understanding of his conflicts and linking the study of the patient's personality to that of his current behavior in the interview. Karl Menninger's case study (1952) is a good example of this approach.

Whitehorn (1944), Powdermaker (1948), Fromm-Reichmann (1950), and particularly Sullivan (1954) are largely responsible for a modified psychiatric interview that concentrates on the patient–therapist interaction as a major source of information. Gill et al. (1954) designed a new model of psychiatric interviewing that stresses a broad appraisal of the patient and a reinforcement of his desire for help. The nature of the disorder, the motivation and capacity for psychotherapy can be evaluated in the current interaction with the interviewer. This approach to interviewing establishes an immediate link between the patient's psychopa-

---

1. For a review of the literature on descriptive and structural characteristics of the borderline personality, see Kernberg, 1975.

thology and the indication for psychotherapeutic treatment. It also focuses on resistances which will probably become major issues in the early stages of treatment. Because the supportive elements inherent in this approach tend to highlight the patient's assets, however, it may miss certain aspects of the patient's psychopathology.

Deutsch (1949) advocated a psychoanalytic method of interviewing that would reveal the unconscious connections between current problems and the patient's past. From a different theoretical background, Rogers (1951) proposed an interview style that encourages the patient to explore his emotional experiences and the connections among them. These unstructured approaches have the disadvantage of minimizing objective data and do not explore the patient's psychopathology and assets in a systematic fashion.

MacKinnon and Michels (1971) describe a psychoanalytic evaluation that stresses the patient–interviewer interaction. Clinical manifestations of the character patterns the patient demonstrates in the interview are used for diagnostic purposes. This approach yields sophisticated descriptive information within a psychoanalytic framework.

The clinical interviews I have described have become crucial tools in evaluating descriptive and dynamic features, but do not, in my view, permit eliciting the structural criteria that differentiate borderline personality organization. Bellak et al. (1973) developed a structured clinical interview in an attempt to achieve a differential diagnosis between normal subjects, neurotic patients, and schizophrenics on the basis of a structural model of ego functioning. Although their study did not seek to differentiate borderline patients, these authors found significant differences between the three groups on rating scales that evaluated ego structures and functions. Their study illustrates the usefulness of a structural approach to differential diagnosis.

In collaboration with S. Bauer, R. Blumenthal, A. Carr, E. Goldstein, H. Hunt, L. Pessar, and M. Stone, I have developed what Blumenthal (personal communication) has suggested calling a *structural interview* to highlight the structural characteristics of the three major types of personality organization. This interview focuses on the symptoms, conflicts, or difficulties that the patient presents, and the particular ways in which he reflects them in the here-and-now interaction with the interviewer.

We assume that the interviewer's focus on the patient's main conflicts will create enough tension so that the patient's predominant defensive and "structural" organization of mental functioning will emerge. In highlighting these defensive operations in the interview, we obtain data that permit us to classify him into one of the three personality structures on the basis of the degree of identity integration (the integration of self and object representations), the type of defensive operations predomi-

nating, and the capacity for reality testing. In order to activate and diagnose these structural characteristics, we have developed an interview
that combines the traditional mental-status examination with a psychoanalytically oriented interview focusing on the patient–therapist interaction and on clarification, confrontation, and interpretation of the identity
conflicts, defensive mechanisms, and reality distortion that the patient
reveals in this interaction, particularly as these express identifiable transference elements.

Before describing the actual interview, a few definitions may be
helpful.

Clarification refers to the exploration, with the patient, of all the elements in the information he has provided that are vague, unclear, puzzling, contradictory, or incomplete. Clarification is the first cognitive
step in which what the patient says is discussed in a nonquestioning
way in order to bring out all its implications and to discover the extent
of his understanding or confusion regarding what remains unclear. Clarification aims at evoking conscious and preconscious material without
challenging the patient. In the end it is the patient himself who clarifies
his behavior and intrapsychic experience to us, thus leading us to the
present limits of his conscious and preconscious self-awareness.

Confrontation, the second step in the interview process, presents the
patient with areas of information that seem contradictory or incongruent. Confrontation means pointing out to the patient those aspects of
the interaction that seem to indicate the presence of conflictual functioning and, by implication, the presence of defensive operations, contradictory self and object representations, and decreased awareness of reality.
First, the patient's attention is drawn to something in the interaction of
which he has been unaware or has taken as natural and which the interviewer perceives as inappropriate, contradictory to other aspects of the
information, or confusing. Confrontation requires bringing together conscious and preconscious material that the patient presented or experienced separately. The interviewer also raises the question of the possible
significance of this behavior for the patient's current functioning. Thus,
the patient's capacity to look at things differently without further regression, the internal relations among the various issues brought together,
and particularly the integration of the concept of self and others are explored. The increase or decrease in awareness of reality reflected in the
patient's response to confrontation and his ongoing empathy with the
interviewer as a reflection of social awareness and reality testing are also
highlighted. Finally, the interviewer relates aspects of the here-and-now
interaction to similar problems in other areas and thus makes a connection between descriptive issues and complaints and structural personality features. Confrontation, thus defined, requires tact and patience; it is

not an aggressive way of intruding into the patient's mind or a move to polarize the relation with him.

Interpretation, in contrast to confrontation, links conscious and preconscious material with assumed or hypothesized unconscious functions or motivations in the here-and-now. It explores the conflictual origins of dissociation of ego states (split self and object representations), the nature and motives for the defensive operations activated, and the defensive abandonment of reality testing. In other words, interpretation focuses on the underlying anxieties and conflicts activated. Confrontation brings together and reorganizes what has been observed; interpretation adds a hypothesized dimension of causality and depth to the material. The interviewer thereby connects the current functions of a specific behavior with the patient's underlying anxieties, motives, and conflicts, which clarifies the general difficulties beyond the current interaction. For example, pointing out to a patient that his behavior seems to manifest suspicion and exploring his awareness of this pattern is a confrontation; suggesting that the patient's suspiciousness or fear is due to his attributing to the interviewer something "bad" that he is trying to get rid of within himself (of which the patient has been unaware before) is an interpretation.

Transference means the presence in the diagnostic interaction of inappropriate behavior that reflects the unconscious reenactment of pathogenic and conflictual relations with significant others in the patient's past. Transference reactions provide the context for interpretations linking the here-and-now disturbance with the patient's there-and-then experience. Pointing out to the patient that he is acting in a controlling and suspicious way toward the diagnostician is a confrontation. Pointing out that he may be seeing the interviewer as controlling, strict, harsh, and suspicious—and therefore may feel he has to be on guard because of his own struggle with such tendencies within himself—is an interpretation. Pointing out that the patient is struggling with the interviewer, who represents an internal "enemy" having such characteristics because he experienced a similar interaction in the past with a parental figure, is an interpretation of the transference.

In summary, *clarification* is a nonchallenging, cognitive means of exploring the limits of the patient's awareness of certain material. *Confrontation* attempts to make the patient aware of potentially conflictual and incongruous aspects of that material. *Interpretation* tries to resolve the conflictual nature of the material by assuming underlying unconscious motives and defenses that make the previously contradictory appear logical. *Transference interpretation* applies all these preceding modalities of technique to the current interaction between the patient and the diagnostician.

Because they focus on the confrontation with and interpretation of defenses, on identity conflicts, on reality testing or distortions in internalized object relations, and on affective and cognitive conflicts, structural interviews subject the patient to a certain amount of stress. Instead of putting the patient at ease and reducing his "defensiveness" by tolerating or overlooking it, the interviewer tries to bring out the pathology in the patient's organization of ego functions so as to elicit information regarding the structural organization of illness. The approach I am describing is, however, by no means a traditional "stress" interview, which attempts to induce artificial conflicts or anxiety in the patient. On the contrary, the clarification of reality required in much initial confrontation requires tact and reflects respect and concern for the patient's emotional reality, an honest engagement in contrast to what may sometimes be an indifferent or "superior" tolerance of the inappropriate. The technique of structural interviewing is described in chapter 2; the clinical characteristics of borderline personality organization that emerge during the structural interview are summarized below.

The Structural Characteristics of Borderline Personality Organization

Descriptive Symptoms as "Presumptive" Evidence

The patient's symptoms and pathological character traits are not structural criteria, but they do direct the clinician's attention to the structural criteria of borderline personality organization. Similarly, the presence of symptoms "presumptive" of a psychotic nature that do not seem to justify or correspond to a clear-cut diagnosis of a major affective disorder (manic-depressive illness), schizophrenia, or an acute or chronic organic brain syndrome should suggest to the clinician that he explore the structural criteria for borderline personality organization. The descriptive symptoms of borderline patients are similar to the presenting symptoms of ordinary symptomatic neuroses and character pathology, but the combination of certain features is peculiar to borderline cases. The following symptoms are particularly important (see Kernberg, 1975).

1. *Anxiety.* Borderline patients tend to present chronic, diffuse, free-floating anxiety.
2. *Polysymptomatic neurosis.* Many patients present several neurotic symptoms, but here I am considering only those patients who tend to present two or more of the following:
   a. Multiple phobias, especially those imposing severe restrictions on the patient's daily life.
   b. Obsessive-compulsive symptoms that have acquired second-

ary ego syntonicity and therefore a quality of "overvaluated" thought and action.

    c. Multiple elaborate or bizarre conversion symptoms, especially if they are chronic.

    d. Dissociative reactions, especially hysterical "twilight states" and fugues, and amnesia accompanied by disturbances of consciousness.

    e. Hypochondriasis.

    f. Paranoid and hypochondriacal trends with any other symptomatic neurosis (a typical combination indicating a presumptive diagnosis of borderline personality organization).

3. *Polymorphous perverse sexual trends.* I refer here to patients who present a manifest sexual deviation within which several perverse trends coexist. The more chaotic and multiple the perverse fantasies and actions and the more unstable the object relations connected with these interactions, the more the presence of borderline personality organization should be considered. Bizarre forms of perversion, especially those manifestating primitive aggression or primitive replacement of genital aims by eliminatory ones (urination, defecation), are also indicative of an underlying borderline personality organization.

4. *"Classical" prepsychotic personality structures.* These include:

    a. The paranoid personality (paranoid trends of such intensity that they determine the main descriptive diagnosis).

    b. The schizoid personality.

    c. The hypomanic personality and the cyclothymic personality organization with strong hypomanic trends.

5. *Impulse neurosis and addictions.* I refer here to those forms of severe character pathology in which chronic repetitive eruption of an impulse gratifies instinctual needs in a way that is ego-dystonic apart from the "impulse-ridden" episodes but is ego-syntonic and actually highly pleasurable during the episode itself. Alcoholism, drug addiction, certain forms of psychogenic obesity, and kleptomania are typical examples.

6. *"Lower-level" character disorders.* Here is included severe character pathology typically represented by the chaotic and impulse-ridden character, in contrast to the classical reaction-formation types of character structure and the milder "avoidance-trait" characters. From a clinical point of view, the typical hysterical personality does not have borderline structures; the same holds true for most obsessive-compulsive personalities and the "depressive personality" structures (Laughlin, 1967) or better-integrated masochistic personalities. In contrast, many infantile per-

sonalities and typical narcissistic personalities present underlying borderline organization; the "as if" personalities also belong to the latter group. All clear-cut antisocial personality structures I have examined have presented a typical borderline personality organization.

All these symptoms as well as the dominant pathological character traits may be elicited by the initial investigation of the symptoms that bring the patient into treatment. The investigation encompasses the characteristics of the patient's interpersonal and social life with regard to his work and family; his sexual and marital relations; his interactions with close relatives, friends, acquaintances; and his interactions in the areas of recreation, culture, politics, religion, and other interpersonal community interests. With all patients in whom the diagnosis of borderline personality organization is to be evaluated, a comprehensive history of the symptomatology and peculiarities of interpersonal interactions is therefore important initial information.

Lack of an Integrated Identity: The Syndrome of Identity Diffusion

Clinically, identity diffusion is represented by a poorly integrated concept of the self and of significant others. It is reflected in the subjective experience of chronic emptiness, contradictory self-perceptions, contradictory behavior that cannot be integrated in an emotionally meaningful way, and shallow, flat, impoverished perceptions of others. Diagnostically, identity diffusion appears in the patient's inability to convey significant interactions with others to an interviewer, who thus cannot emotionally empathize with the patient's conception of himself and others in such interactions.

Theoretically, the following assumptions underlie this lack of integration of self and of the concept of significant others (Kernberg, 1975): (1) In borderline personality organization, there is enough differentiation of self representations from object representations to permit the maintenance of ego boundaries (that is, sharp delimitation between the self and others). In psychotic structures, by contrast, a regressive refusion or lack of differentiation between self and object representations is present. (2) In contrast to neurotic structures, where all self images (both "good" and "bad") have been integrated into a comprehensive self, and where "good" and "bad" images of others can be integrated into comprehensive concepts of others, in borderline personality organization such integration fails, and both self and object representations remain multiple, contradictory, affective–cognitive representations of self and others. (3) This failure to integrate "good" and "bad" aspects of the reality of self and others is presumably due to the predominance of severe early aggression activated in these patients: Dissociation of "good" and "bad" self and object representations in effect protects love and goodness from contamination by overriding hate and badness.

In the structural interview, identity diffusion is reflected in a history of grossly contradictory behavior, or in an alternation between emotional states implying such grossly contradictory behavior and perception of the self that the interviewer finds it very difficult to see the patient as a "whole" human being. Whereas in severe neurotic character pathology contradictory interpersonal behavior may reflect the patient's pathological but integrated view of himself and significant others, in borderline personality organization it is the internal view of himself and of others that is not integrated.

For example, a neurotic patient with predominantly hysterical personality structure said in the interview that she wanted help for her sexual difficulties but was very reluctant to discuss them. Confronted with this contradiction, she explained that she felt that the male interviewers would enjoy the humiliating effect it would have on a woman to talk about her sexual difficulties, that they might get excited sexually while enjoying depreciating her as sexually inferior. This concept of men and of the humiliating nature of sexual experiences and their revelation was part of an integrated—although pathological—concept of herself and others.

In contrast, a patient with predominant infantile character structure and borderline personality organization explained how disgusted she was with men who were only out to use women as sex objects, how she had to escape from the sexual advances of a previous boss, and how she avoided social contacts because of men's predatory sexual approaches. But she also said that she had worked for some time as a "bunny" in a Playboy club, and she was very surprised when the interviewer confronted her with the contradiction between her assertions and her choice of employment.

Identity diffusion is also reflected in descriptions of significant persons in the patient's life that do not permit the interviewer "to put them together," to gain any clear picture of them. The description of significant others is frequently so grossly contradictory that they sound more like caricatures than like real people. One woman who lived in a *ménage à trois* could not describe the characteristics of the man and woman she lived with or the sexual and human relations between them and, particularly, with her. Another borderline patient with masochistic personality structure described her mother at various times in the interview as warm, engaging, sensitive, and alert to the patient's needs; and as cold, indifferent, insensitive, self-involved, and withdrawn. Efforts to clarify these apparent contradictions led first to an increase of anxiety on the patient's part. Later she felt she was being attacked by the interviewer, being criticized for having contradictory images of her mother and, implicitly, for harboring "bad" feelings toward her. The interpretation of the projection of her own guilt feelings upon the interviewer reduced her anxiety but left the patient with the painful experience of a chaotic perception of her mother. A patient may, of course, describe someone who is truly chaotic, so that one has to distinguish a chaotic description of another person from an accurate account of someone who is in fact chronically contradictory. This, in practice, is easier than it might seem.

The structural interview often allows us to explore the patient's perceptions of the interviewer and the patient's difficulty in empathizing with the interviewer's efforts to bring together what he perceives as the patient's perceptions of him. In short, the structural interview constitutes an experimental situation in which the extent of integration of self and of the perception of objects can be explored and tested.

A solid ego identity reflects a neurotic personality structure in a patient with intact reality testing. An abnormal, pathologically integrated identity may appear in some chronic delusional systems in both manic-depressive and schizophrenic patients. Structurally speaking, it is both integration and congruence with reality that differentiate neurotic from psychotic personality organization.

An intimately related structural issue has to do with the quality of object relations: the stability and depth of the patient's relations with significant others as manifested by warmth, dedication, concern, and tactfulness. Other qualitative aspects are empathy, understanding, and the ability to maintain a relationship when it is invaded by conflict or frustration. The quality of object relations is largely dependent on identity integration, which includes not only the degree of integration but also the temporal continuity of the patient's concept of himself and others. Normally, we experience ourselves consistently throughout time under varying circumstances and with different people, and we experience conflict when contradictions in our self-concept emerge. The same applies to our experience of others. But in borderline personality organization, this temporal continuity is lost; such patients have little capacity for a realistic evaluation of others. The borderline patient's long-term relations with others are characterized by an increasingly distorted perception of them. He fails to achieve real empathy; his relations with others are chaotic or shallow; and intimate relations are usually contaminated by their typical condensation of genital and pregenital conflicts.

The quality of the patient's object relations may become apparent in this interaction with the interviewer. Although brief, such diagnostic interactions often permit differentiation of the neurotic personality's gradual buildup of a personal relation of an appropriate kind from the borderline personality's persistently chaotic, empty, distorted, or blocked relation. In the case of psychotic personality organization, where reality testing is lost, even severer distortions of the patient–diagnostician relation may ensue. It is the combination of such distortion within an interaction in which reality testing is maintained that is so characteristic of borderline personality organization. The frequent shift of focus from the present interaction of patient and interviewer to the patient's difficulties in interactions with significant others provides additional material for the evaluation of the quality of his object relations.

Primitive Defense Mechanisms

A further difference between neurotic personality structure, on the one hand, and borderline and psychotic structures, on the other, is the nature of the defensive organization. In the neurotic, as mentioned earlier, this centers on repression and other high-level defensive operations. Borderline and psychotic structures, in contrast, are characterized by a predominance of primitive defensive operations, especially the mechanism of splitting. Repression and such related high-level mechanisms as reaction formation, isolation, undoing, intellectualization, and rationalization protect the ego from intrapsychic conflicts by the rejection of a drive derivative or its ideational representation, or both, from the conscious ego. Splitting and other related mechanisms protect the ego from conflicts by means of dissociation or actively keeping apart contradictory experiences of the self and significant others. When such mechanisms predominate, contradictory ego states are alternatively activated. As long as these contradictory ego states can be kept separate from each other, anxiety related to these conflicts is prevented or controlled.

The mechanism of primitive dissociation or splitting and the associated mechanisms of primitive idealization, primitive types of projection (particularly projective identification), denial, omnipotence, and devaluation may be elicited in the clinical interaction of patient and diagnostician. These defenses protect the borderline patient from intrapsychic conflict but at the cost of weakening his ego functioning, thereby reducing his adaptive effectiveness and flexibility in the interview and in his life generally. These same primitive defensive operations when found in psychotic organization protect the patient from further disintegration of the boundaries between self and object. The fact that the same defensive operations can be observed in borderline and psychotic patients and yet serve different functions has been demonstrated clinically. Interpretation of splitting and other related mechanisms with borderline personality organization integrates the ego and improves the patient's immediate functioning. This immediate (if only transitory) increase in social adaptation and in reality testing can be utilized for diagnostic purposes. In contrast, interpretation of these defenses to the psychotic patient in the diagnostic interview brings about further regression in his functioning. Thus, whether the patient immediately improves or deteriorates under the effect of such interpretation contributes in a crucial way to the diagnostic differentiation of borderline and psychotic organization.

Splitting. Probably the clearest manifestation of splitting is the division of external objects into "all good" and "all bad," with the concomitant possibility of complete, abrupt shifts of an object from one extreme compartment to the other—that is, sudden and complete reversals of all feelings and conceptualizations about a particular person. Extreme repetitive oscillation between contradictory self concepts is another manifestation of the mechanism of splitting. In the diagnostic interview, sudden shifts in the perception of the interviewer or in the patient's perception of himself or a complete separation of contradictory reactions to the same theme may reflect splitting mechanisms in the here-and-now interaction. An increase in the patient's anxiety when contradictory aspects of his self image or his object representations are pointed out to him also indicates the mechanism of splitting. Attempts to clarify, confront, and interpret such contradictory aspects of self and object representations activate the mechanism of splitting in the here-and-now interaction and reflect its functions regarding reality testing (increase or decrease) and the rigidity of the character traits that "fixate" splitting into stable problems.

Primitive Idealization. This mechanism complicates the tendency to see external objects as either totally good or totally bad by increasing artificially and pathologically their quality of "goodness" or "badness." Primitive idealization creates unrealistic, all-good and powerful images; this may be reflected in the interaction with the diagnostician by treating him as an ideal, omnipotent, or godly figure on whom the patient depends unrealistically. The interviewer or some other idealized person may be seen as a potential ally against equally powerful (and equally unrealistic) "all-bad" objects.

Early Forms of Projection, Especially Projective Identification. In contrast to higher levels of projection characterized by the patient's attributing to the other an impulse he has repressed in himself, primitive forms of projection, particularly projective identification, are characterized by (1) the tendency to continue to experience the impulse that is simultaneously being projected onto the other person, (2) fear of the other person under the influence of that projected impulse, and (3) the need to control the other person under the influence of this mechanism. Projective identification therefore implies intrapsychic as well as behavioral interpersonal aspects of the patient's interactions, and this may be reflected dramatically in the diagnostic interview. The patient may accuse the interviewer of a certain reaction to him, a reaction that the patient actually is attempting to induce in the interviewer by his own behavior. For example, one patient accused the interviewer of being sadistic while he himself treated the interviewer in a cold, controlling, derogatory, and suspicious way. Interpretation of this defensive operation in the here-and-now often dramatically permits the differentiation of a paranoid personality (a typical borderline personality constellation) from paranoid schizophrenia.

Denial. Denial in borderline patients is typically exemplified by denial of two emotionally independent areas of consciousness; we might say that denial here simply reinforces splitting. The patient is aware that his perceptions, thoughts, and feelings about himself or other people at one time or another are completely opposite to those he has had at other times, but his memory has no emotional relevance and cannot influence the way he feels now. Denial may be manifested as a complete lack of concern, anxiety, or emotional reaction about an immediate, serious, pressing need, conflict, or danger in the patient's life, so that the patient calmly conveys his cognitive awareness of the situation while denying its emotional implications. Or an entire area of the patient's subjective awareness may be shut out from his subjective experience, thus protecting him from a potential area of conflict. The diagnostician's empathic effort to evaluate the patient's circumstances and the patient's reactions to them in the light of the normal human reactions one would expect often provides the patient with a sharp contrast between this empathic effort and his own apparently indifferent or callous attitude about himself or important others. Denial may also become evident in the patient's discussion of his present life and in the contradiction between his life situation and his reaction to it in the diagnostic interview.

Omnipotence and Devaluation. Both omnipotence and devaluation are derivatives of splitting operations affecting the self and object representations and are typically represented by the activation of ego states reflecting a highly inflated, grandiose self relating to depreciated, emotionally degrading representations of others. Narcissistic personalities, a special subgroup of borderline personality organization, present these defensive operations quite strikingly. Omnipotence and devaluation may become manifest in the patient's descriptions of significant others and his interactions with them and in his behavior during the diagnostic interview. In this connection, the diagnostician should be especially alert to whatever small or subtle indications of pathological behavior can be elicited in the early diagnostic contacts with the patient. Considering that a patient usually tries to present himself at his best in a new situation (and that, if he does not, serious character pathology may be indicated), one must conclude that both grossly inappropriate behaviors, when present, and subtle deviations from otherwise "perfectly normal" behavior require probing in diagnostic interviews.

Reality Testing

Both neurotic and borderline personality organization present maintenance of reality testing, in contrast to psychotic personality structures. Therefore, while the syndrome of identity diffusion and the predominance of primitive defensive operations permit the structural differentiation of borderline from neurotic conditions, reality testing permits the differentiation of borderline personality organization from the major psychotic syndromes. Reality testing is defined by the capacity to differentiate self from nonself, intrapsychic from external origins of perceptions and stimuli, and the capacity to evaluate realistically one's own affect, behavior, and thought content in terms of ordinary social norms. Clinically, reality testing is recognized by (1) the absence of hallucinations and delusions; (2) the absence of grossly inappropriate or bizarre affect, thought content, or behavior; and (3) the capacity to empathize with and clarify other people's observations of what seem to them inappropriate or puzzling aspects of the patient's affects, behavior, or thought content within the context of ordinary social interactions. Reality testing needs to be differentiated from alterations in the subjective experience of reality, which may be present at some time in any patient with psychological distress, and from the alteration of the relation to reality that is present in all character pathology as well as in more regressive, psychotic conditions. By itself, it is of diagnostic value only in very extreme forms (Frosch, 1964). How is reality testing reflected in the structural diagnostic interview?

1. Reality testing can be considered present when the patient's information indicates that he has not suffered from and is not suffering from hallucinations or delusions, or, if he has had hallucinations or delusions in the past, that he now has the capacity to evaluate them fully, including the ability to express appropriate concern or puzzlement over such phenomena.

2. In patients who have not had hallucinations or delusions, reality testing can be evaluated by the interviewer's focusing sharply on whatever inappropriate affect, thought content, or behavior can be observed. Reality testing is reflected in the patient's capacity to empathize with the interviewer's perception of these characteristics and, in a subtler way, in his capacity to empathize with the interviewer's perception of the interaction with the patient in general. The structural interview, as I have pointed out, therefore constitutes an ideal opportunity for reality test-

ing and thus for the differentiation of borderline from psychotic organization.

3. For reasons mentioned earlier, reality testing may also be evaluated by interpreting primitive defensive operations in the patient–interviewer interaction. An improvement in the patient's immediate functioning as a consequence of such interpretation reflects maintenance of reality testing, while an immediate deterioration of the patient's functioning as a consequence of such intervention indicates loss of reality testing.

Table 1 summarizes the differentiation of personality organization in terms of the three structural criteria of identity integration, defensive operations, and reality testing.

Nonspecific Manifestations of Ego Weakness

The "nonspecific" manifestations of ego weakness include the absence of anxiety tolerance, of impulse control, and of developed channels of sublimation. These are to be differentiated from the "specific" aspects of ego weakness: the ego-weakening consequences of the predominance of primitive defensive mechanisms. Anxiety tolerance refers to the degree to which the patient can tolerate a load of tension greater than what he habitually experiences without developing increased symptoms or generally regressive behavior; impulse control refers to the degree to which the patient can experience instinctual urges or strong emotions without having to act on them immediately against his better judgment and interest; sublimatory effectiveness refers to the degree to which the patient can invest himself in values beyond his immediate self-interest or beyond self-preservation—particularly to the degree to which he is able to develop creative resources in some area beyond his natural background, education, or training.

These characteristics, although reflecting structural conditions, are manifest in direct behavior, which may be elicited in the course of the patient's history. Nonspecific manifestations of ego weakness differentiate both borderline personality organization and the psychoses from neurotic personality structures, but they have a less precise and clear differentiating function between borderline and neurotic structures than is true for identity integration and levels of defensive organization. Many narcissistic personalities, for example, present fewer indications of nonspecific symptoms of ego weakness than one might expect.

Lack of Superego Integration

A relatively well-integrated although excessively severe superego characterizes the neurotic types of personality organization. Borderline and

Table 1. *Differentiation of Personality Organization*

Structural Criteria	Neurotic	Borderline	Psychotic
	Self representations and object representations are sharply delimited.		
		Identity diffusion: contradictory aspects of self and others are poorly integrated and kept apart.	
Identity integration	Integrated identity: contradictory images of self and others are integrated into comprehensive conceptions.		Self representations and object representations are poorly delimited, or else there is delusional identity.
	Repression and high-level defenses: reaction formation, isolation, undoing, rationalization, intellectualization.	Mainly splitting and low-level defenses: primitive idealization, projective identification, denial, omnipotence, devaluation.	
Defensive operations	Defenses protect patient from intrapsychic conflict. Interpretation improves functioning.		Defenses protect patient from disintegration and self/object merging. Interpretation leads to regression.
	Capacity to test reality is preserved: differentiation of self from nonself, intrapsychic from external origins of perceptions and stimuli.		
		Alterations occur in relationship with reality and in feelings of reality.	
Reality testing	Capacity exists to evaluate self and others realistically and in depth.		Capacity to test reality is lost.

psychotic organizations reflect impairments in superego integration and are characterized by nonintegrated superego precursors, particularly primitive sadistic and idealized object representations. Superego integration can be evaluated by studying the degree to which the patient identifies with ethical values and has normal guilt as a major regulator. Regulation of self-esteem by excessively severe guilt feelings or depressive mood swings represents a pathological superego integration (typical of neurotic organization) in contrast to the modulated, specifically focused, self-critical functions of the normal individual in terms of ethical values. The degree to which the person is able to regulate his functioning according to ethical principles; to abstain from the exploitation, manipulation, or mistreatment of others; and to maintain honesty and moral integrity in the absence of external control indicates superego integration. This criterion is diagnostically less reliable than the ones previously described. Even patients employing predominantly primitive defenses may give evidence of superego integration, although it may be sadistic in nature, and there are patients with borderline personality organization who maintain a relatively good superego integration in spite of severe pathology in the area of identity integration, object relations, and defensive organization. Also, information regarding superego integration can be elicited more effectively from the patient's history and from long-term observation than in the diagnostic interview. Nevertheless, the prognostic utility of the degree of superego integration makes it an enormously important structural criterion for the indication or contraindication of long-term, intensive psychotherapy. In fact, the quality of object relations and the quality of superego functioning are probably the two most important prognostic criteria stemming from a structural analysis.

Genetic-Dynamic Characteristics of Instinctual Conflicts

Although the characteristic instinctual conflicts of borderline personality organization become manifest in long-term therapeutic engagements with borderline patients, they are relatively difficult to discern in diagnostic interviews and are described here in the interest of completeness.

Borderline personality organization presents a pathological condensation of genital and pregenital instinctual strivings, with a predominance of pregenital aggression (Kernberg, 1975). This assumption explains the bizarre or inappropriate condensation of sexual, dependent, and aggressive impulses found clinically in borderline (and also psychotic) organization. What appears as a chaotic persistence of primitive drives and fears, the pansexuality of the borderline case, represents a combination of various pathological solutions of these conflicts.

It should also be stressed here that the discrepancy between the patient's actual historical development and his internal, fixated experience of it is enormous. What we find out in psychoanalytical exploration of these cases is not what happened in external reality but how the patient experienced his significant object relations in the past. By the same token, we cannot take the patient's initial history at face value: The more severe the character pathology, the less reliable the initial history. In severe narcissistic personality disorders and in borderline personality organization generally, the initial history of early development is frequently empty or chaotic or misleading. Only after years of treatment is it possible to reconstruct an internal genetic sequence (in the sense of intrapsychic origins) and relate it in some way to the patient's actual past experiences.

The characteristics of instinctual conflict listed below derive from the literature, summarized elsewhere (Kernberg, 1975), and from my own experience with intensive psychoanalytic psychotherapy and psychoanalysis of borderline patients.

First is an excessive aggressivization of oedipal conflicts so that the image of the oedipal rival typically acquires terrifying, overwhelmingly dangerous, and destructive characteristics; castration anxiety and penis envy appear grossly exaggerated and overwhelming; and superego prohibitions against sexualized relations acquire a savage, primitive quality, manifested in severe masochistic tendencies or paranoid projections of superego precursors.

Second, the idealizations of the heterosexual love object in the positive oedipal relation and of the homosexual love object in the negative oedipal relation are exaggerated and have marked defensive functions against primitive rage. There is thus both unrealistic idealization of and longing for such love objects and the possibility of rapid breakdown of the idealization, with a reversal from the positive to the negative (or negative to positive) relation in a rapid and total shift of the object relation. As a consequence, the idealizations appear both exaggerated and frail, with the additional complication in the case of narcissistic character pathology of easy devaluation of idealized objects and total withdrawal.

Third, the unrealistic nature of both the threatening oedipal rival and the idealized, desired one reveals, on careful genetic analysis, the existence of condensed father–mother images of an unreal kind, reflecting the condensation of partial aspects of the relations with both parents. While sexual differences in the object relations are maintained, the fantasied relation with each of these objects is unrealistic and primitive and reflects the condensation of idealized or threatening relations stemming from preoedipal and oedipal developments and a rapid shift of both libidinal and aggressive relations from one parental object to the other. Each particular relation with a parental object turns out to reflect a more complex developmental history than is usually the case with neurotic patients, except for the most severely neurotic, in whom the transference developments are more closely related to realistic events of the past.

Fourth, the genital strivings of patients with predominant pre-oedipal conflicts serve important pregenital functions. The penis, for example, may acquire characteristics of the feeding, withholding, or attacking mother (basically the feeding function of her breast), and the vagina may acquire functions of the hungry, feeding, or aggressive mouth; similar developments occur regarding anal and urinary functions. Although many neurotic patients and patients with less severe character pathology also present these characteristics, their existence in combination with the excessive aggressivization of all the pregenital libidinal functions is typical of patients with borderline personality organization.

Fifth, borderline patients typically show what could be described as a premature oedipalization of their preoedipal conflicts and relations, a defensive progression in their instinctual development which is reflected clinically in early oedipalization of the transference. This transference phenomenon often turns out to be spurious in that it eventually leads back to severe and chaotic preoedipal pathology; yet it is at the same time significant in indicating the defensive organization of oedipal conflicts that eventually, sometimes after years of treatment, predominate in the transference. In this regard, our developing knowledge about early genital awareness in both sexes and the difference in mother–infant relations depending on the infant's sex (Money and Ehrhardt, 1972; Galenson and Roiphe, 1977; Kleeman, 1977; Stoller, 1977) may provide information on early infant behavior that relates to the intrapsychic processes by which an escape from preoedipal conflicts into oedipalization of object relations takes place.

In both sexes, the displacement of frustrated dependency needs from mother to father colors the positive oedipal relation of the girl and the negative oedipal relation of the boy. The displacement of oral-aggressive conflicts from mother onto father increases castration anxiety and oedipal rivalry in boys, and penis envy and related character distortions in girls. In girls, severe pregenital aggression toward the mother reinforces masochistic tendencies in their relation to men, severe superego prohibitions against genitality in general, and the negative oedipal relation to the mother as a defensive idealization and reaction formation against the aggression. The projection of primitive conflicts around aggression onto the sexual relation between the parents increases distorting and frightening versions of the primal scene, which may become extended into hatred of all mutual love offered by others. More generally, the defensive displacement of impulses and conflicts from one parent to the other fosters the development of confusing, fantastic combinations of bisexual parental images condensed under the influence of a particular projected impulse.

All these characteristics of instinctual conflicts of patients with borderline personality organization may be reflected in the initial symptomatology and in their sexual behavior, fantasies, and interpersonal relations. But, as mentioned before, they do not often lend themselves to an analysis in depth during the early diagnostic interviews.

Conclusion

A number of issues require further clinical and experimental research. These relate to the structural diagnosis of borderline personality organization at times of temporary regression, such as the brief psychotic episodes that borderline patients have under the influence of severe emotional turmoil, alcohol, or drugs. Preliminary clinical experience suggests that the structural diagnostic interview here proposed may still differentiate borderline personality organization under these conditions, in effect temporarily reducing the loss of reality testing in these patients. Further exploration, however, will be necessary to confirm this. The descriptive characteristics of such brief psychotic episodes and the fact that they are embedded in a personality structure typical of borderline personality organization constitute the positive diagnostic criteria at this time.

Another problem is presented by psychotic reactions under the influence of psychotomimetic drugs, which often, during their acute stage, raise the question of differential diagnosis between acute psychotic episodes in borderline personality organization and acute schizophrenic reactions (Schizophreniform Disorder in American Psychiatric Association, 1980 [DSM-III]). Again, preliminary evidence seems to indicate that loss of reality testing in drug-induced psychosis in borderline personality organization may transitorily improve with the structural diagnostic evaluation proposed, in contrast to the temporary increased regression when primitive defenses are interpreted in the case of schizophrenic reactions. This is, however, only a preliminary impression.

A major issue is that of the structural characteristics of patients with chronic schizophrenic illness during periods of remission. My colleagues and I have observed various types of personality organization in such patients. Some chronic schizophrenic patients seem to "seal over" and present a neurotic personality organization during periods of latency; others seal over and present a borderline personality organization; still other chronic schizophrenic patients present a typical psychotic regression when examined with the structural approach during periods of clinical remission, thus indicating the permanence or persistence of an essentially psychotic structure. Thus, the underlying personality structure of chronic schizophrenic patients during remission may not be uniform, and it may be possible to differentiate, with structural criteria, chronic psychotic personality organizations proper from patients with a higher level sealing-over. If so, this may have prognostic and therapeutic implications in terms of the preconditions for and characteristics of shifts in the predominant personality organization that we observe in some schizophrenic patients during remission.

The structural criteria proposed, particularly that of reality testing, can be regarded as extremely useful diagnostic tools to be used in conjunction with an evaluation of the descriptive symptoms of the various psychotic conditions. The structural diagnostic approach may significantly enrich the sharpness, precision, and accuracy of our differential diagnoses and add important elements to the prognostic and therapeutic considerations of each individual case. Some cases will nonetheless probably continue to defy our capacity for differential diagnosis, at least when it is attempted in a relatively brief period of time.

The structural approach to the differential diagnosis of borderline personality organization stresses the importance of diagnosing the patient as a total individual and of appraising his internal life of object relations in terms of his concept of himself and of significant others. Paradoxically, this dynamic approach based on object relations theory, which seems to run counter to a more descriptive form of diagnosis based on symptoms and behavior, enriches descriptive diagnosis. From the viewpoint of research methodology, it is easier and apparently more "objective" to break down human behavior into clusters of behavioral manifestations than to study the human individual in his totality. However, despite the methodological difficulties implied by such a study of the totality of the individual, it may in the long run provide a firmer basis for research on personality organization and personality change.

The diagnosis of borderline personality organization affects both the prognosis and the treatment. Where structural diagnosis determines the presence of borderline personality organization rather than ordinary symptomatic neurosis and character pathology it indicates limitations to the possibility of psychoanalytic treatment; it suggests that intensive, long-term expressive psychoanalytic psychotherapy rather than supportive treatment would be most appropriate; it signals the need to carefully evaluate whether and how to structure the patient's external life while such intensive psychotherapy proceeds; it means that, under conditions of acute crisis, crisis intervention is indicated. The decision will ultimately have to be made which treatment approach to adopt—expressive or supportive psychotherapy. For those cases where expressive psychotherapy is contraindicated and a supportive approach elected, the possibility may have to be accepted that a patient may need support over many years or perhaps for life.

In my opinion, this diagnosis has a better prognosis for many patients today than it had only 20 or 30 years ago. In the case of patients with chronic schizophrenic illness, the diagnosis of borderline personality organization (in contrast to psychotic structure) during periods of remission indicates the possibility of psychoanalytic psychotherapy and, implicitly, the possibility of fundamentally improving the personality structure and thus affording the patient additional protection against psychotic breakdown.

CHAPTER 2: *The Structural Interview*

My principal objective in this chapter is to illustrate the clinical useful-ness of structural interviewing, particularly in the differential diagnosis of borderline conditions. The detailed clinical descriptions of different patterns emerging during structural interviews should also illustrate the limits of the usefulness of structural interviewing. To put it briefly, the more a clear-cut psychotic or organic syndrome emerges, the more the structural interviewing resembles the traditional mental-status examina-tion. But for patients within the borderline or neurotic spectrum of psy-chopathology, the advantages of structural interviewing quickly become apparent. The structural interview not only sharpens the differential diagnosis but also reveals information with important prognostic and therapeutic implications. It tells us about the patient's motivation, his capacity for introspection and for collaboration in psychothera-peutic treatment, and his potential for acting out and for psychotic decompensation.

An important question is whether a standard psychiatric history should be taken before a structural interview, which, under these condi-tions, then replaces the traditional mental-status examination; or whether both the standard history-taking and the traditional mental-status examination should be replaced by a structural interview, which may end up with selective history-taking in the light of the findings of the interview itself.

The advantages of starting out with classical history-taking are that this method conforms more easily to psychiatric residents' training in medical history-taking and examination, it permits the psychiatrist quickly to diagnose obvious psychotic and organic psychopathology (where structural interviewing is much less important), and, because this approach is more traditional, it decreases the initial anxiety for the

27

patient by fitting into the ordinary expectations of the patient/doctor interaction. To start with taking a history also avoids the consequences of a severe premature flare-up of primitive defenses (with activation of intensely negativistic or oppositional developments, particularly in the case of paranoid patients).

The disadvantages of starting with a traditional history-taking before structural interviewing are that it allows the patient's predominant defensive operations to go underground, and, especially with borderline and neurotic personality structures, makes it easier for the patient to "adapt" protectively to the interview, which decreases anxiety while obscuring areas of current conflicts and early transference developments.

In weighing these advantages and disadvantages, I think that the less time the interviewer has for a full evaluation of the patient, and the less experience the interviewer has had in structural interviewing, the greater is the advantage in beginning with a standard history and then shifting to structural interviewing. In contrast, the more time available, the more experienced the interviewer, and the more the differential diagnosis focuses on the boundaries between neurotic and borderline, and between borderline and psychotic structure, the more useful it is to start with a structural interview, with the understanding that the historical information required in individual cases will fit naturally into the advanced phases of the structural interview.

The interviewer begins by asking the patient to present a brief summary of his reasons for coming to treatment, his expectations of treatment, and the nature of his predominant symptoms, problems, or difficulties. While the search pattern that follows the initial opening questions may vary in different approaches to structural interviewing (Stone, 1980; Selzer, 1981), my preference is to follow the initial inquiry with a systematic search, surveying the cycle of "anchoring symptoms" of key psychopathology indicated on the perimeter of the circle in Figure 1.

The survey completed, the interviewer focuses on the significant symptoms that have emerged in its course, exploring them as they appear in the here-and-now interaction of the interview, followed by clarification, confrontation, and tentative interpretation, with careful attention given to the patient's reactions to these interventions. The patient's capacity to empathize with the interviewer's query, to further clarify issues regarding his ego identity, object relations, reality testing, and current defense–impulse configurations, gives an indication of his capacity for introspection. The structural diagnosis depends heavily upon how the patient handles clarifications, confrontations, and interpretations.

If, for example, the initial survey has revealed some evidence of identity diffusion and defects in reality testing, the interviewer first attempts to amplify the expression of these characteristics in the here-and-

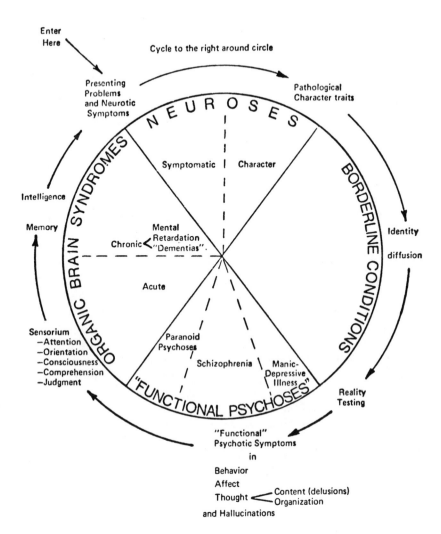

Figure 1. *Cycling of Anchoring Symptoms.*

now interaction of the interview. Then he confronts the patient by calling attention to discrepancies in what the patient has said or to other incongruities that indicate the possible defensive nature of his behavior. In addition, the interviewer tentatively interprets the possible significance of the discrepancies, which further challenges the patient to explore his behavior and motivations. The patient is asked how he sees these inconsistencies, how he feels about them, and what other information might clarify what has been occurring.

The patient's responses are of primary importance in differentiating neurotic, borderline, and psychotic structures. Given their intact capacity for reality testing, borderline patients reveal an often surprising reorganization and improvement in functioning with these clarifications, confrontations, and interpretations. They are able to empathize with the interviewer's "confusions," to clarify and correct their perceptions, and to use these corrections constructively in subsequent phases of the interview. In addition, borderline patients demonstrate some capacity for introspection and insight concerning the basis for the incongruities. As noted earlier, patients with psychotic structures lack this ability to empathize with ordinary social criteria of reality, and attempts to clarify may therefore reveal further distortions in reality testing. Neurotic patients, unlike the borderline cases, emerge with an integrated concept of themselves, which, in turn, tends to increase the interviewer's empathy with various aspects of their conflicts and reality and with their integrated concepts of significant others. The latter give the interpersonal reality and past history of these patients a sharp presence. Whereas borderline patients may increase their realistic behavior during the interview, they simultaneously make plain the emptiness, chaos, and confusion in their life situation and object relations.

With patients who are inarticulate and communicate poorly, information from sources other than the interview must be brought to bear on the diagnostic process. Inferences about anchoring symptoms can be made from such information. Then the focus on the symptoms in the here-and-now and clarification, confrontation, and interpretation can be attempted. This more detailed investigation may be carried out for several of the presenting anchoring symptoms until the interviewer feels comfortable with the structural diagnosis.

The structural diagnostic interview, then, combines a psychoanalytic focus on the patient–interviewer interaction with a psychoanalytic technique for interpreting conflictual issues and defensive operations in this interaction in order to highlight simultaneously the classical anchoring symptoms of descriptive psychopathology and the underlying personality structure.

A significant feature of the proposed model for structural interviewing is its cyclical nature. The concept of the anchoring symptoms as located on the perimeter of a circle makes it possible for the interviewer, as he proceeds from one cardinal symptom to the next, to return eventually to the starting point and reinitiate a new cycle of inquiry, in sharp contrast to a "decision tree" model of inquiry, which has a fixed pattern of progression. "Recycling" along the anchoring symptoms permits the interviewer to return as often as is necessary to the same issues in different contexts, retesting preliminary findings at later stages of the interview. As will be seen, it is not intended that the anchoring symptoms invariably be explored systematically, one by one. Depending upon early findings, different approaches to this cycling of inquiry are recommended.

The Initial Phase of Structural Interviewing

It is useful to start the interview with several questions (direct or indirect) presented in sequence, thus providing both a clear idea of what you expect from the patient and several possible ways for him to answer. In addition, the patient's very capacity to understand a series of questions and to remember them tests his functioning on several key anchoring symptoms. A typical initial inquiry might go as follows: "I am interested to hear what brought you here, what is the nature of your difficulties or problems, what you expect from treatment, and where you are now in this regard." If the interview occurs in the context of a hospital consultation or a research setting, or if the interviewer has previous information about the patient from other sources, he might add an explanatory comment such as: "I have had the opportunity of hearing something about your difficulties, but I am very interested to learn from you directly how you see all of this," or "I should like to tell you that although I shall have opportunity to learn about your difficulties from the members of the staff [or the person who referred you for a consultation, etc.] at this point I have no information about you at all."

This opening permits the patient to talk about his symptoms and the main reasons for his coming to treatment, as well as to expand on the nature of other difficulties. It permits the interviewer to evaluate indirectly the patient's awareness of his illness and of the need for treatment and the realistic or unrealistic nature of his expectations from treatment and reactions to already suggested treatment recommendations.

In response to these questions, patients without psychotic or organic psychopathology may talk freely about neurotic symptoms and difficulties in the psychological aspects of their social life that would point to pathological character traits; thus, indirectly, they give the first sign of good reality testing. The capacity to remember these questions, to respond to them in a cohesive, well-integrated way, also indicates a clear sensorium, good memory, and probably normal or even high intelligence. It represents, therefore, an automatic first "cycling" along the entire perimeter of anchoring symptoms.

In contrast, patients with alterations in the sensorium (decreased attention, orientation, consciousness, comprehension, or judgment) may have difficulties in responding to such questions, and the same is true for patients with memory or intellectual deficits (particularly, limited capacity for abstraction)—that is, patients with acute or chronic organic brain syndromes.

Patients may also be excessively concrete, vague, confused, or evasive in their responses to these questions. The interviewer can then tactfully clarify the discrepancy between the questions and the responses. It is helpful to inquire whether the patient feels he has responded fully to what he was asked or believes that the questions have not been clear enough, or perhaps are overwhelming. If the patient now acknowledges difficulties in following or understanding the interviewer, the questions should be repeated, worded somewhat differently, and the interviewer should then explore whether the patient still has difficulty in understanding. If this is the case, he should explore next what the nature of the difficulty is. In this fashion, often "entering" the diagnostic cycle through evaluation of symptoms, the interview may now lead rapidly to clarification, confrontation, and interpretation of the difficulty, which permits the interviewer to differentiate confusion stemming from intense anxiety and from psychotic misinterpretation of the total situation, negativism, and alteration of the sensorium, or serious memory or intelligence deficits.

The patient may respond in ways that have little or no apparent relation to the initial question. A severely disorganized schizophrenic patient, one with a hypomanic syndrome or with severe character pathology, may make use of the initial inquiry to express, for example, paranoid evasiveness or obsessive perfectionism by clarifying every one of the interviewer's statements. A masochistic patient may start to cry as if presented with an excessively burdensome task. All these responses may be tactfully explored, clarifying the questions once again while attempting to elicit more information about the nature of the difficulty the questions evoked. In this way, early manifestations of loss of reality testing, psychotic symptoms, and acute or chronic organic symptoms may be elicited, together with premature transference developments characteristic of patients with severe character pathology.

If a patient first responds appropriately to the initial questions but then gets lost in details in attempting to clarify them further, the interviewer should again explore for various symptom complexes. Within the realm of neurotic symptoms, is the patient getting lost in details because of obsessive tendencies? Is he vague and cautious in expressing paranoid tendencies? Within the realm of loss of reality testing and psychotic symptoms, is the patient evasive because of underlying paranoid delusions or other psychotic interpretations of the present interaction? Does he get lost in details because of problems in his cognitive functions, either because of alteration in the sensorium or because of chronic loss of memory and intelligence? Again, tactful clarification, exploration with the patient of his difficulty in responding (confrontation), and tentative exploration of the reasons for the difficulty in communication (interpretation) may focus attention on one or another of the major anchoring symptoms and provide early clues to the patient's descriptive and structural characteristics.

If the patient is able to understand and respond fully and clearly to the initial questions, and at the same time to present a coherent picture of the major symptom that brought him to consult and of other problems and difficulties as well, the interviewer may then raise subsidiary questions derived from the information already presented. For example, he may ask about more precise aspects of symptoms, the approximate date of their appearance and their development, and additional related symptoms; this may complete the information regarding neurotic symptoms and at the same time indirectly indicate that the patient has a normal sensorium, no major memory deficits, and at least a normal level of intelligence functioning. Nevertheless, if in the course of the patient's description of his difficulties he refers specifically to concentration, memory, and his cognitive functions in general, the interviewer would now have good reason to focus further on symptoms of acute and chronic organic brain syndromes, but with ɑ preliminary understanding that reality testing is maintained (and the patient, therefore, even if organic, is not demented).

When the patient's responses do not lead in an "organic" direction but convey information indicating an excellent level of functioning in terms of sensorium, memory, and intelligence, it may be assumed that the most important information regarding neurotic symptoms has been obtained. The focus of the interview may now shift along the perimeter to the investigation of pathological character traits (see Figure 1).

The investigation of pathological character traits, fundamental in evaluating not only the type of character or personality pathology but also its severity (and, by the same token, the presence or absence of borderline personality organization, with its key anchoring symptom of identity diffusion), is a crucial focus of the structural interview. The first question, once this point of inquiry has been reached, may be formulated as follows: "You have told me about your difficulties, and I would now like to hear more about you as a person. Could you describe yourself, your personality, what you think is important for me to know so that I can get a real feeling for you as a person?" This question represents a new challenge, a deeper level of inquiry which, under optimal circumstances, may lead a patient to a self-reflective mood. He may then describe feelings about himself, the important areas of his life (studies or work, family, social life, sex, cultural and political interests, leisure time), and particularly, his key relations with significant others.

If the patient can spontaneously present such information about himself, he thus provides one indication of good reality testing. Psychotic patients with the capacity to maintain a certain semblance of an appropriate relation to reality may have arrived at this point in the interview without showing major disturbances. For them to answer such an open-ended question satisfactorily, however, is virtually impossible since this requires the capacity for maintaining empathy with ordinary aspects of social reality (such as the interviewer's interest in the patient's personality). A patient's ability to explore his personality in depth may now indicate that he has probably maintained reality testing. The interviewer can therefore discard psychotic illness (in addition to the previously discarded acute and organic brain syndromes) from the spectrum of diagnostic possibilities.

Sometimes a patient has great difficulty talking about himself in such an unstructured way because of cultural as well as personality factors. The interviewer may then suggest that the patient describe his relations with the people who are most important to him and tell about his life, studies or work, family, sex life, social relations, how he spends his leisure time. Patients with severe character pathology, especially those with severely repressive or paranoid traits, may find it hard to provide even this more concrete, circumscribed information. Failure to respond to this more direct question would be a first indication of severe character pathology. The interviewer would then investigate identity diffusion (for the differential diagnosis of borderline personality organization) and even reevaluate reality testing.

The procedure in this instance would be for the diagnostician to point out to the patient that he seems to have difficulty talking about himself as a person. The interviewer may then ask to what extent the patient believes that this difficulty is due to the circumstances of the interview itself, apprehensions about being interviewed in general, or specific fears about the interviewer or the diagnostic situation (thus probing for possible paranoid features), or whether the difficulty reflects a general problem the patient has in clarifying to himself who he is or what his relations with the surrounding world and others are (which probes for possible schizoid features). As a response to this probing, patients with borderline personality organization may present primitive defensive operations, such as projective identification, splitting, primitive dissociation of contradictory aspects of the self experience, denial, grandiosity, fragmentation of affects, omnipotence, or devaluation. The interview has now become focused on a specific segment of the perimeter of anchoring symptoms, namely, that extending from pathological character traits through identity diffusion to reality testing.

I described in chapter 1 how to recognize clinically the maintenance of reality testing. If the patient's affect, behavior, or thought content in the early stages of the interview is clearly inappropriate, indicating the possibility of a major organic or psychotic illness, the existence of hallucinations or delusions may be explored more directly. (This aspect of the interview is discussed more fully below.) If, however, no gross evidence of psychosis has yet been obtained in the interview and the patient's information has given the interviewer no reason to think that he has had hallucinations or delusions in the past or, if he has had them, that they are still with him, the interviewer may now focus sharply on what seems most inappropriate, strange, or bizarre in the patient's affect, thought content, or behavior.

As mentioned before, encouraging the patient to talk about himself freely, particularly patients with borderline personality organization or psychotic syndromes that have so far gone undetected, may activate primitive defensive operations and the interpersonal features of these defenses that are manifest in the immediate patient/interviewer interaction. The diagnostician may at first experience this distortion as a sense of stress or strain; his internal sense of freedom in interacting with the patient diminishes. He may eventually find that a specific, regressive object relation has been activated and superimposed on the appropriate, reality-oriented one of the interview.

If, at this point, the interviewer, focusing on the patient's affect, thought content, and behavior, shares with the patient what seems to him most unusual in any of these aspects and asks the patient whether he can explain the interviewer's sense that the patient's presentation has a strange or puzzling aspect, the patient's reponse may shed light on his reality testing. Reality testing is reflected in the patient's capacity to empathize with the interviewer's perception of these characteristics of the interaction and, in a subtler way, in his capacity to empathize with the interviewer's perception of the patient in a broader sense.

For example, the interviewer may say: "As I asked you to tell me more about yourself, you first seemed puzzled and then began talking about the way your husband treats you. A little later, when I asked you whether you had any problem in relating to your husband under such circumstances and why you were mentioning this particular example, you responded by telling me about other aspects of your husband's behavior. It is as if, when I asked you to talk about yourself, you seemed to be obliged to talk about how you are treated by your husband. I find this puzzling. Can you see that I have difficulties with your attitude?" The patient may understand what puzzles the interviewer and explain, for example, that she feels so overwhelmed by her husband that it is as if she did not have the right to examine how she feels about herself (thus indicating reality testing in this situation). Or she may say, in a fearful and suspicious tone, that she is trying to point out that her husband is treating her badly and ask whether the interviewer is insinuating that these difficulties are all her fault (thus raising doubts about her reality testing, in addition to pointing to paranoid trends).

Should the latter be the case, the interviewer may now ask the patient why his asking if she might be making any contribution to the difficulties with her husband suggested the insinuation that the difficulties were all her fault. He thus follows the technique of carrying out cycles of clarification, confrontation, and interpretation around an area of disturbance in the interaction that may provide further information about the patient's personality, at the same time clarifying the patient's ability to test reality.

It is important first to clarify whether the patient has a psychotic structure—that is, absence of reality testing (which, by definition, would indicate that the patient is not a borderline patient)—before investigating identity diffusion. The patient's sense of identity differentiates borderline character pathology (characterized by identity diffusion) from nonborderline character pathology (where identity integration is intact).

If, in the course of exploring the patient's personality characteristics or pathological character traits, the question of loss of reality testing never arises (or is rapidly answered satisfactorily in the sense that reality testing is maintained), the interview then enters the middle phase, in which the evaluation of identity diffusion (and therefore the differential diagnosis of borderline personality organization) becomes the major objective. But if, in evaluating the patient's personality, it clearly emerges that reality testing is lost, the interview then focuses on the nature of the patient's psychosis.

It should be clear by now that, although the interview begins in standard ways in all cases, the nature of the questions, the interaction, and the entire quality of the interview will vary considerably according to the nature of the patient's psychopathology. In structural interviewing, this is a desirable effect, a consequence of the interviewer's systematic connection of the patient's information with the nature of the patient/diagnostician interaction.

The Middle Phase of Structural Interviewing

Neurotic Personality Organization

Patients with symptomatic neuroses and nonborderline character pathology are those who are able to respond in the initial phase of the structural interview with a pertinent summary of what brought them to treatment, what their main difficulties are, what they expect from treatment, and where they are at this point. These are also patients who give no evidence of bizarre, strange, or absurd behavior, affects, or thoughts. Their ability to test reality permits the interviewer to rule out the possibility of psychotic illness, and they present an obviously normal sensorium, normal memory, and at least normal intelligence, thus ruling out an organic brain syndrome as well. These patients are able, when the interviewer asks for further information, to expand on their presenting symptoms or difficulties in meaningful ways. They clearly understand not only the manifest content of the interviewer's questions but the subtler implications of these questions.

Such an interview may appear to an outside observer remarkably similar to a traditional or standard psychiatric interview. Now, the interviewer's main area of focus along the perimeter of the circle of anchoring symptoms is the area of pathological character traits. The questions should now focus on the patient's difficulties in interpersonal relations, in adjusting to the environment, as well as on his internally perceived psychological needs.

Whatever cues the patient provided earlier about difficulties in any of these areas should now be explored, and this exploration should be followed with a more general question such as: "I would now like to learn more about you as a person, the way you perceive yourself, the way you feel other people perceive you, whatever you think might help me to form a picture of you in depth within this limited time." This question probes for further information regarding characterological problems and leads to a more specific diagnosis regarding the predominant type of pathological character traits, the dominant pathological character constellation. At the same time, the question also makes possible an evaluation of identity diffusion.

If the patient now conveys information that the interviewer cannot put together in his mind, particularly contradictory data that do not fit with the internal image of the patient that the interviewer is building up, a tactful probing of such potential or apparent contradictions is indicated. The interviewer's aim is to evaluate the extent to which contradictory self representations are present (an indication of identity diffusion) or the extent to which the patient presents a solid, well-integrated conception of himself. Quite frequently there are peripheral areas of self experience that are contradictory to a well-integrated, central area of subjective self experience, peripheral areas that the patient himself experiences as ego-alien or ego-dystonic, not fitting into his otherwise integrated picture of himself. These isolated areas may be an important source of intrapsychic conflicts or interpersonal difficulties but should not be equated with identity diffusion. In other words, we do not expect total harmony in neurotic patients, but there should be central subjective integration of the self concept on the basis of which the interviewer can construct a mental image of the patient.

The next question deals with significant others in the patient's life. Once the interviewer has tentatively answered in his own mind the question regarding integration of the self concept, he may then explore the patient's integration of the concepts of significant others. Patients with borderline personality organization and the corresponding syndrome of identity diffusion typically present an incapacity to integrate the representations of significant others in depth. These patients have more trouble presenting a picture endowed with life of people who are important to them than they do of people they know only casually. A lead question here might be: "I would like to ask you to tell me something about the people who are now most important in your life. Could you tell me something about them so that, given our limited time here, I might form a clear impression of them?" Now the extent of integration of object representations versus lack of integration may be explored and, in this context, the degree of pathology of the patient's interpersonal life. Both identity integration or diffusion (a cross-sectional structural criterion) and the nature of the patient's object relations (a longitudinal, historical-structural criterion) may become clarified in the process.

Again, whenever internal contradictions emerge in the patient's narrative, the interviewer may clarify these first, then tactfully confront the patient with these apparent or potential contradictions and evaluate the patient's capacity to reflect on the interviewer's observations. The interviewer can thus study the patient's capacity for introspection. Finally, if obvious conflictual issues emerge in the exploration of such contradictory areas—within either the self concept or the concept of significant others—clarification and confrontation may be followed by a tentative interpretation, in the here-and-now only, of potentially dynamic or conflictual implications of these issues.

While this part of the interview with a typical neurotic patient is proceeding, the interviewer should focus on the effects the exploration is having on the actual interaction between himself and the patient. Exploration of areas of confusion, internal contradictions, and potential conflicts may increase the patient's anxiety as well as mobilize his predominant defensive operations. Characteristically, in the neurotic patient, these defenses will be fairly unobtrusive, so that in practice it is often quite difficult to diagnose the existence of repression, displacement, rationalization, or intellectualization in evaluating the patient's early interaction with the interviewer. Only reaction formations and inhibitory character traits that assume immediately defensive functions and pathological character traits in general (which, of course, always assume defensive functions) may be detected early in the interaction with neurotic patients. High-level defenses may be inferred indirectly from the content of what is being discussed but rarely show directly in the early interviews.

As noted, with borderline personality organization the exploration of identity diffusion (along the lines of dissociation of the self concept and of the concepts of significant others) typically activates primitive defensive operations which emerge in the interaction with the diagnostician rather than simply in the content of verbal communications. The more the immediate interaction between patient and diagnostician becomes transformed, altered, or distorted by such defensive processes, the more likely it is that primitive defensive operations are predominating. Thus a significant structural criterion for the diagnosis of borderline personality organization is confirmed.

In the case of patients who show no indication of identity diffusion or primitive defensive operations, dominant areas of conflict, emotional inhibitions, or symptomatic development may then be explored to the point where the limits of the patient's conscious or preconscious awareness are reached—in other words, to the limits of his repressive barriers. In these cases, the diagnostician may formulate dynamic hypotheses regarding unconscious intrapsychic conflicts. Often those are strengthened by the natural continuity between the patient's current experiences and his recall of past experiences, but such dynamic hypotheses must remain highly speculative. The healthier the patient, the easier it is for the diagnostician in early interviews to hypothesize connections between the conscious past and the present but, paradoxically, the harder it is for the patient to link present and past because these links are repressed.

With neurotic personality organization, the careful exploration of presenting symptoms, overall personality, and the interactional aspects in the interview that enrich or complement other information practically coincides with a systematic history-taking. In these cases the information gathered by structural interviewing is usually much more complete, richer, and more immediately relevant for treatment considerations than the standard approach. The relevant information regarding the patient's past follows naturally from the investigation of his current personality. In all cases with neurotic personality structure, after completing the information regarding the current illness, it is helpful to obtain a brief history of the past. In the context of such data gathering, it is often possible to link findings regarding the patient's personality tentatively with information regarding his past, a linkage intended not to test dynamic hypotheses but to test the limits of the patient's spontaneous understanding and integration of his past and present.

Borderline Personality Organization

I have already stressed the extent to which patients with borderline personality organization usually contaminate information about the past with current personality difficulties. Such contamination is even more extreme in the case of functional psychotic illness. A careful exploration of the borderline patient's current life, with particular emphasis on the syndrome of identity diffusion—and, in this context, the nature of his object relations—usually proves a rich source of data for clarifying the type and severity of his character pathology. This information should be complemented by an exhaustive investigation of currently manifest neurotic symptoms. In these cases it is preferable to explore the past only very generally and not attempt to clarify, confront, or interpret the patient's characterization of his past experiences; rather, information about the past should be registered as it is presented.

Patients with borderline personality organization typically present identity diffusion, but narcissistic personalities present an important complication in this respect. The narcissistic personality usually has an integrated self concept, but the concept is pathological and grandiose. However, the narcissistic personality clearly presents a lack of integration of the concept of significant others—thus facilitating the diagnosis of identity diffusion and a predominance of primitive defensive operations, particularly omnipotence and devaluation.

The structural characteristics of the narcissistic personality tend to emerge more slowly in structural interviewing than those of non-narcissistic borderline pathology. It is usually in the middle phase of the interview, with a patient who clearly presents good reality testing and no initial evidence of lack of integration of the self concept, that a strange superficiality or unavailability of descriptions in depth of significant others gradually emerges, together with a subtle yet pervasive expression of self-aggrandizement and often a subtle or not so subtle derogatory attitude toward the interviewer. At times, in better-functioning narcissistic personalities, the diagnosis emerges first in these patients' descriptions of their relations with others rather than in the interactions with the interviewer proper.

In contrast, in non-narcissistic borderline pathology, the initial inquiry regarding patients' motives for the consultation and expectations from treatment may immediately bring forth an apparently thoughtless, chaotic jumble of information about themselves, their unrealistic expectations of treatment, and strange or inappropriate ideas, behavior, or affects in relation to the diagnostician, which require evaluation of their reality testing. For example, a patient may start to cry in presenting her reasons for consultation, and when the diagnostician explores with her what makes her cry (particularly the possibility of acute or severe depression), the immediate response may be that she cries because she knows nobody is going to pay attention to what she says, and everybody, and therefore also this psychiatrist, will agree with her mother, with whom she has severe conflicts. In contrast, crying as a manifestation of emotional lability in an essentially neurotic personality structure (for example, in a hysterical personality) may easily disappear under exploration. The patient will acknowledge her quick change of moods and the inappropriate nature of that affect, and she will maintain a spontaneous, immediate empathy with the reality of the present social interaction.

Whenever the immediate emotional interaction of the session becomes deeply intensified in the early phase of structural interviewing (by the expression of behavior, affects, or thoughts that strongly affect that interaction), an exploration is indicated, after completing the exploration of the patient's responses to the initial inquiry, of these manifestations in the here-and-now. A delicate decision now has to be made: Where the severity of the patient's interpersonal disturbances in the immediate interaction raises the question in the interviewer's mind of whether reality testing is being maintained, an immediate exploration of these disturbances is warranted. Under these circumstances, clarification and confrontation in the here-and-now of these interactional disturbances may clarify the existence of reality testing and assure the interviewer that he is not in the presence of a psychotic structure. He can then return to the exploration of the patient's character pathology in terms of other aspects of the patient's life and at the same time focus further on primitive defensive operations manifested in the interview.

But where reality testing is not in question, there may be an advantage in following the first inquiry with a second set of questions investigating further the patient's current life and relations with others. The purpose here is to search for confirmation of indications of identity diffusion in the patient's information about himself and his social life. Only later would the interviewer return to the manifestations of primitive defensive operations and pathological object relations in the here-and-now. Here the key question is: "What you have told me about your life makes me think of something I have observed here, in this hour, and reminds me of these difficulties you mentioned. Could it be that (such and such behavior here) is a reflection, in your relation with me, of what you have said troubles you with other people?"

To put it somewhat differently, from the viewpoint of the strategy of exploring various anchoring symptoms, if a patient with obvious indications of character pathology reveals such disturbance in affect, thought content, or behavior that his reality testing is in question, an exploration of these issues takes precedence over further exploration of his pathological character traits outside the present diagnostic situation. If, however, reality testing is assured, there is an advantage in first obtaining further information about pathological character traits and in gathering more evidence about difficulties in the patient's life outside this concrete situation. The objective is to gather information regarding both identity diffusion and primitive defensive operations in a relatively "neutral" area first, and only then to link this information with the exploration of the emotional implications of these characterological manifestations in the hour.

The issue of identity diffusion can thereby usually be fully clarified, and, to some extent, primitive defensive operations also diagnosed. Sometimes, however, in patients whose reality testing at first seems appropriate, other evidence gradually accumulates regarding their lack of tact, social inappropriateness, general immaturity and arbitrariness of judgment, and the like, which may require a second exploration of reality testing. The interviewer must evaluate the extent to which these patients are able to maintain empathy with social criteria of reality by raising questions regarding their descriptions of relations with other people and exploring the socially inappropriate nature of some of the behavior that they may be describing in a matter-of-fact way.

In the typical borderline patient, neurotic symptoms tend to merge with diffuse, generalized, chaotic difficulties, reflecting serious personality malfunctioning. When there is lack of identity integration, it is often difficult or impossible to obtain a comprehensive view of the patient's life. By the same token the past histories of such patients are usually unreliable, highly distorted in the light of the current psychopathology. In other words, the severer the character pathology, the less reliable—and the less immediately relevant—is the past history. Here, therefore, in contrast to patients with neurotic personality structure, it is difficult or impossible to link predominant current conflicts with past psychodynamically significant material, and the attempt to do so is thus a highly questionable procedure. Paradoxically, however, mutually dissociated intrapsychic conflicts may make their appearance rather quickly in the manifest content of the borderline patient's communications. Key conflicts may therefore be more directly available in the initial interviews with borderline patients than with neurotic patients, while the dynamic links to their past remain obscure. By the same token, investigation of the current personality of patients with neurotic personality organization naturally leads into information about their past. In contrast, the initial information about the past obtained from patients with borderline personality organization is often no more than a retrospective expansion of current conflicts with significant others.

In patients with borderline personality organization, particularly those with narcissistic personality structure (whether or not their overt functioning is borderline), it is extremely important to evaluate antisocial behavior. Antisocial features, together with the quality of object relations, are crucial prognostic variables for intensive psychotherapy with borderline personalities and should always be probed before treatment is undertaken. Especially in patients with narcissistic personality, it is helpful to explore tactfully whether the patient has had difficulties with the law and to what extent such antisocial behaviors as stealing, shoplifting, chronic lying, and inordinately cruel behavior are significant antecedents. In practice this inquiry should be integrated with relevant information that the patient presents in other areas. When such questions are asked directly and naturally in the context of related information from the patient, the answers are often surprisingly direct and open.

(Naturally, the patient who freely admits chronic lying or "storytelling" is only giving a warning that he may soon be tempted to do the same with the therapist.)

Psychotic Personality Organization

The presence or absence of identity diffusion differentiates borderline from nonborderline character pathology in structural interviews. The presence or absence of reality testing differentiates borderline personality organization from psychotic structures.

I am referring here to patients with "functional" psychotic illness in contrast to psychotic developments secondary to an acute or a chronic organic brain syndrome. This group includes the entire spectrum of schizophrenic illness, major affective disorders, and paranoid psychoses that do not fit into the other two major psychotic syndromes. All these patients present loss of reality testing. In a typical case of a psychotic illness, the patient's response to the initial inquiry may already indicate absence of reality testing and, beyond that, such an incapacity to respond intelligibly to the interviewer's questions that the entire spectrum of functional psychotic illness, acute and organic brain syndrome, has to be evaluated.

In the extreme case of a patient who is totally unresponsive to the initial inquiry, the interviewer should first try to explore with him whether he has heard the question and has understood it. If the patient has been able to walk into the room and is obviously aware of and alert to the immediate environment, such total mutism is likely to indicate a functional psychotic illness rather than an organic brain syndrome. Nevertheless, it is helpful for the interviewer to proceed along the entire perimeter of the cycle of anchoring symptoms. Explore the sensorium, then memory and intelligence, before recycling to further focus on reality testing and major psychotic symptoms in behavior, affect, thought content and organization, and hallucinations.

The focus on the sensorium can be carried out by first testing the patient's attention: "I asked you some questions, and you have not responded; were you able to hear and understand what I asked?" If the patient continues to be unresponsive, it is helpful to find out whether he can indicate that he hears, understands, and agrees or disagrees with various questions asked by nodding his head or by any other signal. Under such extreme circumstances, it is important to clarify whether he understands and is trying to communicate, even though he may not be able to speak.

A lack of response to this probing behavior usually indicates negativism as part of a catatonic syndrome or schizophrenic illness in general or severe psychomotor retardation in extreme degrees of depressive illness. Sometimes, in the totally unresponsive patient, direct testing of catatonic features, particularly negativism, may elicit behavior directly opposed to the instructions given, flexibilitas cerea, and/or stereotyped posture or behavior that points to schizophrenic illness. In other cases, only a full exploration of the history of the present illness, obtained from other sources, will provide more definite information. Organic patients whose degree of consciousness is sufficient to be alert to their environment are usually able to respond to simple questions that would complete the exploration of the sensorium, such as the patient's orientation, consciousness, comprehension, and judgment of the immediate situation. (Because these areas are amply covered in guides to standard mental-status examination, I am not illustrating them with further concrete questions.)

If, in the course of the initial inquiry, it turns out that the patient's sensorium is clear, one can then explore whether the lack of response or the confusing response to the initial set of questions was due to loss of memory or lack of intelligence—that is, an incapacity to understand clearly what was asked or to retain the questions sufficiently while preparing an answer. Again, without going into a detailed analysis of the loss of cognitive functions that would characterize an organic brain syndrome, I want to stress the general point that, when a patient demonstrates severe incapacity to respond to the initial set of questions, the anchoring symptoms reflecting abnormalities in the sensorium, memory, and intelligence should be explored before returning to the examination of the major anchoring symptoms of functional psychosis.

If it is evident that the patient shows severe disturbance in verbal or nonverbal behavior but no alteration of the sensorium, memory, or intelligence, then the interviewer should return to the initial set of questions regarding what brings the patient to treatment, the nature of his difficulties, what he expects from treatment, and where he is now. If the response to this second cycle of inquiry is still inappropriate, confused or confusing, or accompanied by affect or behavior that seems inappropriate, the interviewer should now focus on such pathological thought content, affect, and behavior, tactfully share his observations with the patient, and explore in detail the extent to which the patient can empathize with the diagnostician's experience of the patient's responses as strange or puzzling.

If it is clear that reality testing has been lost regarding any aspect of the patient's behavior, thought, or affect during the interview, the diagnosis of a functional psychosis should be considered, and the diagnostician may then shift to a different approach to the patient's disturbed manifestations by attempting to explore with him possible meanings of these manifestations in terms of the patient's present subjective experience. In other words, once the loss of reality testing has been confirmed, there is an advantage in temporarily abandoning a confronting approach and in pursuing the patient's internal experience corresponding to his behavioral manifestations. Further exploration of the patient's subjective experiences may lead to an understanding of the connections among his affect, thinking, and behavior and open the road to a differential diagnosis. Is the patient suffering from a schizophrenic illness (with disorganization of these linkages) or an affective illness (in which an internal organization links inappropriate affect, behavior, and thought so that a degree of internal harmony among these psychic functions is maintained within a highly pathological organization of them)? The evaluation of hallucinatory experiences may now enrich the diagnosis of loss of reality testing formulated earlier on the basis of interactional processes. The confirmation of hallucinations indicates, by definition, loss of reality testing. Similarly, the diagnosis of delusions also confirms loss of reality testing and usually provides further clues about the nature of the psychotic illness.

A general principle of structural interviewing with psychotic patients is that, once clarification and tactful confrontation confirm loss of reality testing, the patient's thought processes, reality distortion, and internal experience are no longer challenged. To the contrary, an effort should now be made to empathize maximally with the patient's internal reality in order to deepen the understanding of the psychotic process itself. By the same token, in the middle and termination phases of structural interviewing of psychotic patients, the diagnostician may implicitly adjust his interventions to the severe distortions in the interaction with the patient, helping the patient to achieve a nonthreatening or anxiety-reducing termination phase of the interview.

In the case of some psychotic patients, with whom the initial communication is much more appropriate and freer, where only the exploration of what initially appeared as severe character pathology leads the interviewer into evaluating reality testing and eventually to the decision that reality testing is lost, the interview may appear much more similar to that of the typical borderline patient. In fact, patients with true hallucinations and delusions sometimes initially present their delusions or hallucinations as, respectively, overvalued (even obsessive) ideas or illusions (or pseudohallucinations). Under these conditions, it may be helpful to explore to what extent the patient is trying to maintain a "reasonable" or "normal" evaluation of his thought or sensory perceptions because he is afraid that otherwise he might be considered "crazy."

For example, an illustrative question might be: "You have told me that at times you feel you are Jesus Christ, but that, of course, you are aware that you are really not Jesus Christ. Could it be that, deep down, you are really convinced that you are Jesus Christ but afraid that this conviction will be interpreted as 'crazy' by me or by others?" In other words, when delusional or hallucinatory phenomena are potentially present, reality testing should include a confrontation not only with external reality but also with psychotic reality, in a nonthreatening way.

When the exploration of inappropriate behavior, affect, or thought content does not clarify the issue of reality testing and when there is no clear indication of hallucinations or delusions, a further, more complex interviewing technique may be utilized—namely, the interpretation in the here-and-now of the patient's primitive defensive operations. As I have suggested (see chap. 1), the interpretation of primitive defensive operations in the here-and-now tends to increase reality testing in patients with borderline personality organization but to decrease it in psychotic patients.

For example, a typical intervention interpreting a projective identification might be: "I notice that you have been talking in a very cautious and fearful way with me, as if you were afraid of some danger connected with me. I also notice that you have been frowning at some of my questions (for example, . . .). Could it be that you are afraid I might think badly of you or attack you in some way because you are afraid of some similar tendencies in yourself, such as feeling critical or angry toward me?"

The interpretation of primitive defensive operations is difficult. The diagnostician must develop a hypothesis about the nature of the primitive, fantastic, dissociated object relations activated. He must also develop a hypothesis about the defensive function of that primitive defensive operation. Then he must share his hypothesis with the patient.

Sometimes there may be dramatic shifts toward improvement or worsening in the immediate interaction following such an interpretive hypothesis. At other times, the response is uncertain. Patients with paranoid psychotic illness who have preserved sufficient awareness of reality to hide their real thoughts or fears may simply show increased evasiveness after such probing interventions. Some of the most difficult challenges to structural interviewing (as well as to all diagnostic approaches) are presented by paranoid patients in whom the differential diagnosis between paranoid personality and paranoid psychosis is unclear. Repeated diagnostic interviews may be required to reach a more definite conclusion.

In the case of patients with active psychotic illness, particularly schizophrenia and manic-depressive illness, the main emphasis of the structural interview should be on the nature of the presenting symptoms, with the objective of differentiating the major psychoses as well as subtypes within them. In these cases and in patients with organic brain syndrome and loss of reality testing, systematic investigation of the history of the present illness, as well as of the past history, usually requires input from other sources and does not form part of the structural interview itself.

Acute and Chronic Organic Brain Syndromes

As mentioned before, a patient's incapacity to respond appropriately to the initial set of questions may indicate an alteration of the sensorium (typical of an acute organic brain syndrome) or severe deficit of memory and intelligence (typical of a chronic organic brain syndrome). When the patient is apparently conscious yet unresponsive to the initial inquiry or, though responding to it, reveals severe disorganization in his response, a minimal or an inadequate reaction, or a general attitude of confusion or perplexity, cycling from the presenting problems to the evaluation of the sensorium, memory, and intelligence is indicated.

The evaluation of the sensorium, including the patient's spontaneous and induced attention, his orientation, the degree of consciousness, his comprehension and judgment, may clarify whether a confusional state exists characteristic of an acute organic brain syndrome or whether this confusional state represents an acute functional psychosis, particularly acute schizophrenia (a schizophreniform disorder in DSM-III). The tactful evaluation of the patient's awareness of his difficulties in grasping the interviewer's questions or the total interviewing situation may gradually produce evidence of disorientation, decrease of consciousness, and diffuse difficulty in understanding concepts—all of which are typical of an acute organic brain syndrome. In contrast, highly idiosyncratic responses in which perplexity and confusion coexist with bizarre yet organized formulations are more characteristic of schizophrenia. A series of direct questions having to do with clarifying and confronting the difficulties the patient experiences in communicating and exploring his ability to introspect may contribute to the differential diagnosis of organic and schizophrenic confusional states.

With patients whose difficulty in grasping and responding to the initial inquiry appears to reflect mostly a deficit in memory and intellectual understanding, an open ventilation of such difficulties may facilitate a systematic evaluation of memory and intelligence functions (particularly abstraction). For example, the interviewer might comment: "I have the impression from your reaction that you are struggling with problems in concentrating or memory. May I ask you some questions to clarify whether, indeed, you have some difficulties with your memory?" This inquiry may initiate the transition toward a more standard systematic evaluation of memory and intelligence.

If and when deficits in memory and intelligence have been confirmed, the interviewer may tentatively explore with the patient the extent to which he is aware of or preoccupied with his difficulties in remembering or formulating his thinking clearly, and how upsetting this is to him. If the patient is unable to grasp his obvious difficulties or vehemently denies them, tactful confrontation may test the discrepancies between what the diagnostician observes and the patient's reaction.

If such confrontation increases the denial, loss of reality testing regarding such organic deficits may be assumed, and the interviewer may ascertain a tentative diagnosis of dementia (that is, a chronic organic brain syndrome with secondary loss of reality testing).

In a less severe case of chronic organic brain syndrome, the patient may present some awareness of his difficulties and acknowledge them. Nevertheless, there may be a lack of appropriate anxiety or depression over this loss, which also may indicate personality changes and loss of reality testing commensurate with dementia. Under these conditions, before exploring the discrepancies between the patient's memory and intellectual deficits, on the one hand, and his affect state, on the other, it is helpful to explore whether he has experienced similar difficulties in relation to studies, work, other people, and his social life in general. The investigation of the symptoms of chronic organic brain syndrome is thus expanded via "recycling" through the evaluation of neurotic symptoms and pathological character traits in the patient's social life.

In this manner, structural interviewing may contribute to the differential diagnosis of confusional states (organic versus schizophrenic) and to the evaluation of the severity of personality deterioration and loss of reality testing in chronic organic brain syndrome—that is, the evaluation of dementia.

By and large, when the interviewer sees that the patient is having severe difficulty responding to the initial inquiry or seems very anxious, depressed, or confused, he should share his impressions with the patient. Further, he should ask whether these impressions correspond to the patient's feelings about himself and whether part of his apprehension or fearfulness may relate to the interview itself. In fact, this approach to the expression of intense fear and apprehension should be applied to patients along the entire spectrum of psychopathology. Psychotic and organic cases and patients with severe paranoid personality traits and severe degrees of social inhibition (shyness, timidity, and the like) may appear intensely anxious in the interview, especially in the early phase. On the other hand, the initial inquiry, with its structuring properties, may have a tranquilizing or reassuring effect on nonorganic, nonpsychotic patients by modifying their unrealistic fantasies about the interview itself. Therefore, persistence of intense anxiety after the initial inquiry usually indicates severe psychopathology of some kind.

The Termination Phase of Structural Interviewing

Having completed the exploration of neurotic symptoms and pathological character traits, predominant defensive operations, and identity diffusion, reality testing, and the major psychotic or organic anchoring symptoms, the interviewer should now acknowledge to the patient that he has completed his task. He should then invite the patient to provide him with information regarding additional issues that the patient considers important or thinks the interviewer should know about. A very helpful question (suggested by Robert Michels in a personal communication, 1981) is "What do you think I should have asked you and have not yet asked?" This inquiry may sometimes lead to significant new information or to further reflections on areas already explored. It also provides an opportunity for the patient to express anxieties activated during the interview, which can now be explored further and reduced by bringing in reality considerations.

It is important to leave enough time at the end not only for the patient to raise questions but also for the interviewer to respond to them and to deal with unexpected anxiety and other complications. The interviewer may decide that further interviews are warranted before a definite diagnosis can be arrived at, or perhaps that both participants will need more time to think before discussing treatment recommendations, or perhaps that a treatment disposition can be completed now. In any case, the decision-making process should be shared with the patient. The interviewer may tell the patient that he has learned enough about him to make a recommendation or feels he would like to continue the diagnostic process; in either event, the interviewer may wish to obtain pertinent information from other sources.

The termination of the structural interview is a crucial opportunity for evaluating the patient's motivation for continuation of the diagnostic process and/or treatment, the management of acute dangers that have been diagnosed and require urgent action (for example, acute suicide risk in severely depressed patients), and the extent to which the patient can tolerate and respond positively to statements regarding his problems as perceived by the interviewer. Every consultation should carry with it the possibility for the diagnostician to extend it with a number of additional interviews if necessary. The patient's magical assumption that all diagnostic conclusions can be made in one or two interviews should be realistically explored if necessary. Most patients are usually appreciative when a psychiatrist honestly acknowledges that, although he has learned much, he does not yet know enough to decide what, if any, the treatment needs are.

Some Further Considerations on the Interviewer's Attitude

Structural interviewing requires time, including time for experiencing and thinking while the interview goes on. Therefore, I recommend that at least an hour and a half be reserved for an initial interview. In our borderline diagnosis research project (Kernberg et al., 1981), after much experimenting, we settled on two 45-minute periods, separated by a 10-

to-15-minute intermission. In my private practice I often set aside the last two treatment hours of the day for the initial interview of a new patient.

The diagnostician should be comfortable, relatively "at his best" in the sense of not being disturbed by extraneous considerations, and able to remain emotionally alert and receptive, yet very much in the background, while all his attention is focused on the patient. In spite of (or because of) his unobtrusive attitude, the interviewer may initially appear as an "ideal" person to the patient; he may elicit strong tendencies toward idealization or dependency in patients with a capacity for basic trust, regardless of the anxieties and difficulties that brought them to treatment. In patients with severe disturbances in their object relations, an incapacity for basic trust, paranoid dispositions, or intense unconscious envy, the very calmness, receptivity, and "untroubledness" of the diagnostician may evoke suspicion, resentment, fear, or derogation.

In any case a double relationship is quickly established between the patient and interviewer: a realistic, socially appropriate one of patient and therapist, and an underlying, more or less subtle one reflecting the patient's predominant transference dispositions and the diagnostician's potential corresponding countertransference dispositions. The latter jointly activate a conflictual, "fantastic" object relationship (in the sense of both a fantasy and its unrealistic nature). Early expression of conscious or unconscious erotic, aggressive, and/or dependent affective dispositions on the patient's part creates not only a cognitive awareness of them in the diagnostician but also concordant or complementary affective dispositions in him (Racker, 1968).

The diagnostician faces the task of simultaneously (a) exploring the patient's subjective, inner world, (b) observing the patient's behavior and interactions with him, and (c) utilizing his own affective reactions to the patient in order to clarify the nature of the underlying activated object relation. This underlying object relation is the basic material that should permit the interviewer to formulate tentative interpretations in the here-and-now of the patient's defensive operations, if such operations become apparent, dominant, and require exploration.

From a different perspective, the diagnostician also builds up in his own mind a model of the patient's image of himself, his self representation. At the same time, he explores the extent to which the communications from the patient really lend themselves to building up such a model. The diagnostician also attempts to build up a model in his mind of the significant others with whom the patient is interacting in his life and raises the same question: whether it is possible to obtain an integrated representation of them. Here, of course, the diagnostician is evaluating identity integration versus identity diffusion.

From a still different perspective, the diagnostician is evaluating what appears to be most inappropriate in the patient's affect, thought content, or behavior, preparing himself to explore his perceptions with the patient in an honest yet tactful way, evaluating, in this context, the patient's capacity to empathize with the diagnostician's experience— which will reflect, at one level, the patient's capacity for introspection or insight and, at a different level, the patient's capacity for reality testing.

To carry out all these tasks is difficult; it requires knowledge of and experience with the standard mental-status examination, psychotherapeutic experience in working interpretively with transference developments, and clinical experience with a broad spectrum of psychiatric patients. It is, however, a technique that can be taught to and acquired by gifted third-year psychiatric residents and further developed with personal experience and practice. The structural interview represents what might be called a "second generation" of the earlier "dynamic interview," which reflected the impact of a psychoanalytic frame of reference on the diagnostic interview in descriptive psychiatry.[1]

1. For the research implications of diagnostic interviewing see Carr et al. (1979), Bauer et al. (1980), and Kernberg et al. (1981).

CHAPTER 3

Differential Diagnosis in Adolescence

General Diagnostic Considerations

In the older literature on identity disturbances in adolescence, identity crises and identity diffusion were not clearly differentiated. Therefore one can still find the question raised whether all adolescents might present some degree of identity diffusion and hence be indistinguishable from later borderline personality organization. I think one can differentiate borderline and nonborderline character pathology quite easily, utilizing the structural approach to diagnosis. The descriptive and psychodynamic characteristics of severe character pathology and borderline conditions in adolescence have been reviewed by Geleerd (1958), Masterson (1967, 1972), Paz (1976), Michael Stone (1980), and Paulina Kernberg (1982).

In applying structural criteria to the initial evaluation of adolescent patients, the clinician is faced with several complicating features. First, the relative severity of the disorganizing effects of symptomatic neuroses in adolescence, typically severe anxiety and depression, may affect the adolescent's overall functioning at home, in school, and with peers to an extent that may resemble the severer social breakdown typical of borderline conditions.

Second is the adolescent tendency toward identity crises, characterized by rapidly shifting identifications with this or that social ideology or group, so that what looks like radical change in the personality may appear in the course of a few months. These sudden alterations in identification raise the question of whether the much severer syndrome of identity diffusion is present.

Third, conflicts with parents, siblings, and/or school authorities may be misinterpreted. These conflicts may reflect neurotic dependent and rebellious needs, or they may reflect severe pathology in the area of object relations and a manifestation of the syndrome of identity diffusion. In fact, nonborderline neurotic conflicts with parents and authority figures may intensify and activate the potential for primitive defensive operations in an essentially nonborderline patient, so that what appears as omnipotent control, projective identification, and devaluation may become manifest in certain object relations of some nonborderline patients.

Fourth, antisocial behavior in adolescence may be an expression of a "normal" or neurotic adaptation to an antisocial cultural subgroup (and thus be relatively nonmalignant), or it may reflect severe character pathology and borderline personality organization masking as an adaptation to an antisocial group. Accordingly, the frequently misused label "adjustment reaction in adolescence" is not so much a diagnosis as an alarm signal indicating the need to evaluate in depth the personality structure of an adolescent in social conflicts.

Fifth, the normal, neurotic, and infantile narcissistic reactions so frequent in adolescence may mask a severe narcissistic personality structure, particularly when there are no antisocial features to immediately alert the diagnostician to the evaluation of narcissistic, in addition to antisocial, pathology. Narcissistic pathology may present not as typical conflicts around omnipotent control, grandiosity, and devaluation but rather as a strange oscillation between excellent school functioning and puzzling failure in competitive tasks.

Sixth, the normal emergence of multiple perverse sexual trends in adolescence may imitate the condensation of genital and pregenital features (with the predominance of aggressive conflicts) that is typical in borderline personality organization. As I have already said, the nature of the predominant unconscious conflicts is not a good diagnostic criterion.

Finally, the more slowly developing psychotic conditions, such as chronic schizophrenic illness, may mask as borderline conditions because of the predominance of severe pathology of object relations, social withdrawal, and severe character pathology in general. Also, although hallucinations are rather easily diagnosed, insidious delusion formation may at first be misinterpreted as, for example, hypochondriacal tendencies or excessive preoccupation with physical appearance.

In what follows, I shall attempt to illustrate these difficulties in the differential diagnosis of borderline pathology in adolescence, as well as the application of the general diagnostic criteria mentioned.

Clinical Illustrations

Miss A. An 18-year-old college freshman was referred to me with a presumptive diagnosis of borderline personality organization and severe neurotic depression. Miss A had been failing in her schoolwork, isolating herself socially, and had oscillated between periods of depressiveness and withdrawal and other periods of vehement arguments with friends and family. She had had both homosexual and heterosexual affairs, and the referring physician had found her aloof and distant. The predominant symptom was the severe breakdown of social life at school and failure in her studies despite high intelligence.

In the exploration of her difficulties, it turned out that Miss A had always had sexual inhibitions, manifested in severe guilt over any sexual activity and in masturbation fantasies of being humiliated, beaten, and enslaved by powerful, sadistic men. Although she had fallen in love with several men, she had always been revolted by actual sexual intercourse with them. Fearful of other women with whom she felt she could not compete, she attempted to establish submissive relations with dominant women. She had had a few sexual relations with girlfriends without experiencing much sexual pleasure. In high school she had always felt that good work and hard studies would permit her to find her own professional identity without having to get involved in sex relations with men or having to compete with other women for men. At college, she felt that all roads to sexual intimacy were closed to her, and her increasing despair over her incapacity to overcome these difficulties, combined with increasing guilt feelings over engaging in "forbidden" sexual activities, finally triggered the depression that intensified to the point of interfering seriously with her studies.

Miss A was able to convey differentiated and vivid descriptions of the most significant people with whom she was involved and of her relations with them. She had an integrated concept of herself in spite—or because—of severe repressive features, and she presented rather typical traits of a predominantly hysterical/masochistic personality structure. She showed a clear commitment to values and ideals, a definite and authentic interest in certain cultural and political areas, and surprisingly good functioning in interpersonal situations where important age differences made potentially sexualized relations less pressing. Having worked as a volunteer in a social organization where she was by far the youngest participant, she was able to function excellently for several months while living "like a nun." In this case, an integrated concept of the self and of others indicated that there was no identity diffusion; the apparently chaotic sexual life corresponded to an underlying sexual inhibition regarding men and guilt-determined submission to powerful women. Miss A was able to establish object relations in depth in areas not "contaminated" by sexual conflicts, and she gave evidence of an overly sadistic and strict but definitely integrated superego. The final diagnosis was hysterical personality with masochistic features, frigidity, and severe neurotic depression. The patient's depression improved with a short-term, psychoanalytically oriented psychotherapy, and she was then able to function much better in her school and social life. Later, she was referred for psychoanalysis in order to deal with her deeper underlying character problems.

Miss B. A 15-year-old high school sophomore was referred for consultation because of a recent dramatic change in her personality. Miss B had been close to her family, timid with others, and a hard worker at school. Suddenly, according to her parents, she had adopted a dramatically accentuated "hippie style" attire, entered upon a stormy and apparently quite subservient love relation with a boy several years older than herself, and participated in a "drug scene" with a social subgroup of rebellious, unconventional youngsters. The quiet atmosphere at home had been replaced by ongoing arguments and mutual recrimination, and the parents were disturbed by the emergence of frequent lying and what they saw as manipulative and secretive—implicitly dishonest—behavior, which they had never observed in their daughter before. The girl had been seen by a psychotherapist who had urged the parents to be more flexible and tolerant in their attitude toward their daughter. For reasons that were not clear, strong tensions had developed between the psychotherapist and the parents, with the patient in the role of "innocent" bystander.

Although the referring physician wondered whether this was a patient with borderline personality organization, clinically Miss B impressed me as intellectually and emotionally more mature than one would expect at her age. After exploring her initial distrust and fearfulness of me, her seeing me as an "agent" of her parents, I was able to convey to her my attitude of neutrality regarding her lifestyle, ideology, and relation with her boyfriend. She then opened up, describing what appeared to me to be a deep and meaningful relationship with the boy—a normal, romantic falling in love, and a satisfactory sexual relation with him. Miss B was indeed "rebelling" against what she saw as the overconventional values of her home, but at the same time she seemed to be making realistic plans for her own career and future. She was keeping up her schoolwork, was fairly responsible regarding various tasks and social commitments, and openly acknowledged her enjoyment of occasional pot smoking and being part of a "protest" group but did not seem to be addicted. Nor had she abandoned her long-standing interests in culture and art or her close relations with a few long-time friends. She had an integrated way of presenting herself, a differentiated concept of significant others, a thoughtful and emotionally open response to my questions regarding the conflicts with her parents and the relation with her psychotherapist.

My principal concern was the sudden change in her overall appearance and outlook, and I raised this matter with her over a period of nine sessions. In the course of these meetings, the change seemed less pathological than it had originally; it seemed to reflect an essentially normal effort to separate from family ties that she experienced as too close and overwhelming. I concluded that Miss B was a relatively normal adolescent. The separate and joint meetings with the patient and her parents reconfirmed her psychotherapist's recommendation that the parents respect the patient's distancing and her development of a social life that did not conform with their own standards. These parents were in fact unusually understanding and flexible. A one-year follow-up indicated that the difficulties with the parents had markedly decreased and the relation with the boyfriend had terminated six months after the first consultation; she was dating another boy, and she was pursuing her work and social life quite normally.

Mr. C. A 19-year-old college student was referred for what appeared to the referring physician as almost psychotic grandiosity, self-absorption, and severe pathology of object relations. This young man had long had an interest in history and art and had been writing essays attempting to integrate widely divergent approaches to certain problems in historical and art criticism. While the referring physician could not evaluate the actual quality of that work, he was impressed by the patient's high intelligence but also concerned over the grandiose tone the patient used in conveying his information and his somewhat childish, self-congratulatory attitude. Mr. C also generally derogated most of the people who were relatively close to him. His world of object relations seemed to consist of very few, highly idealized models, on the one hand, and a great many devalued "mediocrities" (including his parents, other family members, and most of his teachers, friends, and acquaintances), on the other. There were times when the referring physician wondered whether he was faced with a genius, a psychotic patient, or a combination of both.

The immediate reason for the consultation had been Mr. C's growing apprehension over his incapacity to establish a satisfactory relationship with a girl. Those women he admired seemed unapproachable or strongly rejecting of him, and the patient was extremely shy and inhibited with them; he was not able to provide much information about how his internal attitude affected his relations with these girls. At the same time, girls who had shown interest in him and with whom he had developed some kind of relationship he soon depreciated and escaped from, fearful lest they exert demands on him. He had had occasional and rather unsatisfactory sexual affairs with girlfriends, occasional impotence, and some rapidly shifting idealizations of inaccessible women.

In general, Mr. C experienced a sense of great loneliness, which derived from his actively separating himself from peers (because he depreciated them) and from the pattern of his relations with women. At college, his performance was irregular; he made a name for himself because of his outstanding knowledge and awareness in certain areas, and at the same time (for reasons that were not clear to him) he received poor grades in other subjects and experienced frank rejection from some professors and instructors, who became sharply critical of him.

It needs to be stressed that the combination of timidity and inhibition with the "bravado" attitude with which he expressed his intellectual superiority, the difficulties with girls, and his sharply oscillating moods might have led one to think of him as a not too atypical adolescent. His commitment to intellectual and cultural values, his hard work in certain areas, his creativity in his own field suggested that he had the capacity to sublimate for superego integration. He had good impulse control and anxiety tolerance and, except for occasional mild impotence, no neurotic symptoms.

On an extended evaluation, what most impressed me was Mr. C's incapacity to describe adequately the nature of his difficulty with girls and the reasons certain teachers and peers rejected him. In spite of his intelligence he could not convey a picture of his parents, his admired teachers, or the two or three girls with whom he was involved at that time. In short, the quality of his object relations seemed remarkably poor, and there was a definite indication of marked splitting and a lack of integration of object representations.

In contrast, his self image and self concept seemed consistent and integrated, reflecting a pathological grandiose self. He adequately conveyed his understanding of the contradiction between his concept of himself as a kind of a genius, a still unacknowledged major contributor to contemporary culture in a certain area, on the one hand, and his feelings of uncertainty and insecurity regarding girls and social situations, on the other. He explained that he had emotional needs for other people and that without other people he was bound to feel alone. Insofar as he needed other people and was concerned over his inability to establish relationships with them, he felt insecure. This is what he wanted treatment for: to feel secure and reassured in his relations with women so that this area of "limitation" to his self-satisfaction would be substantially reduced and he could then dedicate himself without distraction to the pursuit of his writing.

Reality testing was maintained, and he was able to evaluate realistically manifestations of his sense of superiority in the diagnostic interviews. He quickly came to perceive me as a friendly but somewhat confused, not too bright, rather unattractive, unmasculine, and aging psychiatrist. Because I had been highly recommended to him, he was willing "to give me a chance," but he was seriously concerned about whether he could be helped in his difficulties with women by a man who himself did not look like somebody who would be very attractive to women.

This case illustrates a surface pathology imitating certain mild adolescent features and an underlying severe character pathology: namely, a narcissistic personality functioning better than on an overt borderline level.

Mr. C was referred for psychoanalysis, and a follow-up after two years indicated that he was able to continue his treatment to that point and that he had established a typical constellation of narcissistic resistances in the transference. At that time, no major change had yet occurred in his difficulties with women, although his awareness of his contributions to the difficulties at work, particularly with his teachers and superiors, had gradually increased.

I have so far described cases in which the surface functioning indicated the possibility of borderline personality organization but the diagnosis of a neurotic personality organization—and even normality—had to be seriously entertained. The following cases illustrate the opposite end of the spectrum: namely, cases in which the differential diagnosis was between borderline and psychotic personality organization.

Miss D. The manifest illness of a young artist began at age 17, when she entered her first year of college. At that time, she became more and more preoccupied with bizarre sexual thoughts that interfered with her capacity to concentrate, a growing sense of estrangement, and a desperate need to remain close to her mother at all times. Miss D secretively began to cut her skin, withdrew socially, remained in her room most of the time, felt more and more depressed, and made several suicide attempts when cutting herself. The initial diagnosis (arrived at elsewhere) of severe depression (presumably psychotic depression) was followed by electroshock treatment; after some temporary improvement, all her symptoms returned. Short-term hospitalization in several treatment centers and standard psychopharmacological treatment combining tranquilizers and antidepressant medication did not bring any definite improvement. Finally, a long-term hospital treatment was carried out, in the course of which the question was raised as to whether Miss D presented a chronic schizophrenic illness or a borderline personality organization. Most of the psychiatrists who saw her made the diagnosis of a schizophrenic illness.

In an extended diagnostic evaluation over a period of several weeks I found the following features: She was deeply suspicious of the motivations of her family and all the people surrounding her in the hospital. She gave no clear indication of delusional thinking but did show a general paranoid orientation. Her speech was vague and circumstantial, with prolonged silences and blocking, raising in my mind the question whether she presented formal disorganization of thought processes. Careful evaluation did not reveal hallucinations or delusions. Her descriptions of herself and of significant others were vague, chaotic, and contradictory. Her affect fluctuated between periods of confusion and bewilderment, moments of depression, and other moments of subtle bemusement.

When I confronted Miss D with her suspicious, strangely withdrawn attitudes toward me, she showed a surprising awareness of her own behavior and of how it was influencing the therapist/patient relationship. Interpretation of the predominant projective mechanisms (for example, of her fears that I would not be interested in her or would be sharply critical of her, when she was indirectly giving evidence of these same trends herself) increased her awareness of the immediate reality situation and sharply reduced the vagueness of her communications. In short, the absence of hallucinations and delusions, her capacity for empathizing with ordinary social criteria regarding the immediate patient/therapist interaction, and an integrated response with transitory improvement of ego functions to the interpretation of primitive defensive operations in the early transference, all reconfirmed a solid maintenance of reality testing.

I formulated the diagnosis of a borderline personality organization with predominant schizoid, masochistic, and paranoid features. I recommended intensive psychoanalytically oriented psychotherapy and discontinuation of all medication and also suggested that the beginning of psychotherapy be carried out in a structured hospital setting until such time as she was able to control her self-mutilating and suicidal behavior.

This recommendation was followed; Miss D remained in the hospital for another six months and then continued in outpatient psychotherapy four sessions a week over a four-year period. A follow-up after three years of this treatment revealed a growing sense of autonomy; a growing capacity to study and work (to the extent that she had completed her college education and was developing a career as an artist), the beginning of normal heterosexual relations with appropriate men, the capacity to move away from home and achieve a sense of internal autonomy, and complete disappearance of the self-mutilating and suicidal tendencies. This case illustrates the crucial function of the evaluation of reality testing in the differential diagnosis of borderline from psychotic—particularly schizophrenic—disorders.

Miss E. This was an 18-year-old girl with a history of several episodes of severe depression, gradual deterioration at school over the previous two to three years, severe and chronic arguments with her parents, and increasing social isolation. Miss E presented sexual inhibition in relation to boys and a tendency to gravitate toward those who were rebellious and socially isolated, keeping a few friendships with some persons with these characteristics over several years. She was hospitalized because of her parents' concern that her depression might again become severe and that she might become suicidal.

In the hospital she was haughty, controlling, suspicious, and manipulative. She insisted that nothing was wrong with her psychologically; her only problem, she said, was a chronic pain in her arms, which presumably had developed gradually because of the difficulty she had experienced in sleeping during the previous extended depression. She thought her problems were originally emotional and had caused the depression—and the depression the sleeplessness—but that the pain in her arms was an organic consequence of lack of sleep. Nothing would help her, she insisted, except the right kind of medication, which she was willing to fight for as long as necessary.

The symptom of pain in her arms gradually emerged as a major organizing axis in all her interpersonal dealings. She reacted quite violently to confrontations of her manipulative behavior, and her tendencies to split staff and patients alike in her dealings on the ward increased with confrontations. Because of the combination of clearly predominant primitive defensive operations—particularly denial, splitting, and projective tendencies—and her lack of an integrated self concept and a differentiated concept of others, she was initially thought to present a borderline personality organization.

In my diagnostic interviews I felt that reality testing was maintained regarding her empathy with external observations of her immediate behavior and that she did not show further disintegration under the effect of interpretation of primitive defensive operations. However, I felt that I could never go beyond her denial of all psychological difficulties and that the hypochondriacal orientation regarding the pain in her arms could never be reduced by ordinary reality testing. Therefore, the question remained to what extent this was a chronic hypochondriacal delusion, probably indicating—in a patient who at that time did not present any other manifestations of severe depression—the possibility of a schizophrenic (or schizoaffective) illness.

Long-term hospitalization was recommended and a probing, expressive approach carried out in order to further clarify this differential diagnosis. Under the effect of this treatment approach, Miss E's behavior gradually began to disorganize further; eventually, clear-cut hallucinations and other hypochondriacal and paranoid delusions became manifest; the final diagnosis was that of chronic schizophrenic illness.

This case illustrates the diagnostic difficulties with patients who present a chronic monosymptomatic delusional symptomatology and points again to the crucial importance of reality testing as part of the diagnostic study. Both borderline and schizophrenic patients present severe identity diffusion and clear predominance of primitive defensive operations. It is the presence or absence of reality testing in a strict sense that permits the diagnostic differentiation. The embedding of an isolated chronic delusion in a constellation of what seems to be a more or less severe adolescent rebelliousness may obscure the underlying psychotic personality organization.

Narcissistic Pathology in Adolescence

It should be said at the outset that it is probably only the severer types of narcissistic personality who come to us for treatment in adolescence. Many of the better-functioning narcissistic personalities consult only much later in life, in connection with other symptoms or when the beginning of the aging process threatens narcissistic defenses. Some adolescents with narcissistic personality also consult for other symptoms—school failure, for example, or depression or sexual deviation—but usually these difficulties have to be fairly severe to bring an adolescent patient with narcissistic personality to a psychiatrist. Therefore, the diagnosis of narcissistic pathology in adolescence usually implies that the pathology is severe.

I describe elsewhere (chap. 11) a continuum of severity of narcissistic personality features. Here I shall limit myself to describing some characteristic features of adolescent patients with narcissistic personality proper. These are first, a contradictory school record, with ambitiousness and driving efforts, on the one hand, and almost inexplicable failure and withdrawal from other activities, on the other. The explanation lies in the adolescents' need either to be the best or to devalue those fields in which they cannot triumph or could achieve their goal only through persistent effort. This pattern is often masked by symptomatic depression related to failure at school. Only a careful evaluation reveals the predominant narcissistic features of that depression (feelings of defeat and shame over not having triumphed) and the devaluation of what does not come easily or is not immediately rewarding. Difficulty in accepting being a "beginner" is characteristic of—although not exclusive to—narcissistic patients.

Another frequent feature of narcissistic adolescents is what one might call an "innocently" charming hedonism, a search for pleasure and enjoyment that often goes with an easygoing, superficially friendly nature, a kind of adolescent playboy attitude that can be quite engaging. Such an attitude, combined with talents and high intelligence, may obscure the difficulty these adolescents have in committing themselves to any life goals or to relationships in depth. The superficial warmth and social engagingness reveal, on further exploration, the typical poverty of object relations and the absence of long-range investment in value systems and goals other than self-aggrandizement.

Patterns of sexual behavior of narcissistic adolescents may include feelings of inferiority (concern over a "small penis") and sexual inhibition toward the other sex, combined with sexual promiscuity. The differentiation from more normal kinds of adolescent sexual promiscuity requires a study in depth of the nature of each of the sexual relationships these adolescents engage in, their capacity for romantic falling in love, and their capacity for a differentiated experience of their sexual partner.

The combination of omnipotent control, grandiosity, and devaluation with violent rebelliousness against the parents requires differentiation from more normal adolescent emotional turmoil. A normal or neurotic—in contrast to borderline and narcissistic—adolescent patient may also present violent conflicts with the parents and a tendency to criticize and devalue them bitterly, but this is usually mitigated by the capacity to value other aspects of the parents. Furthermore, the neurotic patient would have other relationships that are not affected by this self-affirmative and devaluative trend. Nonborderline patients do not present a division between overall devaluation of others and a few extremely idealized models and show a differentiated and more integrated conception of at least some objects. In short, as I have pointed out elsewhere (1975), the differentiation of borderline and narcissistic cases from their normal and neurotic counterparts depends upon the nonborderline adolescents' capacity for experiencing guilt and concern, for establishing lasting, nonexploitative relationships with friends, teachers, or others, and for realistically assessing these people in depth. The nonborderline has a consistently expanding and deepening set of values, which may conform or be in opposition to the surrounding culture.

With severe family pathology (frequent in all borderline conditions and narcissistic personalities), it is often difficult to disentangle the contribution of the adolescent from that of the parents and siblings. In this connection, the diagnostic use of family investigation in difficult cases and the observation of initial transference patterns in the individual psychotherapeutic treatment situation complement each other and may make a crucial contribution to the diagnosis. The differential diagnosis of antisocial behavior in these cases is a fundamental aspect of the diagnostic evaluation of narcissistic adolescent patients.

Various combinations of the narcissistic features mentioned may constitute a more "adaptive" and, paradoxically, a more malignant type of adolescent narcissistic pathology. One patient, the 17-year-old son of a powerful politician, fought his father's traditional, overbearing style by chronic temper tantrums at home but identified himself with what he saw as his father's authoritarian attitude by using his father's influence in the town they lived in. He attempted to terrorize teachers at school, salespeople, and other adults by invoking the power of his father to retaliate if and when his own demands were not met. At the same time, making use of the affluence of his background, he rationalized his pleasure-seeking and pleasure-centered lifestyle in a superficial but intelligent manner as his particular identification with the "antiestablishment." For the diagnostician, this kind of patient raises the question to what extent he presents a relatively nonmalignant adaptation to an exceptional social environment, or to what extent environmental factors are protecting the deeper underlying narcissistic personality structure.

Because narcissistic character pathology is usually reinforced at some point by some adaptive narcissistic features within the family, the problem of disentangling the patient's from the family's pathology often presents difficulty. Once again, a careful focus on the quality of the patient's object relations and of his superego integration, together with individual and family evaluation, usually provides the answer.

Before offering some clinical illustrations of these diagnostic issues, it should be stressed that true narcissistic pathology usually stems from early childhood and is not a consequence of the currently observable family dynamics and structure. Therefore, the assumption that family therapy alone may resolve true narcissistic pathology in an adolescent seems to be highly questionable. Even in the case of adolescent patients with the severest family pathology, true borderline personality organization is not dependent upon the immediate family pathology and will require individual long-term treatment. At the same time, a good many cases cannot be approached exclusively or initially in individual treatment because the adolescent's psychopathology is successfully protected by the family's psychopathology and by the family's conscious or unconscious collusion in keeping the patient under its control.

For example, a 19-year-old patient with narcissistic personality and antisocial features insisted that he would come for treatment only if his parents bought him a car. His father was willing to do so although I expressed my concern about this arrangement as representing a continuation of chronic attempts on the parents' part to buy the patient off. It eventually became clear that, without further exploitation of his family, the patient was not going to accept the recommendation for treatment with me or any of the arrangements I had insisted on as conditions for such treatment to begin. I faced the family with the alternatives of consulting someone who might be willing to take their son into treatment under different arrangements or restricting our future contacts to my seeing them without their son in order to help them cope better with their very difficult situation. In this case, a two-year supportive relationship with the family permitted them finally to undo the omnipotent control that their son had exerted over them in the past, to expose him to the direct consequences of his antisocial behavior, and thus indirectly to bring home to him the need for treatment.

Here are a few illustrations of the condensation of narcissistic pathology in adolescence with family pathology. A 17-year-old girl who shot and seriously wounded her boyfriend during a quarrel had a father who also had a violent temper. He used to say proudly that if worse came to worst he could triumph in his business ventures by banging his fist on the table. His efforts to intimidate psychiatrists and treatment agencies if his wishes to protect his daughter from the law were not met were perhaps more threatening than her impulsive handling of the gun.

Another 17-year-old girl, who had engaged in part-time prostitution, colluded with her mother to discontinue treatment. The patient promised her mother that she would "behave well" until she was out of the hospital—and out of the control of the treatment team—so that mother could put pressure on everyone to release her daughter and thus avoid continuing to pay what she considered wasted money for the treatment.

A further example is that of a painter in her early twenties, with narcissistic personality, multiple drug addictions, homosexual and heterosexual promiscuity, and obesity, whose efforts to control the treatment situation and utilize it for her own ends and to escape from any external control or supervision (which she experienced as a humiliating insult) were subtly supported by her influential family. The patient hated what she experienced as the "confronting" therapist. The family, following the patient's wishes, pressed the hospital for a change in therapist and managed to select a therapist they thought would be more compliant with their own demands. The "confronting" therapist was reprimanded by the hospital authorities, and the treatment situation was corrupted to the extent that the family seemed to be dictating treatment arrangements for the purpose of assuring their own maximum comfort and minimum guilt feelings. The patient finally died of a drug overdose, perhaps a suicide, a few months after leaving the second therapist and the hospital.

The next, and final, case illustrates further aspects of the diagnostic problems created by adolescent borderline patients with narcissistic personality and antisocial trends. The diagnosis of antisocial personality emerged only over a lengthy period of evaluation and follow-up.

Mr. F. The patient, a 17-year-old high school senior, was brought by his parents because of his chronically poor school performance (in spite of demonstrated above-average IQ), his lack of motivation for any further pursuit of studies or a profession, his violent temper tantrums when his wishes were not immediately fulfilled by his parents, and his threats of physical violence to them. He would throw around objects in the house, and over the years the parents had become very much afraid of antagonizing him.

The oldest of five siblings, Mr. F was extremely envious of anything his younger brothers and sisters got that he did not have. During a careful investigation of any past history of lying, stealing, or antisocial behavior, the parents were very reluctant to provide me with full information. They acknowledged that he had occasionally stolen things from them and other members of the family but added an explanation of why he had to do this in terms of his emotional reactions. They were also very much concerned about the "bad company" he was keeping, which they believed was "contaminating" him. Reports from various school psychologists showed that he was considered a very angry and suspicious youngster. He was passive, impatient, and quickly abandoned tasks that did not seem immediately achievable. At the same time, he had high aspirations for success but was unwilling to put any effort into what he was doing. It was rather difficult to get a picture of him as perceived by the authorities at school and his parents. He emerged as a guarded and isolated youngster, except when he made threatening demands on those around him.

In his appointments with me, Mr. F was guarded, vague, and aloof, but this behavior changed when he felt that there were no further "threats" of probing or unknown action from me. When, for example, I mentioned that he had answered all the questions I wanted to ask him and that he should feel free now to tell me whatever about himself he felt might help me to know him better, he began to talk quite freely but in a somewhat ingratiating, superficial, and essentially uninvolved way.

My efforts to explore the apparent contradiction in the patient's father between the high standards he set for himself and his hard work, on the one hand, and his tendency to justify wherever possible what appeared to me as antisocial manifestations in his son led to increasing tension between the parents. Mother accused father of giving in to his son, of not providing sufficient structure and firmness, and she said she felt afraid of her son.

It was very difficult for me to obtain any clear image of this young man's social life; he seemed interested only in driving a sports car, parties, and drinking. He denied taking drugs, but I had a feeling that he was not telling me the truth. He gave a superficial impression of being afraid of not being accepted, but I detected an underlying note of defiance and self-affirmation throughout the entire evaluation.

Because of the difficulties in obtaining full information from the patient and his family, I combined my own clinical evaluation with that of a psychiatric social worker who knew the total family structure. Psychological testing was carried out by an experienced psychologist. The testing revealed severe character pathology and no indication of psychotic functioning. The psychiatric social worker concluded that chronic marital conflict between the parents was also acted out in their arguments regarding the patient. Father was very demanding of his son but also strangely condoning of his antisocial behavior. The social worker felt that there was more stealing and blackmail in the home (and perhaps also in other areas of the patient's life) than our first impression indicated. Mother seemed to be somewhat narcissistically withdrawn from her son and preoccupied with herself but eventually acquired a clearer awareness of the severity of the situation and a sense of impotent rage regarding what was going on.

My final diagnosis was of a narcissistic personality with antisocial features, and I was concerned about the family's collusion with Mr. F's pathology as a major negative prognostic indicator. Because of the antisocial features, I considered an external social structure and feedback indispensable as part of the general treatment arrangements.

The final recommendation was for family therapy for the entire nuclear family and intensive psychotherapy for Mr. F, by a different therapist. I also recommended that treatment start with the patient's moving to a residential school or some equivalent alternative to living at home.

The family never accepted this recommendation. The patient obtained support from his father for a long trip to another state and money to finance an extended stay away from home regardless of any other plans he might have for work or studies. Father also consulted several other psychiatrists and finally reached a more "optimistic" attitude regarding his son, a wish to give him a chance "to grow out of all of this" rather than put pressure on him to continue treatment.

A two-year follow-up provided the following information: Mr. F had just returned home in order to get his father's help with legal proceedings against him. He had been in an armed fight apparently connected with groups pushing drugs.

Psychiatric evaluation at this time revealed a young man who seemed much more self-assured, more depreciatory, and haughtier than I had remembered from two years earlier. He now conveyed the impression that he was beginning to engage in a criminal career. Reevaluation of the quality of object relations and of any evidence that might indicate that he did not have an antisocial personality proper (for example, nonexploitative relationships, any manifestation of concern or guilt, any honest awareness of the highly inappropriate nature of his lifestyle) was unsuccessful, and I concluded with the diagnosis of an antisocial personality proper.

I have pointed out earlier (Kernberg, 1975) that in all cases of antisocial behavior in adolescence, a number of important factors should be considered when formulating a differential diagnosis. Is the label *antisocial* legal or social, or is it truly psychiatric? Is the adolescent truly antisocial, or should the label more properly be applied to the social subgroup to which the adolescent is adjusting? Does the antisocial behavior merely reflect a typical neurotic reaction to adolescent dependency and rebelliousness issues, or is it part of severe character pathology, particularly in a narcissistic personality (the initial diagnosis in the case just mentioned)? Or is it a case of antisocial personality proper (the final diagnosis in this case)? All antisocial personalities have borderline personality organization, as is true of narcissistic personalities. Although many patients with narcissistic personality do not have antisocial features, the frequency of such features in these cases and their prognostically negative significance cannot be overemphasized.

CHAPTER 4: *Personality Disorders in Old Age*

In her sociological study of old age, Simone de Beauvoir (1972) passionately indicts society for condemning the large majority of the aged to extreme poverty, uncomfortable dwellings, and loneliness, and then spells out the possibilities for old age. These possibilities, in her view, are now granted to only a handful of privileged people. She states:

> There is only one solution if old age is not to be an absurd parody of our former life, and that is to go on pursuing ends that give our existence a meaning—devotion to individuals, to groups or to causes, social, political, intellectual or creative work. In spite of the moralists' opinion to the contrary, in old age we should wish still to have passions strong enough to prevent us turning in upon ourselves. One's life has value so long as one attributes value to the life of others, by means of love, friendship, indignation, compassion. When this is so, then there are still valid reasons for activity or speech. People are often advised to "prepare" for old age. But if this merely applies to setting aside money, choosing the place for retirement and laying on hobbies, we shall not be much the better for it when the day comes. It is far better not to think about it too much, but to live a fairly committed, fairly justified life so that one may go on in the same path even when all illusions have vanished and one's zeal for life has died away. (pp. 541–543)

For the clinical psychiatrist, such a state of affairs would require certain minimal preconditions: first, an absence of or sufficient control of general physical illness to protect the individual from unbearable pain; second, absence of or sufficient control of restrictions in perceptive, locomotive, and communicative skills, such as those derived from organic brain disease and psychosis; third, the capacity to invest in relations with other people and to care about the outside world in all its aspects. This last capacity implies that whatever personality disorders are pres-

68

ent are relatively mild. It further implies that, in addition to the socio-economic and medical factors that might interfere with optimal function-ing in the aged, the question of personality disorder emerges as a significant factor.

Gianturco and Busse (1978), in a survey of psychiatric problems en-countered during a long-term study of normal aging volunteers, pointed to the frequency of hypochondriasis as a psychoneurotic reaction in this age group. Bromley (1978), raising methodological issues regarding the study of personality changes in adult life and old age, points to the com-plex problem of differentiating normal adaptive behavior from general personality disorders. He stresses the importance of evaluating geriatric patients in terms of individual disposition, current psychosocial situa-tion, and interactional issues in order to arrive at diagnostic categories. Bergmann (1978) has studied the prevalence of neurosis and personality disorders in old age and presents a critical review of the literature. He leaves the impression that, although the facts point to the existence of serious neurotic reactions to the stresses of aging and to significant suf-fering of elderly patients because of personality disorders, we do not yet have ways of evaluating and diagnosing these conditions that are pre-cise enough to be very useful.

I agree with Bergmann that we have remarkably little information regarding the diagnosis of personality disorders in old age and, other than a few clinical reports, very little information about treating individ-ual patients with personality disorders. Insofar as the clinical experience of working with geriatric patients points to a significant prevalence of personality disorders in advanced age, one cannot avoid the impression that there must be professional or cultural biases or prejudices that have inhibited empirical research into these fundamental issues. The ancient assumption in the psychoanalytic literature that psychoanalysis should not be attempted with patients beyond their late forties seems to have persisted. The reluctance on the part of psychoanalysts to explore psy-choanalytic psychotherapies with older people leaves the field of psychi-atric interventions to those who attempt to alleviate suffering by general medical, social-rehabilitational, and psychopharmacological means.

Psychoanalytic exploration of patients in their forties and fifties has indicated that the prognosis for psychoanalytic treatment of some per-sonality disorders—the narcissistic and the hysterical personality, for example—improves with age, while the prognosis for others—the in-fantile or hysteroid personality, for example—is poorer. These observa-tions are clinical impressions rather than empirical research findings and do not apply to patients in their sixties and seventies. They nonetheless do raise the possibility that psychotherapeutic interventions with some personality disorders in older patients deserve to be explored.

In addition to the general cultural biases and the specific psychoan-

alytically derived ones there is the possible reluctance of young psychiatrists to treat patients who by their very appearance activate universal
parental conflicts and threaten the generational boundaries linked to
profound infantile taboos. The clinical exploration of personality disorders requires not only the knowledge of simple checklists of behavioral
traits but also profound life experience. Only solid experience, enriched
by the technical knowledge of character pathology, makes it possible realistically to explore rigidity of behaviors, incongruity of interpersonal
interactions, and emotional inhibitions in pursuing important life tasks.
Only the combination of knowledge and experience permits the therapist to confront patients with areas of difficulty in their functioning as
against being "brainwashed" by their rationalizations of their rigidities.
A young psychiatrist may feel that he does not have the necessary experience to adopt the perspective of a patient who is 20 or 30 years older
than he is. As I have pointed out elsewhere (1980, chap. 7), in middle
age we expand the time boundaries of our ego identity. It is only as we
reach middle age that we identify with our parents as we experienced
them when we were young and they were middle-aged. This identification is facilitated as we repeat in our interactions with our own children
our parents' past interactions with us. Our newly acquired ability to
identify with our parents as they were in the past improves our ability
to identify with them as they are now advancing into old age. And expansion of our ability to identify into the future enhances our ability to
identify with older patients.

On the basis of my clinical experience, I suggest that this normal
process of developing a capacity for identifying with older people can be
enormously accelerated by experience in treating older patients during
the years of psychiatric residency training. We know that the normal
sexual boundaries (which under ordinary circumstances are never
crossed but are nonetheless involved in the frustrating yet exciting tensions, encounters, and misunderstandings between men and women)
are temporarily overcome dramatically in the psychoanalyst's experience
of identifying himself with patients of the other sex. By the same token,
I think that the treatment of older patients may accelerate the emotional
maturity of the clinical psychiatrist in evaluating normal and abnormal
personality functioning in all age groups. Furthermore, once the psychiatrist develops an internal freedom to explore the personality of older
patients without succumbing to cultural prejudices and inhibitions (for
example, the proverbial reluctance to exploring the sexual life of older
patients), his diagnosis of personality disorders in older patients may be
significantly enhanced.

A few clinical illustrations might be in order at this point.

Miss G. A single 63-year-old woman who suffered from relatively
mild but chronic depression, diabetes, moderate obesity, and a fear of

participating in large social gatherings presented a hysterical personality with masochistic features. In the course of four years of psychotherapy, the patient's feelings of bitterness and mourning over having lost her opportunities for satisfactory relations with men and marriage became a central issue that gradually expanded into the analysis of her masochistic interactions with men, her persistent unconscious submission to her mother (who had died three years before the beginning of treatment, a time when Miss G's depressive symptoms had intensified), and her strong sense that a growing physical unattractiveness was making her distasteful and ridiculous in the eyes of men in whom she was interested. I should add that she was one of my first psychotherapy cases, that I treated her under supervision during the first two years of treatment, and that at the beginning of the treatment I was 26 years old. The fact that I was undergoing psychoanalytic training and a personal psychoanalysis at the same time proved very helpful at difficult stages of the treatment.

Miss G had restricted her social life because she felt inferior to other women. She oscillated between periods when she felt so unattractive that she did not dare go to religious and cultural community meetings and other times when she felt better about herself. But when she felt better about herself she also felt painfully reminded of her age and unattractiveness and distressed by the thought that she could no longer be taken seriously as a sexual person and a potential sexual partner.

She surprised me by her sense of humiliation, not only at having to tell me about her masturbatory activities and fantasies but at having such sexual desires and at masturbating at all. She broke off a sexual relationship with a man that began in the middle of the treatment because she was afraid he would find her disgusting. Her mother's prohibitive attitude toward sexuality became a prominent theme of the treatment. In the transference, she eventually dared to accuse me of hypocrisy: How could I question her sexual self-denigration when I obviously could not feel attracted by a woman like her? After my initial guilt feelings because, indeed, I could not imagine having a sexual relation with her, I discovered, in the private exploration of my own fantasies and motives, underlying sexual fantasies about older women that were quite obviously disturbing because of their oedipal implications. Once I could accept these fantasies internally, I was able to explore without guilt feelings what it was that made her unattractive to me and, presumably, to other men, namely, the subtly self-demeaning aspects of her presentation of herself, including physical neglect—in short, her masochistic tendencies.

In the last two years of psychotherapy, I became much more challenging of her cultural clichés (some of which I had originally shared) regarding behavior appropriate for a woman in her middle sixties and less afraid to explore with her her competition with and envy of younger women, as well as her similar feelings toward men who, in her view, never aged but, unlike women, remained eternally attractive. Deep sources of envy of men gradually emerged and could be explored as codetermining her reluctance to participate actively in social and political affairs as well as in her having dropped out of a professional career much earlier in her life. She resumed studies that permitted her to improve her functioning as an administrator of a religious relief organization, and she felt freer about friendships and social relations with men. She eventually established a sexual relation with a man who had been a friend for many years, was now a widower, and whose long-standing interest in her she had previously devalued for unconsciously masochistic reasons.

I have described in earlier writing on love relations in middle age (1976, chap. 8) how women with hysterical personality have a better prognosis for psychotherapeutic treatment when they are in their forties than in their early twenties, whereas women with infantile personality tend to present a poorer prognosis at that point than during adolescence and early adulthood. In this connection, Kahana (1979) has pointed to similarly favorable results in psychoanalytic psychotherapy with patients suffering from obsessive-compulsive and masochistic personalities. The increasingly satisfactory prognosis for the hysterical personality may also hold true for old age. Berezin and Fern (1967) describe the satisfactory outcome in the psychotherapy of a 70-year-old woman with a hysterical character disorder. In contrast, my experience with patients presenting severer personality disorders within the borderline spectrum has been much less satisfactory.

I have elsewhere discussed (1977) some of the prognostic and psychotherapeutic issues regarding pathological narcissism in old age in reference to a case reported by Berezin (1977). I have also written about the deterioration that narcissistic personalities undergo in middle age (1980, chap. 8). Narcissistic personalities experience throughout the years a deterioration of their world of internalized object relations, including the unconscious devaluation of both their own past (in order to not feel envy of that past) and of what others have (in order to not envy others). Hence these people do not have at their disposal the normal gratifications that come from memories of past experiences and of others they love. Pathological narcissism thus leads to increasing social isolation and an internal sense of emptiness. In many cases, the vicious circle of devaluation and emptiness becomes insurmountable.

Mr. H. An outstanding historian with a severe narcissistic personality disorder lost all interest in contemporary political affairs after his forced retirement at age 65. A gradually deepening depression was clearly secondary to the dramatic devaluation of his major life interest and his envy of those in his family who, unlike himself, persisted in their own interests and professions. He became intensely resentful of me because I was younger than he was. A major battle was waged in the transference, and for several months I felt that, if the patient could overcome his intense envy and resentment of me and accept my help in mourning over his lost work and the enormous professional opportunities that had gone with it, he would also be able to better understand how his revengeful devaluation of his past interests impoverished his present life. But his inability to work through his envy in the transference led to a premature disruption of the treatment. Despite that particular failure, other cases have suggested that patients who have some need for dependency and a capacity for mourning over lost opportunities can often be helped.

Some middle-aged patients with narcissistic personality, in spite of, or rather because of, the worsening of depressive symptoms secondary to their narcissistic personality structure, have a better prognosis for psychoanalytic treatment than they would have had in their early twenties or thirties. Whether the treatment of narcissistic personalities in old age can provide additional positive prognostic features seems an extremely important research question. Melanie Klein, in one of her last writings (1963, chap. 4), first pointed to the crucial prognostic value, in dealing with loneliness in old age, of the equilibrium between envy and gratitude. The diagnosis and appropriate treatment of narcissistic character pathology may have significant relevance for adaptation to old age.

My experiences in the treatment of infantile personalities in old age have been limited but interesting. *Mrs. J*, a 68-year-old woman with hypochondriacal complaints, multiple drug abuse of minor tranquilizers, and increasing social isolation, was referred for psychotherapy by her internist, who was concerned because of her uncontrolled ingestion of sedatives. While it was possible to reduce the amount of medication and obtain her commitment to use minor tranquilizers only under very specific and restricted circumstances, the loss of social contacts and interests and the emptiness of her personal life proved almost insurmountable. Her husband had divorced her 23 years earlier, and her now-adult children maintained minimal contact with her.

She lived alone in a small apartment and experienced contacts with other people as an invasion of her privacy. She liked to attend community affairs and church groups, but, for reasons that remained obscure to her, she could not make friends with anybody, and some people had made it clear to her that they wanted to keep their distance. Her impulsive, childlike, aggressive style of communication tended to alienate others. She nevertheless tried desperately to cling to relationships with people who either were inappropriate or had indicated their unavailability. She was interested in dating men and was invited out by apparently appropriate men from time to time. However, her inordinate demanding-ness and her inability to interest herself in the life of others after a while seemed to turn these men away. She felt that her masturbatory activity was quite satisfactory and that sex at her age with men she did not want to relate to in a more consistent way was awkward and demeaning.

A prescription of activities and a regulated life with group involve-ments without too much demand for intimacy turned out to be the optimal solution for her. Mrs. J benefited from supportive psychother-apy. Her case raises another research question: whether different types of personality disorder and different degrees of severity of personality disorder in old age call for a supportive or an expressive approach.

This patient, with a college education and a rich cultural back-ground, had remarkably little interest in the intellectual and cultural as-pects of her community life and depended for entertainment mostly on gossip. In terms of my own countertransference reaction I was con-cerned for quite some time about whether my sense of helplessness and hopelessness in working with her derived from my anxiety over her problems in reality or from a pessimism related to her age. Only gradu-ally did I become aware that I was facing the final stages of a severe de-terioration of personality functioning that had been developing over many years. Mrs. J illustrates the fact that the most devastating psycho-social problems in old age may frequently relate not simply to the imme-diate social circumstances but to long-standing personality disorders that gradually become unmasked as external life supports fall away.

From his review of the literature of the functioning of paranoid, schizoid, and inadequate personalities in old age Bergmann (1978) con-cludes that, paradoxically, these patients may make better adjustments than would be expected from their psychopathology. The inadequate person, he suggests,

provides a focus for help for family, for friends, and even sometimes for quite casual contacts. They show gratitude, their dependency and lack of achievement allow them to fit into the setting that many people with more normal pride and self respect would find most uncongenial. On the other hand the fighting stance of the hostile paranoid personalities keeps them intact, failure is never their own, ill health could be remedied if only the doctor gave adequate treatment, etc. The world, at large, has to be taken on in single combat; life presents a very busy and diverting struggle against the dangerous and hostile forces from with-out and there is little time for despair, depression, fear, and anxiety. (p. 62)

In my own experience, some paranoid personalities in old age have indeed been able to maintain a lonely fighting stance in the environ-ment, but the extent to which such patients become physically depen-dent on others and therefore exposed to an intensification of their para-noid anxieties is an important factor. In addition, in psychotic regression, lonely old people with paranoid personality may develop extreme degrees of social isolation and physical neglect before any help comes their way.

Mr. K. A 65-year-old man, a paranoid personality, was a chronic alcoholic and pathologically jealous of his wife. He was forced to retire prematurely because of a breakdown in work related to both his alcoholism and his belligerent interactions with superiors. He was brought to treatment by his wife because of severe marital conflicts and his continual drinking. Although Mr. K initially agreed to see me only because his wife threatened to leave him, it eventually became possible for him to understand that I was not his wife's agent, that if I was going to see him it was in terms of a contract involving himself and me. I carried out an essentially supportive psychotherapy along the lines I have outlined elsewhere (see chap. 9), tactfully but consistently confronting him with his arrogant and bellicose behavior toward me and relating this behavior, once he could recognize its inappropriateness, to what had happened at his work.

His increased insight led to an intensification of his depression, to his blaming himself for having lost his work, and to a temporary increase in drinking. I then discussed with him the self-defeating cycles of guilt and self-destructiveness and raised the question with him whether he had anything better to expect from life than to drown himself in alcohol. Knowing of Mr. K's paranoid assumption that his former colleagues would be depreciating him if they knew he was in psychotherapeutic treatment, I utilized his pride in helping him to control the drinking "in order to demonstrate to them that he could deal with life on his own." I used his passionate and paranoid views about politics and national events to stimulate him to participate more actively in local political affairs. I also was able to help him avoid personal relations that were too intense, to accept his limitations in terms of intimacy, and to concentrate on making himself a desirable member of political action groups.

One area in which I was never able to reduce fully the nature of his paranoid distortions of reality was in his jealousy of his wife. In fact, Mr. K's attempt to convince me that I was too young to know how women really are, permitted him to maintain an attitude of superiority over me. At the same time, he did agree to try to control his behavior toward her and to be more tolerant of her "faults." The final outcome was a marked lessening in marital conflict, abstinence from drinking over a period of at least three years (before I lost contact with him), and a growing sense of satisfaction with his new activities.

I trust that these examples have illustrated my assumptions that the prognosis for individual types of personality disorder may vary in different age groups, that it may become significantly improved for personality disorders functioning at a neurotic level in contrast to those functioning at a borderline level of personality organization, and that the adaptive–maladaptive equilibrium related to pathological personality traits may change with the differing tasks and psychosocial environment in old age.

CHAPTER 5: *Problems in the Classification of Personality Disorders*

Classifying personality disorders is problematic for several reasons. One is quantitative: How intense must the disturbance be to warrant calling it a disorder? Another is semantic: A variety of terms—character neuroses, neurotic characters, character disorders, personality trait disturbances, personality pattern disturbances, personality disorders (the term used in the *Diagnostic and Statistical Manual-III*)—have been applied to the same clinical syndromes. And behind these semantic differences loom important conceptual, clinical, and ideological issues—for example, the wish to eliminate the term *psychoneuroses* from a classification system, as stated in the introduction to DSM-III. One's choice of terminology can thus arise from theoretical assumptions regarding the determinants of personality organization. For example, a psychodynamic rather than a behavioristic frame of reference will strongly influence the observer's ordering or grouping of pathological personality features.

In clinical psychiatric practice the terms *character* and *personality* have been used interchangeably. For the purpose of this discussion I am using the term *personality disorders* to refer to constellations of abnormal or pathological character traits of sufficient intensity to imply significant disturbance in intrapsychic and/or interpersonal functioning. Regardless of the theoretical assumptions of psychoanalysis, the data derived from close involvement with patients supply, in my view, the strongest clinical evidence available for use in connection with any effort to classify personality disorders. This viewpoint is theoretically in harmony with the criteria spelled out by Spitzer in the introduction to DSM-III:

> There is no assumption that each mental disorder is a discrete entity with sharp boundaries (discontinuity) between it and other mental disorders, as well as between it and No Mental Disorder. . . . The approach taken in DSM-III is atheoretical with regard to etiology or pathophysiological process except for

those disorders for which this is well established and therefore included in the definition of the disorder.

. . . This approach can be said to be "descriptive" in that the definitions of the disorders generally consist of descriptions of the clinical features of the disorders. These features are described at the lowest order of inference necessary to describe the characteristic features of the disorder. . . . For some disorders . . . particularly the Personality Disorders, a much higher order of inference is necessary. For example, one of the criteria for Borderline Personality Disorder is "identity disturbance manifested by uncertainty about several issues relating to identity, such as self-image, gender identity, long-term goals or career choice, friendship patterns, values and loyalties." (pp. 6–7)

Elsewhere, the introduction lists the goals of DSM-III as follows:

—clinical usefulness for making treatment and management decisions in varied clinical settings; reliability of the diagnostic categories;
—acceptability to clinicians and researchers of varying theoretical orientations; usefulness for educating health professionals;
—maintaining compatibility with ICD-9, except when departures are unavoidable;
—avoiding the introduction of new terminology and concepts that break with tradition, except when clearly needed;
—reaching consensus on the meaning of necessary diagnostic terms that have been used inconsistently, and avoiding the use of terms that have outlived their usefulness;
—consistency with data from research studies bearing on the validity of diagnostic categories;
—suitability for describing subjects in research studies;
—being responsive during the development of DSM-III to critiques by clinicians and researchers. (pp. 2–3)[1]

From both a clinical and a research standpoint, it is important that the constellations of pathological character traits described in any classification of personality disorders truly correspond to well-documented clinical experience. If the therapeutic and prognostic implications of different personality disorders were reflected in the criteria used to differentiate them, the differences, if any, would be much more meaningful. A classification that respected the relationships between personality structure and the disposition to other types of psychopathology would strengthen the descriptive definitions, regardless of theoretical differences about how such relationships are to be conceptualized. And the

---

1. ICD-9 is the current international classification of disease of the World Health Organization.

more criteria converge in justification of any particular constellation of pathological character traits, the more reason for including that type of personality disorder. This would be a truly atheoretical frame of reference (if that is what is wanted at this time).

I seriously question a classification of personality disorders based upon any single preconceived typology that sets out a theoretical diagram of trait dimensions and then attempts to fill it in with potential clinical types. I question even more seriously classifications that clearly correspond to only one particular model of psychopathology and more or less idiosyncratic classification systems that do not have a broad base in clinical psychiatry. Finally, I question the grouping of pathological character traits on the basis of preconceptions not related to clinical psychiatry and classifications in which there is gross overlapping of various personality types. In other words, the individual categories or specific personality disorders should be broadly representative and capable of being differentiated from one another. In what follows I explore the classification of personality disorders in DSM-III in the light of these considerations with particular concern for internal consistency, clinical relevance, and correspondence to DSM-III's own stated goals.

To begin, DSM-III ignores important and frequently encountered types of personality disorders, particularly the hysterical and depressive-masochistic personalities. DSM-III argues that the Histrionic Personality Disorder corresponds to the hysterical personality (p. 314), a point made elsewhere by Spitzer and Williams (1980). This equation, in my view, is an error reflecting an attempt to condense the entire spectrum of character pathology ranging from the hysterical personality per se to the hysteroid (Easser and Lesser, 1965), infantile (Kernberg, 1975), or "Zetzel Type IV" (Zetzel, 1968) personality. It thus overlooks the important clinical contributions that have provided clarifying differentiations of this spectrum. DSM-III also presumably includes the depressive-masochistic personality with the "other specific affective disorders," namely, the Cyclothymic Disorder or the Dysthymic Disorder. Dysthymic Disorder is a new term for the depressive neurosis. DSM-III, in referring to cyclothymic disorder and dysthymic disorder, states, "Other terms for these disorders are Cyclothymic and Depressive Personality Disorders" (p. 218). In my view, to confuse depressive neurosis with depressive personality and to ignore the characteristics of depressive personality proper is an error. It could also be argued that the newly coined term Avoidant Personality Disorder corresponds to the depressive personality, but this is clearly not so. Spitzer and Williams (1980) describe the Avoidant Personality Disorder as part of what DSM-II (American Psychiatric Association, 1968) called the Schizoid Personality (together with the Schizotypal Personality Disorder and the Schizoid Personality Disorder proper). Further contradictions can be found between the as-

sumed characteristics of the Avoidant Personality Disorder and the depressive personality proper.

The hysterical personality, particularly the modern concept of it, is
a much more differentiated, effectively functioning type than the infantile or hysteroid personality. The latter seems to imitate it superficially,
but in the infantile personality both intrapsychic and interpersonal distortions of the relations with self and others are much severer and more
pervasive. The literature on the hysterical personality is abundant (Abraham, 1920; Marmor, 1953; Chodoff and Lyons, 1958; Easser and Lesser,
1965; Shapiro, 1965; Blinder, 1966; Easser, 1966; Laughlin, 1967; Zetzel,
1968; Lazare, 1971; MacKinnon and Michels, 1971; Kernberg, 1975;
Blacker and Tupin, 1977; and Krohn, 1978). The last two references
stress the structural rather than the psychodynamic aspects of the hysterical personality, enrich its clinical description, and clarify its different
manifestations in men and women.

Clinically, the hysterical personality (as differentiated from the more
regressive personality types with which it has tended to be confused in
the past) emerges as having emotional lability and warmth, a histrionic
but controlled and socially adaptive quality, a proneness to emotional
crises (but a presence of emotional depth and stability apart from such
crises), and the capacity for appropriate social interactions with the exception of specific object relations that have sexual implications. In more
general terms, hysterical personalities present good ego strength and
show infantile, regressive behavior only in circumstances that are actually or symbolically sexual. They are impulsive, but their impulsiveness
is restricted to these sexual interactions or to occasional emotional temper tantrums. They are essentially extroverted in the sense of being out-
going and involved with others. They have a tendency to "clinging
dependency" only in sexual relations, and their dependent and exhibitionistic needs also have a sexual component. Hysterical personalities want to be loved, to be the center of attention and attraction, again
only in circumstances with sexual implications. Women with hysterical
personality show a combination of pseudohypersexuality and sexual inhibition, reflected in sexual provocativeness and frigidity and in sexual
involvements that typically have "triangular qualities" (as with older or
unavailable men, rejection of available men) and that satisfy masochistic
needs. The hysterical personality is competitive with both sexes and in
the case of women typically competitive with other women for men.
Competitiveness with men contains implicit fears and conflicts around
consciously or unconsciously assumed inferiority to men. Various subtypes of a "submissive" or "competitive" kind of hysterical personality
reflect characterological fixations of these masochistic and competitive
patterns. What typically emerges in the treatment, where regressive infantile behavior clearly acquires defensive functions against the more

adult aspects of sexual involvement, is flirtatiousness combined with warm, highly differentiated relations in depth with others.

In contrast, the infantile personality (with which the hysterical personality tended to be confused in the past) shows diffuse emotional lability, undifferentiated relations with significant others, and shallow emotional investments. In contrast to the socially appropriate extroversion of the hysterical personality, the infantile personality overidentifies with others and projects unrealistic, fantasied intentions onto them. Infantile personalities have difficulty understanding others, as well as themselves, in depth. They typically show the syndrome of identity diffusion, and the childlike, clinging nature of all their relationships contrasts with the general maturity of the hysterical personality in this respect.

Dependent and exhibitionistic traits are less sexualized in the infantile personality than in the hysterical personality, in the sense that the infantile personality wishes for a childlike dependency in itself rather than as a defense against more mature sexual commitments. The infantile personality crudely and inappropriately uses sexualized behavior to express exhibitionistic needs. This personality tends to have fewer sexual inhibitions and is more frequently promiscuous than the hysterical personality. There are fewer repressive features in the infantile personality's sexual life and more generalized dissociative features, such as the alternation of contradictory sexual fantasies and engagements (expressed in polymorphous infantile sexual behavior). In the pathology of interpersonal relations, there is much less differentiation of specified object relations in the infantile personality than in the hysterical personality, and the degree of disturbance in any particular interpersonal relationship is proportional to the intensity of involvement or intimacy with the other person.

This differentiation of the hysterical and infantile personalities has therapeutic and therefore prognostic implications. It corresponds to a long history of descriptive and psychodynamic observations as well as to observations made outside a psychoanalytic frame of reference. The description of the Histrionic Personality Disorder in DSM-III quite clearly relates to the infantile personality and not to the hysterical personality. For example, histrionic patients are described as quickly becoming bored with normal routines, appearing shallow and lacking genuineness, and presenting manipulative suicide threats, feelings of depersonalization, and, during extreme stress, transient psychotic symptoms of insufficient severity or duration to warrant an additional diagnosis (DSM-III, pp. 313–14).

To complicate matters further, DSM-III describes the Borderline Personality Disorder as presenting traits similar to those presented by the Histrionic Personality. Both are described as impulsive or unpredictable, with patterns of unstable and intense interpersonal relations, showing inappropriate, intense anger or lack of control of anger and affective instability, prone to suicide gestures and attempts, and presenting incessant efforts to attract attention and reassurance. While DSM-III explicitly describes the Borderline Personality Disorder as presenting an identity disturbance, the characteristics of the Histrionic Personality in practice equally indicate identity disturbances. And both Histrionic and Borderline Personality Disorders are described as prone to developing brief psychotic episodes.

The diagnosis Histrionic Personality Disorder is therefore equivocal, corresponding to the more regressive pole of the hysterical–infantile spectrum. In all fairness, however, it should be pointed out that DSM-I (American Psychiatric Association, 1952) had also forgotten the hysterical personality in its time, and that DSM-II "rediscovered" it. Hope therefore remains for future rediscoveries of this highly prevalent personality disorder.

Another prominent absentee from DSM-III is the depressive-masochistic personality disorder, most frequently referred to as the "masochistic personality" or, in psychoanalytic literature, as the "moral masochist." The depressive personality was referred to by Kraepelin (1904), Tramer (1931), and Schneider (1950) and described by Fenichel (1945b) and Laughlin (1967). Further clinical descriptions are provided by Gross (1974) and Kernberg (1975).

Before proceeding, however, it should be noted that clinical descriptions arrived at by means of psychoanalytic exploration, with its eminently phenomenological characteristics, must be differentiated from the etiological, psychopathological, and psychodynamic theories of psychoanalysis. To throw out prevalent clinical syndromes because they were discovered, studied, and described by psychoanalysts is not an expression of "atheoretical" objectivity but may reveal a theoretical bias against psychoanalysis. Frances and Cooper (1981), in a related critique of the artificial separation of descriptive and dynamic criteria in DSM-III, state: "Some clinical observations concerning the 'dynamic unconscious' are no more inferential than observations considered descriptive in DSM-III. . . . The tendency of DSM-III to exclude observations derived from a dynamic framework seems arbitrary and unnecessarily limiting" (p. 1199).

Patients with depressive-masochistic personality disorders usually function quite well, typically within the spectrum of "high level" character pathology (in my view, a neurotic rather than borderline personality organization). They have well-integrated ego identity, show nonspecific manifestations of ego strength (good anxiety tolerance and impulse control), and have an excessively guilt-ridden but well-integrated moral conscience. They are able to establish well-differentiated object relations in depth.

Following Laughlin's (1967) description, one may break down the character traits of the depressive-masochistic personality disorder into three categories: (1) traits reflecting excessively severe superego functioning; (2) those reflecting overdependency on support, love, and acceptance from others; and (3) those reflecting difficulties in the expression of aggression. In many ways, all three categories have the faulty "metabolism" of dependency needs as a predominant issue. These patients feel guilty because of intense ambivalence toward loved and needed objects, and they are easily frustrated if their dependent longings are not gratified.

The conspicuous "superego" features of the depressive-masochistic personality are reflected in a tendency to be very serious, responsible, and concerned about work performance and responsibilities. There is a somberness about them, an overconscientiousness. These patients usually do not have much of a sense of humor but they are highly reliable and dependable. Psychological exploration reveals their tendency to judge themselves harshly and to set extremely high standards for themselves. These usually considerate, tactful, and concerned people may also be very harsh in their judgment of others. Under certain circumstances, the cruelty of their superego may be directed toward others in the form of "justified indignation" (see Schneider, 1950). When these patients do not meet their own high standards and expectations, they display the clinical manifestations of depression.

Under optimal circumstances, hard work and external success may eventually provide these patients with a sense of having fulfilled their duties and responsibilities, and life may be easier for them in later years. But if they attempt the impossible, they may become increasingly depressed as life goes on. These are the moral masochists who unconsciously put themselves into circumstances that will induce suffering or who experience such suffering as the price of whatever enjoyments they can permit themselves.

Still other moral masochists are psychodynamically closer to the hysterical personality disorder, particularly women with depressive-masochistic character features and severe unconscious prohibitions against sexual freedom and enjoyment. They may tolerate a satisfactory sexual experience only when it is carried out under conditions of objective or symbolic suffering.

Patients characterized by the depressive-masochistic personality disorder also show an abnormal vulnerability to disappointment by others, especially the loss of love or interest, and may go out of their way to obtain sympathy, love, and affirmation. In contrast to narcissistic personalities, who are overdependent on external admiration without responding internally with love and gratitude to those who admire and love them, the depressive-masochistic personality typically is able to respond deeply with love, to be grateful. However, these patients become unconsciously clinging and demanding and may develop an abnormal degree of compliance to the other person, together with a gradual increase of the demands implied in their excessive reliance on the other. If the pathology of the other fits, the result can be a highly satisfying relation in love and marriage.

The less fortunate of these patients display an excessive sensitivity to loss of love, an unconscious sense of being rejected and mistreated as a reaction to relatively minor slights, and the tendency to retaliate for such perceived behavior in others by attempting to make the others feel guilt or by rejecting behavior on their own part. Their attitude of "How could you do this to me?" may cause others to reject them in fact, thus initiating a vicious cycle that may eventually threaten even deep personal relations. These patients' subjective sense of being rejected, as well as actual frustrations and losses, tends to lead them to clinical depression. Throughout the years, as Laughlin (1967) has pointed out, awareness of their enormous needs from others, the danger of raising hopes too high and then being frustrated, may bring about a secondary reaction of cynical withdrawal from interpersonal relations.

The faulty "metabolism" of aggression in the depressive-masochistic personality disorder shows in these patients' tendency to become depressed under conditions that would normally produce anger or rage. Unconscious guilt over such anger (reinforcing the guilt unconsciously experienced because of aggression toward earlier love objects) may complicate their interpersonal relations. They tend to experience cycles in which they express anger toward those they "rightfully" attack or feel rejected by, then get depressed, overly apologetic, even submissive and compliant, until secondary anger over the compliance or submission builds up into the next rage attack. The traditional psychoanalytic view that patients who are depressed direct anger against themselves rather than against others seems typically illustrated by these cases.

The early psychoanalytic literature used to include these personalities as subcategories of the "oral" character in an attempt to classify character pathology on the basis of "libidinal fixation points." In this schema the hysterical character corresponded to genital fixations, the obsessive-compulsive character to anal-sadistic fixations, and the oral character to oral-dependent fixations. This early classification broke down for many reasons. Clinically, however, the hysterical personality disorder, the obsessive-compulsive personality disorder, and the depressive-masochistic personality disorder are types of character pathology that reflect a high level of personality organization, a good differentiation of the tripartite intrapsychic structure, solid ego identity, and a predominance of defensive operations centering on repression. These patients may be suffering severely from their character pathology and yet have a very good prognosis with psychoanalytic treatment. The fact that two of these three categories have been omitted from the classification of personality disorders in DSM-III seems a serious shortcoming.

The Avoidant Personality Disorder in DSM-III appears to be somehow related to the depressive personality, but this is not, apparently, the understanding of Spitzer and Williams (1980), who point out that the "distinction between the DSM-III categories of Schizoid and Avoidant Personality Disorders is based on whether or not there is a defect in the motivation and capacity for emotional involvement (Millon). It is expected that this descriptive distinction will have therapeutic and prognostic implications" (p. 1065).

Millon, one of the members of the Task Force on Nomenclature and Statistics responsible for DSM-III and of the Advisory Committee on Personality Disorders, has developed his own theoretical system of classifying personality disorders based on a combination of learned coping patterns. These "may be viewed as complex forms of instrumental behavior, that is, ways of achieving positive reinforcement and avoiding negative reinforcements" (Millon, 1981, p. 59). The following table summarizes the correspondence between Millon's classification and DSM-III.

Millon	DSM-III
passive-dependent pattern	Dependent Disorder
active-dependent pattern	Histrionic Disorder
passive-independent pattern	Narcissistic Disorder
active-independent pattern	Antisocial Disorder
passive-ambivalent pattern	Compulsive Disorder
active-ambivalent pattern	Passive-Aggressive Disorder
passive-detached pattern	Schizoid Disorder
active-detached pattern	Avoidant Personality Disorder

Millon has also developed two computerized diagnostic self-report inventories, the Millon clinical multiaxial inventory and the Millon behavioral health inventory. His recent textbook (1981) provides detailed illustrations of his views on classification and documents the influence he has had on the DSM-III Task Force, to the extent that at least 2 of the 11 categories of personality disorders in DSM-III (the Dependent Personality Disorder and the Avoidant Personality Disorder) relate directly to his thinking. The scholarly quality of Millon's analysis, the historical dimension of classifications of personality and character pathology he outlines, and the internal consistency of his personal classification system should be of great interest to everyone struggling with these issues. At the same time, the fact that Millon's terminology, derived from a highly personal theoretical system not directly linked to ordinary clinical psychiatric experience, should have so strongly influenced this sector of DSM-III raises questions regarding the assumed atheoretical nature of the proposed classification and the explicit goals of developing a terminology acceptable to clinicians and researchers of varying theoretical orientations and of avoiding the introduction of new terminology and concepts that break with tradition, except when clearly needed. The candor of Millon's description of his complex relation to and influence on the Task Force of DSM-III speaks for him, if not for the personality-disorders section.

The Avoidant Personality Disorder is described in DSM-III as presenting hypersensitivity to rejection, humiliation, or shame and a tendency to interpret innocuous events as ridicule. These characteristics do not correspond to depressive personality features so much as to the narcissistic and paranoid personality disorders. The avoidant personality is described as unwilling to enter into relationships unless given unusually strong guarantees of uncritical acceptance. The depressive-masochistic personality, by contrast, has an enormous sense of personal responsibility and the feeling that he has to make maximal efforts to encounter and relate to others, which is reflected socially in remarkably good surface relations with others at the cost of great stress, tension, and constant doubts that he deserves others' love and friendship.

In DSM-III the Avoidant Personality Disorder is described as socially isolated, similar to the schizoid personality except for a desire for social involvement and a particular alertness to criticism. The depressive personality does not present social isolation of the kind and severity shown by the schizoid personality. Further, that schizoid personalities do not present a desire for social involvement and are not sensitive to criticism is open to question; intense clinical involvement with schizoid personalities reveals them to possess a much more complex intrapsychic reality than they initially convey. Here the neglect of psychodynamic explorations of the schizoid personality impoverishes its description. In short, whatever clinical meaning or usefulness is provided by the concept of the Avoidant Personality Disorder, the depressive-masochistic personality disorder is definitely missing from DSM-III. The so-called Dysthymic Disorder—neurotic depression or depressive neurosis, we would say—does not correspond to the depressive-masochistic personality but to a symptomatic complex that can be activated by the decompensation of other personality disorders, such as, typically, the narcissistic personality. Or the Dysthymic Disorder might be simply a direct expression of unconscious intrapsychic conflict not structuralized into character pathology.

Other personality disorders are also missing from DSM-III. For example, the "as if personality," the "sadomasochistic personality," and the "hypomanic personality" are missing, and the Inadequate Personality from DSM-I and DSM-II has also been withdrawn from circulation. It could be argued that these were omitted because their descriptive basis is too narrow or they are too closely linked to psychoanalysis as one theoretical system or their clinical frequency is low. In my view, although the "inadequate personality" was rarely met with, it corresponded to a clinically existing constellation.

On the other hand, the 11 personality disorders selected for discussion in DSM-III include at least 3 newcomers of questionable status: the Avoidant Personality mentioned above; the Dependent Personality, another apparent contribution from Millon; and the Schizotypal Personality. I have already raised some questions regarding the Avoidant Personality; here I would add only that I found the clinical illustrations of all three of these types in the *DSM-III Case Book* (American Psychiatric Association, 1981) problematic. The case of the "bookkeeper" (p. 59), one illustration of Avoidant Personality Disorder, is presented in a two-paragraph description that I would find highly inadequate for any personality diagnosis. The case of the "sad sister" (p. 175) is about a lonely woman who has been extremely fearful of men and cuts off potential relationships with them because she fears that they will eventually reject her, champions good causes, is competent and responsible in her work as a teacher's aide, and has as her only contacts a sister and one close friend from high school. On the basis of this capsule description, one could raise the possibility of the presence of a schizoid personality disorder or, on further exploration, perhaps important hysterical features. In any event, there is little evidence of her desire for affection and acceptance "on unconditional approval," supposedly central in the Avoidant Personality.

The cases of Dependent Personality Disorder in the *DSM-III Case Book* immediately raise the question of the relationship between the Dependent Personality Disorder and the Passive-Aggressive Personality Disorder. The latter is a category that first emerged in DSM-I and has survived through DSM-II into DSM-III. The original descriptions (Whitman et al., 1954; Rabkin, 1965; Small et al., 1970) provided a relatively narrow yet descriptively clear and clinically relevant base, and this category has been a useful diagnostic grab bag for disorders that do not fall easily into any other major category. This category, then, is a good illustration of a relatively atheoretically arrived at and clinically useful one.

In DSM-III, the Dependent Personality Disorder has reemerged with a newly assumed independence. The manual makes no reference to the diagnostic problems or to any reasons for distinguishing this classification from the Passive-Aggressive Personality Disorder. The corresponding cases in the *DSM-III Case Book* illustrate this ambiguity.

The "stubborn psychiatrist," diagnosed as a Passive-Aggressive Personality Disorder (p. 40), shows strongly implicit, inappropriate (and unacknowledged) dependent attitudes toward his wife; the "blood is thicker than water" patient (p. 47), who broke up with his girlfriend because his mother disapproved of her, is diagnosed as dependent while yet very clearly showing passive-aggressive behavior toward his mother. The other case illustration of a Dependent Personality Disorder (p. 73), "pushed around," a homosexual who resents his excessively passive role with his boyfriend but has difficulties obtaining erections with other men, seems to present a much more complex personality disorder than can be subsumed under the label Dependent Personality Disorder. Although in this case the diagnosis was only "provisional," the reason was that "dependent behavior is clearly present in his current relationship, but there is inadequate information to determine whether this is characteristic of his long-term functioning." In other words, the provisional nature of the diagnosis did not derive from the distortions and complexity of his sexual life. This patient, by the way, also received the diagnosis of Inhibited Sexual Excitement, but his homosexuality was not referred to diagnostically. We may assume, therefore, that this patient was comfortable with his homosexuality.

The Schizotypal Personality Disorder presents important clinical and theoretical problems. Spitzer and Williams (1980, p. 1065) state: "The criteria for Schizotypal Personality Disorder were developed to identify individuals who had been described as having Borderline Schizophrenia (Spitzer et al.). There is evidence that Chronic Schizophrenia is more common among family members of individuals who were described as having Borderline Schizophrenia than in the general population (Rosenthal and Kety)." Here is a clear theoretical bias; a category was created that would fit with a schizophrenia spectrum concept based upon research on genetic features in schizophrenia.

The evidence for the concept of a schizophrenia spectrum is convincing enough, but it should be kept in mind that some of the biological relatives of schizophrenic patients who present what Hoch and Polatin (1949) called "pseudo-neurotic schizophrenia," and others have called "borderline schizophrenia" or "ambulatory schizophrenia," may be suffering from milder or subclinical versions of schizophrenic illness rather than a personality disorder. In fact, the entire contemporary literature on research on borderline conditions stemmed from an effort to clarify whether "borderline schizophrenia" exists and the extent to which one can differentiate this group into (a) patients with "psychotic personality" structures or "atypical" or "latent" or "simple" or "residual" forms of schizophrenic illness, and (b) borderline personalities proper who are definitely not psychotic. Epidemiological studies, including clinical interviews of biological relatives of schizophrenic probands, may not provide the kind of subtle discriminatory evidence that would answer these questions, in contrast to long-term, intensive diagnostic and therapeutic involvements with patient populations, or the empirical research conducted by Grinker et al. (1968), Gunderson (1982), Perry and Klerman (1980), Kroll et al. (1981), and others.

In the *DSM-III Case Book*, the "clairvoyant" (p. 95), diagnosed a Schizotypal Personality Disorder, presents depersonalization, derealization, magical thinking, ideas of reference (which were not challenged regarding their delusional quality), odd speech, suspiciousness, and reality testing evaluated only to the extent of determining that she had no hallucinations or delusions. We have no way of knowing whether her ideas of reference and her suspiciousness were properly explored. The case book commentary states: "The clinician might be concerned about the likelihood of a previous psychotic episode in this patient, in which case the current symptoms would be indicative of the residual phase of Schizophrenia. In the absence of such a history, however, a diagnosis of Schizotypal Personality Disorder is most appropriate" (p. 96). The other case of Schizotypal Personality presents social isolation, magical thinking, inadequate rapport, odd speech, and hypersensitivity to criticism (reading in criticism where none was intended). Again, the commentary (p. 235) says: "There are many similarities between Schizotypal Personality Disorder and the symptoms seen in the Residual subtype of Schizophrenia, but the absence of a history of overt psychotic features rules out that diagnosis."

In my view, the diagnosis of Schizotypal Personality Disorder is problematic. A careful evaluation of reality testing in the clinical situation may identify patients with actual loss of reality testing and psychotic personality structure in contrast to those in whom the maintenance of reality testing corresponds clearly to the diagnosis of Schizoid Personality. It is as if a tail end of schizophrenia has been inserted in the section on personality disorders, the counterpart of the remarkable restriction of schizophrenia to a psychosis of at least six months' duration, so that any schizophrenic illness lasting even a few days less than six months would be classified as a Schizophreniform Disorder. It would be preferable, it seems to me, not to restrict schizophrenia so artificially and, from a clinical viewpoint, to be able to make the diagnosis even in cases who do not have the florid picture and where the treatment approach and the prognosis are different from those corresponding to personality disorders.

In all fairness, one could also argue that the introduction of the diagnosis of Schizotypal Personality Disorder as intermediary between Schizophrenic Disorder and Schizoid Personality Disorder reflects a sophisticated approach to the interrelation of the various diagnostic sectors, the delimitation of an obscure area that links personality disorders with the psychoses. We find, however, that the corresponding personality disorders on the affective side have now been classified among the

Affective Disorders. Thus, as mentioned earlier, the Cyclothymic Disorder (corresponding to the Cyclothymic Personality in DSM-II) is classified together with the Dysthymic Disorder or Depressive Neurosis within the Affective Disorders. Here the problem mentioned in discussing the depressive personality is compounded.

If we conceive of personality disorders in a sequence of severity from the depressive personality to the hypomanic and cyclothymic personalities, with an area in which affective disorders and personality disorders overlap, the entire affective spectrum of personality disorders would remain together, as do the schizoid and schizotypal disorders. DSM-III, however, inconsistently restricts schizophrenia and expands the affective disorders. Frances (1980) has called attention to a similar inconsistency in the handling of spectrum disorders in DSM-III. This inconsistency extends to a third dimension as well, perhaps even more important than the relation of the personality disorders to schizophrenia and the affective disorders, namely, the relation of the personality disorders to the symptomatic neuroses or psychoneuroses. Because the neuroses have been dispersed throughout DSM-III, the relation between depressive reactions and personality disorders is severed, and the relation between the hysterical personality and conversion hysteria and dissociative disorders has disappeared. Conversion hysteria has been divided into Somatization Disorder (when a woman has more than 14 symptoms or a man more than 12) and Conversion Disorder (14 or fewer symptoms in women, 12 or fewer symptoms in men). The Obsessive Compulsive Personality of DSM-II has been renamed the Compulsive Personality Disorder "in order to avoid confusion with Obsessive Compulsive Disorder."

This artificial dissociation of personality disorders from symptomatic neuroses and the renaming and reshuffling of symptomatic neuroses throughout DSM-III increase rather than reduce the problems of the relation between personality disorders and psychopathology in general. In addition, several personality disorders have been placed outside the sector of personality, such as the already mentioned Cyclothymic Disorder, the Disorders of Impulse Control Not Elsewhere Classified, which include the explosive personality (under the name Intermittent Explosive Disorder), and various impulsive personality disorders (under the heading of Pathological Gambling, Kleptomania, and Pyromania), in addition to Atypical Impulse Control Disorder.

On the diagnosis of borderline personality disorder, the DSM-III Task Force was faced with the sometimes idiosyncratic terminology used by individual clinicians, researchers, and theoreticians and with their varying ideas about exactly what this diagnosis included. For example, Gunderson (1977, 1982; Gunderson and Singer, 1975; Gunderson et al., 1981) considers borderline personality disorder a narrow, strictly delimited diagnostic entity, with clinical characteristics that correspond quite closely with those defined in DSM-III and roughly corresponding to the infantile personality or the severer types of infantile personality referred to earlier. In contrast, Grinker (1975) presents a very broad spectrum of borderline conditions, as do Rosenfeld (1979a, 1979b), Searles (1978), Giovacchini (1979), Masterson (1980), and Rinsley (1980). Stone (1980) and Kernberg (1975; see also chaps. 1 and 2, above) adopt an intermediary position which considers borderline personality organization to be a psychostructural diagnostic entity in which genetic predispositions, psychodynamic predispositions, and temperamental dispositions converge. For practical purposes, the decision had to be made whether borderline personality organization should be introduced as a structural concept (indicating severity of character pathology or personality disorder) or in a restricted sense corresponding to Gunderson's and others' concepts.

DSM-III opted for the restricted definition but the decision has not been consistent. First, Gunderson's emphasis on the development of brief psychotic episodes in these patients was not included among the essential criteria—in spite of the significant clinical and research evidence—and is mentioned only as an afterthought: "Dysthymic disorder and major depression as well as psychotic disorders, such as a brief reactive psychosis, may be complications" (DSM-III, p. 322). In addition, DSM-III shows a striking overlap of Borderline Personality Disorder and Histrionic Personality Disorder (referred to above). Both are described as presenting severe pathology of object relations, affective instability, physically self-damaging acts, impulsivity, self-dramatization, and transient psychotic disorders. The disturbance of identity, correctly mentioned for the borderline personality disorder, is also mentioned for the histrionic personality. Pope et al. (1983) concluded that although borderline personality disorder could be distinguished readily from DSM-III schizophrenia and did not appear to represent "borderline affective disorder," it could not be distinguished on any of the indices from histrionic and antisocial personality disorders.

It seems that the inclusion of borderline personality and histrionic personality represents some kind of compromise solution, with confusing effects. Perhaps the term Histrionic Personality Disorder and the corresponding description relate to D. Klein's (1975, 1977) interest in classifying the borderline spectrum according to psychopharmacological response, and perhaps his participation in the task force influenced that labeling, just as the selection of the avoidant and dependent personality disorders reflects Millon's thinking. On the general concept of the borderline personality disorder, I agree with Millon's emphasis on the importance of a classification of personality disorders that would consider severity of illness in addition to a particular constellation of pathological character traits. Millon writes:

An early aspiration of the committee was the differentiation of personality types along the dimension of severity; unfortunately, criteria for such distinctions were never developed. Rather than drawing severity discriminations, as proposed by both Kernberg and Millon, associates of the Task Force grouped the personality syndromes into three symptomatological clusters. The first includes the paranoid, schizoid, and schizotypal disorders, unified as a group in that their behaviors appear odd and eccentric. The second cluster subsumes the histrionic, narcissistic, antisocial, and borderline disorders, grouped together on the basis of their tendency to behave dramatically, emotionally, or erratically. The third cluster groups the avoidant, dependent, compulsive, and passive-aggressive personalities on the grounds that these types often appear anxious or fearful. A memo distributed by the author [that is, Millon] for discussion at the Task Force meeting of June 1978 addressed these recommended clusters as follows:

> I never quite understood the importance of those dimensions that led us to cluster personality disorders in the manner described. Any number of different dimensions could have been selected to group the eleven personality disorders in any of an almost infinite number of arrangements of sets or combinations. Why the specific one suggested in the text was selected out of these is not clear to me. Does it have some prognostic significance, some etiological import, logic in terms of a deductive theoretical model? If I were to develop a cluster or factorial framework for the personality disorders I am sure I would come up with a different schema than the one suggested. The characteristics specified are clear enough, but of what value is it to know that three are "eccentric," that four are "emotional," and that four appear "anxious"?
>
> My own preference would be either to drop the grouping entirely and list them alphabetically or to group them in terms of their known prevalence or potential severity. (1981, p. 63)

Millon then compares his views with mine, accurately pointing out that I give "primary attention . . . to the *internal* structural characteristics of the personality, whereas for Millon the *external* social system and interpersonal dynamics are given a status equal to that of internal organization" (Millon, 1981, p. 63).

On the positive side of this troubled sector of personality disorders in DSM-III, the descriptions of the Paranoid Personality Disorder and of the Narcissistic Personality Disorder are essentially satisfactory. The first of these is a good illustration of a classical description from clinical psychiatry which has maintained its clinical usefulness regardless of the various theoretical conceptions of its etiology, psychopathology, and treatment. The description of the Narcissistic Personality Disorder includes recent contributions from psychoanalytic studies and acknowledges the descriptive criteria derived from psychoanalytically oriented clinical investigations. The only omission is mention of these patients' strong conflicts around envy, both conscious and unconscious, and the degrees of clinical severity.

The description of the Antisocial Personality Disorder is based largely on the work of Robins (1966), who was a member of the advisory committee on personality disorders of the DSM-III Task Force. I agree with Frances (1980), also a member of that committee, who has stated: "The DSM-III diagnostic criteria specifying antisocial personality are indeed clear and reliable and have been the most carefully studied . . ., but they may have missed the most important clinical point. Using criteria comparable to those in DSM-III, approximately 80% of all criminals are diagnosed as antisocial." Frances then points to the absence from DSM-III of such crucial clinical criteria as "the individual's capacity for loyalty to others, guilt, anticipatory anxiety, and learning from past experiences" (p. 1053).

I have already referred briefly to the diagnosis of Schizoid Personality Disorder, which is essentially acceptable but is somewhat impoverished by its failure to include consideration of the contemporary contributions to the study of clinical and dynamic features of patients with such disorder (Fairbairn, 1954; Guntrip, 1968; Rey, 1979). Schizoid personalities may experience an acute awareness of their surrounding environment, an emotional attunedness to others, and yet a sense of unavailability of feelings. In contrast to what DSM-III states (p. 310), many of them are not "humorless or dull and without affect in situations in which an emotional response would be appropriate," and they experience very intense suffering because of their lack of easy access to their feelings for others. However, for practical purposes, the diagnostic category does permit the clinical diagnosis of this common type of personality disorder.

Elsewhere (1976) I have suggested a classification of character pathology based on psychoanalytic, psychostructural criteria. In a highly simplified summary, this classification conceives of a high-level or neurotic type of character pathology including, predominantly, the hysterical, obsessive-compulsive, and depressive-masochistic personalities; an intermediary level of character pathology that includes the better functioning narcissistic personalities, some infantile personalities, and passive-aggressive personalities; and a "lower-level" or "borderline personality organization" that includes most cases of infantile and narcissistic personalities and practically all schizoid, paranoid, and hypomanic personalities, in addition to the "as if" and all antisocial personalities. The descriptive-phenomenological criteria of the various types of character pathology and the structural criteria of borderline personality organization mutually strengthen the accuracy of clinical diagnosis and have prognostic and therapeutic relevance.

I think, in sum, that the DSM-III classification of personality disorders requires revision. It is remarkable how many diagnostic problems have been created by this relatively small section of the DSM-III classification system and how the criteria and goals outlined in the introduction to DSM-III have been disregarded. New terminology has been introduced for reasons that are unclear; clinical experience and clinicians' needs have been neglected; and overlapping categories have been included unnecessarily while essental constellations are missing. DSM-III is not, of course, unique in problematic classifications; there were significant problems with DSM-I and DSM-II as well. While we may hope that DSM-IV will improve matters, it is only realistic to expect new problems together with new solutions. At bottom, the field is in flux, and strong, conflicting theoretical biases find expression in the political maneuvers activated by the bureaucratic method by which DSMs are produced. For maximal effectiveness in the light of our current knowledge, an optimal classification of personality disorders should include both a categorical approach to different types of personality constellations and a dimensional approach that refers to the degree of severity of these disorders and to the internal relations of the subgroups to one another.

PART TWO: *Treatment of Borderline Personalities*

CHAPTER 6: *Expressive Psychotherapy*

Theoretical Background

Because major contributors to the study of the psychotherapeutic treatment of borderline conditions gravitate toward a broad definition of borderline personality, the patients they write about might be classified under different headings in DSM-III and by researchers who tend to prefer a narrower definition.

Rinsley (1980) and Masterson (1976, 1978, 1980), for example, concern themselves primarily with patients who, in my view (see chap. 5), correspond to the infantile personality. Their patients also seem to correspond with Gunderson's (1977, 1982) concept of borderline personality disorder and with what DSM-III designates the Histrionic Personality Disorder and the Borderline Personality Disorder. Rosenfeld (1979a) focuses mostly on borderline patients with predominantly narcissistic and paranoid features, comparable to what DSM-III describes in the criteria for Narcissistic Personality Disorder and Paranoid Personality Disorder. Fairbairn (1954) and Rey (1979) focus mostly on the schizoid features of borderline conditions characteristic of the Schizoid and Schizotypal Personality Disorders in DSM-III. In short, the literature on intensive psychotherapy of borderline conditions covers a spectrum of psychopathology related to various types of character pathology or personality disorders. In my view, all these types share the structural characteristics of borderline personality organization; in the view of the other authors cited, they share common genetic (in a psychoanalytic sense) and developmental characteristics.

Mahler (1971, 1972; Mahler and Kaplan, 1977) has provided clinical and theoretical frameworks for these genetic and developmental characteristics. All the clinical descriptions in the works of the psychotherapists mentioned and in the works of others who have carried out inten-

97

sive psychotherapy with borderline patients include features common to patients with borderline pathology (Winnicott, 1958, 1965; Bion, 1967; Khan, 1974; Volkan, 1976; Green, 1977; Little, 1981). With the exception of Bion, these authorities make a distinction between the way they treat borderline patients and the way they treat neurotic patients, patients with nonborderline character pathology, and psychotics. Elsewhere I have attempted to synthesize the clinical characteristics of borderline patients, in the process developing an explanatory frame of reference—a psychostructural object relations theory—that links their descriptive and structural characteristics with their transference developments and the psychotherapeutic process (1975, 1976, 1980). The psychoanalysts and psychotherapists mentioned have reached conclusions similar to mine: Object relations theory constitutes a valuable frame of reference and provides an explanatory formulation for both the clinical characteristics of these patients and their psychotherapeutic process. In the past, under the influence of Knight's pioneering work (1953a), the treatment considered optimal for borderline patients was supportive psychotherapy. Gradually, however, many clinicians who worked intensively with borderline patients shifted to a psychoanalytic (or expressive) psychotherapeutic approach for most of those patients. Unmodified psychoanalysis was still considered possible for some patients.

The Menninger Foundation's Psychotherapy Research Project (Kernberg et al., 1972) attempted to compare the effects of psychoanalysis, expressive psychotherapy, and supportive psychotherapy—the entire spectrum of psychoanalytically derived psychotherapies—for patients with "good ego strength" (mostly neurotic character pathology and symptomatic neuroses) and those with "ego weakness" (borderline character pathology). The research results led to the conclusion that the best treatment for patients with ego weakness may be an expressive approach, with little structure provided during the treatment hours and as much concomitant hospitalization (environmental structuring) as the patient needs. This approach contrasts with a purely supportive treatment, which provides a good deal of structure during the treatment hours, but not hospital support.

Other psychoanalytically derived psychotherapeutic approaches to borderline conditions employ more modifications of technique. Masterson (1972, 1976, 1978), for instance, has designed a special form of psychotherapy geared to the resolution of "abandonment depression" and the correction and repair of the ego defects that accompany the narcissistic oral fixation of these patients by encouraging growth through the stages of separation-individuation to autonomy. He has proposed that psychotherapy with borderline patients should start out as supportive and that intensive, reconstructive, psychoanalytically oriented psychotherapy is usually an expansion and outgrowth of supportive psycho-

therapy. Masterson stresses the importance of analyzing primitive transferences and offers an expanded description of two mutually split-off
part-object-relations units (the rewarding or libidinal unit, and the with-
drawing or aggressive unit), thus combining an object relations viewpoint with a developmental model based on the work of Margaret
Mahler.

Rinsley (1977) and Furer (1977) are others among a growing group
of psychoanalytically oriented therapists who are combining a psychostructural object-relations theory with a developmental model stemming
from Mahler's work (Mahler, 1971, 1972; Mahler and Furer, 1968;
Mahler and Kaplan, 1977). Giovacchini (1975), Bergeret (1970), Green
(1977), Searles (1977), and Volkan (1976) have also been applying models
derived from object relations theory. Searles has focused particularly on
understanding the characteristics of transference and countertransference developments in the treatment of borderline and psychotic patients. Comprehensive overviews of some of these approaches can be
found in Hartocollis (1977) and in Masterson (1978).

Whereas the American authors base their approach essentially on
an ego-psychology model that incorporates recent developmental findings and psychostructural object-relations theories, the British school of
psychoanalysis (originally identified with certain object-relations theories) has continued to influence the technical approaches to borderline
patients. Little's work (1957, 1960, 1966) focused mostly on technique.
Although she assumed that most of the patients she described were borderline, her implication that these patients presented a lack of differentiation between self and object and her technical proposals for helping
them develop a sense of uniqueness and separateness seemed to focus
on the pathology of the early differentiation subphase of separation-
individuation. Her views are somewhat related to those of Winnicott,
but her patients seem to be more regressed than those he described.

Winnicott (1960b) stressed the therapist's need to permit the patient
to develop his "true self" by avoiding "impinging" upon him at certain
stages of therapeutic regression. The optimal function of the therapist
under these conditions, he said, was as a "holding" object, akin to basic
mothering for patients who lacked normal mothering. At such moments, Winnicott suggested, a silent regression takes place to what
amounts to a primitive form of dependency on the analyst experienced
as a "holding mother." Winnicott thought that the analyst's intuitive,
empathically understanding presence was more useful than the disturbing, intrusively experienced effects of verbal interpretation.

This concept is related to Bion's theory (1967) that mother's intuitive
daydreaming (Bion calls it "reverie") permits her to incorporate the
baby's projected, dispersed, fragmented primitive experiences at points
of frustration and to integrate them by means of her intuitive

understanding of the baby's total predicament at that point. Mother's intuition, Bion says, thus acts as a "container" which organizes the projected "content." Similarly, the dispersed, distorted, pathological elements of the regressed patient's experience are projected onto the analyst so that the patient can use him as a "container"—an organizer, one might say—of what the patient cannot tolerate experiencing in himself.

In short, both Winnicott and Bion stress the ability of the therapist working with borderline patients to be able to integrate both cognitive and emotional aspects in his understanding of the therapeutic situation, with Bion focusing on the cognitive ("containing") aspect in contrast to Winnicott's emphasis on the emotional ("holding") one. A source of some confusion in the literature is that some who write on the psychotherapy of borderline personality tend not to differentiate expressive psychotherapy from psychoanalysis. To me it seems that these writers —for example, Giovacchini (1978), Little (1981), Searles (1979), and Winnicott (1958, 1965)—actually modify their technique sufficiently so that what they do in practice is not standard psychoanalysis. The advantage, I think, of clearly distinguishing between expressive psychotherapy and psychoanalysis is that it permits a sharper delimitation of a specific psychotherapeutic approach for borderline patients.

This review would be unbalanced, however, if it did not mention that clinical practice often diverges from the expressive treatment recommended in most of the literature. A large number of borderline patients, perhaps the majority, are treated with a mixture of expressive and supportive techniques or in a treatment modality that employs infrequent sessions (one a week or fewer), signifying a shift from an intended expressive modality to a supportive modality. The clinical response to crisis intervention and brief hospitalization, along with clear and firm environmental structure, indicates that a supportive approach is effective, at least in short-term types of psychotherapy. Another everyday clinical observation is that many borderline patients are maintained on an outpatient basis by means of a long-term supportive psychotherapeutic relationship.

The specific literature on supportive psychotherapy of borderline conditions is very scanty. The "purely" supportive approaches earlier recommended by Knight (1953b) and Zetzel (1971), and still advocated by Grinker (1975), have shifted, as I have noted, to the recommendation that supportive techniques be used only for the initial stages of psychoanalytic psychotherapy with such conditions (Masterson, 1978). Adler and Buie (1979), Modell (1976), and Volkan (1979) stress the supportive effects of the holding function of the therapist but propose an essentially expressive technique for borderline patients from the beginning of the treatment.

On the basis of the findings of the Menninger project, I have proposed rejecting the traditional assumption of Knight (1953b) and Zetzel (1971), among others, that the more distorted or weaker the patient's ego, the more supportive the treatment he needs (Kernberg, 1975). I also question the long-standing tradition of mixing expressive and supportive techniques, particularly with borderline personality organization. The consistent clinical observation is that the use of supportive techniques eliminates technical neutrality and, by the same token, eliminates the possibility of interpreting the transference. Because the borderline patient induces in the therapist strong emotional currents that tend to cause the therapist to abandon a position of technical neutrality, interpretation of these central transference areas becomes impossible. At the same time, the therapist, in an effort to maintain an essentially analytic attitude while mingling expressive and supportive techniques, tends to restrain himself or herself in the use of supportive measures, thus weakening both the expressive and the supportive features of the psychotherapy.

Using Gill's (1954) specifications, one may define the technique of psychoanalysis by the analyst's (1) consistent adherence to a position of technical neutrality; (2) consistent use of interpretation as a technical tool; and (3) facilitation of the development of a full-fledged transference neurosis and of its psychoanalytic resolution solely by interpretation. In fact, a spectrum of psychoanalytic psychotherapies ranging from psychoanalysis to supportive psychotherapies can be differentiated in terms of these three basic features. What follows is a description of expressive psychotherapy for patients with borderline personality organization.

Technique of Expressive Psychotherapy

Expressive psychotherapy for borderline conditions may be described in terms of variations in Gill's three technical essentials. Because primitive transferences are immediately available, predominate as resistances, and in fact determine the severity of intrapsychic and interpersonal disturbances, the therapist can and should focus upon them immediately, starting by interpreting them in the here-and-now. Genetic reconstruction should be attempted only at late stages of the treatment, when primitive transferences determined by part-object relations have been transformed into higher level transferences or total-object relations. At that point, the transferences approach the more realistic experiences of childhood that lend themselves to such reconstructions. Interpretation of the transference requires maintaining a position of technical neutrality, for primitive transferences cannot be interpreted without a firm, consistent, and stable maintenance of reality boundaries in the therapeutic situation. The therapist must also be ever alert to the possibility of being sucked into reactivation of the patient's pathological primitive object relations. Insofar as both transference interpretation and a position of technical neutrality require the use of clarification and interpretation and contraindicate the use of suggestive and manipulative techniques, clarification and interpretation are the principal techniques.

Transference analysis, however, in contrast to psychoanalysis proper, is not systematic. Transference analysis must focus both on the severity of acting out and on disturbances in the patient's external reality which may threaten the continuity of the treatment as well as the patient's psychosocial survival. Because of this and also because the treatment, as part of the acting out of primitive transferences, easily comes to replace life, transference interpretation must be codetermined by three sets of factors: (1) the conflicts predominating in immediate reality; (2) the overall specific goals of treatment, as well as the consistent differentiation of life goals from treatment goals (Ticho, 1972); and (3) what is immediately prevailing in the transference.

In addition, technical neutrality is limited by the need to establish parameters of technique (Eissler, 1953). In certain cases such parameters include structure in the external life of patients who cannot function autonomously during long stretches of their psychotherapy. Technical neutrality is therefore a theoretical baseline from which deviations occur again and again, to be reduced by interpretation. The therapist's interpretation of the patient's understanding (or misunderstanding) of the therapist's comments is an important aspect of this effort to reduce the deviations from technical neutrality.

With these cautions and observations in mind, the three technical essentials and their specific effects on borderline personality organization can be examined in greater detail.

Interpretation

Interpretation is a fundamental technical tool in psychoanalytic psychotherapy with borderline patients. In fact, as I have noted above, in order to protect technical neutrality as much as possible, suggestion and manipulation are practically contraindicated here. An exception is made when the potential for severe acting out requires structuring the patient's external life and using a team approach, which implies setting limits and other interventions in the social field. Such social structuring and interventive efforts should be considered parameters of technique, to be interpreted as soon and as comprehensively as possible so that they can gradually be dissolved.

Some have questioned whether patients with severe psychological illness and ego weakness can respond to interpretation. Do these patients accept the interpretations because of their actual meaning or because of their magical, transference meanings? Empirical evidence indicates that patients with severe psychological illness are indeed able to understand and integrate the therapist's interpretive comments, particularly if their distortions of these interpretations are examined and interpreted in turn (Frosch, 1970). In other words, the patient's difficulty in integrating verbal communications is itself a product of primitive defensive operations, and this difficulty can be interpreted, particularly as the defensive operations are activated in the patient's reactions to the therapist's interpretations.

However, as a result of the very fact that the patient's interpretations of the therapist's interpretations must be explored so fully, clarification takes precedence over interpretation. This technical demand creates quantitative differences between expressive psychotherapy and psychoanalysis.

Maintenance of Technical Neutrality

This is an essential technical tool, an indispensable prerequisite for interpretive work. Technical neutrality by no means excludes empathy. There are times when the patient's regressive aggression in the transference brings about counteraggressive reactions in the therapist. Under such circumstances, technical neutrality depends on the therapist's emotional capacity to maintain an empathic attitude or "holding" action (Winnicott) and his cognitive capacity to integrate or "contain" (Bion) the fragmentarily expressed transferences.

Technical neutrality means maintaining an equal distance from the forces determining the patient's intrapsychic conflicts, not a lack of warmth or empathy. One still hears comments implying that borderline patients need, first of all, empathic understanding rather than a focused theory and cognitively sharpened interpretations based on such a theory. All psychotherapy requires at minimum the therapist's capacity for authentic warmth and empathy. But empathy is not only the therapist's intuitive emotional awareness of the patient's central emotional experience at a certain point; it must also include the therapist's capacity to empathize with what the patient cannot tolerate within himself. Therapeutic empathy, therefore, transcends that involved in ordinary human interactions. It also includes the therapist's integration, on a cognitive and an emotional level, of what is actively dissociated or split off in borderline patients.

However, the patient's potential for severe acting out, the development of life- or treatment-threatening situations, or both may require structuring, not only of the patient's life, but of the psychotherapy sessions themselves. Technical neutrality is thereby constantly interfered with, threatened, or limited, and a good part of the therapist's efforts will have to be concentrated on returning to it repeatedly. Again, this reduction in technical neutrality represents a quantitative difference from psychoanalysis proper.

The therapist's deviation from technical neutrality in the form of directive behavior may be of such intensity and/or duration that technical neutrality cannot be achieved or recovered. Modifications, instead of parameters, have been established. Under optimal circumstances, gradual interpretation of temporary deviations from technical neutrality permit a reversion to a neutral stance, which maximizes the possibility for transference interpretation and resolution of primitive transferences.

Transference Analysis

As mentioned earlier, transference interpretation is limited in expressive psychotherapy and is codetermined by a constant focus on the immediate reality of the patient's life and the ultimate treatment goals. Also, because the interpretation of primitive transference gradually leads to the integration of part-object relations into total-object relations and, by the same token, to a transformation from primitive transference to an advanced or neurotic transference, relatively sudden shifts occur in the transference of borderline patients. More neurotic or advanced transferences, reflecting more realistic childhood developments, appear at first infrequently and then with increasing frequency throughout the treatment. The shifting of transference phases throughout the treatment gives an overall timelessness to genetic reconstructions and interferes with their historical placement. The transference must therefore be interpreted in an atemporal "as if" mode over extended periods of time—an additional reason for considering transference interpretation in these cases as less than systematic, and therefore different from transference interpretation in the standard psychoanalytic situation.

Nevertheless, the interpretation of defensive constellations under these conditions is systematic. In contrast to exploratory psychotherapy with better-functioning patients, where certain defenses may be selectively interpreted and others not touched, the systematic interpretation of defenses in severe psychopathology is crucial to improving ego functioning and to transforming and resolving primitive transferences. The interpretation of the constellation of primitive defensive operations centering on splitting therefore should be as consistent as possible, given their predominance in the patient's transference and in his extratherapeutic relationships.

Guidelines for Managing the Transference

Because interpretation of the transference plays so vital a part in expressive psychotherapy with borderline patients, I have reserved a description of the strategy and tactics I recommend for a separate chapter (chap. 7). Here I offer more general guidelines.

1. The predominantly negative transference of these patients should be systematically elaborated only in the here-and-now, without attempting to achieve full genetic reconstructions. With borderline patients, the lack of integration of the self-concept and the lack of differentiation and individualization of objects interfere with the ability to differentiate present and past object relationships. Patients confuse transference and reality and fail to differentiate the therapist from the transference object. Full genetic reconstructions, therefore, must await advanced stages of the treatment. A premature genetic interpretation (for example, "You react to me this way because you see in me your mother's attitude in your past") may bring about a condensation of past and present ("You are right, and it is terrible that, having had such a mother, I have to have a therapist exactly like her").

2. The typical defensive constellations should be interpreted as they enter the transference, for their interpretation strengthens the patient's ego and brings about structural intrapsychic change, which contributes to resolving the borderline personality organization. Primitive ego defenses do not strengthen the patient's ego, but weaken it! Their systematic interpretation therefore has powerful "supportive" effects.

3. Limits should be set in order to block acting out of the transference, with as much structuring of the patient's life outside the sessions as is necessary to protect the neutrality of the therapist. Although interventions in the patient's external life may sometimes be needed, the therapist's technical neutrality is essential for the treatment. Moreover, it is important to avoid allowing the therapeutic relationship, with its gratifying and sheltered nature, to replace ordinary life lest the patient gratify his primitive pathological needs by acting out the transference during and outside the sessions. The therapist must be alert to this secondary gain of treatment, be willing to interpret it, and, if external limits are required, try to use auxiliary social support systems (a social worker, nurse, counselor, and others) rather than intervene directly in the patient's outside life and thus eliminate technical neutrality.

4. The less primitively determined, modulated aspects of the positive transference should not be interpreted. Respecting these aspects of the transference fosters gradual development of the therapeutic alliance. With borderline patients the focus on interpretation should be on the primitive, grossly exaggerated idealizations that reflect the splitting of "all good" from "all bad" object relations. These must be interpreted systematically as part of the effort to work through the primitive defenses. The negative transference should be interpreted as fully as possible. This is the major vehicle for indirectly strengthening the therapeutic alliance while dealing directly with the primitive conflicts around

aggression and intolerance of ambivalence characteristic of borderline patients.

5. Interpretations should be so formulated that the patient's distortions of the therapist's interventions and of current reality, especially the patient's distorted perceptions in the hour, can be clarified systematically. In other words, the patient's magical utilization of the therapist's interpretations requires interpreting. For example, the patient's tendency to listen to the "amount" of verbal communication from the therapist rather than pay attention to its content should be consistently interpreted. Also, it is indispensable that interpretations be based on a frame of reality shared by patient and therapist: there can be no interpretation of unconscious motivations before the patient can agree with the therapist on what the *reality* in their interaction is. Only ego-dystonic distortions of reality can be interpreted!

The strategy of interpreting the transference with borderline patients may be conceived as requiring three consecutive steps, representing, in essence, the sequence involved in working through the primitive transferences and their transformation into advanced or neurotic transferences. Primitive transferences express part-object relations: that is, units of "split-off" aspects of the self concept relating to "split-off" aspects of object representations in the context of a primitive affective link of self and object representations. Advanced or neurotic transferences involve integrated or total-self and object representations and more closely reflect actual experience in childhood. The first step consists of an effort to reconstruct, on the basis of the psychotherapist's gradual understanding, the nature of the primitive or "part-object" relation that has become activated in the transference. The therapist must evaluate what, at any point, from the contradictory bits of verbal and behavioral communication of the patient's confused and confusing thoughts, feelings, and expressions, is of predominant emotional relevance in the patient's current relation with him or her. In other words, the therapist, by means of interpretation, transforms the prevalent meaninglessness or futility in the transference—what literally amounts to a dehumanization of the therapeutic relationship—into an emotionally significant, though highly distorted and fantastic, transference relationship. In practice, the therapist uses his own fantasies, intuition, and previous knowledge of the patient to construct a basic human interaction—strange or bizarre or unrealistic as it may appear—that approximates optimally the central organizing fantasy activated in the current therapeutic situation.

As a second step, the therapist evaluates this crystallizing predominant object relation in the transference in terms of the self representation and object representation involved and clarifies the affect of the corresponding interaction of self and object. The therapist may represent one aspect of the patient's dissociated self and/or primitive object representation, and patient and therapist may exchange their enactment of self or object representation. These aspects of the self and object representations should be interpreted, and the respective internal object relation must be clarified in the transference. In practice, the patient's reaction to, clarification of, and associations derived from the therapist's effort to describe what seems to be going on between them at this time lead to gradual enrichment and clarification of "who is doing what to whom," or "who is experiencing what from whom," in this fantastic object relation in the transference, and to "tagging" the patient's self and object representations through cycles of projection and reintrojection.

As a third step, the particular part-object relation activated in the transference has to be integrated with other part-object relations, reflecting other related and contradictory, defensively dissociated part-object relations, until the patient's real self and internal conception of objects can be integrated and consolidated. In this process, positive and negative aspects of the self concept are linked and simultaneously integrated with corresponding positive and negative aspects of the patient's object representations.

Integration of self and object representations, and thus of the entire world of internalized object relations, is a major strategic aim in the treatment of patients with borderline personality organization. Integration of the patient's affects with his fantasied or real relations with significant objects is another aspect of this work. The patient's affect dispositions reflect the libidinal or aggressive investment of certain internalized object relations, and the integration of split-off, fragmented affect states is a corollary of the integration of split-off, fragmented internalized object relations. When such a resolution of primitive transferences has occurred, the integrative affect dispositions that then emerge reflect more coherent and differentiated drive derivatives. The integrated object representations then reflect more realistic parental images as perceived in early childhood. At this point, the borderline patient may be helped to come to terms with the past more realistically, in the context of profound transformations in his relation to the therapist and to significant others in his current life.

Prognostic Considerations

There are few systematic prognostic studies of long-term psychotherapy of borderline conditions. The findings of the Menninger project indicated that patients with initially low ego strength, especially those with initially low quality of interpersonal relationships, showed the least improvement. On the basis of a detailed clinical evaluation of the patient population of that project, I suggest that prognostic features included the predominant type of character constellation, certain ego and superego distortions reflected in individual character traits, self-destructive-ness as a character formation, the particular type and intensity of nega-tive therapeutic reactions, the degree and quality of superego pathology, and the quality of the patient's object relationships (Kernberg, 1975).

Michael Stone's findings (unpublished) in evaluating the distribu-tion of personality types among borderline office patients with respect to treatment outcome agree with the prognostic considerations I have sug-gested. Borderline patients of predominantly hysteric, obsessive, de-pressive, phobic, infantile, and passive personality types had a compar-atively successful outcome. In contrast, the majority of borderline patients with personality types that were predominantly paranoid, narcissistic, schizoid, explosive, hypomanic, inadequate, and antisocial ended in treatment failure. Masterson (1980) stressed the prognostic im-portance of the degree of early-life stress, the level of early ego develop-ment, the degree of mastery of early developmental tasks, and the ef-fectiveness of early social relationships (object relations).

Although other prognostic references appear throughout the litera-ture on intensive psychotherapy of borderline conditions, the evidence regarding most postulated prognostic features does not yet seem to be conclusive. My current view is that the two most important prognostic indicators are the presence of antisocial features—which definitely worsen the prognosis for psychotherapeutic treatment—and the quality of object relations. In addition, the development of negative therapeutic reactions is an important process variable with significant negative prog-nostic implications. The importance of other personality and environ-mental variables and of the techniques, skill, and personality of the ther-apist, as well as his or her countertransference, all require further systematic research. The relationship between the process and the out-come of long-term psychotherapy, a crucial factor in daily clinical prac-tice, remains a relatively neglected area of psychotherapy research.

A Case Illustration

The following case focuses on the development of transference patterns reflecting primitive internalized part-object relations and their gradual transformation into more advanced or neurotic transferences. It also shows the development of significant intrapsychic structural change over a period of four years of expressive psychotherapy, four ses-sions a week.

Miss L. A Latin American artist in her late twenties presented a bor-derline personality organization with predominant masochistic and schizoid features and severe sexual inhibition, to the extent that she was unable to reach orgasm in masturbation. Her sexual fantasies were of mutilation of her own and her fantasied male partner's genitals in sexual intercourse. She had been studiously avoiding any real involvement with men whom she found attractive.

In the transference, the following major patterns developed sequentially over the first four years. First she wished that the therapist would rape her and kill her in intercourse because only in hatred and the infliction of death could true love and commitment be found. A sadistic, primitive oedipal father image lay at the core of these fantasies. Later she fantasied being the dependent child of a motherly father and believed that if she were permitted to suck the therapist's penis all her needs for warmth, love, sex, and protection would be met. She now wished that the therapist would hold her as a mother holds a baby while she sucked his penis with its never-ending flow of semen or milk. It became clear that a major reason for her incapacity to engage in relations in depth with men was her terror over the confusion of these two contradictory attitudes and her terror that her love and hatred would come together in an unbearable situation of danger: She was afraid that her hatred would destroy both partners.

Still later in her treatment, when sexual fantasies about men acquired more integrated qualities, Miss L's fears of orgasm emerged as fears of "uncontrollable wetness." She could not show sadness in the sessions because crying also meant uncontrollable wetness. Crying, orgasm, and urinating at times of sexual excitement represented the threat of loss of control, with dangerous dependency on an unreliable object—her cold and frustrating mother. She also feared that orgasm would result in a dissolution of her personality into impersonal fragments. In summary, the predominance of splitting mechanisms, the fear of conflicts related to severe oral frustration, and the regressive dangers of the oedipal situation all blocked sexual excitement and orgasm. At a still later time Miss L was able to fantasize more elaborate sexual experiences with men, the therapist in particular, which centered upon "letting herself go" and urinating during orgasm and which expressed her longings for dependency and sexual gratification in more synthetic ways. She now began to date men more freely, engaged in heavy petting with one of them, and (three and a half years after beginning treatment) developed severe blocking during the sessions, with long periods of silence. She also became aware of internal prohibitions against any further improvement or good experiences with the therapist or men in general. This could be traced back to a primitive maternal superego introject of an extremely sadistic nature. A primitive type of negative therapeutic reaction now developed, in which her submission to a sadistic superego constellation emerged, combining the hated and hateful pregenital mother with the feared oedipal rival. It turned out that the earlier fantasy of a sadistic father represented a displacement onto him of this very mother image. Only after a prolonged working through of her primitive superego pressures was Miss L finally able, for the first time in her life, to establish a sexual relation with an appropriate love object.

How do these transference developments reflect significant intrapsychic structural change? The shift from the wish for the therapist to rape her and kill her to the wish to be the dependent child of the motherly father actually reflected a permanent feature of Miss L's conflicts: her terror over the confusion of her two contradictory attitudes and fears regarding men. This sequence, then, reflected only one pattern of internalized object relations, a pattern that changed when she became aware of and able to tolerate the fact that her hatred, death wishes, and fear of being destroyed were directed toward the same object on whom she wished to depend. In the transference she became able to both fear and hate the therapist, to express criticism of him, attack him, and be suspicious of him, and yet also to express longing and feelings of warmth and dependency upon him. Her gradually increasing capacity to tolerate these contradictory attitudes permitted her to overcome this major transference constellation and represented the first transformation in her transference pattern, reflecting a transformation from a primitive to a more integrated internalized object relation.

This transformation was reflected behaviorally in an impressive diminution in Miss L's suspiciousness and fearfulness without the use of medication. (She had previously been massively medicated for her panic attacks, without satisfactory response.) Miss L could now talk more coherently, consistently, and thoughtfully in the sessions and began to take the first steps toward more realistic and less fear-provoking relations with other people.

A second major transformation occurred when Miss L began to describe her sexual fantasies and fears in more detail in the hours; this occurred in connection with her increased tolerance for enjoying genital and dependent longings in fantasied relations with the therapist and other men. At this point, she started to have sexual experiences with men. She also improved in her creative activities and work. Only then did it emerge that one major reason for her blocking in her artistic work had been the uncontrollable sexual fantasies that were triggered by various subjects she was attempting to explore. For example, a reference to the differences between men and women immediately evoked pervasive sexual fantasies of penises and urinating. This difficulty now subsided.

A third major transformation occurred at the time of the severe blockings in the sessions and the negative therapeutic reaction related to the activation of a primitive maternal superego introject. Overcoming this major transference pattern, again reflecting a primitive object relation, permitted Miss L to become objectively more independent of her parents, to separate from her mother's values, and to become more self-affirming in her daily life.

I should stress that very little information about these issues was available at the beginning of treatment. The patient had consulted for severe and chronic anxiety and depression, breakdown in her social functioning, inability to perform in her artistic work, and several suicide attempts. Previous psychotherapeutic efforts had failed. The sessions with previous therapists (all of them men) had consisted of long, stubborn silences. Only in hindsight was it possible to diagnose the nature of the blocking in the previous therapeutic experiences: It was related to the activation of the same primitive sexual fantasies that terrorized the patient. Her negative behavior torward her previous therapists reflected the wish to provoke sexual attacks and punishment from men and to punish herself for her efforts to overcome her problems—that is, for rebelling against the primitive mother introject. These needs had motivated her suicide attempts, which had interfered with and complicated previous treatment efforts.

To stress again my principal point: In this case it took considerable time with several transference developments to diagnose the significant sequence of internalized object relations that jointly constituted a persistent constellation in the transference. It took even more time to bring about a significant transformation of these major constellations in the transference. This transformation was a precondition for bringing about change in other areas of the patient's life. It needs to be underlined that the changes that occurred in this case were not derived from the therapist's supportive, suggestive, or manipulative efforts but followed naturally, spontaneously, and unpredictably the transformations in significant object relations in the transference.

CHAPTER 7: *Transference Management in Expressive Psychotherapy*

Perhaps the most striking characteristic of the treatment of patients with borderline personality organization is the premature activation in the transference of very early conflict-laden object relationships in the context of ego states that are dissociated from one another. Why "premature"? It is as if each of these ego states represents a highly developed, regressive transference reaction within which a specific internalized object relationship is activated. This transference is in contrast to the more gradual unfolding of internalized object relationships as regression occurs in the typical neurotic patient.

The ordinary transference neurosis is characterized by the activation of the patient's infantile self: The patient reenacts the emotional conflicts of this infantile self with the parental objects experienced in infancy and childhood. In contrast, the self and object representations of borderline patients are activated in the transference in ways that do not permit the reconstruction of infantile conflicts with the parental objects as perceived in reality. With these patients, the transference reflects a multitude of internal object relations of dissociated or split-off aspects of the self with dissociated or split-off object representations of a highly fantastic and distorted nature.

The basic cause of these developments is the borderline patient's failure to integrate libidinally determined and aggressively determined self and object representations. The problem is that the intensity of aggressively determined self and object representations makes it impossible to integrate them with libidinally determined self and object representations. Because of the implicit threat to the good object relations, bringing together opposite (loving and hateful) images of the self and of significant others would trigger unbearable anxiety and guilt. Therefore, an active defensive separation of such contradictory self and object im-

112

ages occurs. In other words, *primitive dissociation* or *splitting* becomes a major defensive operation.

In working through the transference developments with borderline patients, the overall strategic aim is to resolve these primitive dissociations and thus to transform the primitive transferences into the higher level transference reactions characteristic of the neurotic patient. Obviously, this requires intensive, long-term treatment, usually not fewer than two or three sessions a week over a period of five to seven years.

The conflicts that typically emerge in connection with the reactivation of these early internalized object relations may be characterized as a particular pathological condensation of pregenital and genital aims under the overriding influence of pregenital aggression. Excessive pregenital, and especially oral, aggression tends to be projected and determines the paranoid distortion of the early parental images, particularly those of the mother. Through projection of predominantly oral-sadistic and also anal-sadistic impulses, the mother is seen as potentially dangerous. Hatred of the mother extends to hatred of both parents when the child subsequently experiences them as a united group. A "contamination" of the father image by aggression primarily projected onto mother and lack of differentiation between mother and father tend to produce combined, dangerous father–mother images and, later on, a conceptualization of all sexual relationships as dangerous and infiltrated by aggression. Concurrently, in an effort to escape from oral rage and fears, a "flight" into genital strivings occurs; this flight often miscarries because of the intensity of the pregenital aggression, which contaminates the genital strivings (Heimann, 1955a).

The transference manifestations of patients with borderline personality organization may at first appear completely chaotic. Gradually, however, repetitive patterns emerge, reflecting primitive self representations and related object representations under the influence of the conflicts just described. These appear in the treatment as predominantly negative transference patterns. The defensive operations characteristic of borderline patients (splitting, projective identification, denial, primitive idealization, devaluation, and omnipotence) become the vehicle of the transference resistances. That these defensive operations in themselves have ego-weakening effects seems to be a crucial factor in the severe regression that soon complicates the premature transference developments.

Once a borderline patient embarks on treatment, the crucial decompensating force is the patient's increased effort to defend himself against the emergence of the threatening primitive, especially negative, transference reactions by intensified utilization of the very defensive operations that have contributed to "ego weakness" in the first place. One main culprit in this regard is probably the mechanism of projective identification, described by Melanie Klein (1946), Heimann (1955b), Money-Kyrle (1956), Rosenfeld (1963), and Segal (1964). Projective identification is a primitive form of projection, called upon mainly to externalize aggressive self and object images. "Empathy" is maintained with real objects, onto which the projection has occurred, and is linked with an effort to control the object, now feared because of this projection. Insofar as the patient maintains emotional awareness of the projected impulse (empathy with "others'" aggression), he illustrates the absence or failure of repression (which characterizes higher levels of projection). To the extent that the patient rationalizes his own "counteraggression" as motivated by the other's aggression toward him, projective identification may be complicated by a secondary rationalization.

In the transference, projective identification is typically manifested as intense distrust and fear of the therapist. The therapist is experienced as attacking the patient, while the patient himself feels empathy with that projected intense aggression and tries to control the therapist in a sadistic, overpowering way. The patient may be partially aware of his own hostility but feel that he is simply responding to the therapist's aggression and that he is justified in being angry and aggressive. It is as if the patient's life depended on his keeping the therapist under control. The patient's aggressive behavior, at the same time, tends to provoke counteraggressive feelings and attitudes from the therapist. It is as if the patient were pushing the aggressive part of his self onto the therapist and as if the countertransference represented the emergence of this part of the patient from within the therapist (Money-Kyrle, 1956; Racker, 1957).

It should be stressed that what is projected in a very inefficient and self-defeating way is not "pure" aggression but a self representation or an object representation linked with that drive derivative. Primitive self and object representations are actually linked as basic units of primitive object relationships (Kernberg, 1976). Characteristic of borderline patients is a rapid oscillation between moments of projection of a self representation while the patient remains identified with the corresponding object representation, and other moments in which it is the object representation that is projected while the patient identifies with the corresponding self representation. For example, a primitive, sadistic mother image may be projected onto the therapist while the patient experiences himself as the frightened, attacked, panic-stricken little child; moments later, the patient may experience himself as the stern, prohibitive, moralistic (and extremely sadistic), primitive mother image while the therapist is seen as the guilty, defensive, frightened, but rebellious child. These complementary role reenactments in the transference may also induce corresponding countertransference reactions in the therapist, an example of "complementary identification" (Racker, 1957).

The danger in this situation is that, under the influence of the expression of intense aggression by the patient, the reality aspects of the transference–countertransference situation may be such that it comes dangerously close to reconstituting the originally projected interaction between internalized self and object images. Under these circumstances, vicious cycles may be created in which the patient, in the grip of the projected aggressive drive derivatives, projects his aggression onto the therapist and reintrojects a severely distorted image of the therapist, thus perpetuating the pathological early object relationship. Heimann (1955b) has illustrated these vicious cycles of projective identification and distorted reintrojection of the therapist in discussing paranoid defenses. Strachey (1934) has referred to the general issue of normal and pathological introjection of the analyst as an essential aspect of the effect of interpretation, especially in regard to modifying the superego.

Rapidly alternating projection of self images and object images representing early pathological internalized object relations produces a confusion of what is "inside" and "outside" in the patient's experience of his interactions with the therapist. It is as if the patient maintained a sense of being different from the therapist at all times, but concurrently he and the therapist were interchanging their personalities. This is a frightening experience for the patient, in that it reflects a breakdown of ego boundaries. As a consequence there is a loss of reality testing in the transference. It is this loss that most powerfully interferes with the patient's capacity to distinguish fantasy from reality, past from present, and projected transference objects from the therapist as a real person. Under such circumstances, the possibility that a mutative interpretation will be effective is seriously threatened. Clinically, this appears as the patient's experiencing something such as "Yes, you are right in thinking that I see you as I saw my father. That is because you and he are really identical." It is at this point that a "transference psychosis" is reached (Kernberg, 1975, chap. 5).

I prefer to reserve the term *transference psychosis* to designate the loss of reality testing and the appearance of delusional material within the transference that does not very noticeably affect the patient's functioning outside the treatment setting. Hospitalization may sometimes be necessary for such a patient, and it is often quite difficult to separate a transference-limited psychotic reaction from a broader one. Nevertheless, in many borderline patients this delimitation is easy, and it is frequently possible to resolve the transference psychosis within the psychotherapy (Little, 1951; Reider, 1957; Romm, 1957; Holzman and Ekstein, 1959; Wallerstein, 1967).

Acting out the transference becomes a principal resistance to further change; therefore it is important that the therapist introduce parameters of technique to control it. The danger is that the therapist may appear to the patient as prohibitive and sadistic, thus initiating a vicious cycle of projection and reintrojection of the patient's sadistic self and object representations. The therapist can counteract this danger by interpreting the transference situation, then introducing the structuring parameters as needed, and finally interpreting the transference situation again, without abandoning the parameters. Some aspects of this technique have been illustrated by Sharpe (1931) in demonstrating how to deal with acute episodes of anxiety.

The nature of primitive transferences in borderline patients presents certain technical problems and dangers. The therapist may be tempted to interpret these transferences directly, as if they reflected the actual earliest or most primitive human experiences; he might even go so far as to interpret them as a genetic reconstruction of the first few years or even the first few months of life, thus confusing or condensing primitive fantasy and actual earliest development. This kind of condensation is characteristic of some Kleinian work. The Kleinian approach contains, in my opinion, two errors: It mistakes the primitive bizarre intrapsychic elaboration of psychic experience for actual developmental features; and it telescopes complex, slowly developing structural organization of internalized object relations into the first few months of life.

Because the transference acting out appears to be such a meaningful reproduction of the patient's past conflicts, fantasies, defensive operations, and internalized object relations, the therapist may be tempted to interpret it as evidence of a working through of these conflicts. The repetition compulsion expressed through this transference acting out cannot be considered as working through, however, so long as the transference relationship provides the patient with instinctual gratification of pathological, especially aggressive, needs. Some patients, indeed, obtain much more gratification of their pathological instinctual needs in the transference than would ever be possible in their extratherapeutic interactions. At this regressed level, the patient's acting out overruns the therapist's effort to maintain a climate of abstinence.

A second danger can result from assuming that, because of the intense activation of affects in a patient with little capacity for observing what he is experiencing, the therapist should focus on ego functioning, to the neglect of the object relations implications of what is activated in the transference. The therapist may focus, for example, on the patient's difficulty in experiencing or expressing his feelings or overcoming silence, his tendency to impulsive actions, or his temporary loss of logical clarity instead of on the total primitive interaction (or the defenses against it) activated in the transference. A mistake in the opposite direction would be to interpret the object relation "in depth" without paying sufficient heed to the patient's ego functions. A still further danger is that the therapist may focus exclusively on the here-and-now in the context of conceptualizing the transference as a corrective emotional "encounter," neglecting the task of gradually integrating self and object images into more realistic internalized object relations and advanced types of transference that will permit more realistic genetic reconstructions. Here, the therapist unwillingly or unwittingly may contribute to the stability of primitive transferences (as the treatment replaces life), thus interfering with the patient's ego growth.

Simultaneous attention should be given to the here-and-now and to the underlying past primitive internalized object relations activated in the transference so that what is on the surface and what is deepest are integrated into emotional experiences of ever-growing complexity. In this process, whatever capacity for self-observation and autonomous work on his problems the patient has must be explored, highlighted, and reinforced so that attention is given to the patient's ego functioning, particularly to his self-observing function, hand in hand with the clarification and verbalization of primitive object relations reflected in his conscious and unconscious fantasies.

Fenichel's (1941) general rule of interpretation—to proceed from surface to depth—certainly applies to borderline patients. It is helpful if we first share our observations with the patient, stimulate him to integrate them a step beyond what is immediately observable, and interpret beyond his own awareness only when it is clear that he cannot do so himself. Further, whenever we interpret beyond the patient's awareness of the transference situation, we should include in the interpretation the reasons for his unawareness. Inasmuch as primitive transference dispositions imply a rapid shift to a deep level of experience, the therapist working with borderline patients must be prepared to shift his focus from the here-and-now to the past fantasied object relation activated in the transference—one that often includes bizarre and primitive characteristics which the therapist has to dare to make verbally explicit as far as his understanding permits. Moreover, the therapist should be alert to the danger that the patient may interpret what he has said as a magical statement derived from a magical understanding rather than as a realistic putting together of what the patient has communicated to him.

Integrative aspects of the interpretations therefore include consistent interpretation of surface and depth. The same procedure applies to the patient's communications. When apparently "deep" material comes up in these communications, it is important first to clarify the extent to which the patient is expressing an emotional experience, an intellectual speculation, a fantasy, or a delusional conviction. One question the therapist often has to ask himself in the treatment of borderline patients—"Should I now clarify reality, or should I now interpret in depth?"—can usually be answered by evaluating the patient's reality testing at the moment, his capacity for self-observation, and the disorganizing effects of primitive defensive operations in the transference. Ideally, clarification of reality and interpretation in depth should be integrated, but that is often not possible.

Surprisingly, as one's experience with this kind of treatment of borderline patients grows, one finds more and more that what at first seemed a simple manifestation of ego weakness or ego defect turns out to be the effect of very specific, active, primitive defensive operations directed against full awareness of a dissociated transference relation reflecting intrapsychic conflicts. In other words, this treatment approach permits us to diagnose areas of ego weakness, to evaluate the ego-weakening effects of primitive defensive operations and of dissociated internalized object relations, and to foster ego growth by essentially interpretive means. Clarifications of reality made by the therapist often subsequently turn out to have been an unnecessary support feeding into a certain transference situation. Whenever this occurs, it is very helpful to interpret to the patient how an apparently necessary clarification by the therapist was actually not necessary at all.

The question often arises whether to further clarify the reality of the patient or to interpret the meaning of his distortion of reality. If one proceeds from surface to depth, first testing the limits of the patient's understanding and then interpreting the defensive aspects of his lack of awareness of an appropriate perception of (or reaction to) reality, one can usually resolve this question in a basically analytic fashion. The danger always exists that the patient will perceive the therapist's interpretation of his defensive denial of reality as a subtle attempt to influence him. Therefore, in addition to an introspective evaluation of whether the patient may be right in this regard, this distortion of the therapist's interpretation has to be interpreted as well. In essence, technical neutrality, interpretation of the transference, the therapist's introspective exploration of his countertransference, and the focus on the patient's perceptions in the session are intimately linked technical tools.

A related problem for the therapist working with borderline conditions concerns the extent to which he should interpret rather than wait until the patient is ready to do further work on his own. In general, once operational understanding has been achieved, I think few advantages are gained from simply waiting. Insofar as primitive transferences are activated rapidly in the sessions and tend to perpetuate themselves in a repetition compulsion, there is an advantage in interpreting the material fully as soon as it is clear enough and whenever a certain transference disposition becomes a predominant transference resistance. Some borderline patients activate one kind of transference pattern in an endless repetition over many months and years; for them early interpretation may not only save much time but may protect them from destructive acting out. At the same time, an interpretive approach that deals rapidly with the developing transference resistances does not imply by-passing the patient's capacity for self-observation: I wish to stress again that interpretation in depth should include an ongoing evaluation of the patient's capacity for self-observation and should never justify the patient's hopes (or fears) of a magical relation with an omnipotent therapist. Very often, simply waiting for the patient to improve in his self-observing capacities is of little use and risks bringing about chronic countertransference distortions that gradually undermine the therapist's position of technical neutrality.

There are areas in which the therapist must let patients know that he cannot or will not do for them what they cannot or will not do for themselves. The intense and deepening object relation involved in each psychotherapy session throughout weeks, months, and even years of treatment has a totally different quality from an ongoing real-life relation, and this is something the patient must eventually accept. The therapist's empathic attitude, derived from his emotional understanding of himself and from his transitory identification with and concern for the patient, has elements in common with the empathy of the "good-enough mother" with her infant (Winnicott). There is, however, also a totally rational, cognitive, almost ascetic aspect to the therapist's work with the patient which gives their relation a completely different quality from that of a mother–infant one.

Because patients with good ego strength frequently use either intellectualization or excessive affective reactions as a defense (obsessive-compulsive versus hysterical pathology), we tend to overlook the intimate connection between affects and cognition at the earlier levels of development and in the more pathological or primitive psychological functioning that retains modes of such early development. In addition, the traditional focus on "catharsis" in psychoanalytic psychotherapies (and the distortion of this concept in some currently employed psychotherapeutic modalities, which naively assume that affective discharge will produce fundamental psychological change by itself) has prevented us from recognizing that cognitive clarification and integration are basic and potent psychotherapeutic tools.

The therapist's cognitive formulations strengthen or broaden the patient's integration of affects and internalized object relations. The therapist's holding function includes both affective and cognitive aspects. To formulate interpretations with patients in a state of severe regression is to interpret primitive defensive splitting, which results in an integration of defensively dissociated affects and object relations and increases the patient's cognitive capacities. Not all intellectual knowledge is "intellectualization"; authentic knowledge both fosters and is a concomitant of any emotional growth.

The therapist who carries out an interpretive psychotherapy with borderline patients will necessarily frustrate the patient's wishes by carefully avoiding making decisions for him. The patient may for a long time remain unaware that what he is receiving is consistent alertness, interest, and concern in the face of the many temptations for the therapist, under the onslaught of the patient's aggression, to become angry, sleepy, withdrawn, indifferent, impatient, and the like.

I have elsewhere (1975) said it is necessary to deepen the level of interpretation rapidly when the patient begins to act out. Although there is a risk of interpreting beyond the level of emotional understanding the patient has reached at that point—and a risk, therefore, that the interpretation will be either rejected or incorporated in intellectualized or magical ways—the focus on the patient's relation to the interpretation will make it possible to correct such potential misfirings of quick interpretations of the transference.

Another important aspect of the analysis of the transference of borderline conditions is the tenuous nature of the therapeutic alliance compared with that of neurotic patients in psychoanalysis. The therapeutic alliance (Zetzel, 1956; Greenson, 1965) links the analyst with the observing part of the patient's ego, however limited it may be, in the treatment situation. Insofar as there is a sufficient observing part of the neurotic patient's ego, the therapeutic alliance (or, one might say, the task-oriented alliance between the patient's observing ego and the analyst) is a given, ordinarily not requiring too much attention. However, even under ideal circumstances, in the typical psychoanalytic case there are times when the intensity of the transference relation threatens temporarily to overwhelm the patient's observing ego. At such times it may be necessary to focus the patient's attention on that complication. In contrast, the observing ego in the typical borderline case is so limited and frail that the question has been raised to what extent it is necessary to focus attention strongly, consistently, on the therapeutic alliance: Are there times when the therapist needs to take active measures to strengthen the therapeutic alliance by reality-oriented, supportive comments or by providing the patient with information regarding the therapist's reality aspects?

In my opinion, to focus on the defensive use or nature of the distortions of the patient's perceptions, particularly on his distortions of the therapist's interpretations, is the best means of strengthening the patient's observing ego without shifting from an essentially analytic model. It seems to me that various aspects of the real relation between therapist and patient are a nonspecific, potentially therapeutic aspect of the treatment in all cases. However, this aspect of the total treatment relationship is limited in the ordinary psychoanalytic case, and the systematic analysis of all transference paradigms in the unfolding transference neurosis should lead to a systematic working through of the patient's efforts to use the therapeutic relationship as a parental function in the transference. In other words, the nonspecific supportive implications of the real aspects of the relationship in terms of the patient's unfolding transference will automatically become part of the analytic work and remain in the background. In borderline patients, on the other hand, the nonspecific, "real" human relationship reflected in the therapeutic alliance may constitute an important corrective emotional experience, not in the sense that the therapist adopts an active, manipulative stance but in the sense that such a positive working relation, which often goes far beyond anything the patient has previously experienced, is normally gratifying. To the extent that chronically traumatizing or frustrating circumstances of early development, and therefore of the patient's former relations with the real parents, are an important aspect of the genetic and historical background of borderline patients, the real relation with the therapist may perform parental functions the patient has never experienced before.

In addition, the therapist's availability as a "container" (Bion, 1967), as an absorber, organizer, and transformer of the patient's chaotic intrapsychic experience (which the therapist first attempts to clarify in his own mind and then conveys to the patient as part of his interpretive comments), does provide cognitive functions that the neurotic patient undergoing psychoanalysis is expected to carry out for himself. In other words, the therapist does provide auxiliary cognitive ego functions for the borderline patient in addition to the implicit reassurance given by his ability to withstand and not be destroyed by the patient's aggression, by his not retaliating, by his maintaining a general attitude of concern for and emotional availability to the patient. Others have stressed the importance of the therapist's "holding" functions with borderline patients (Little, 1958, 1960; Winnicott, 1960b). These aspects of the therapeutic relationship undoubtedly play a vital role in the psychoanalytic psychotherapy of borderline patients, and, as long as they occur within a setting of technical neutrality, they constitute a legitimate use of the psychotherapeutic relationship. This use has to be differentiated from the patient's intense transference demands that the therapist gratify needs that were previously frustrated, that he act in loco parentis, thus abandoning the position of technical neutrality and increasing the supportive aspects of the therapeutic relationship. I cannot emphasize strongly enough the need for the psychoanalyst and psychotherapist working with borderline patients to analyze carefully all these attempts on the patient's part. What really strengthens the patient's ego is not the gratification of needs in the here-and-now that were denied in the there-and-then but a coming to terms with past frustrations and limitations in the context of an understanding of the pathological reactions, impulses, and defenses that were activated under those earlier traumatic circumstances and that contributed importantly to the development and fixation of ego weakness.

The question of insight in borderline patients deserves discussion. In some borderline patients, one finds what at first looks like insight into deep layers of the mind and into unconscious dynamics. Unfortunately, this is actually an expression of the ready availability of primary-process functioning, which is part of the general regression of their ego structures. Insight that comes without any effort, unaccompanied by any change in the patient's intrapsychic equilibrium and, above all, by any concern for the pathological aspects of his behavior or experience, is questionable insight. Authentic insight is a combination of intellectual and emotional understanding of the deeper sources of one's psychic experiences, accompanied by concern and an urge to change the pathological aspects of those experiences.

I have stressed the importance of maintaining an attitude of technical neutrality in order to be able to interpret the primitive transferences occurring in the patient–therapist interaction. I cannot emphasize strongly enough that a heavy price is paid whenever the therapist yields to the temptation of introducing supportive techniques; immediate improvement is followed by the patient's later rationalizations of transference developments that cannot be resolved fully and thus limit the fundamental personality changes the treatment aims for.

However, as Loewald (1960) has pointed out with reference to the standard psychoanalytic situation, the therapist's function in interpreting the patient's emotional reality itself is to reflect the fact that his ego is functioning at a more integrative level than the patient's ego is capable of achieving at the time of transference regression. The patient's identifying himself with the interpreting function of the therapist is therefore a growth experience. Under such conditions it implies, as Loewald observes, an identification with an object image of the therapist and with a self-image as well: namely, the image of the patient himself as perceived by the therapist.

To put it differently, the patient's identification with the therapist's interpreting function reflects an identification with a dyadic object relation of a good or helpful kind. This process, which normally occurs in subtle and unobtrusive ways in the treatment of neurotic patients, is strongly accentuated in the psychoanalytic psychotherapy of borderline conditions, where identity diffusion interferes with precisely the integrative function that the therapist can provide. Whereas the integrative, cognitive-emotional function is more important in the therapeutic situation with borderline patients than with the standard psychoanalytic cases in providing a basis for potential growth, this function may, at the same time, stir up intense experiences of hatred and envy in borderline patients: hatred because significant learning about oneself—as opposed to defensive dissociation—is always painful, and thus the therapist's helping attitude, paradoxically, is painful as well; envy because primitive aggression frequently takes the form of envious strivings to destroy the therapist as a giving maternal image. Therefore, the interpretation of the patient's unconscious need to reject or destroy the therapist's integrative function may be an important aspect of interpretive work within an essentially technically neutral position.

The effect of primitive defensive operations, particularly projective identification, is not only to attribute a certain mental disposition to the therapist but to induce in him a certain emotional disposition which complements the patient's own affective state, an urge to act in a certain direction which complements the transference needs. Neutrality is thus challenged or threatened, although by the same token every momentary threat to or deviation from technical neutrality imparts important transference information.

The primitive nature of the transference activated in the borderline patient leads the therapist, as he strives to empathize with the patient, to whatever capacity he may have for awareness of primitive emotional reactions within himself. This is reinforced by the patient's nonverbal behavior, especially those aspects that attempt to control the therapist, to impose on him, so to speak, the role assigned to the self or object image within the primitive activated transference. We probably still do not know enough about how one person's behavior may induce emotional and behavioral reactions in another. The therapist's empathy, his creative use of evenly hovering attention—an activity akin to daydreaming—and the direct impact of behavioral perception combine to bring about a temporary regressive reaction that permits him to identify with the patient's primitive levels of functioning.

In order to maintain the optimal degree of inner freedom for exploring his own emotional reactions and fantasy formations in connection with the patient's material, the therapist who treats borderline patients must be particularly concerned that he intervene only when he has again reached a technically neutral position. It is especially important to maintain a consistent attitude of "abstinence"—in the sense of not giving in to the patient's demands for transference gratification—but, instead, to interpret these demands fully and consistently. The therapist's humanity, warmth, and concern will come through naturally in his ongoing attention to and work with the patient's difficulties in the transference and in his ability to absorb and yet not react to the demands stemming from the patient's primitive dependent, sexual, and aggressive needs.

Paradoxically, it may be very helpful for the therapist who treats borderline patients in long-term psychoanalytic psychotherapy or in analysis also to have active experience with brief, crisis-intervention type treatment of other such patients. When the therapist feels secure conducting short-term, supportive psychotherapy or crisis intervention and can adhere firmly to an analytic stance, he will feel less pressure for "action." A broad level of experience, the capacity to carry out alternative modalities of treatment, and a careful, complete diagnostic evaluation all contribute to the therapist's ability to maintain a serene and firm position while interpreting the patient's acting out and complex transference developments.

Clinical Illustrations

Miss M. A graduate student in her late twenties had begun psychoanalytic psychotherapy (three sessions a week) because of a severe depressive reaction with weight loss and suicidal ideation, alcoholism, and a general breakdown in her functioning at school, in her social life, and in her love relation with her boyfriend. The diagnosis was infantile personality with borderline features, severe depressive reaction, and symptomatic alcoholism. The treatment was carried out in face-to-face sessions since I use the couch only for psychoanalysis (see Kernberg, 1975). In the beginning of the treatment, I had established certain conditions under which I would be willing to see Miss M on an outpatient basis. If she could not fulfill these conditions, I would see her in psychotherapy until she became ready to do so, and she would remain in the hospital. Hospitalization had been suggested by other psychiatrists who had seen Miss M, and I, too, had contemplated it as an alternative in case she proved unable to take responsibility for her functioning in reality.

Insofar as I made these conditions, one might say that a selective process took place, that only a limited range of borderline patients would accept and be able to undergo the kind of treatment approach proposed. However, it must be pointed out that Miss M had available as an alternative the possibility of short-term (or long-term) hospitalization and that I would expect hospitalization, if needed, at a minimum to develop her capacity to take responsibility for such functions as are indispensable for outpatient treatment in any case. The opposite approach—to accept outpatient treatment on a less than realistic basis—would probably bring about a more complicated and potentially disastrous course of treatment. In other words, a therapist cannot do justice to his patient's needs if the therapist does not have the minimal requirements and freedom for full deployment of his special technical knowledge and capabilities.

Miss M had committed herself to stop drinking, not to act on suicidal impulses but to discuss them openly with me if and when they occurred, and to maintain a minimum weight by eating sufficiently, regardless of her mood and appetite. A psychiatric social worker was beginning an evaluation of Miss M's total social situation, including her relation with her parents, who lived in a different town, and was available to the patient for suggestion and advice, if needed, regarding problems in her daily life. Our understanding was that the social worker would convey full information about Miss M to me and that I would communicate to the social worker only the information that I considered crucial and that the patient had explicitly authorized me to transmit. My psychotherapeutic approach was essentially psychoanalytic, and I attempted to maintain a consistent position of technical neutrality.

In the session to be described, which took place a few weeks after the start of treatment, Miss M looked haggard and distraught; it was raining heavily, and she had not taken precautions to dress appropriately so that she arrived without raincoat or umbrella, drenched, the thinness of her body apparent under her wet clothes. Her blouse and pants were dirty, and she looked somewhat disheveled. She began talking immediately about a difficult test she had to take at school that she was afraid she would not pass. She then talked about a serious fight with her boyfriend; she felt jealous because of his interest in another woman, a former girlfriend of his whom, the patient had discovered, he had met secretly. She also expressed concern over whether her parents would send her the monthly check (which produced in me the fantasy that she wanted to reassure me: She would be paying for her treatment; therefore, even if I were fed up with her otherwise, it would still be in my interest to continue seeing her in spite of her "unlikable" nature).

Miss M's flow of verbal communication seemed to be disrupted by a variety of nonverbal behaviors. Sporadically, she fell silent and looked at me with a searching, distrustful, and somewhat withdrawn expression; there were moments of inappropriate, artificial gaity and forced laughter, which conveyed to me her conscious efforts to control our interaction. She became "confused" in telling me where she had met her boyfriend and the other woman—which made me wonder whether she had been drinking without daring to let me know about it. Information from the psychiatric social worker came to my mind: Miss M had casually remarked to her that she had recently had stomach aches and had been vomiting, and the social worker wondered whether the patient needed another medical checkup.

I now oscillated between moments of concern and strong urges to express this concern to the patient in terms of the deterioration of her physical appearance, her health, and the question of whether she would really be able to maintain the outpatient treatment setting we had agreed upon. I was also tempted to confront her with those aspects of her behavior that made me wonder whether she was telling me the truth. I perceived an underlying fearfulness in her and felt that she was experiencing me as a potentially critical and inflexible parental figure who would scold her for not being truthful or for behaving poorly. (All this was superimposed on my feeling that she desperately wanted me to take over and run her life.) I now become aware of a growing sense of impatience in myself, a combination of worry for the patient and irritation that the treatment program as set up was falling apart and inordinate demands were being made on the psychiatric social worker and on me to change the treatment arrangements, mobilize Miss M's parents, and protect her against the impending threat of dismissal from school (another reality aspect that had brought her into treatment).

I finally felt that the predominant human relationship enacted at that moment was of a frightened little girl who wanted a powerful parental figure (whose particular sexual identity was irrelevant) to take over and protect her from pain, fear, and suffering in general. At the same time, I thought, she hated that parental figure because to be so taken over could occur only because she was suffering and not because of natural concern, love, and dedication to her. And she was afraid of a retaliatory attack from that needed and yet resented parental figure because she projected her own angry demands onto it. Therefore, I felt, she had to escape from that dreaded relationship, perhaps by drinking herself into oblivion and creating a chaotic situation in which she would be rescued without having to acknowledge or emotionally relate to the rescuer as an enemy.

I told Miss M that, on the basis of what she seemed to be communicating, I had the feeling that she was expressing contradictory wishes: She wanted to reassure me that she was still in control of her life, and at the same time she was conveying quite dramatically that things were falling apart, that she was unable to handle her life, and that she was running the risk of illness, expulsion from school, and loss of her boyfriend. I added that, if I was correct, whatever I might do under these circumstances would be disastrous to her. If, on the one hand, I explored further whether she was really able to handle her immediate life situation, she would experience this as an attack. For example, if I raised the question whether, under these circumstances, she felt able to continue to refrain from drinking, she would consider it a "cross-examination" revealing my basic harshness and suspiciousness of her. If, on the other hand, I listened sympathetically without raising such questions, she would regard this as an expression of indifference and callousness. In either case, she would expect only suffering and disappointment from my potential reactions to her.

Miss M replied that she had been worried because she had been drinking and was afraid I would hospitalize her if I knew. She had also thought that, because of her parents' tardiness in sending her the money, I might be worried about receiving my fee, and she had been angry with her parents and embarrassed about this lateness. She said she felt completely hopeless about herself and did not know how this psychotherapy could help her. I said I thought she was worried not so much about whether the psychotherapy would help her as about whether I was genuinely interested in her or just concerned about getting paid for the sessions. I also said that I wondered whether she felt the only way of obtaining anything from me was by forcing it from me, extracting it, so to speak, by presenting herself as a completely helpless human wreck. I added that, under these circumstances, any help from me would be like the irritated, angry reaction of a parent who would prefer not to be bothered but had no alternative but to take care of an unwanted child.

Miss M burst into tears and said how desolate she felt because her boyfriend was leaving her, adding with real feeling that she felt she had no right to be helped by me, there were many people like her, and only because of the fortunate circumstance that her parents had money was she able to afford treatment that would otherwise be unavailable. Why should she be treated when there was so much suffering in the world? It was better to give up. . . .

At this moment, I felt that a change had occurred: Now her verbal communications and her behavior coincided. She was telling me about what had actually happened during the previous two days, with awareness of and worry about her sense of failure, mixed with a strange sense of relief for failing because she felt she did not deserve better. I felt that Miss M was becoming concerned for herself in the process of this interchange, that the pressure on me to take over was decreasing, and that she was beginning to feel guilty for having failed to keep her part of our agreement while also beginning to understand that this failure was an expression of her feeling that she did not deserve to be helped.

What I wish to stress is that the transference situation had now become more coherent; a masochistic character pattern was being expressed in a mostly pregenital, conflictually dependent relation to a frustrating parental image. The intersystemic conflict between superego features (unconscious guilt) and the dependency conflictually expressed by her ego now reflected a typical neurotic object relation in the transference. This development was in marked contrast to the earlier chaotic, contradictory manifestations of implicit suspicion, projected anger, aggressive demandingness, concealment, and withdrawal. I would also stress that the reduction of the chaotic transference manifestations into the predominant object relation expressed in the transference permitted the full exploration of the transference and life situations. Ego resources were activated that made it unnecessary for me to intervene on the patient's behalf. In other words, the approach from a position of technical neutrality permitted a strengthening of the patient's ego, even if only temporarily, and a fostering of her capacity to combine understanding in the session with an increasing sense of responsibility for her life outside the treatment hours.

Miss N. In contrast to that of Miss M, the case of Miss N illustrates the oscillation in the transference, at an advanced stage of treatment among various levels of internalized object relations, with alternating progression toward advanced, neurotic, or total-object relations, and regression toward primitive, part-object, or borderline object relations.

Miss N was a lawyer in her early thirties, presenting borderline personality organization with predominant obsessive and schizoid features. I saw her in psychoanalytic psychotherapy three times a week, for more than five years.

In the third year of treatment, after interpretation of primitive defensive operations in the context of condensation of oedipal and pre-oedipal material centering on her masochistic search for a warm, giving, but also powerful and sadistic father, the following transference pattern emerged. Miss N now experienced her oedipal and preoedipal mother combined as a powerful force preventing her from any further improvement. Vague and imprecise speech, serious blocking in the hours with a sense of futility, unending demands for demonstrations of my motherly love and interest, and accusations that I was cold and rejecting (that is, mother attacking her internally and externally) alternated with sexualized transference reactions in which she experienced me as a sexually exciting but dangerous and powerful man who frightened her. The oedipal qualities of the material become stronger in the context of an integration of the transference that seemed to reflect more realistic aspects of her childhood, while the conflict between her wishes for a sexual relation with a powerful father and her fear of punishment from the oedipal mother acquired intersystemic qualities. That is, her mother introject coincided more with broader superego features, and the intrapsychic conflicts were now intersystemic, in contrast to the previously predominant chaotic and conscious conflicts between mutually dissociated aspects of the relations with both parents. She also established, for the first time, a sexual relation with a man but eventually attempted to escape from the relationship out of an unconscious sense of guilt. Interestingly, she experienced her boyfriend as rather passive and sexually nonthreatening and at first found this helpful. But then she perceived his inability to withstand the forces in her that tended to destroy a good sexual relationship (her mother introject) as disappointing.

At this point, in the midst of my interpreting Miss N's fears of sexual longings for me as father (because they were forbidden by her internal mother), a relatively sudden deterioration occurred, and over a period of several weeks she seemed to regress to what had characterized the early stages of her treatment. She now presented an almost disorganized verbal communication (at the beginning of treatment she had presented an obsessive rumination that almost amounted to a formal disorganization of thought processes), an incapacity to listen to what I was saying, and a growing sense that my understanding of her was terribly incomplete, imperfect, and arbitrary. For the first time in her treatment, she expressed a strong wish to shift to another, presumably warmer and more understanding therapist. Efforts to interpret these feelings as a regressive escape from the oedipal aspects of the transference led nowhere.

At one point, Miss N let me know that she wanted me to say only perfect and precise things that would immediately and clearly reflect how she was feeling and would reassure her that I was really with her. Otherwise, I should say nothing but listen patiently to her attacks on me. At times, it became virtually impossible for me to say a word because Miss N would interrupt me and distort almost everything I was saying. I finally did sit back for several sessions, listening to her lengthy attacks on me while attempting to gain more understanding of the situation.

I now limited myself to pointing out that I understood her great need for me to say the right things, to reassure her, to give her indications that I understood her almost without her having to say anything. Also, I pointed out that I understood that she was terribly afraid that anything I might say was an attempt to overpower, dominate, or brainwash her. After such an intervention, Miss N would sit back as if expecting me to say more, but I did not. Then she would smile, which I privately interpreted as her acknowledgment that I was not attempting to control her or say anything beyond my acknowledgment of this immediate situation.

I must stress that in the early stages of this development I had intended to interpret the patient's attitude as an effort to control me omnipotently and as a reflection of her identification with the attitude of her sadistically perceived mother (her superego) toward herself (represented by me). But at this stage, any such efforts at interpretation exacerbated the situation and were not at all helpful (in contrast to similar interventions that had been very helpful months earlier). Surprisingly, after several weeks of my doing nothing beyond verbalizing the immediate relationship between us as I saw it, Miss N felt better, was reassured, and again had very positive and sexual feelings toward me. However, my efforts to investigate the relationship between these two types of sessions—those in which she could not accept anything from me and had to take over and those in which she seemed more positive but afraid of her sexual feelings—again led to stalemate.

After a few more weeks, I finally formulated the interpretation that she was enacting two alternate relations with me: one in which I was like a warm, receptive, understanding, and not-controlling mother and another in which I was again a father figure, sexually tempting and dangerous. Miss N now said that when I interpreted her behavior she saw me as harsh, masculine, invasive; when I sat back and just listened to her she saw me as soft, feminine, somewhat depressed, and somehow very soothing. She said that when she felt I understood her in that way—as a soothing, feminine, depressed person—she could, later on, listen to me, although I then "made the mistake" of again becoming a masculine and controlling figure.

I now interpreted her double split of me (as masculine and feminine, and good and bad) as an effort to avoid the conflict between the need for a good, warm relation with a mother who could understand and give her love—but who also forbade sex with father—and the need to be a receptive feminine woman to a masculine man standing for a father who was able to "penetrate" her in spite of her acting as if she rejected him (but, by the same token, threatening her relation with mother). I also interpreted her "getting stuck" in that situation as reflecting a condensation of a very early relationship with her mother, probably stemming from the second or third year of life, in which she felt that her mother could listen to her only when mother was depressed and listless, while any active interest of her mother seemed like intolerable control and dominance. I added that this reflected one more deep reason for her incapacity to shift into a dependent relation with a man who, at the same time, would be sexually attractive to her: Not having the security of a basic acceptance of love from a mother who also respected her autonomy, she felt she could not tolerate her sexual feelings for her father.

Months later, I was able to point out to Miss N that her perception of her father as a cruel, controlling, and sexually aggressive man represented a condensation of his masculinity and those qualities of dominance displaced from mother onto him. But the patient could not integrate these understandings, and the treatment continued to advance in the direction of further work on her oedipal conflicts.

This brief vignette illustrates how, in an advanced stage of psychoanalytic psychotherapy with a borderline patient (after years of working through primitive defensive mechanisms and object relations in the transference), a gradual predominance of oedipal conflicts occurred, simultaneously with a shift toward intersystemic conflicts. However, there was, at the same time, a regressive shift toward a very early stage of separation-individuation from mother that required a temporary shift in my attitude and my interpretive comments. During such regressive states, my interpretations focused less on typical borderline mechanisms and part-object transferences and more on the patient's conflicting needs to differentiate herself from me and to elicit perfect understanding and caretaking from me. In short, differentiation conflicts seemed temporarily to predominate over pathological rapprochement conflicts.

CHAPTER 8: *Expressive Psychotherapy with Adolescents*

The therapist's fundamental tasks during the early evaluation of the adolescent patient and his family include establishing the diagnosis, recommending treatment, and, above all spelling out the arrangements that should make treatment possible. It hardly needs to be stressed that the psychiatrist evaluating an adolescent patient and his family should maintain a technically neutral attitude. He should have total respect for the adolescent as an independent, autonomous person and should approach him without preconceived notions about what would or would not be proper in terms of the patient's negotiations with his family.

The therapist should avoid either being judgmental or romanticizing adolescence. He should be alert to the adolescent's tendency to think of him as a representative of his parents and equally aware that adolescents do not necessarily have special insight into basic truths denied to adults. On this basis, the therapist may explore the internal consistency of the adolescent's picture of himself, his significant object relations, and the integration and adequacy of his view of the world. Accepting the adolescent within his own assumptions and value systems is most likely to permit an evaluation of the consistency of his self and object representations and these value systems. At the same time, the therapist should maintain the appropriate distance, in contrast to either protective remoteness or chumminess. The adolescent has as much right to privacy as an adult patient.

If an adolescent wants the consultation, the psychiatrist should see him before seeing his parents. How his parents come into the picture—if at all—should be negotiated with him. If the parents request a consultation, either the adolescent should be seen first or the entire family should be seen together. If the therapist has preliminary meetings with the parents before the consultation or treatment starts, whatever

131

paranoid potential exists in the adolescent will be reinforced, and the therapist's neutral stance will become more difficult to establish. The same right to privacy applies to the adolescent's information. The patient may agree to allow some of the information he has provided to be discussed in the meetings with the family, but he should be given the option to decide that certain information is not to be shared.

Naturally, if there is evidence that the patient is withholding important information, the therapist may have to draw on a team that may include a psychiatric social worker, a school counselor, a psychologist, a teacher, and others. This immediately raises the issue of the patient's and/or his family's attempts to achieve control of the treatment situation, a complication frequently encountered in adolescent cases. Typically, the family or the patient tries to dictate conditions under which the treatment or the evaluation will be carried out. It seems to me preferable to discontinue an evaluation or treatment rather than accept it under less than optimal conditions. Very often, an early and quiet expression of the therapist's intention to reserve the right to evaluate or treat the patient or refer him to somebody else if the therapist finds it impossible to obtain sufficient freedom of action helps to prevent severer acting out subsequently or striving for omnipotent control. Sometimes the best help that can be given is to tell the family that if treatment cannot be carried out under certain circumstances, treatment efforts might be futile.

Paradoxically, the more severely disturbed the late-adolescent patient, the more the treatment should resemble that given to an adult patient, for this reason: In the psychotherapy of adolescent patients who are functioning fairly well, the early focus is on the normal developmental tasks of adolescence. With adolescents who are not functioning well, it is necessary to work on the severely distorted primitive transference dispositions, and these are similar to those found in adult borderline patients. When (as with borderline patients) the normal developmental tasks of adolescence have not been accomplished, psychoanalytic psychotherapy as conceptualized for the treatment of adult patients best serves the purpose of resolving primitive transferences, primitive defensive operations, and the ego and superego distortions that militate against carrying out these developmental tasks. The resolution of borderline psychopathology by analytic means will permit the spontaneous resumption of normal developmental processes later on.

Because of the significant age difference and therefore the difference in role and status between the adolescent patient and the psychotherapist, the patient is usually tempted to see himself as "an adolescent" relating to a stereotyped "adult." For example, the borderline adolescent's contention, with the slightest of justifications, that the therapist thinks, behaves, and treats him exactly as the patient's parents do may be less a specific transference manifestation than an effort on the patient's part to avoid awareness of his confusion, suspicion, derogatory behavior, and so forth regarding the significant adults in his life by simplistically lumping them all together.

As part of the systematic examination of the therapeutic interaction, therefore, the therapist may have to examine the patient's denial of the therapist's individuality as well as of his own individuality by taking refuge in the stereotyped behavior of a cultural subgroup. A position of technical neutrality does not mean that the therapist permits the patient to unload on him all the accumulated biases and stereotypes that both protect the patient against and reflect his identity diffusion. It is possible to clarify such distortions without telling the patient, "No, I'm not the way you see me." The general statement, "You have no reason to see me this way rather than in many other ways; therefore, there must be meaning to the fact that it is so important to you to see me in precisely this way," covers the issue.

Adolescent borderline patients often strenuously attempt to induce in the therapist the very attitudes they accuse adults, especially their parents, of having toward them. This reflects, particularly, the mechanism of projective identification. The therapist's alertness to such developments may permit him to interpret the patient's unconscious effort to make him into one more parental image. At the same time, the therapist may have to resist a tendency to behave in the opposite way from the adolescent's family as the patient describes them as behaving; the therapist must beware of trying to foster a good therapeutic relationship by seductive means.

A seductive attitude toward adolescents is also nurtured by a general idealization of adolescence, so prevalent in our culture, and by the therapist's unconscious efforts to defend himself against unconscious envy of adolescents by romanticizing or imitating them. Sometimes the therapist's effort to resist the patient's attempts to stereotype him as conventional may result in a wish to show the patient that he is not conventional. Of course the therapist has to be unconventional in withstanding cultural stereotypes enacted in the transference; but his unconventionality should emerge by means of his consistent, empathic, warm, yet detached stance as he raises questions about what is going on in the treatment. He must refuse to allow the patient to suck him into certain role models and must maintain technical neutrality.

In short, the analysis of cultural stereotypes as secondary defenses against full emergence of identity diffusion in the transference is an important aspect of treatment, particularly in the early stages of psychotherapy with borderline adolescents.

Expressive Psychotherapy and Family Structures

There seems to be mounting evidence, derived from clinical data and research, that borderline adolescents come from severely pathological families (Shapiro et al., 1975; Goldstein and Jones, 1977). The question is often raised to what extent the borderline adolescent patient "simply" reflects severe family psychopathology or is suffering from "internalized, structured" illness. I think that whenever a careful study of the adolescent patient demonstrates the existence of identity diffusion and the predominance of primitive defensive operations, we must assume that, regardless of what the family contribution to this illness has been, the patient has a bona fide structuralized borderline pathology that will require intense individual treatment.

Whereas the family, particularly the parents, may have made fundamental contributions to borderline psychopathology in their child, the diagnosis of borderline personality organization implies severe, long-standing pathological intrapsychic structures that now have an autonomous existence.

For the purpose of carrying out expressive psychotherapy, I think it is crucial that the therapist have an exclusive relationship with the adolescent and that family therapy, if indicated, be carried out by another therapist. if the patient is to be included in that family therapy, the family therapist should have the family's and the adolescent patient's authorization to communicate his observations to the patient's psychotherapist, thus establishing a teamwork approach similar to what I recommend for those borderline patients whose severe acting-out potential cannot otherwise be controlled.

To combine family therapy and intensive psychoanalytically oriented psychotherapy for the adolescent borderline patient presents various complications. First, the objectives of family therapy need to be clarified in an effort to differentiate short-term and long-term goals for all the participants. Sometimes there are no particular reasons for involving the family; the indication for family therapy should derive not from the therapist's ideological predilection for that type of therapy but from concrete, well-documented needs of the specific patient.

Family treatment may be needed because of the contribution the family is making to the patient's psychopathology or because the patient's pathology is being supported by the family structure or in order to prevent, avoid, or resolve the family's interference with the patient's treatment. The extent to which the family treatment will relate to, support, or be detrimental to the individual treatment must be explored.

There is always a danger of dilution of the transference, transference splitting, and acting out for the adolescent who is treated simultaneously in individual and family therapy. This danger is greater if the family therapist and individual therapist do not constitute a harmonious treatment team. In general, splitting of the transference is best avoided if the therapists conceptualize the entire constellation of family, patient, and themselves as one system regarding which all information flows to the individual psychotherapist.

The predominance of primitive defensive operations, particularly projective identification, omnipotence, devaluation, splitting, and denial, may permit the adolescent borderline patient to induce complementary pathology in the key family members with whom he lives and bring about self-fulfilling prophesies in all his interactions, which can become an extremely powerful resistance in the treatment. It is important for the therapist to evaluate the extent to which the patient is responding to pathological pressures from his parents and, conversely, is exerting such pressures on them.

The answer to these questions is usually found in the transference developments, especially in the patient's unconscious efforts to reproduce his parents' behavior in the therapist. Systematic analyses of such attempts in the transference may be the first step in helping the patient become aware of how he perpetuates pathological conditions at home. For example, the patient's pathological submission to what he perceives as his parents' sadistic behavior is usually reflected in the re-creation of the situation with inverted roles in the psychotherapy. Unconsciously, adolescent patients may treat the therapist in omnipotent and sadistic ways, projecting onto him their masochistically suffering, mistreated, devalued self representation, while identifying themselves with a triumphant, sadistic, grandiose parental image.

The therapist's understanding that primitive transferences reflect the activation of such part-object relations with role reversal will permit him to interpret this transference relationship and then apply his interpretation to the patient's relations with his family. Systematic analysis of the therapeutic interaction, with a sharp focus on the activation within it of primitive part-object relations, is the first step to the interpretation of the patient's pathological interactions at home. It is important to keep in mind that such interpretation is not a genetic reconstruction and that the current pathological interactions with the parents may, in turn, reflect a part-object relation. This part-object relation may be defensively split off from contradictory part-object relations that need to be examined first. Only thus can an understanding be gained of the total underlying pathogenic object relation against which both the current relation with the parents and the transference developments are defenses.

Borderline Pathology and Developmental Tasks of Adolescence

By definition, late-adolescent borderline patients have not accomplished the normal developmental tasks of adolescence, particularly (1) consolidating a sense of ego identity; (2) reconfirming a normal sexual identity, predominantly heterosexual in nature, with subordination of partial polymorphous to genital strivings and the beginning integration of tender and erotic trends into a relatively stable object relation, reflected in the capacity to fall in love; (3) loosening the ties to the parents, in reality linked with the appropriate differentiation of sexual and generational roles in the expanding social interactions with other adults and peers (and the corresponding intrapsychic individualization and stability of object relations); and (4) replacing infantile superego regulations by a relatively abstract and depersonified, firmly internalized, yet flexible system of unconscious and conscious morality which integrates adult sexual tolerance with firm repression of direct oedipal strivings.

In contrast to normal adolescents, who experience a real loosening of ties to the infantile objects, reflected in increasing distance from and yet deepening object relations with the parents, borderline adolescents, suffering as they do from lack of differentiation of internalized object representations, manifest excessive involvement, violent rebelliousness, overdependency, and general chaos in the relatively unstructured interpersonal relations at home.

Similarly, in psychotherapy, the patient not only overidentifies the therapist with his parental images or defensively experiences him as different in a fantastic way, but develops a chaotic alternation of mutually split-off, partial parental, and combined father/mother images, and a defensive refusal to experience the therapist as realistically different from the parents. For the adolescent borderline patient, differences between the therapist and the parents often signify only greater chaos; the individuality of the therapist cannot be grasped.

This situation can easily lead the therapist to assume, mistakenly, that the adolescent patient needs new "identification models" and that direct educational efforts may be warranted as a means of establishing the therapist himself as such a model. But the developmental task of the borderline adolescent who needs to complete his processes of individuation and differentiation are better served by interpretation and working through of primitive transferences. Otherwise, new surface adaptations to the therapist may evolve, activating an "as if" quality in the therapeutic interaction and the presence of what Winnicott (1960a) called the false self.

In contrast, resolution of primitive transference by analytic means and resumption of normal growth processes in borderline adolescents go hand in hand. In advanced stages of the treatment, when the adolescent patient gradually recognizes the therapist as a differentiated individual, integration of and differentiation from the parental images will occur in parallel fashion.

This process can be illustrated by the vicissitudes of the two defense mechanisms of idealization and devaluation. The primitive idealization of poorly differentiated adult or peer models which represent split-off part-object relations will gradually shift into idealization processes that reflect reaction formations against guilt and, later on, into the normal projection of sophisticated idealized values and aspirations that emerge in normal falling in love and the idealization of admired teachers. And the primitive devaluation of the parents (the counterpart of split-off primitive idealizations) will gradually become integrated into an age-appropriate, hypercritical, but ambivalent recognition of their realistic features, a disappointment reaction that now contains elements of guilt and mourning and acceptance of the loss of primitive idealized parental images.

If the analytic stance is maintained consistently, the patient's real relation with the therapist will eventually become the testing ground for a resumption of normal developmental processes.

Another area of severe borderline pathology—the lack of integration of superego structures—may superficially resemble the normal adolescent features of partial redissolution and reprojection of the superego (Jacobson, 1964). The emergence of primitive dissociated sexual and aggressive drive derivatives in borderline conditions may mask as the instinctual eruptions of normal adolescence. It is at first difficult to differentiate drive derivatives that emerge in consciousness in the context of an integrated self concept and object constancy from drive derivatives that express dissociated part-object relations. However, a consistently analytic approach to this material, the therapist's exploring homosexual and polymorphous perverse impulses in the light of their functions within part- or total-object relations activated in the transference, will differentiate normal developmental-drive eruptions from structured part-object relationships and permit the integration of object relations rather than the premature suppression of certain drive derivatives.

The neurotic or normal adolescent will quickly repress certain polymorphous perverse drive derivatives and integrate others into his conscious ego. The borderline adolescent patient, in contrast, may have to experience consciously and express in the transference (or in transference acting out) sexual and aggressive drives that are dissociated and/or condensed in various ways, over many months or years of treatment. Here, the normal integrative and repressive tasks of adolescence will eventually follow the integration of the self and the superego and of repression barriers of the ego. In other words, integration of part- into total-object relations will eventually bring about the replacement of dissociative by repressive defenses.

In short, I believe that completion of the normal developmental tasks of adolescence does not require special modifications of the psychotherapeutic technique proposed for borderline personality organization in general; as a consequence of the resolution of primitive transferences, it will be resumed and completed naturally in the advanced stages of the treatment.

It is helpful for the therapist to evaluate at the beginning to what extent severely pathological behavior patterns must be controlled in order to permit psychotherapy to get under way. If in his judgment the psychotherapeutic relationship will not be able to "contain" impulsive behavior patterns that threaten the adolescent's life or the treatment, he should establish a team approach. Another team member should carry out the responsibility of providing sufficient social structuring to permit stability of the therapeutic situation. It should be stressed that external control needs to be instituted not only to restrict certain behaviors but also to increase the adolescent's participation in ordinary life and to provide him with new challenges in order to avoid allowing the treatment situation to become his only meaningful social experience.

Types and Management of Acting Out

My focus on the psychotherapeutic interaction is very far from a simplistic model that relates the patient's current interpersonal interactions to past interactions on a one-to-one basis. In borderline personality organization the current interaction expresses pathological intrapsychic structures that reflect primitive types of interaction of a fantastic nature—fantastic both in the sense that they are unreal, emotionally threatening, and uncanny, and in the sense that they manifest a fragmented, distorted, part-object relation—which only indirectly reflects the actual pathogenic relations of the past. The focus on current interactions in the treatment of borderline conditions, in adolescence as with all borderline patients, really starts out as a focus on the intrapsychic life of the patient as it is expressed in the therapeutic interaction.

Adolescent borderline patients, with their intolerance of painful subjective experience, rapidly begin to act out in the transference as a defense against experiencing and introspection. The importance of the therapist's technical neutrality lies precisely in the need to maintain objectivity, so as to highlight the patient's distortion by action, which reflects a primitive transference relationship.

Borderline personality organization always involves severe character pathology and hence the expression, mostly by nonverbal means, of unconscious intrapsychic conflicts in the form of chronic, repetitive behavior patterns. Therefore, the nonverbal aspects of the interaction with the therapist supply fundamental information, replacing to a considerable extent what the content of verbal communication conveys in the standard psychoanalytic situation.

Through his nonverbal behavior, and by a particular use of language as action and as a means of controlling the interpersonal situation, the patient attempts to activate his intrapsychic part-object relations in the current interpersonal one. In fact, primitive transferences may be conceived of as mutually dissociated units of strange, bizarre, primitive units of interaction that the therapist by his interpretations transforms into the patient's subjective experience. One might say that in this transformation of intrapsychic conflict into interpersonal action, the patient is resorting to a means of communication and relationship that, genetically speaking, predates the predominance of verbal communication: Regression in the form of communication is perhaps the most important aspect of regression in the transference of borderline patients.

To reformulate this in a still different way, the patient's expression of his intrapsychic past in terms of interpersonal action, rather than in remembering (in thoughts or feelings), illustrates the prevalence of acting out as a characteristic of transference developments in borderline patients.

Acting out is a concept that has been expanded to include a broad range of phenomena (Fenichel, 1945a; Greenacre, 1950, 1963, 1968; Limentani, 1966; Panel, 1957; Rosenfeld, 1966; A. Freud, 1968; Grinberg, 1968; Kanzer, 1968; Moore, 1968; Rangell, 1968; Panel, 1970), from the appearance of concrete acts or behaviors in the course of psychoanalytic or psychotherapeutic sessions—acts that express an emerging transference disposition the patient cannot yet tolerate subjectively—to the development of complex behaviors toward the therapist that express, in a conscious emotional development toward him, the aspect of related past pathogenic conflicts that is still repressed as an awareness of a past (in contrast to present) experience; to the development of behaviors outside the analytic setting that correspond to split-off aspects of the transference; to the patient's disturbed interpersonal relations that drain off significant intrapsychic conflicts during the treatment in general.

Psychoanalytic discussions of the origin, mechanism, and functions of acting out are constantly complicated by the inclusion of this broad range of phenomena, and it seems to me that efforts to restrict the meaning of the term or to redefine subsets of it (for example, "acting in" as temporary behavior expressing transference in actions in the hours) have not been particularly helpful (see Rexford, 1978).

I have found it useful to consider acting out in the broadest sense as an essential aspect of transference developments in borderline patients. Insofar as the adolescent's rapidly changing social and interpersonal world temporarily reduces the stability of his surrounding social structures and fosters the expression of old and new experimental behaviors in all areas, acting out in this broad sense is especially prevalent in borderline adolescents. One crucial task is to diagnose when living out becomes acting out—that is, the expression in action of transference material that cannot yet be tolerated in subjective awareness.

When can severely pathological behavior that predated the beginning of psychotherapy and continues apparently unchanged by the psychotherapeutic relationship itself be considered acting out? First, if and when significant changes occur in such preexisting behavioral patterns, they should be explored in terms of the developments in the transference. It is important that the therapist really explore their signifi-cance rather than implicitly reward or punish behaviors that are favor-able or unfavorable. The reasons for "positive" changes should be ex-plored with the same technically neutral attitude as the reasons for deteriorating patterns.

Second, the development of a striking contrast between a psycho-therapeutic relationship in which "nothing seems to happen" and dra-matic actions occurring in the patient's external life—regardless of whether such actions predated the treatment—usually is a clear expres-sion of transference developments. Here, the typical situation of border-line pathology obtains, in which the patient, incapable of tolerating the intrapsychic experience of his conflicts, has to express them in actions, particularly in splitting the transference. The availability of the therapeu-tic relationship should ideally provide a new channel for expressing dis-sociated or repressed urges. When this does not occur—when, to the contrary, an atmosphere of emptiness in the psychotherapeutic relation-ship prevails—this should be interpreted systematically. "Emptiness" does not mean only that the patient feels he has nothing to say to or to tell the therapist. Emptiness may also represent the use of language as a smoke screen in the hours, the filling up of the void of the hours with statements that reflect the patient's learning to "talk psychotherapy lan-guage." The therapist's consistent exploration of the reality and mean-ings of his interaction with the patient will provide the frame against which emptiness or fake content reflects, in contrast, the specific part-object relationship activated in the transference that requires interpreta-tion as the split-off counterpart of where the action seems to be—namely, in the patient's outside life.

Third, acting out should be interpreted under the subtle yet fre-quent conditions in which action takes place in the hours and has the ef-fect of distorting, fragmenting, or temporarily destroying the reality as-pects of the patient/therapist relationship. This third category of conditions is really the most important aspect of work with primitive transferences. What follows are some special types of acting out in this third, restricted, sense. These clinical examples also illustrate the general principles involved in transference interpretation with borderline patients.

Clinical Data

Transformation of a Part-Object Relation in the Transference into Action

Miss O. A 17-year-old borderline adolescent girl with predominantly in-fantile or histrionic features swallowed a Darvon pill before entering her session. She was not addicted to any particular drug but occasionally took a variety of drugs as a way of making herself "feel good." This pattern predated the beginning of treatment but had now changed into the patient's casual report to me that she had taken a pill before a session. It was our understanding on initiating the treatment that I expected her to be off all drugs and that I would not prescribe any medication for her as part of treatment. In fact, by this time, there had been several episodes of relatively severe anxiety and/or depression that could be resolved by interpretive means alone, thus illustrating the defensive nature of the patient's request for medication.

Efforts to stimulate Miss O to explore her understanding of taking the Darvon this time led nowhere, except to her saying, "You know, I do this quite frequently." She denied any particular feelings about coming to the session or surrounding the impulsive decision to take a pill. She had looked rather relaxed and at ease on entering the session. However, as I sat back, implicitly inviting her to continue talking, she became increasingly uneasy, finally expressing her fear that I would criticize her for having taken the pill.

At first, I did not know how important it was to focus on her taking the pill and was expecting new subject matter to emerge. Now, however, I felt that this was indeed the predominant subject at hand and speculated privately that she might have taken the pill as an expression of defiance or to provoke me into critical behavior toward her and thus to allay her feelings of guilt for experiencing herself in a good relation with me. (We had clarified in the past that there were deep-seated internal prohibitions against a good relation with me as a fatherly image.)

I also speculated in my mind that Miss O's telling me that she had taken the pill contrasted with her secretive behavior in the past, but then I felt that it was an "honesty" not leading anywhere else and perhaps an expression in action of her sense that honest relationships led nowhere. At that point, Miss O started to discuss entirely different matters; I could not connect these with her having taken the pill, and I felt distracted by my thoughts about her having taken the pill, and then guilty for not paying full attention to the new issues she was commenting on.

A few minutes later Miss O suddenly glanced at me inquisitively and said that she was boring me. When I asked what made her think so, she said that I looked puzzled and distracted. I acknowledged that her perception was accurate and expressed my puzzlement over her change of subject, over the casual nature of her comment about having taken the pill—as if she were indifferent to its meaning—in contrast to her concern over my being indifferent to something she was saying after that. I added, however, that she was right in observing that, as a consequence of my having taken her behavior more seriously than she had, I had become distracted. Miss O said she felt that I paid attention to her only when she had a problem. I replied that I wondered whether she had taken the pill and told me about it as an expression of her sense that only if she misbehaved would I pay any attention to her. At this point, she evidenced surprise and became thoughtful. She remembered that she was indeed worried about whether she would have anything important to tell me before she decided to take the pill. I now experienced our interaction as reflecting, at the level of this transference aspect, the relationship between child and indifferent mother who pays attention to her child only when he or she misbehaves, while the patient was reenacting the role of the defiant yet guilt-ridden, submissive yet suspicious child. Further material in the hour confirmed that impression.

This case illustrates a relatively simple transformation of an emotional experience into an action, with concomitant initial denial of the emotional experience. The following case illustrates a more complex form of acting out.

Action as an Accretion of Meanings

Miss P. An 18-year-old borderline girl with markedly narcissistic features who repeatedly burned herself with cigarettes (and who had been treated on several occasions for third-degree burns on her arms and legs) casually mentioned in a session that she might feel like burning herself during the forthcoming two-week absence of her therapist. Her comment, made in the context of an ongoing discussion over many weeks of whether she would be able to control her tendency to burn herself if she were permitted to stay outside the hospital (where she had been an inpatient), led to renewed discussion of whether outpatient treatment for her would be feasible at this point. The realistic concerns of the therapist were in sharp contrast to Miss P's apparent indifference to the situation and to her attitude of expectation that all those who were taking care of her would naturally be worried and do something to prevent her from burning herself. On repeated occasions, the therapist had explored with her the implicit atmosphere of violence and blackmail that she created around herself, "innocently" forcing her parents, her therapist, and her social worker to go into elaborate analysis of how to deal with her while she smilingly announced her temptation to burn herself. At the beginning of one of the last sessions before the therapist's absence, Miss P said she had made plans to spend the time of his absence at the house of a religious group that had been very supportive of her in the past; she felt that would provide her with spiritual stimulation over this period.

The therapist's reaction to this announcement was a momentary flash of anger and then a feeling of helplessness, followed by the idea of resigning himself to let her do as she pleased without exploring the issue further. In the course of discussing this particular session with the therapist, I learned that to understand the patient's comment fully, it had to be kept in mind that she was changing her plans suddenly and, in so doing, discarding with one gesture all the serious and lengthy discussions that had taken place between her parents, herself, and her social worker regarding plans for her during the therapist's forthcoming absence. The therapist had provided her and the social worker with the name of another psychiatrist who would be available if needed during his absence. Her change of plans now made these arrangements irrelevant. In addition, Miss P had previously spent some weeks at that religious house at a time when violent rebelliousness against her parents was expressed in frequent escapes from home, self-mutilating behavior, and a search for ideal substitute parents, all of which had been explored in great detail in earlier stages of the psychotherapy.

Thus her casual comment about her plans reflected her symbolic elimination of the substance of an important aspect of her psychotherapy. In addition, it reflected a very concrete depreciation of the therapist as the key element in the changed constellation of her life. It was as a consequence of psychotherapy that the diffuse, destructive, chaotic behavior in all aspects of her life (of which living at the religious house was part) had been changed.

Miss P's statement also reflected an almost studied thoughtlessness, presented in a natural and yet pseudothoughtful way that belied its impulsive nature. Furthermore, her attempt to convince the therapist of the seriousness of this new plan, arrived at so suddenly, between two sessions, illustrated the spurious way in which she had been using verbal communication to convey apparent thoughtfulness in the preceding sessions.

What is significant is the easy, relaxed, well-organized way in which Miss P presented a plan that was completely dissonant and destructive in terms of everything that had been going on in the treatment. And she did it in a few seconds, while the analysis of the implications of that statement took literally an hour of my consultation time.

In other words, that statement represented a "microscopic" but extremely violent and severe form of acting out, which reflected, rather than a condensation of various meanings into one, an intense accretion or compression of multiple meanings in so rapid and immediate a way that it temporarily exploded the therapist's capacity to hold or contain, to integrate the total-object relationship being enacted.

Such episodes are frequent in the treatment of borderline adolescent patients. The immediate impact of the patient's behavior on the therapist may be precisely the kind of rage, helplessness, and discontinuity of the emotional relationship that the patient unconsciously attempts to avoid experiencing subjectively: This is the emotional reality that has been translated into action and into violent projective identification affecting the therapist.

The optimal way of dealing with this kind of acting out is for the therapist to spell out the meanings of the behavior, gradually and very fully, including the reasons for expressing in action what the patient cannot subjectively tolerate. The net effect of an attempt at interpretation at such points is that a brief comment by the patient may have to be followed by lengthy statements from the therapist. It is as if the therapist, in a reconstruction, has to spell out what, in action, was compressed into a moment of time—and the patient may often accuse the therapist of making a mountain out of a molehill. What is required from the therapist here is a full emotional awareness of his own reactions to the patient's action, combined with the capacity to contain this reaction within himself without, in turn, having to act on it, and then the gradual development or re-creation of all the emotional aspects of the relationship that were compressed into that brief action.

The Isolation of Meaningful Communication within Chronic Action in the Transference

The situation to be described here represents the opposite polarity of the accretion of meanings in sudden actions just described. I am referring to borderline patients who, in concrete developments within one hour or a brief sequence of sessions, provide the key to the understanding of complex transference patterns that appear chaotic, although they have a strangely repetitive quality over a period of weeks or even months.

Miss Q. A borderline adolescent with severe schizoid and masochistic features came to understand at one point how she experienced her mother as becoming depressed every time Miss Q was successful or felt happy. Her mother, the patient felt, could not stand her growing up and becoming independent. She mercilessly bombarded Miss Q with questions, criticisms, and ironic comments until she made her daughter feel completely helpless and defeated. But when Miss Q was feeling resigned and depressed, mother became very warm and supportive; in fact, the patient felt that when things were going poorly, there was really no one who could be so warm and giving as her mother.

This understanding, gained in the context of an analysis of various part-object relations that reflected mutually split-off aspects of this general transference pattern, was followed by a period of rapid improvement in self-confidence, autonomy, and the capacity to study and broaden her social life. However, a few months later, Miss Q reverted to periods of chronic dissatisfaction with the therapist and repeated complaints that the therapist was controlling, rigid, dominant, that he could not tolerate the idea of her becoming more independent, and so forth. The interpretation of this experience as an attribution to the therapist of the characteristics of her own mother led nowhere. On the contrary, Miss Q seemed to enjoy ironic paraphrasing of the therapist's interpretations, "outguessing" him step by step. A long period of time ensued in which no understanding gained in the hours seemed to have any meaning.

Retrospectively, it seemed rather easy to interpret Miss Q's refusal to listen, her almost joyful destruction of everything received from the therapist, as a repetition of the relationship with mother with inverted roles: Miss Q had now become a sadistic, intruding mother who could not tolerate the therapist's success. However, during the many weeks in which Miss Q successfully enacted this pattern, the therapist's only hold on his conviction that this was the meaning of her behavior was by keeping in mind the understanding of the total transference transitorily gained in an earlier episode. Here, the acting out consisted not only in creating a smoke screen that would destroy earlier understanding the patient had achieved but also in the very isolated nature of understanding that the patient could tolerate in herself. In short, isolation of brief moments of understanding in depth may in itself be a form of acting out, an expression of the intolerance of learning as a continuous process because of, for example, severe unconscious guilt.

The Central Function of the Therapist as a Dyadic Polarity and the Dangers of Countertransference Acting Out

The therapist's efforts to integrate what is going on affectively and cognitively, by using his subjective experience as a starting point, must expand his understanding with whatever objective evidence becomes available to him through the very process of repetition—the characteristic sequence within the repetitively predominant transference paradigms that are so typical of borderline conditions. Careful attention to the sequences of dominant behavior patterns that he has repeatedly interpreted in the past permits the therapist to transform his subjective experience in the present into an interpretive statement. The main risk is his overdependence on his emotional reactions, which may in turn reflect countertransference issues.

There are narcissistic temptations for the therapist when he puts himself at the center of understanding the patient/therapist interaction. Many borderline patients, especially those with severely narcissistic tendencies, will accuse the therapist of grandiosity, of injecting himself artificially into a situation that, as far as the patient can see, has no emotional relevance for him at all. Reevaluating the knowledge he has about the patient's current life outside the hours, keeping in mind the problems that brought the patient to treatment and the therapeutic goals, and, above all, the determination to evaluate the immediate reality of the therapeutic situation before indulging in speculation will help the therapist to withstand the threats to his objectivity.

Perhaps the most difficult aspect of the therapeutic interaction is the therapist's subjective experience as a reflection of a projected aspect of his patient's self experience. In other words, it may be most difficult for the therapist to tolerate what the patient, by means of projective identi- fication, induces in him while the patient enacts the experience of his object representation. It is usually less difficult to tolerate the interaction when the therapist represents the patient's object representation di- rectly. Insofar as the patient usually sees himself as the victim of a frustrating, overwhelming, unavailable, or sadistic object, identification with the patient's self-image at such points may threaten the therapist's ability to contain that reaction within himself and use it for interpreta- tions. Again, the theoretical understanding of the nature of reciprocal activations of part-object relations, of primitive self and object represen- tations in an alternating way, should help the therapist organize his ex- perience at such moments. The therapist's ability to tolerate his emo- tional experience without having to transform it into action, to derive his interpretation from the situation rather than act upon it directly, is a ma- jor factor in helping the patient transform action into subjective experience.

It seems to me that we have underestimated the normality of many adolescents and the severity of the psychopathology of many adolescents who come to our attention. Psychopathology in these adolescents needs to be approached with a long-range, strategic outlook instead of with simple, short-term supportive measures.

CHAPTER 9: *Supportive Psychotherapy*

In the context of comparing the appropriate application of psychoanalysis, expressive psychoanalytic psychotherapy, and supportive psychoanalytic psychotherapy, I have suggested (1980, p. 200) that "our understanding regarding supportive psychotherapy may have to be
reexamined and reformulated in the light of what we now know about
severe psychopathology." In what follows, I undertake that reformulation.

Some type of supportive psychotherapy, in relatively "pure" form
or in combination with expressive psychotherapeutic techniques, has
long been a major modality of treatment in the daily practice of
psychotherapists. It is therefore surprising to find so few detailed descriptions of the principles and techniques of supportive psychotherapy
in the psychoanalytic literature of the past 40 years.

Before 1950 the psychoanalytically oriented literature on supportive
psychotherapy was concerned with the application of psychoanalytic
principles and techniques to psychotherapy in general. At that time the
focus was on enriching psychoanalytically oriented psychotherapy, and
no clear efforts were made to distinguish between supportive and expressive techniques. Nevertheless, in applying psychoanalytic theory
and technique to such an enrichment of "commonsense psychotherapy," many techniques were described that later on became part of what
we now see as supportive psychotherapy.

Perhaps the most comprehensive early contributions are the texts
by Schilder (1938), Levine (1942), and Alexander et al. (1946). Schilder
described giving advice and persuasion, appealing to willpower, discussing the past, changing the patient's surroundings, the analysis of
social adaptation, and hypnosis for catharsis, for clearing up amnesias,
for repeating a traumatic scene, and for suggestion. Indeed he strongly

advocated suggestion in general. All these techniques were consonant with what was subsequently called supportive psychotherapy.

He did not make a sharp distinction between what we would today call the theory of therapy and practical techniques, but he did differentiate the techniques to be used by the "general practitioner" from methods to be used by the specialist. The latter included hypnosis, psychoanalysis, and modified psychoanalytic methods, such as short-term psychotherapy.

The title of Levine's book, *Psychotherapy in Medical Practice* (1942), suggests the audience he was aiming for. He covered pretty much the same ground Schilder did and focused on what might now be termed supportive techniques. Indeed, it is impressive to see how many of the techniques described by both Schilder and Levine are still widely practiced.

Although Alexander et al. (1946) discussed principles of psychoanalytic therapy, they included under the heading "the principle of flexibility" manipulation of the transference relationship, probably an important supportive technique. Supplying a "corrective emotional experience," which they recommend, is now generally considered a variety of supportive technique.

In the early 1950s, such ego psychologists as Gill (1951, 1954), Knight (1952, 1953a), Eissler (1953), and Bibring (1954) criticized Alexander (and Fromm-Reichmann, 1959) for blurring the distinctions between psychoanalysis and psychotherapy. In the context of this controversy, these theoreticians attempted to define more clearly the differences between psychoanalysis and psychotherapy and, within psychotherapy, between supportive and expressive modalities. Gill (1951, 1954) in particular differentiated exploratory, insight, uncovering, or, simply, expressive psychoanalytic psychotherapy from suppressive or supportive psychotherapy and differentiated all psychotherapy from psychoanalysis. It was Gill (1954) who most clearly spelled out the theoretical assumption that the purpose of supportive techniques was to strengthen the patient's defenses and thus improve his overall functioning, whereas expressive techniques were intended to weaken the patient's defenses, reorganize the ego, and promote personality reorganization by bringing about structural intrapsychic change. Both Gill (1951) and Bibring (1954) stated that supportive and expressive techniques are usually combined in any psychotherapeutic treatment. Bibring proposed that the employment of some techniques over others determined to what extent a treatment was supportive or expressive.

The Menninger project made operational the definition of supportive and expressive modalities of psychotherapy (Wallerstein and Robbins, 1956). The treatment of each patient was defined according to where it fell along the continuum from the most expressive (psychoanal-

ysis) to the least expressive and most supportive (supportive psychotherapy), which was determined by studying the use each made of the
basic techniques and principles suggested by Bibring (1954), namely,
suggestion, abreaction, manipulation (supportive), clarification, and interpretation (expressive) (Luborsky et al., 1958).

The results of the Menninger project indicated, unexpectedly, that
patients with ego weakness who were treated with supportive
psychotherapy—following the traditional conceptualization that such
patients need to reinforce their defensive operations and that resolution
of resistances by interpretation is therefore risky—did rather poorly
(Kernberg et al., 1972). In contrast, many patients in this same category
who were treated with expressive psychotherapy did remarkably well.
As predicted, such patients did rather poorly with unmodified psychoanalysis.

Throughout the 1960s a number of clinical contributions helped to
specify and clarify the supportive components of psychotherapy. Novey
(1959), initiating the trend, concluded that support is used in all psychotherapeutic approaches. Although he did not believe that supportive
psychotherapy represented a complete system of therapy in itself, he
described specific technical procedures that had supportive aspects,
such as direct verbal support and the supportive implications of forth-
right statements and other verbal behavior, as well as of the psychotherapist's nonverbal behavior.

Hollon (1962) described the technique of supportive psychotherapy
for depressed outpatients, and MacLeod and Middelman (1962) reported
on a supportive outpatient treatment for chronically disturbed patients
with severe ego weakness. Several psychoanalytic contributions on
supportive techniques expanded on the idea of Gill and Bibring that selective reinforcement of certain defensive strategies may support ego
functioning while still permitting an exploratory or interpretive approach in this context. Tarachow (1963), for example, suggested measures that were profoundly supportive within a psychoanalytic psychotherapy. His overriding principles were to supply the infantile object in
reality, to supply displacements and stability. In contrast to an emphasis
on verbal support, he proposed that the most effective support is the
therapist's permitting himself to be real to the patient in some implied
or indirect way.

Gedo (1964), in agreement with Grinker (Grinker et al., 1961), recommended supportive psychotherapy for patients "whose ego integrative capacity is insufficient to tolerate the anxiety generated by interpretations of derivatives from the unconscious, whose object relationships
consist predominantly of transferences whose irrationality they are unable to perceive, and whose self-representation is that of a child lacking
autonomy" (p. 534).

Perhaps the most comprehensive text describing, within a psychoanalytic frame, the spectrum of expressive versus supportive aspects of technique throughout all phases and vicissitudes of psychotherapy is Dewald's (1971). An overall critical review of the literature of psychoanalytic psychotherapy can be found in Wallerstein's book essay (1966) and his related later paper (1969).

Miller (1969) and Langs (1973) point to the supportive aspects of interpretive approaches in psychotherapy, continuing the tradition of the 1950s and 1960s, which saw psychoanalytic psychotherapy as a combination of supportive and interpretive techniques and the effects of the psychotherapist's interventions also as frequently having both expressive and supportive features. In contrast, two significant contributions from England regard supportive psychotherapy as a specific treatment modality and provide comprehensive summaries of its techniques (Stafford-Clark, 1970; Bloch, 1979).

Schlesinger (1969) presents an interesting analysis of the effects of supportive psychotherapy as it is usually practiced, in potentially restricting the therapist's range of exploration and interventions because of the fear of becoming "expressive" with a patient who presumably would only be able to respond to a supportive modality of treatment. He stresses the supportive purpose and effects of techniques that are exploratory or expressive and concludes by recommending that the terms *supportive* and *expressive* no longer be used to denote different kinds of psychotherapy. He prefers to use them to describe specific purposes, effects, and techniques within each concrete mode of therapy. While I disagree with his idea of expanding the meaning of the term *supportive psychotherapy* to include purposes and effects rather than only techniques, I find his observations regarding the negative effects of the rationale for supportive and expressive psychotherapy on the practice of psychoanalytic psychotherapy in the 1950s and 1960s an important contribution.

The definitions I have given of psychoanalysis and expressive psychotherapy (chap. 6) are based upon the *techniques* employed in the treatment. The *effects* of the techniques employed in expressive psychotherapy vary, however, according to the severity of the patient's psychopathology. As I have noted elsewhere (1980, p. 199), these techniques have different effects in the treatment of borderline conditions and ordinary neurosis and nonborderline character pathology.

I would define supportive psychotherapy technically by saying that it does not use interpretation, partially uses clarification and abreaction, and mostly uses suggestion and what I call environmental intervention (similar to the older concept of *manipulation*). Although the therapist must remain acutely aware of the transference, monitor its developments, and carefully consider transference resistances in relation to his technique in dealing with patients' character problems and their connection to life difficulties, transference is not interpreted, and the use of suggestion and environmental intervention eliminates technical neutrality.

In conclusion, psychoanalysis, expressive psychotherapy, and supportive psychotherapy may be defined in terms of (1) the principal technical tools used (clarification and interpretation versus suggestion and environmental intervention), (2) the extent to which the transference is interpreted, and (3) the degree to which technical neutrality is maintained.

The indications and contraindications for supportive psychotherapy are spelled out in detail in chapter 10. Here I will say only that supportive therapy is usually appropriate as a treatment of last resort—that is, when other modes must be ruled out. One other point bears stressing. For reasons described in chapter 10, it is easier to move from expressive to supportive psychotherapy than in the other direction.

Treatment Goals and Patients' Responsibilities

It is important when recommending supportive psychotherapy (and also expressive psychotherapy and psychoanalysis) to clarify early in the consultation or at the start of treatment the general goals and specific objectives of the treatment, to define at least one area in which patient and therapist are in agreement regarding these goals, to distinguish treatment goals from life goals (Ticho, 1972), and to emphasize that psychotherapy is work carried out jointly by patient and therapist. The therapist's function is to contribute knowledge that may help the patient to understand himself and his conflicts better and accordingly to work more effectively on his conflicts and problems in reality. Precisely because opportunities for systematic analysis of the patient's primitive transferences and magical perceptions and expectations are less available in this treatment modality than in expressive forms, it is even more important in supportive psychotherapy to create a rational basis for the treatment that will constitute a boundary of reality against which transference distortions may later be diagnosed and modified. The patient's continuing responsibilities for his own life should be spelled out, and if the need for external support is anticipated, its structure and relation to the psychotherapy should be defined.

One major advantage of supportive therapy is that the frequency of sessions can be adjusted, from two or three per week to one per week, one every other week, or even fewer. The less frequent the sessions, however, the more important it is to evaluate the work the patient carried out between the treatment hours in relation to what has been learned in the sessions, and the more important it is that the therapist actively connect the contents of one session with another. Indeed, this is one noninterpretive way of working with the mechanism of splitting: An active dissociation of the patient's life from his psychotherapy sessions or a defensive splitting off of one session from the next can be explored in terms of the reality of the patient's tasks in the treatment. It is essential for the therapist to explore fully the patient's life—the conflicts and patterns of interactions outside the treatment hours—and in the process to challenge vagueness, lack of information, and the distorting effects of primitive mechanisms of denial, fragmentation of emotional experience, devaluation, and the like. An active exploration of the patient's life—in contrast to the therapist's passive submission to the patient's defensive suppression or vagueness—tends to highlight the patient's primitive defense mechanisms and their resistance functions and constitutes the first step in a challenge to such defensive operations.

While the decision regarding the frequency of sessions can be made with more flexibility in supportive than in expressive therapy, there are dangers in setting up a frequency unrelated to the nature of the task and the goals of the treatment. For example, a patient's primary motivation for treatment might be the existence of an urgent life problem, and a treatment frequency of one session per week may not do justice to his objective needs to make rapid decisions in major areas of his life. A frequency of less than one session per week may easily foster in some therapists the idea that little is to be expected from the patient under such circumstances; this in turn may foster the patient's passivity and a parasitic attitude toward the therapy. There is generally a danger of associating relative infrequency of sessions with treatment that is "second best" in quality. (The opposite danger, of course, is to attempt to carry out expressive psychotherapy on a once-a-week basis or less, which is equivalent to misusing or even abusing interpretation as a technique.)

The objectives of supportive psychotherapy may range from ambitious to modest, but even modest goals may exceed the patient's capacities. A modest goal for the patient who is not expected to be able to function independently in the foreseeable future is to enable him to function autonomously within his limitations, with ongoing psychotherapeutic support. In other cases, supportive psychotherapy may have the function of enabling the patient gradually to seek out and make use of alternative supportive environmental structures, so that the psychotherapy can end when the patient is able to replace it with these other supports (Robert Michels, personal communication).

It is generally preferable to set goals and objectives that aspire to increase the patient's level of functioning and autonomy and to shift to a more "custodial" form of supportive psychotherapy only when it becomes clear that the patient's capacity for cooperation, his intrapsychic and social resources, are insufficient for this ambitious goal. In all cases, it is necessary to be alert to the presence of secondary gain of treatment in the form of chronic social parasitism. There are nowadays quite a number of patients who have become "experts" in maintaining themselves in day hospitals and other social institutions that provide shelter and some minimal life amenities without requiring any individual responsibility or active work from them (John Cody, personal communication). Some forms of psychotherapy may unwittingly foster such secondary gain.

Misconceptions

There are a great number of misconceptions regarding supportive psychotherapy. The first is that it is "easy" to conduct such therapy. It is unfortunate that, even within psychoanalytically oriented psychiatric residency programs, the less experienced therapists are often assigned "supportive" cases and the more experienced therapists are assigned "expressive" ones. In fact, it requires more skill to apply psychoanalytic principles to supportive than to expressive therapy. The reason is that, as part of expressive therapy, transference phenomena are consistently explored in depth, thus naturally helping the therapist to highlight the patient's defensive constellations as they become manifest in transference resistances and, by the same token, to clarify the dominant themes of unconscious intrapsychic conflicts, their drive-derivation and object relations implications. In supportive psychotherapy, by contrast, the manifestations of defenses and resistances, of pathological character traits and their activation in the transference, of transference resistances, and of acting out are less evident, and their handling requires a great deal of experience and technical skill. Ideally, supportive therapy should be taught after a solid basis in expressive therapy has been achieved. Supportive psychotherapy is, as I trust I am making clear, not simply "commonsense therapy." Psychotherapy begins where the effectiveness of common sense ends.

A second misconception about supportive psychotherapy is that primitive ego defenses have to be left undisturbed because, given the supposedly frail equilibrium of impulse-defenses, interpreting them may produce further regression. In this connection, the traditional view is that even frequent sessions have a regressive effect, so that the weaker the patient's ego, the less frequent the therapy sessions should be. This assumption fails to take into account that regression in the treatment depends upon the management of the transference and the effects of interpreting primitive defensive operations. Both the psychotherapy research project of the Menninger Foundation and my clinical work with borderline conditions have provided evidence indicating that primitive defensive operations are themselves ego weakening, but that the interpretation of these primitive defenses has ego-strengthening effects. This is one of the basic reasons that I advocate expressive psychotherapy for borderline conditions. It may be summarized in the following dictum: Although transference interpretation within the expressive psychotherapy of borderline conditions cannot be systematic, the interpretation of primitive defenses in the therapeutic interaction should be as systematic as possible.

But what does this new understanding of the ego-strengthening effect of interpretation of primitive defenses have to do with a supportive treatment technique that, by definition, is not interpretive? In my view, one of the main technical requirements of supportive psychotherapy is noninterpretive but consistent work with primitive defenses in the therapeutic interaction.

Another misconception about supportive psychotherapy is that transference itself, because it is not to be interpreted, should not be focused on. But to ignore transference manifestations results in a gradual distortion of the therapeutic relationship, with the therapist making a pseudoadaptive adjustment to aspects of the patient's transference instead of clarifying and confronting it and, therefore, risking the activation of turmoil reflecting primitive transference acting out. A silent collusion develops between therapist and patient regarding key areas of the patient's conflicts, a cessation of active expression of these conflicts in the treatment situation, and the fostering of splitting mechanisms and acting out in the patient's outside life. These developments typically are reflected in a chronic, superficially friendly but basically distant relationship in the therapy hours, while all the action seems to occur somewhere else in the patient's life.

Still another common misconception is that if the therapist ignores negative transference developments and attempts to maintain a consistently friendly, patient, "permissive" attitude, the patient will be able to carry out an "identification with the therapist." Accordingly, within an atmosphere of benign idealization of the therapist, the patient will resume his psychological growth. In other words, ignoring the negative transference will permit bypassing or transforming the patient's pathological character organization and will strengthen his ego in the process. This assumption is illustrated by the traditional supposition that the therapist's silence is therapeutic per se, or by the misunderstanding and overextension of Winnicott's (1960b) concept of "holding," as if there were no unconscious distortions in the patient's perceptions of the therapist derived from the projection onto him of primitive sadistic superego functions and aggressive, dissociated object relations. The commonly observed paradoxical negative reaction to psychopharmacological medication included as part of supportive psychotherapy illustrates the effects of acting out undiagnosed negative transference aspects in relation to the medication. A heavy price is usually paid when the therapist attempts to utilize the patient's magical assumptions and related dissociated idealizations as part of a supportive treatment modality.

A final misconception, perhaps the most widespread of all, is that the sicker the patient, the less he can be expected to participate actively in psychotherapy. Therefore, almost by definition, patients who are in supportive psychotherapy are not to be expected to take responsibility for themselves or to participate actively in the treatment process; supportive psychotherapy becomes a treatment modality that is "done" or "administered" *to* the patient. This misconception fosters passivity and makes a large contribution to treatment stalemates.

Basic Techniques

The basic technique of supportive psychotherapy consists in exploring the patient's primitive defenses in the here-and-now, with the objective of helping him achieve control over their effects by nonanalytic means and fostering a better adaptation to reality by making him aware of the disorganizing effects of these defensive operations. In the process, manifest and suppressed (as opposed to unconscious or repressed) negative transference can be highlighted, reduced by means of consistent examination of the reality of the treatment situation, and utilized for clarification of related interpersonal problems in the patient's life.

Consider, for example, a patient with paranoid personality who uses projective identification, is hypersensitive to criticism, experiences himself as attacked by others while unconsciously provoking them to attack, and experiences himself as being sadistically controlled while subtly exerting such control over others by means of his suspicious and controlling behavior. Such a patient may be gradually helped by focusing in a tactful, persistently challenging, yet nonthreatening way on how the patterns of his interactions with others tend to repeat themselves. The analysis of these difficulties with others will naturally be helped by the fact that the therapist has already observed similar behaviors in the patient's relation to himself. Very often, however, the systematic analysis of the patient's behavior in relation to others may be the first stage in the later exploration of the same behavior in the treatment situation. In other cases, to the contrary, early exploration of the transference in the here-and-now should precede exploration of these issues in extratherapeutic interactions. This latter order of priority is particularly useful when manifest negative transference predominates. If it is not resolved, this transference may threaten the continuity of the treatment and constitute a major challenge to the treatment alliance.

Or consider the patient whose splitting operations are reflected in primitive idealization of some people and total devaluation of others. A careful exploration of the patient's relationships may reveal how former idols are suddenly devalued or how his judgments about others rapidly shift from extreme idealization to total devaluation. The therapist may show the patient how these predictable sequences tend to weaken the objectivity of the patient's judgment of others and to threaten his relationships with them and how a critical reflection about any extreme judgment of others may help him to discriminate his reality.

Still another example is the clarification of denial manifested in a patient's neglect of serious responsibilities in his work, together with magical assumptions that what is denied will not have any effect.

There is an important difference between giving a patient advice on how to handle his life and helping him understand how certain "automatic" ways of functioning are detrimental to his interests. The therapist should not give a patient advice about issues the patient may be able to handle on his own but is defensively avoiding. The therapist's function is to acquaint the patient with the primitive defenses and their effects upon his evaluation of reality and decision-making processes. In contrast to efforts to override pathological character traits and primitive defenses by advice regarding more "normal" behavior, the therapist attempts to acquaint the patient with the conscious and preconscious aspects of his intrapsychic difficulties and to help him use such knowledge, which the patient potentially has and is actively avoiding.

Supportive psychotherapy can be very "permissive" in increasing the patient's internal freedom for decision making by an actively confronting approach; on the other hand, what often looks like the therapist's tolerant, permissive attitude may actually reflect unconscious collusion with the patient's self-defeating tendencies.

In contrast to the position of technical neutrality that characterizes psychoanalysis and is a constant point of reference in expressive psychotherapy as well, in supportive psychotherapy the therapist is deliberately partisan to the needs of external reality and mindful of the patient's emotional needs—in other words, the therapist is promoting both adaptation and impulse expression. There may be occasions when adaptation conflicts with impulse expression, in which case the therapist should acknowledge the conflict and be available to explore it with the patient. Let me illustrate this point with an example in which the therapist is clearly siding with the patient's "id."

Mr. R. A man in his thirties dared not masturbate because he thought his religion forbade it. Mr. R never went to church or gave any other indication that religious considerations were of importance to him. Rather than help him directly to overcome his sexual inhibition, I focused consistently on the contradiction between this particular religious interdiction and his generally casual attitude toward religion. The patient responded by alternately suspecting me of provoking him to drop his religion and making him feel guilty so that he would become more religious in other aspects of his life as well.

Eventually, he tried to convince me of the dangers of masturbation, implicitly identifying with his sadistic superego while projecting his sexual impulses onto me. I was gradually able to convey to him how judgmental his attitudes about sexuality seemed to be, regardless of his religious convictions. I pointed out to him that, although he assumed that I was not a member of his religious group, he would be very upset if my behavior were not to conform to the mores of that group. Mr. R was able to recognize that, and later on he also became aware of how condemnatory his attitude was regarding the sexual activities of other people in his life. This development in turn led to my observation that he was very critical toward himself as well regarding sexual matters, and that his religious conviction served only as a rationalization for a deep-rooted, pervasive emotional attitude. Mr. R himself then related this critical attitude toward sexuality to experiences in his past and to his harshly prohibitive parents.

In this connection, I would add that whenever such insight occurs as a by-product of an essentially supportive approach it is most welcome, but it should not tempt one immediately to go beyond the general boundaries of the supportive approach. In other words, supportive therapy does not discourage patients from deepening their knowledge about themselves but works exclusively with conscious and preconscious material. Because defensive operations are usually the primitive ones of denial, projective identification, or splitting rather than repression or other higher level types, primitive fantasy material emerges in consciousness and the corresponding defensive operations in behavioral manifestations, all of which facilitates therapeutic work with these defenses and contents in supportive therapy.

Returning to Mr. R, I was here clearly on the side of impulse gratification, the "id," but instead of challenging the patient's rationalizations of his superego-determined sexual inhibition directly, I explored with him the conflict in the here-and-now in the transference, in the object relation activated when the patient identified himself with a sadistic superego figure while projecting onto me an impulse-ridden self representation. In the following example, in contrast, I stood on the side of external reality.

Mr. S. A man in his late forties alternated between inordinately submissive and rebellious behavior toward people in a position of authority. Shortly after he had started to work in a position he had very much wanted, he began to make highly critical remarks about his boss. I realized that he was jeopardizing the job he had worked long and patiently to obtain, and as soon as the first manifestations of these renewed conflicts with authority emerged in the treatment, I addressed the question. I said that if his boss was indeed, as he claimed, a hypersensitive and revengeful man, would not even any mild expression of anger or resentment on the patient's part threaten his future in that job? Mr. S immediately accused me of wanting him to behave submissively and of taking the side of his wife (who had warned him about losing his job) and of other authorities who were always blaming him. Mr. S also accused me of wanting him to continue in a work situation which was paying him well so that he could pay for his treatment with me, regardless of the humiliations and sacrifices this job entailed.

The activation in the transference of this life pattern escalated rapidly, with massive use of projective mechanisms. I started out by clarifying fully the reality of the treatment situation; namely, that indeed I expected him to pay me our agreed-upon fee and would not be able to see him if he was unable to do so. I added that should he lose his present job I trusted that he would be able to find another that would permit him to continue the treatment. As far as I was concerned, whether or not he continued in this present job was not of the essence, but he should think through whether he would be more or less satisfied with reasonably available alternatives to it. I drew his attention to how in the past he had bitterly complained because he had lost jobs that in retrospect had seemed attractive to him.

Over several sessions, this reality-oriented approach to the intense manifest negative transference led to increased reality testing in the treatment situation, to a decrease in the intensity of that transference, and to Mr. S's acceptance of the possibility that it might be reasonable for him to attempt to control his behavior at work in order not to jeopardize his job, while still exploring his feelings about his boss with me. It was only then that I pointed out to him how, in his escalating anger and suspiciousness toward me, he had almost re-created with me the situation he described in his job, thus illustrating his propensity to misjudge persons in positions of authority. I also told him that he seemed to be acquiring a new and quite impressive capacity to step back, observe his behavior, and change it in the light of better understanding.

This example illustrates the exploration, clarification, and reduction by repeated confrontation with reality of manifest negative transference; the activation and clarification of projective identification in the context of here-and-now exploration of a primitive, activated object relation in the transference; and a generally supportive approach to paranoid character pathology.

Another general principle of supportive psychotherapy is to refrain from the use of advisory, "supportive" statements and environmental "manipulation" if to do so would exploit unanalyzed primitive transference dispositions. Clarification, confrontation, environmental intervention, and directly conveying the therapist's opinion in matters in which the patient objectively needs advice should all operate through rational channels and convey that the therapist has confidence in the patient's own critical judgment, in his capacity for understanding and for using his understanding constructively.

I am rejecting the traditional concept of *manipulation* as one supportive technique, in spite of its benign use by psychoanalysts interested in supportive psychotherapy. I think it has denigrating implications for both patients and supportive psychotherapy. We certainly cannot avoid the suggestive effects of rational interventions, or, at a deeper level, powerful yet undiagnosed transference reverberations related to all we say and do during the patient's treatment in supportive psychotherapy. Nevertheless, if the therapist provides information, carefully considered and limited advice, and direct expression of support on the basis of rational consideration, some directly supportive effects may be obtained and the boundaries of reality in the treatment situation may thus be reinforced. It is only against these boundaries of reality that we can detect primitive defenses and transference distortions in the treatment and the patient's acting out in external reality.

This also means that when we wish to introduce medication as part of supportive therapy we should explain its rationale and what the patient can expect from it. Medication should be used in pharmacologically effective doses rather than for placebo effects. If placebo effects do develop, they should be diagnosed without necessarily interpreting them, but without attempting to exploit them either. Similarly, if direct behavior-modification techniques are introduced into supportive psychotherapy—such as sex therapy, hypnosis, or active guidance to confront phobic avoidance—an essentially rational approach should be pursued. The reasons for introducing such techniques should fit into the context of the overall treatment objectives and procedures. If these techniques are introduced arbitrarily, the patient's sense of responsibility, which the therapist has been trying to cultivate, will be undermined; he will treat such techniques magically or will obscure the transference by splitting off transference reactions from the therapist onto the newly introduced technique. In other words, it is important that the therapist maintain the internal logic and consistency of his conceptual scheme, his techniques, and the verbalized understandings that define the goals and responsibilities of patient and therapist in the treatment situation.

Still another general principle is that the patient's actions throughout the treatment need to be evaluated in terms of their relation to both transference acting out and gratification of basic emotional needs in adaptive ways in the patient's social reality. It is true that, because a systematic analysis of the transference is not attempted in these cases, a full exploration of transference acting out is less available. But acting out itself is also less undesirable than in expressive treatment modalities, and the new adaptive learning potentially involved in such acting out should be diagnosed and supported.

Initial Stages of Treatment

It is crucial to define at the start major issues in the patient's life and in his psychopathology that are to be explored and modified in the course of treatment. This is a precondition for defining the objectives of the treatment and of the roles of patient and therapist in obtaining them. The goals of treatment should be realistic, to be achieved by mechanisms that can be explained to and discussed with the patient rather than by the assumption that, simply by getting together, patient and therapist will magically and jointly bring about a solution of the patient's problems. It is important to raise the question early whether direct environmental intervention is warranted or necessary, how it will be carried out, and whether there is any need to set limits to the patient's behavior as a prerequisite for treatment. Severely destructive or self-destructive tendencies in the patient's immediate life may require such realistic precautions. It is necessary to stress the patient's responsibility to communicate honestly with the therapist. The patient should know that he is expected to carry out work on his own between the sessions. The therapist should set up a monitoring function by which he can evaluate from session to session how the treatment is influencing the patient outside the hours. The patient should be expected to keep the therapist well informed about developments in his life and to communicate promptly and fully on areas of conflicts and difficulties.

The initial instructions to the patient should convey these expectations and invite him to communicate freely and openly in the sessions; if no pressing problems, new information, or "reporting back" is to be discussed, the patient then should express freely what comes to his mind during the hours.

Indications and contraindications for psychopharmacological treatment and/or other special therapeutic techniques should be evaluated fully in the initial stages of treatment rather than introduced haphazardly later on in response to the patient's failure to improve. In other words, a strategic integration of various treatment techniques as part of an overall treatment plan is preferable to a haphazard introduction of new modalities in response to transference—and countertransference—developments.

A careful and detailed evaluation of the patient's personality and his interactions in his external life should provide information regarding his dominant character patterns and the related patterns in his significant object relations. This information makes it possible to predict future developments in the patient's life, to plan for diagnostic and therapeutic interventions in these areas, and to carry out working through in an essentially noninterpretive frame. Within the therapeutic setting itself, the therapist should diagnose predominant primitive defenses and anticipate technical interventions geared to working with them. Damaging environmental factors, antitherapeutic influences stemming from the patient's environment and from environmental sources of secondary gain, should be diagnosed for exploration in the sessions and for potential direct environmental intervention.

One major problem in the practice of supportive psychotherapy may be the therapist's unwarranted imitation of psychoanalytic technique in the sense of "sitting back" and leaving the initiative for structuring the content of the hours entirely to the patient. This usually fosters subtle forms of transference acting out; the patient shifts into a passive-dependent attitude toward the treatment, and primitive defenses go underground in the transference. The patient should be expected to talk openly, not only about his conflicts, thoughts, and feelings but also about significant developments between the hours.

While the patient should be encouraged to begin each hour by spontaneously informing the therapist about his life, the therapist should ask himself the following questions: Is what the patient is telling me really important or crucial? Is it related to his initial complaints or to the problems we are now exploring? Is it related to our common treatment goals? Is it related to issues that we are currently exploring? Does it reflect what the patient has done with what we examined in our last session or sessions? Does it include new issues important for psychotherapeutic exploration? The therapist thereby evaluates the patient's active collaboration with the treatment, the presence or absence of continuity versus splitting mechanisms, and, at a deeper level, the nature of transference developments.

Transference Management

To put it most generally: Moderately intense positive transferences may be utilized for psychotherapeutic work, but intense primitive idealization has to be treated cautiously because of the concomitant devaluation processes that are usually active in some other area of the patient's life. Latent negative transferences should be detected for strategic planning, and manifest negative transference should be actively explored, clarified, and reduced by realistically and fully examining the relevant conscious and preconscious fantasies, feelings, and behaviors and by reinforcing reality considerations. As I said earlier, the careful exploration of repetitive behavior patterns in the patient's life may permit the exploration of similar patterns in the transference later on. The examination and realistic reduction of a certain transference pattern in the sessions may open the way for exploring similar difficulties in other areas of the patient's life.

It is important for the therapist to keep in mind that, insofar as he tolerates the patient's expression of intense ambivalence toward him, he is carrying out a holding function, in Winnicott's (1960b) sense. This reassures the patient of the therapist's permanence; the patient discovers that the therapist does not crumble under the impact of the patient's aggression, that it is possible to maintain a good relation with the therapist even in the presence of frustration and anger, which reduces the patient's fears over his own impulses and fosters strengthening of integrative ego functions. The therapist certainly should support the patient's spontaneous search for origins of his present behavior to the degree to which these refer to conscious or preconscious memories. The therapist working mostly with conscious and preconscious material, however, must remind himself constantly that reports about the patient's past will necessarily be colored by defensive functions and that often what appear to be causes in the past actually reflect justifications and rationalizations of present characterological difficulties. Pseudogenetic reconstructions, by means of which the therapist uses the magic of an assumed analytic approach in linking the conscious present to the conscious past, may reinforce the patient's own myths about his past and provide him with justification for his present views and behavior. But a general attitude of "We may not know where all this comes from, but this is what it means now and how it affects you and what we have to work with" represents a more realistic, less magical base for introspective work on the patient's part.

A frequent and complicated type of transference acting out is the patient's presenting himself as the helpless victim of mistreatment or frustration by other people. If a patient explains all his symptoms as a natural consequence of the "reality" of a hostile spouse, it is important to acknowledge the patient's unfulfilled needs but also to point out his own contributions to his frustrations. Whereas in expressive psychotherapy or psychoanalysis there is the possibility of working through sadomasochistic patterns in the transference by means of interpretation, in supportive psychotherapy such interactions should be explored directly in terms of their reality. The therapist tactfully yet consistently confronts the patient with how he contributes to his own difficulties. This may temporarily increase manifest negative transference developments, which then will permit the exploration of the same difficulties in the here-and-now of the hours. At the same time, a full and detailed exploration of the patient's difficulties—for example, in the interactions with his spouse—may surprisingly open up the road for new sources of gratification and the patient's masochistic ignoring or undermining of them. Often careful work with the "hidden logic" of other people's reactions to the patient may indirectly increase the patient's knowledge about himself.

At this point, it may be helpful to compare the approaches to the transference in psychoanalysis, expressive psychotherapy, and supportive psychotherapy.

In psychoanalysis, the patient's defenses against a full awareness of his transference dispositions are systematically explored, which leads to a gradual transformation of latent into manifest transferences. Transference reactions evolve into a full-blown transference neurosis. The systematic analysis of the transference neurosis permits its resolution as a resistance against awareness of the unconscious past. Then the information about the past contained in the transference can be integrated with the patient's recovery of the previously unconscious past through memory and reconstruction.

In expressive psychotherapy, the focus on the transference is less systematic. The combined focus on the predominant transference pattern, the predominant conflicts in the patient's immediate life situation, and the long-range treatment goals permits the therapist in any one session to decide how extensively and deeply the predominant transference pattern should be explored. This approach, carried out with patients with good ego strength, evolves into a limited analysis of transference patterns. With patients presenting ego weakness—that is, borderline personality organization—the availability of dissociated yet conscious primitive transference material permits interpretation of primitive transferences, which leads to their transformation into more advanced, "neurotic" transferences. These can be interpreted in depth, although a full reconstruction of the unconscious past is usually not achieved.

In supportive psychotherapy, the therapist works with the transference manifestations, particularly the manifest negative transference. The effort to work in a clarifying and confronting way with the disorganizing and regressive effects of primitive defensive operations (in order to reduce their ego-weakening effects) may lead to the activation of manifest negative transference developments in the hours, which then have to be explored and resolved, as illustrated earlier.

In all types of treatment, work with the transference starts with conscious and preconscious transference manifestations and is pursued until the patient's here-and-now fantasies about the therapist are fully explored and clarified. In supportive psychotherapy, however, this exploration is not connected interpretively with the pateint's unconscious relation to the therapist or with his unconscious past. It is, instead, used for confronting the patient with the reality of the treatment situation and with parallel distortions in his external life. The beginning of work with transference manifestations is the same in all three modalities of treatment, but the end point is very different. If a patient in supportive psychotherapy presents the therapist with very primitive regressive fantasy material, the communication is not neglected but is traced back to reality issues. In expressive psychotherapy, the direction is reversed: the usual path is from reality to exploration of the underlying fantasy.

Mechanisms of Change

What are the mechanisms by which change in the direction of therapeutic objectives is obtained in supportive psychotherapy? First of all, in a direct, nonmanipulative, nonmagical therapeutic approach the patient's ego functions are tested, activated, and strengthened, particularly in the areas of reality testing and self-awareness and in tolerating and integrating contradictory affects, experiences, and behaviors. The careful exploration of primitive defensive operations, even without their analytic resolution, should permit a decrease in their previously unchecked control over the adaptive functions of the ego and thus should increase ego strength.

At a deeper level, the controlled activation of primitive object relations in the transference, partially acted out at times of relatively stable manifest negative transference as well as at times of rapid shifts from idealizing to devaluating transference, permits a consolidation of basic trust of the libidinally invested self and object representations and should indeed permit some partial identification with the therapist. This identification, however, is in contrast to the dissociated, primitive identification with the therapist that occurs on the basis of narcissistic idealization or by the reinforcement of splitting mechanisms that divide the world into all-good and all-bad objects. The direct stimulation of more adaptive expression of both defensive operations and impulse gratification may gradually bring about an overall improvement in the impulse/defense equilibrium. The nonspecific effects of all therapeutic interventions (see Kernberg, 1980, chap. 10) also operate here; the affective "holding" and cognitive "containing" functions of the therapist are of significant importance in patients with ego weakness.

CHAPTER 10: *Indications and Contraindications for Psychoanalytically Based Treatment Modalities*

Having described the distinguishing characteristics of the various types of psychoanalytically based psychotherapies, it might be appropriate to spell out the general indications and contraindications for each, as well as for psychoanalysis proper.

These criteria cannot be based exclusively on the diagnosis of the predominant personality organization (neurotic vs. borderline) or on that diagnosis together with the predominant constellation of pathological character traits. The practice of allowing external or circumstantial factors—for example, the patient's financial circumstances, social or geographic factors, the psychotherapist's personal preferences and skills, or external pressures on the therapist—to determine the choice of treatment is regrettable. What is optimal treatment for each case should take precedence. Sometimes, however, these external factors may require shifting from the optimal to the feasible. Very often, sharing with a patient what we think would be the optimal treatment for him as well as our concern over the absence of realistic conditions for such treatment may mobilize the patient's active participation. The patient's capacity to mobilize his own psychological and psychosocial resources is often surprising.

Psychoanalysis

Although most borderline patients, as has been stated, do best with modified psychoanalytic psychotherapy, there are some who can be analyzed without modifications of technique, and I have recently become more optimistic in this regard. In addition to the potential for early severe acting out and the extent to which there is an observing ego, perhaps the most important criteria for whether a borderline patient is ana-

165

lyzable are first, the extent to which there exists a certain superego integration, so that the patient presents only very limited antisocial trends; and, second, the extent to which object relations have evolved so that at least some advanced, neurotic transferences (in contrast to more primitive ones) are available. When antisocial trends are marked, there is usually a danger that conscious distortion and lying will invade the treatment, which make psychoanalysis proper very difficult indeed, even impossible. When the patient has some capacity for differentiated relationships in depth with other people, there is less risk that primitive transferences will have disorganizing effects on the analytic situation. Hence, when differentiated oedipal features are strongly present from the beginning of treatment, and realistic, integrated kinds of transferences are available in addition to the chaotic, bizarre, and fragmented ones of borderline conditions, psychoanalysis may be indicated. This is particularly the case with infantile personalities with hysterical features functioning on a borderline level.

Psychoanalysis is the treatment of choice for patients suffering from hysterical personality, obsessive-compulsive personality, and depressive-masochistic personality. Psychoanalysis may also be indicated for patients with infantile or hysteroid or Zetzel-type-two and type-three hysterics—that is, patients with a mixture of infantile and hysterical features. (Zetzel-type-one hysterics correspond to the hysterical personality proper, and Zetzel-type-four to the severest cases of infantile personality.) Here, individual considerations may determine that even if borderline personality organization is present, the treatment should be psychoanalysis. A similar consideration obtains with narcissistic personalities who, in spite of an underlying borderline personality organization, do not present overt borderline features (general absence of impulse control, anxiety tolerance, and sublimatory channeling) or other prognostically negative indicators (infiltration of the pathological grandiose self with aggression, antisocial qualities, extreme deterioration or poverty of object relations).

In short, psychoanalysis is the treatment of choice for patients with neurotic personality organization, for narcissistic personalities *not* functioning on an overt borderline level, and for patients manifesting some mixed infantile and hysterical structures.

Certain requirements, however, exist for psychoanalysis. Given the fact that psychoanalysis requires four or five sessions weekly, time and money must be available, except in large cities where psychoanalytic institutes offer low-cost treatment as part of their educational functions.

It is helpful to consider for psychoanalysis patients whose personality and social and cultural potential are promising. The issue here is an effort to maximize the benefit of such an expensive and lengthy treatment. Psychoanalysis usually presupposes at least normal intelligence, a pathology of object relations that is relatively moderate, only mild anti-social features, adequate motivation for treatment, and the capacity for introspection or insight. Nonspecific manifestations of ego weakness should be absent.

Expressive Psychotherapy

Expressive psychotherapy is the treatment of choice for most patients with borderline personality organization, specifically for those with infantile personality, narcissistic personality with overt borderline features, narcissistic personality with condensation of the pathological grandiose self with aggression, and patients presenting a mixture of narcissistic and strong paranoid personality traits. The schizoid personality, the paranoid personality, and the sadomasochistic personality with a predominance of self-destructiveness and without life-threatening sadistic features are other types suitable for expressive psychotherapy. Patients with severe chronic self-destructiveness (such as self-mutilating tendencies, suicidal tendencies as a "way of life," and anorexia nervosa) are suitable for this type of psychotherapy, if sufficient external structure can be provided to prevent or control acting out that may otherwise threaten the continuation of the treatment or the patient's life. The establishment of such social structure should not prevent the therapist from maintaining an essentially neutral stance.

Hypomanic personalities and "as if" personalities with pseudologia fantastica have a less promising prognosis for expressive psychotherapy, particularly for cases of pseudologia fantastica, because of the tendency toward lying.

Expressive psychotherapy also has certain general requirements that cut across the diagnostic categories mentioned. In all cases, it is important that it be possible to carry out the treatment with minimal structuring of the hours. If external structure is provided, the treatment should be carried out by a team so that the therapist's technical neutrality can be maintained. In other words, the therapist should not intervene directly in the patient's life, and whatever intervention becomes necessary should be the responsibility of the other member or members of the team (a caseworker, perhaps, or a counselor or nurse). Patients should be able to preserve basic honesty in their verbal communications, and severe antisocial features even in a patient without antisocial personality proper may contraindicate expressive psychotherapy. Some severe forms of negative therapeutic reactions in which the patient identifies with an extremely sadistic primitive object may contraindicate expressive psychotherapy, but it is difficult to judge this before treatment is under way (except where the corresponding observations have been well documented in previous attempts at psychotherapy). As long

as there is the hope that the acting-out aspects of severe negative therapeutic reactions can be contained by the overall structure of the treatment, the therapist can try expressive psychotherapy.

A patient's commitment to expressive psychotherapy includes a willingness and an ability to fulfill a contract to attend regularly—at least two
or three times a week. In my view, expressive psychotherapy carried out
on a once-a-week basis or less is usually completely inadequate. With
such infrequent sessions, it is impossible to do justice to the analysis of
the transference required in this type of psychotherapy, and there is a serious risk of focusing on the transference, thus dismissing the developments in the patient's life between the hours and artifically separating
transference exploration from the analysis of the patient's life situation.
Or else, in an effort to bring himself up to date, the therapist may be
forced to focus so much on the patient's life situation outside the sessions
that the manifestations of the patient's conflicts in the transference go underground and the treatment comes to a standstill.

Patients who are candidates for expressive psychotherapy should be
willing to abstain from drugs and alcohol and from other physically self-
destructive behavior. If they feel such tendencies are out of control, they
should be willing to acknowledge them openly and to accept brief hospi-
talizations. Patients who are alcoholic, drug addicted, or chronically suicidal should not undergo expressive psychotherapy if those symptoms
cannot be controlled. Finally, we expect at least normal intelligence as a
prerequisite for participating in the highly symbolic and abstract verbal
communication that is part of expressive psychotherapy.

Supportive Psychotherapy

Within the broad spectrum of symptomatic neuroses, character pathology, and borderline conditions—that is, all nonpsychotic, nonorganic
psychopathology—supportive psychotherapy is rarely if ever the treatment modality of choice. In fact, I think that as a general rule the indication for supportive psychotherapy for these patients derives from the
contraindication for expressive psychotherapy.

Insofar as patients with good ego strength—that is, symptomatic
neuroses and nonborderline character pathology—respond to all modalities of psychoanalytically derived treatment but particularly to expressive psychotherapy or psychoanalysis (Kernberg et al., 1972), supportive
psychotherapy would be indicated only if the patient lacks motivation or
psychological mindedness or lacks the capacity or the willingness to participate in the two or three sessions per week minimally required for expressive psychotherapy.

It is preferable when psychotherapy is being considered, first to evaluate the indications and contraindications for expressive psycho-therapy; in fact, strictly speaking, it is preferable first to determine whether psychoanalysis is indicated and whether the patient is analyza-ble. If not, the next question is whether expressive psychotherapy is in-dicated. Only if all expressive modalities are contraindicated should supportive psychotherapy be considered and a strictly defined supportive technique adopted. I want to stress that a patient's apparent lack of time, motivation, introspection, and psychological mindedness—any of which would, if excessive, contraindicate expressive psychother-apy—should be probingly evaluated before settling on supportive psy-chotherapy. It is advantageous in all cases to carry out the patient's ini-tial evaluation with an expressive approach and to allow time before making the decision to undertake supportive psychotherapy. A psycho-analytic approach to the diagnostic study facilitates the evaluation of in-dications and contraindications for the entire spectrum of psychoanalytic modalities of treatment, and leaves the road open for expressive psycho-therapy or psychoanalysis with the same diagnostician.

The patient's past history of psychotherapeutic engagements may be of fundamental importance in evaluating his capacity to participate in any form of psychotherapy. Other issues may tilt the balance toward a supportive rather than an expressive mode. If the patient's illness is pro-viding a substantial degree of secondary gain, the prognosis for expres-sive psychotherapy is not good. Other issues militating against expres-sive therapy include disorganization of external life circumstances severe enough to require environmental interventions; a general sense of ur-gency for such environmental intervention because of potentially damaging developments in the patient's current life; a chronic absence of actual object relations (patients with severe social isolation); and the presence of severe nonspecific manifestations of ego weakness.

The severity of some of these features, however, may contraindicate supportive psychotherapy as well. For example, chronic lying (even without an antisocial personality structure), a history of negative thera-peutic reactions with violent aggressive behavior and destructive or self-destructive acts, and relentless masochistic acting out all may raise doubts whether any kind of psychotherapy could be initiated on an out-patient basis. A period of brief or extended hospitalization may clarify these issues and significantly broaden the potential range for all psycho-therapeutic interventions.

Supportive psychotherapy is an ideal modality for crisis interven-tion. A supportive technique within the sessions combined with direct interventions in the patient's environment provides an effective time-limited treatment. This approach should be differentiated from short-term expressive psychotherapy, a special type of therapy that is currently undergoing renewed exploration (Davanloo, 1980). An interesting and probably still open question is to what extent a mixture of supportive and expressive techniques is less damaging or more effective in brief psychotherapy or crisis intervention than in long-term treatment.

When circumstances militate against any realistic treatment arrangement or indicate an extremely pessimistic prognosis, the question must be raised whether any type of psychotherapy is indicated. The therapist must accept the fact that some patients cannot be helped by any psychotherapeutic intervention. Such an awareness automatically heightens one's alertness to establishing minimal requirements for treatment, the need for a contract with the patient that implies that the patient assume some responsibilities during treatment, and a realistic consonance between treatment objectives and treatment processes. It also reduces possible tendencies toward excessive therapeutic zeal or messianic spirit, which can be very self-defeating.

Within the broad spectrum of borderline personality organization, supportive psychotherapy is indicated for the inadequate personality (as defined by DSM-II) and for patients with severe character pathology and borderline personality organization who present chronically severe antisocial features although not an antisocial personality proper. (See chap. 5 for the corresponding diagnostic discussion.) The antisocial personality has an extremely poor prognosis for all psychoanalytically based modalities of treatment and probably should not be treated by ordinary types of psychotherapy.

Supportive psychotherapy is also indicated for all patients with borderline personality organization who do not meet the requirements for expressive or psychoanalytic psychotherapy although they would be suitable for such a modality on the basis of their predominant constellation of character pathology.

Supportive psychotherapy also has its prerequisites. The patient should present a level of intelligence commensurate with what is still a complex verbal form of treatment—that is, an intelligence quotient of at least 75 to 100. Severe self-destructive behavior should be controllable by providing support in the hours and structuring the patient's life outside the hours. If a supportive psychotherapeutic technique is unable to contain the patient's self-destructiveness, that may be a contraindication for any outpatient treatment at this point, and the patient may require short-term or long-term hospitalization. Similarly, the development of negative therapeutic reactions of the type mentioned earlier as potentially contraindicating expressive psychotherapy must be controlled by direct measures in the sessions, as well as by structuring the patient's life outside the sessions.

Paradoxically, reinforcing reality considerations as part of the technique of supportive psychotherapy tends to reduce the effects of severe negative therapeutic reactions, which may worsen with an expressive approach that provides insufficient structuring of the patient's life. Supportive psychotherapy also requires a life situation that is not so chaotic or destructive that a modification of the patient's behavior rather than of an impossible environment is still a reasonable first task.

General Contraindications for Psychoanalytically Based Modalities of Treatment

First of all, as mentioned before, the diagnosis of an antisocial personality structure practically contraindicates any modality of psychoanalytically based psychotherapy. In addition, where the secondary gain of illness exceeds the patient's suffering, the prognosis for psychotherapy is extremely unfavorable. For example, patients with chronic neurotic symptoms, hypochondriacal traits, and severe interpersonal difficulties who have been declared incapable of any work and assured of a stable pension for the rest of their lives may have realistic reasons (in addition to unconscious ones) for clinging to their symptoms.

Unwillingness or incapacity to attend the sessions regularly, severe disturbances in verbal communication, and a very low IQ are obvious contraindications. There are some patients whose relentless acting out of self-destructive tendencies is not controllable, either because of an unremitting need to destroy themselves or because of a combination of such need with a conspiring psychosocial environment in which key relatives unconsciously or consciously desire the patient's death. Patients with a chronic tendency to lie, even without an antisocial personality structure proper, have a very poor prognosis.

Revising Treatment Modalities

Sometimes a mistake in suggesting psychoanalysis or expressive psychotherapy for borderline patients is unavoidable, and it is necessary, after a period of time, to revise the treatment modality. It is relatively easy or safe to shift the modality from psychoanalysis to psychotherapy. This may be made because of the analyst's awareness that the patient's persistent and severe acting out cannot be controlled by interpretation alone and threatens the continuity of the treatment or even the patient's physical or psychological survival. Sometimes, reality conditions (often brought about in part or totally by the patient's illness) deteriorate and interfere with analytic work. At other times, the prevalence of primitive transferences and primitive defensive operations evolves into a full-fledged transference psychosis, with a loss of reality testing in the treatment hours and the impossibility of reconstituting an observing ego.

Under these circumstances, the analyst may reevaluate the situation with the patient, clarify the nature of the problems that unexpectedly changed the total therapeutic situation, and transform the analysis into psychotherapy. In practice, this usually also means carrying out face-to-face interviews: I see no advantage and only disadvantages in carrying out psychoanalytic psychotherapy on the couch rather than face to face (1975).

When circumstances are reversed—that is, when what started as an expressive psychotherapy should, in the therapist's opinion, be transformed into psychoanalysis—the situation is more difficult. Usually, under these circumstances, the analyst has developed some non-neutral stances and has established parameters or even modifications of technique which may distort the transference relation to such an extent that analysis becomes difficult or impossible. Therefore, the more technically neutral the position of the psychotherapist in an expressive psychotherapy with borderline patients, the easier will be such a shift into psychoanalysis if indicated. Now the analyst has to ask himself searchingly to what extent he has utilized supportive techniques (in the form of manipulative or suggestive comments) or made supportive use of the transference rather than analyzing it. If the analyst can answer these questions satisfactorily in the sense that the major transference distortions or departures from neutrality can be resolved analytically, the case may still be shifted into psychoanalysis.

At other times, especially if a shift from psychotherapy to psychoanalysis seems indicated after months or even years of treatment—that is, when the patient has sufficiently improved in psychotherapy to make psychoanalysis possible—it may be preferable to evaluate the situation fully with the patient, set up certain goals that should be accomplished in psychotherapy itself before terminating it, and then consider the possibility of terminating psychotherapy and starting psychoanalysis—if it is still needed—later on. Under these conditions, the patient should ideally remain without treatment for at least 6 to 12 months so that the total effect of the psychotherapy can be reevaluated after he has functioned independently for a time and the mourning process connected with termination of psychotherapy has had a chance to be resolved. The patient should start psychoanalysis with a different analyst.

Indications for Hospitalization

Certain aspects of the borderline patient's personality structure, symptoms, life situation, and/or attitude toward his illness may make any form of outpatient psychoanalytic psychotherapy practicably impossible. When hospitalization is required, the treatment may be brief (several days to three months) or long-term (three months to a year or more).

Short-term hospitalization is usually indicated when the patient's personality structure, symptoms, and life circumstances make outpatient treatment impracticable. Long-term hospitalization is indicated for the most part on the basis of the patient's attitude toward his illness.

The objectives of short-term hospital treatment include a comprehensive diagnostic evaluation, therapeutic interventions to control symptoms, a diagnosis of the patient's family situation and/or social support systems and traumatic or conflict-triggering circumstances, and an evaluation of the optimal outpatient treatment indicated after discharge, including the patient's capacities for maintaining such outpatient treatment.

The principal objective of long-term hospital treatment for borderline personality organization is the modification of personality features of these patients that militate against their capacity to engage in and maintain outpatient psychotherapy. The key personality features to be modified in long-term hospital treatment include the patient's attitudes toward his illness and the treatment, that is, lack of introspection or insight, poor motivation for treatment, and significant secondary gain of illness. The prognostically most negative features for outpatient psychotherapy, namely, severe antisocial tendencies and deterioration or absence of residual, good, internalized object relations, may be additional indications for long-term hospital treatment.

Therefore, the targets of long-term hospital treatment involve the deepest aspects of personality functioning and require a total exploration of the patient's personality within the hospital (see chaps. 20–22).

Personality features warranting short-term hospitalization include extreme severity of the nonspecific aspects of ego weakness that entails the risk of destructive or self-destructive acting out, a paralyzing sense of chaos with breakdown in all social functioning, and behaviors that, without being acutely dangerous to the patient or to others, endanger the patient's future and imply that he is "burning the bridges" behind him. Personality features (or rather, their interaction with the therapist) also include a pervasive predisposition to the development of negative therapeutic reactions. Symptoms warranting brief hospitalization include those which imply an immediate danger to the patient or others, such as acute suicidal tendencies, uncontrollable rage attacks with a tendency toward physical violence, drug abuse and/or alcoholism that the patient cannot control, and antisocial behavior that, without being intentionally self-destructive, is potentially so because of its effects. Symptomatic features also include acute regression in the transference in the case of patients undergoing outpatient psychotherapy, ranging from psychotic developments in the transference only (transference psychosis) to generalized, acute psychotic reactions. Acute psychotic episodes in borderline patients may reflect transference regression, very severe forms of negative therapeutic reaction, the effects of drug abuse, alcoholism, or extreme emotional turmoil. Obviously, personality features and symptoms as reasons for brief hospitalization cannot always be differentiated sharply, and they reinforce one another.

Life situations that may warrant brief hospitalization of borderline patients include a temporary breakdown of the patient's social support systems; a vicious cycle derived from the patient's disorganizing effects upon his family; and the family's pathological, maladaptive, or inappropriate reactions to the patient's illness. A breakdown brought about by moving away to college or returning home after an absence may generate such a cycle, and a brief hospitalization may protect the patient and stabilize him as well as his social support system.

In short, all the personality, symptomatic, and environmental features mentioned so far usually represent indications for short-term hospitalization, particularly in the case of a first psychotic episode, social breakdown, or development of symptomatic worsening. Repeated episodes of this kind may reveal potential therapeutic interventions that stabilize the patient's functioning without hospitalization, or else suggest the need for long-term hospitalization. The lack of an appropriate treatment structure capable of maintaining the patient in an outpatient treatment setting may justify a brief hospitalization even with patients whose crisis might otherwise be handled without hospital treatment. If it is a first episode of breakdown in a patient who has been engaged in intensive, long-term psychotherapy, the adequacy of this treatment approach needs to be reevaluated, together with the possibility that what happened was the development of a negative therapeutic reaction or an acute transference regression. These diagnostic and prognostic evaluations may be facilitated by a brief hospitalization.

Additional indications for short-term hospitalization derive from diagnostic uncertainties, for example, new symptomatic developments that raise complex diagnostic questions. Also, a disruption of an adequate outpatient psychotherapy may be the consequence of external circumstances that interfere with the regularly scheduled hours. An intensification of severe anxiety or depression within an ongoing outpatient treatment situation may constitute another reason for short-term hospitalization.

Indications for long-term hospitalization in practice coincide with issues relating to the patient's attitude toward his illness. Features referring to the patient's attitude toward his illness include a capacity for introspection, the motivation for treatment, and the secondary gain of illness. Regarding the capacity for introspection, I mean not only the maintenance of reality testing in a strict sense but a combination of cognitive and emotional awareness of and concern over his illness, so that the patient experiences wishes to be helped. There may be evidence of severe personality breakdown, intensification of potentially destructive or self-destructive symptoms, and social turmoil and breakdown in the patient's functioning without his presenting such introspection and concern, and that itself may become an important reason for a brief hospitalization.

In contrast, an absence of introspection over an extended period of time in the face of chronic social malfunctioning, which leads to the rejection of any psychotherapeutic treatment even in the absence of loss of reality testing, may be one indication for long-term hospitalization.

Motivation for treatment usually goes hand in hand with introspection, but there are patients whose motivation for treatment is of a primitive kind, a wish to be taken care of while refusing to take any responsibility for themselves, that may also militate against initiation or maintenance of an outpatient psychotherapeutic relationship. The patient's refusal to accept responsibility for himself may imply the risks of destructive or self-destructive behavior. For example, some patients referred to elsewhere (chap. 16) as presenting "suicide as a way of life" may be perfectly aware of the nature of their symptoms, wish to be helped, and yet refuse to accept responsibility for alerting their psychiatrist about uncontrollable suicidal impulses even in the absence of any other significant secondary gain of illness. Here, what might be called the primary gain of self-destructive behavior as an unconscious triumph over or revenge against a hated parental image may militate against outpatient treatment, justifying short-term hospitalization (in order to prevent an acute suicide attempt) and, in other cases, long-term hospitalization to attain more fundamental changes in the patient's attitude toward his illness as a condition for further outpatient treatment.

In patients with borderline personality organization, secondary gain of illness is, in general, difficult to separate from the primary gain. The obvious gains derived from a parasitic relationship to the family, the financial exploitation of others, the omnipotent control over the environment expressed symbolically by self-destructive symptoms that keep everybody on their toes may all represent an indication for long-term hospitalization geared to modifying the patient's attitudes in this area as well as to helping the family overcome their being controlled by the patient's pathology.

Long-term hospitalization may also be indicated for patients in apparently appropriate intensive psychotherapeutic outpatient treatment if they present a severe form of negative therapeutic reaction, if the treatment is failing to stem the destructive effects of chronic acting out or unremitting, self-defeating life patterns, or if the investment in life's ordinary responsibilities is being replaced by exclusive investment in the psychotherapy itself ("psychotherapy as replacement for life"). In all these cases, the objectives of long-term inpatient treatment include, first of all, the achievement of significant personality change related to permitting the resumption of outpatient treatment.

Additional indications for long-term hospitalization include lack of change in chronically severe impulsivity and acting out, chronic antisocial behavior that cannot be reduced by means of outpatient treatment, and alcohol or drug abuse that, similarly, despite adequate social structuring of the patient's environment and even of the treatment hours within a supportive psychotherapy, cannot be controlled.

There are some cases where either short-term or long-term hospitalization may be indicated but effectively replaced by short-term or long-term part-time hospitalization in day hospitals, by placement in a residential home or half-way house, or by the provision of an additional social support system, such as psychiatric social worker, counselor, or nurse.

Part Three: *Narcissistic Personalities: Clinical Theory and Treatment*

CHAPTER 11: *Contemporary Psychoanalytic Approaches to Narcissism*

All three major approaches to the study of normal and pathological narcissism in contemporary psychoanalytic thinking stem from Freud's (1914) paper on narcissism.

A Kleinian Approach

The first approach, relatively unknown in this country and based on the object relations theory of Melanie Klein, is represented by the work of Herbert Rosenfeld. It has its historical roots in Abraham's (1919) description of narcissistic resistances in the transference, Joan Riviere's (1936) paper on the negative therapeutic reaction, and Melanie Klein's (1957) study on envy and gratitude.

In a series of four highly condensed papers published between 1964 and 1978, Rosenfeld detailed the structural characteristics of narcissistic personalities and their transference developments in the course of psychoanalysis. He thereby linked, for the first time, a Kleinian approach to treatment with a descriptive and characterological analysis of a specific group of patients and developed the first contemporary theory of pathological narcissism.

Narcissistic personalities, Rosenfeld proposes, have omnipotently introjected an all-good, primitive part object and/or have omnipotently projected their own self "into" such an object, thus denying any difference or separation between self and object. This permits such patients to deny any need for dependency upon an external object. Dependency would imply the need for a loved and potentially frustrating object who is also intensely hated, with the hatred taking the form of extreme envy (Rosenfeld, 1964). Envy, Rosenfeld assumes, following Klein, is a primary intrapsychic expression of the death instinct, the earliest manifestation of aggression in the realm of object relations. Narcissistic object relations permit the avoidance of aggressive feelings caused by frustration and of any awareness of envy. Such external objects as the patient realistically needs are often used for the projection of all undesirable parts of the patient "into" them; in treatment, therefore, the analyst is used as a "lavatory." The relationship to a "lavatory analyst" is extremely gratifying to the narcissistic patient because everything unpleasant is discharged into the analyst, and the patient attributes to himself everything good that comes from the relationship.

These patients, Rosenfeld goes on, have a highly idealized self-image and omnipotently deny anything that interferes with this picture. They may quickly assimilate other people's values and ideas and declare them to be their own, or they may unconsciously devalue and destroy what they receive from others (because it would otherwise evoke unbearable envy) and therefore have a chronic sense of dissatisfaction with what they are receiving from others.

Rosenfeld (1971) examines a further complication of these personality structures, derived from the contamination of their self-idealization by idealization of the omnipotent destructive parts of the self. The infiltration of the pathological "mad" self by primitive aggression gives these patients a quality of violent self-destructiveness. Under these conditions, there is an unconscious hatred of everything that is good and valuable, not only in external objects but in the potentially good aspects of the patient's own normal dependent self. In extreme cases, such patients feel secure and triumphant only when they have destroyed everyone else and, particularly, when they have frustrated the efforts of those who love them. The patient's sense of power seems to derive from his imperviousness to all usual human "frailties." In short, extremely narcissistic personalities may have a malignant fusion of libidinal and aggressive drives invested in the "mad" self, in which aggression strongly predominates. It is extremely difficult to "rescue" the dependent healthy parts of the self from their trapped position inside the narcissistic structure.

Rosenfeld (1975) links this theory with the severest forms of negative therapeutic reaction. He also suggests that the unconscious grandiosity of these patients may take the form of fantasies that they have incorporated both the masculine and the feminine aspects of their internal and external objects so that they are totally immune to any sexual needs, as well as to any dependent needs. The breakdown of these narcissistic structures may bring about almost delusional experiences of a paranoid kind, which must be overcome by interpretation so that the patient can advance toward a situation of true dependency: into the depressive position and the experience of oedipal conflicts. The pathological grandiose self of these patients reflects a more primitive, severer, and more intractable resistance to treatment than the unconscious guilt feelings stemming from a sadistic superego that is characteristic of milder forms of negative therapeutic reaction.

Unlike some other Kleinian authors, Rosenfeld has been interested in the phenomenological aspects of character pathology and their differential diagnosis. This has made it easier to integrate his clinical observations—if not his metapsychological thinking—with the mainstream of psychoanalytic thinking. I believe that Rosenfeld has provided us with important descriptions of the clinical characteristics of narcissistic patients as well as of their transferences. I disagree with his assumption that envy is a manifestation of an inborn death instinct and with his tendency to interpret narcissistic conflicts as if they reflected almost exclusively developments in the first year of life. I also disagree with his assumption that narcissistic personalities deny the separateness between self and object. They deny *differences* between self and object but not separateness; only in psychotic structures do we find an actual loss of self–object differentiation.

This is actually a fairly common misunderstanding. It is reflected in Kohut's (1971) "merger" transference and in many other authors' overextension of the concept of "symbiotic" relationships. The same misunderstanding results in a failure to differentiate patients who deny differences with the analyst from patients who actually cannot separate their bodily experiences or thoughts from those of the therapist. The latter situation is characteristic of schizophrenic patients in intensive therapy, but not of nonpsychotic psychopathology. The looseness of the use of the term *psychotic* in Kleinian formulation is one of its major problems.

In addition, I question Rosenfeld's assumption that most narcissistic (as well as borderline) patients can and should be psychoanalyzed. I believe that there are contradictions between his therapeutic recommendations and at least some of the case material he himself presents. In fact, Rosenfeld later (1979a) conceded that some overtly borderline narcissistic patients, particularly those with violently aggressive features, should not be analyzed. In addition, he has suggested modifications in technique with some narcissistic patients at times of severe regression (1978).

Most of all, however, I disagree with Rosenfeld's Kleinian assumption that the major developmental stages occur in the first year of life. Thus, for example, he states (1964): "In narcissistic object relations, omnipotence plays a prominent part. The object, usually a part-object, the breast, may be omnipotently incorporated, which implies that it is treated as the infant's possession; or the mother or breast are used as containers into which are omnipotently projected the parts of the self which are felt to be undesirable as they cause pain or anxiety" (pp.

332–333). This Kleinian collapse of all development into the first year of life and, technically speaking, the treatment of all primitive material as if it reflected an assumed earliest level of development I find highly questionable.

I do agree, however, with Rosenfeld's stress on the need to interpret both positive and negative transferences of narcissistic patients, and I find especially important his focus on specific groups of narcissistic patients in whom the grandiose self condenses aggressive and libidinal strivings. I also find his clinical observations regarding narcissistic transferences very helpful. Although my approach to these transferences differs from his, my interpretation owes much to Rosenfeld's operational clarifications.

My technical approach, unlike Rosenfeld's, focuses on the transference implications of the material without attempting to relate them immediately to their assumed genetic sources; in fact, the more primitive the material, the more caution is required before attempting genetic reconstructions, because at such a level of regression a great deal of intrapsychic restructuralization and condensation of fantasies from many sources also occurs.

My approach, in contrast to general Kleinian technique, also focuses much more on the patient's participation in the analytic exploration; I am reluctant to let the patient "learn" about my theories and am probably much more cautious and gradual than the Kleinians in expanding the patient's awareness of unconscious material. Patients quickly learn their analyst's language and theories; this creates a problem with "confirmatory" material for all theoretical approaches, but perhaps particularly with the authoritative formulation of interpretations that characterizes the Kleinian school. And, of course, as Rosenfeld himself has pointed out, narcissistic patients are most eager to learn their analyst's theories for various defensive purposes.

Kohut and the Psychology of the Self

In a series of papers and two books (1971, 1977) Heinz Kohut proposed a completely different metapsychology, clinical explanations, and therapeutic procedure for narcissistic personality disorders. In essence, Kohut argued that there exists a group of patients whose psychopathology is intermediary between the psychoses and borderline conditions, on the one hand, and the psychoneuroses and milder character disorders, on the other. The group of narcissistic personality disorders that he considers analyzable can, in his opinion, be differentiated only by their transference manifestations, not by purely clinical-descriptive criteria.

One diagnoses the narcissistic personality in the psychoanalytic situation by recognizing the development of two types of transference, idealizing and mirroring. The idealizing transference reflects the therapeutic activation of an idealized parent image and derives from an archaic, rudimentary "selfobject." The patient feels empty and powerless when he is separated from this idealized transference object. Kohut suggested that the intensity of the dependency on these idealized selfobjects is due to the patient's wish to substitute them for a missing segment of the psychic structure. The patient's narcissistic equilibrium is safeguarded only through the interest and approval of current replicas of traumatically missing selfobjects of the past.

Second, the patient develops a propensity toward the reactivation of a grandiose self in the psychoanalytic situation. This activation accounts for the development of mirror transferences in analysis. These mirror transferences can be differentiated according to three levels of regression. The most archaic is a "merger" transference in which the extension of the grandiose self envelops the analyst. A less archaic form is the "alter ego," or "twinship," transference. A still less archaic form is the "mirror" transference in a narrow sense. The most archaic form represents the revival of an early stage of primary identity of self and object. The alter ego, or twinship, transference reflects the patient's assumption that the analyst is either like him or similar to him. Through the mirror transference in a narrow sense the patient experiences the analyst as separate but significant only insofar as he is needed by the reactivated grandiose self for its own purpose.

Kohut proposed that two types of transferences—idealizing and mirroring—represent the activation in the psychoanalytic situation of an arrested stage of development, of an archaic grandiose self. The fragility of that archaic self requires the empathy and normal mirroring functions of mother as "selfobject," whose love and ministrations permit consolidation of the grandiose self first and, later, its gradual development of more mature forms of self-esteem and self-confidence through less and less archaic types of mirroring.

At the same time, optimal relationships with the mirroring selfobject also facilitate the development of normal idealization of the selfobject that stands for the original perfection of the grandiose self, now partially preserved in the relationship with such an idealized selfobject. This idealization culminates eventually in what Kohut calls the "transmuting internalization" of the idealized selfobject into an intrapsychic structure that will originate the ego ideal and provide the idealizing qualities to the superego, thus preserving the new internalized regulation of self-esteem.

Narcissistic psychopathology, in essence, Kohut proposed, derives from the traumatic failure of the empathic mothering function and from the failure of the undisturbed development of idealization processes. These traumatic failures bring about a developmental arrest, a fixation at the level of the archaic infantile grandiose self, and an endless search for the idealized selfobject needed to complete structure formation, all of which are reflected in the narcissistic transferences mentioned above.

In the treatment, the psychoanalyst must permit the development of the patient's narcissistic idealization of him and must not disturb it by premature interpretation or reality considerations. This permits the gradual unfolding of mirror transferences. The patient relives the earlier traumatic experiences with a more mature psyche and acquires new psychic structures, with the help of the analyst as selfobject, by the process of transmuting internalization. The psychoanalyst must be basically empathic, focusing on the patient's narcissistic needs and frustrations rather than on the drive derivatives and conflicts that emerge at times of narcissistic frustration in the analytic situation.

The unavoidable failures in the psychoanalyst's empathy bring about traumatic circumstances in the treatment situation, temporary fragmentation of the archaic grandiose self, with activation of narcissistic rage, experiences of diffuse anxiety, depersonalization, hypochrondriacal trends, or even more pathological regression into a delusional reconstitution of the grandiose self in cold paranoid grandiosity.

In each of these conditions of narcissistic frustration, the psychoanalyst explores with the patient where and how the analyst has failed in being appropriately empathic and how this relates to past failures of the significant objects of the patient's childhood. Kohut insists that this does not require the establishment of parameters of technique and that it represents a modification of the standard psychoanalytic technique for non-narcissistic patients only in that it stresses the analyst's empathy in contrast to "objective neutrality" and focuses on the vicissitudes of the self rather than on drives and (not yet existent) interstructural conflicts.

Kohut has suggested a fundamental difference between preoedipal or narcissistic pathology and oedipal psychopathology linked to the ordinary neuroses and non-narcissistic character disorders. The psychopathology of the stage of development that begins with the cohesion of the archaic grandiose self and ends with the transmuting internalization of the ego ideal needs to be examined in terms of the vicissitudes of what Kohut has called the "bipolar self." He suggested that one pole, the bulk of nuclear grandiosity of the self, consolidates into the nuclear ambitions of early childhood while the other pole, the bulk of nuclear idealized goal structures of the self, is acquired somewhat later. These two polarities of the self derive, respectively, from the mother's mirroring acceptance—which confirms nuclear grandiosity—and her holding and caring—which allow merger experiences with the selfobject's idealized omnipotence. Nuclear ambitions and nuclear ideals are linked by an intermediary area of basic talents and skills.

Kohut considered these component structures of the bipolar self as reflecting both the origin and the seat of early psychopathology, in contrast to the drives and conflict-derived psychopathology of the tripartite structure of the mind that characterize the oedipal period. He has coined the terms *tragic man* to refer to the psychopathology of narcissism and *guilty man* to refer to the oedipal psychopathology that evolves under the influence of drives, unconscious intrapsychic conflicts, and the tripartite structure of the mind. He sees aggression, greed, and voraciousness in narcissistic personality disorders as products of the disintegration of the self, not the motivational factors of that disintegration.

Kohut replaced his earlier (1971) term *narcissistic transference* (derived from libido theory) with *selfobject transference*, thus illustrating his abandonment of his concept of narcissistic and object libido as "qualitatively" different from each other (rather than as determined by the object in which libido is invested). This shift solves the problem created by Kohut's earlier assumption that different qualities were inherent in narcissistic and object-directed libido. It is furthermore consistent with his stress on early intrapsychic development as unrelated to the vicissitudes of drive development of libido and aggression. In fact, Kohut abandoned the consideration of drives and conflict as major motivational forces in the early stages of development. He believed that achieving the normal, transmuting internalization of the idealized selfobject into an intrapsychic structure contributes to the consolidation of the tripartite intrapsychic structure as defined by Freud and permits the development of drive-determined, oedipal, unconscious intrapsychic conflicts.

As I have pointed out in earlier work (1975), I think Kohut has accurately described the importance of idealization in the transference. In fact, he has contributed fundamentally to the clarification of narcissistic transferences in describing both grandiosity and idealization as characteristic of them. But he has missed the differences between the pathological types of idealization activated in narcissistic transferences and the more normal types of idealization reflecting the early defensive operation of idealization and its later modifications under the impact of integration of object relations. He thus collapses (1) idealization reflecting part of a defense against aggression by splitting idealization from devaluation, (2) idealization as a reaction formation against guilt, and (3) idealization as a projection of a pathological grandiose self. In accepting rather than analyzing idealization in the transference, he misses the differences among various developmental levels of this defense mechanism. Also, Kohut has confused the pathological interactions of borderline conditions and pathological narcissism with their rapid exchange of self and object representations, with true merger phenomena that obtain only in psychosis.

Kohut's cases are far from resembling true merger phenomena such as develop in the symbiotic transferences of schizophrenic patients. This is part of a larger problem: the confusion between a patient's statements about his experiences and the actual nature and degree of regression. For example, a patient's saying that he feels confused or as if he is falling apart does not necessarily mean that he is suffering a "fragmentation of his self." In addition, Kohut does not differentiate the pathological grandiose self from normal self formation in infancy and childhood. Consequently, his efforts to preserve the grandiose self and permit its becoming more adaptive result in a failure to resolve the pathology of internalized object relations, with crucial limitations in the effects of the treatment of these patients.

This failure to distinguish normal from pathological grandiosity constitutes a major problem in Kohut's theory. His statement that the self has a line of development independent from that of object relations may well reflect the consequence of a treatment that attempts to preserve, protect, and reinforce the grandiose self. One has the impression that the aim is merely to tone down the grandiose self gradually, so that it will not have too disruptive an effect upon others. Only systematic analysis of the positive and negative transferences of the pathological grandiose self, leading to the gradual uncovering of its defensive functions and its eventual replacement by a normal self, permits the resolution of pathology in the narcissistic and object relations sectors of these patients.

Kohut neglects the interpretation of negative transference and even artificially fosters idealization in the transference. In my opinion, his is a supportive, reeducative approach to narcissistic patients, for he helps them to rationalize their aggressive reactions as a natural result of the failure of other people in their past. This problem appears consistently in the case material presented both by Kohut and in Goldberg's *The Psychology of the Self: A Casebook* (1978).

For example, with Mr. I, referred to in both of Kohut's books and extensively in Goldberg's *Casebook,* the analyst almost always interpreted the patient's rage or anger as a consequence of either the analyst's or other people's failures. The analyst did not explore either the unconscious aspects of the patient's fantasies and reactions toward him or sexual conflicts (regarding both his homosexual impulses toward the analyst and his sadistic sexual behavior toward women) except as they were connected with the frustration of the patient's grandiosity or his idealization of the analyst. Kohut's rejection of drive theory as a theoretical model corresponds to his ignoring of aggression in the transference—except when he sees it as a natural reaction to others' (particularly the analyst's) failures.

Kohut also neglects the analysis of the unconscious aspects of the transference, that is, the defensive nature of the patient's conscious experiences of the analyst. Failure to analyze unconscious experiences and distortions of the psychoanalytic situation that mediate between the conscious present and the unconscious past feeds into the patient's tendency to elaborate the past on the basis of a conscious reorganization of that past, in contrast to the radical reorganization of the unconscious past that evolves as part of working through the transference neurosis. Kohut, of course, implies that such patients cannot experience a full-fledged transference neurosis. Perhaps his patients did not, but if so I believe their failure to do so resulted from the analyst's protection and reinforcement of the pathological grandiose self.

In restricting the concept of empathy to the analyst's emotional awareness of the patient's central subjective state, Kohut neglects the broader function of psychoanalytic empathy whereby the analyst simultaneously becomes aware of what the patient experiences and what he is dissociating, repressing, or projecting. It is very easy for the analyst to consider an intervention "empathic" when it fits with both his own theory and the patient's conscious expectations or needs. Some fundamental truths about himself that the patient is defensively avoiding may produce pain and suffering when he is first confronted with them, even in the most tactful and understanding way. If empathy is taken to mean, in practice, protecting the patient from painful truths about himself, particularly by strengthening certain narcissistic transference resistances, then the concept is severely narrowed. Also, empathy is never illustrated in Kohut's writings or in the *Casebook* as empathy with a patient's excited, lustful, joyful aggression. That cruelty and sadism can be pleasurable is obscured by references to the frustrating conditions that motivate them. For all these reasons, the very concept of transference is thus flattened in Kohut's examples, and the patient's current conscious experience is directly linked to the mostly conscious past.

I think it significant that Kohut failed to differentiate his concept of the *selfobject*—a primitive and highly distorted representation of significant others—from the more or less distorted or realistic object representations of the preoedipal and oedipal stages of development. Libidinally and aggressively invested self and object representations have no place in Kohut's theoretical system. Hence, under conditions of frustration and failure (including, of course, narcissistic frustration and failure) there is only the threat of traumatization or fragmentation of the self. No mention is made of "bad," frustrating object representations—the image of a "bad" mother, for example. Kohut's intrapsychic world contains only idealized images of the self and others (selfobjects). This theoretical restriction fails to explain the reproduction in the transference of internal relations with "bad" objects, a crucial observation not only in pathological narcissism but in all cases of severe psychopathology. This theoretical problem corresponds to Kohut's neglect, at the clinical level, of the interpretation of negative transference. Acknowledging a patient's aggression in the transference as caused by the analyst's "failure" is diametrically opposed to interpreting it as a transference distortion reflecting the activation of unconscious aggression toward an earlier internalized object.

Kohut has pointed to the internal consistency between his theoretical formulations and his clinical approach, an appealing argument that should contribute to the evaluation of his theory. I agree that Kohut's thinking is consistent, but I think it is erroneous. The psychoanalytic approach to the pathological grandiose self that leads to its resolution permits the emergence in the transference not simply of fragmented bits and pieces of drive components but of highly differentiated though primitive part-object relations. These can be explored and resolved with an interpretive approach that permits their transformation into advanced or total-object relations and transferences and thus permits the resolution of primitive intrapsychic conflict and the consolidation of a normal self. By ignoring the transference implications of regressive states, considering them simply as "fragmentations of the self," Kohut has kept himself from learning about the deepest, most primitive layers of the psychic apparatus. He has acknowledged that his approach brings about an improvement in the narcissistic segment of the personality but not in the object-related segment. In contrast, a systematic psychoanalytic interpretation of the pathological grandiose self and of the nonintegrated, primitive, ego–id states that emerge in this process permits the simultaneous resolution of narcissistic pathology and the related pathology of internalized object relations.

As mentioned before, Kohut considered that in patients who have achieved the transmuting internalization of the idealized selfobject into the ego ideal and the consequent integration of the superego, the conditions exist for consolidation of the tripartite structure and for the development of drive-determined, oedipal, unconscious intrapsychic conflict. The question can be raised, however, to what extent this is a compromise solution that will be abandoned by Kohut's followers in favor of a more complete psychology of the self, in total replacement of Freudian metapsychology. This theoretical ambiguity is reflected in Kohut's assertion that, while the vicissitudes of the consolidation and maturation of the self are not derived from drives or intrapsychic conflict, the emergence, at times of traumatic fragmentation of the archaic grandiose self, of sexual and aggressive drive derivatives reflects disintegration products of the self. Thus, in Kohut's thinking, the self does not derive from drives but generates drives by fragmentation.

Kohut's theory has left a series of questions unanswered: If instinct theory is to be abandoned, what motivates the self? What spurs it on? If aggression and libido are disintegration products, how can their presence be explained? Why do selfobjects not undergo developmental transformations? And what, if any, role do object relations play in the preoedipal stages of development?

Whatever the answers to these questions, I think that the adherents of Kohut's theory of the self eventually will have to deal with the issues of motivation, early development, and the role of object relations.

Ego-Psychology Object Relations Approach

The foregoing critiques have incorporated many of my own theoretical ideas on normal and pathological narcissism. (See also Kernberg, 1975, 1976, 1980.) In summary, I might add that my approach differs from the traditional psychoanalytic viewpoint stemming from Freud's (1914) pioneering examination of narcissism, according to which there first exists a narcissistic libido and later an object libido. It also takes issue with Kohut's (1971) views that narcissistic libido and object libido start out together and then evolve separately and that aggression in narcissistic personalities is secondary to their narcissistic lesions. It is my belief that the development of normal and pathological narcissism always involves the relationship of the self representations to object representations and external objects as well as instinctual conflicts involving both libido and aggression. If my formulations are valid, it would seem that the study of narcissism cannot be divorced from the study of the vicissitudes of both libido and aggression and of internalized object relations.

The concept of the self I am proposing remains harmoniously close to Freud's original concept of the *Ich*, the I, the ego (see chap. 14). It remains related to and dependent on the dynamic unconscious as a constant, underlying current that influences psychic functioning. The basic reason I propose to define the self as the sum total of integrated self representations from all developmental stages rather than as simply a "composite" self representation derives from the central function that this organization or structure plays in development. I strongly believe that the importance of differentiating the normal self from the pathological (grandiose) self of narcissistic personalities and from the conflictually determined, dissociated or split-off self in borderline personality organization justifies the use of this term. My concept treats the self as a purely psychological entity whose origin and normal and pathological development I will now briefly explore.

Jacobson (1971) and Mahler (Mahler and Furer, 1968; Mahler et al., 1975) expanded our understanding of the genetic and developmental continuity that exists in a broad range of nonorganic psychopathology. Both Jacobson and Mahler used a structural concept. The regressive pathological refusion and even fragmentation of self and object representations in manic-depressive illness and schizophrenia that Jacobson described correspond to the undifferentiated self and object representations in the symbiotic psychosis of childhood that Mahler described. Mahler's research on normal and pathological separation-individuation, particularly her specifying the rapprochement subphase as related to borderline psychopathology, applied Jacobson's concept to the under-standing of the incapacity to achieve object constancy in borderline con-ditions. Mahler provided the clinical evidence that permitted us to estab-lish timetables for the developmental stages of internalized object relations proposed by Jacobson. My own work on the pathology of internalized object relations of borderline conditions evolved in the con-text of that theoretical frame.

Thus, it is now possible, within Freudian metapsychology, to ana-lyze developmentally and genetically the relation between various types and degrees of psychopathology and a failure to achieve normal stages of integration of internalized object relations and the self.

(1) Psychotic illness is related to a lack of differentiated self and ob-ject representations, with a consequent blurring not only of boundaries between self and object representations but of ego boundaries as well. Loss of reality testing is therefore a key structural characteristic of psychosis.

(2) Borderline conditions are characterized by differentiation of self and object representations and therefore by the maintenance of reality testing but also by an incapacity to synthesize the self as an integrated concept and the concepts of significant others. A predominance of split-ting mechanisms and related dissociated or split-off multiple self and ob-ject representations characterizes the ego structure of these conditions and explains the defensive fixation at a level of lack of integration of the self and the failure of superego integration (Kernberg, 1975).

(3) My research into the psychopathology and treatment of narcis-sistic personalities has provided clinical evidence in support of the fol-lowing ideas:

(a) Although normal narcissism reflects the libidinal investment of the self (as defined earlier), the normal self actually constitutes a struc-ture that has integrated components invested with both libido and ag-gression. Integration of "good" and "bad" self representations into a re-alistic self concept that incorporates rather than dissociates the various component self representations is a requisite for the libidinal investment of a normal self. This requirement explains the paradox that integration of love and hate is a prerequisite for the capacity for normal love.

(b) The specific narcissistic resistances of patients with narcissistic character pathology reflect a pathological narcissism that differs from both ordinary adult narcissism and fixation at or regression to normal infantile narcissism. In contrast to the latter, pathological narcissism re-flects libidinal investment not in a normal integrated self structure but in a pathological self structure. This pathological grandiose self contains real self, ideal self, and ideal object representations. Devalued or aggressively determined self and object representations are split off or dissociated, repressed, or projected. The psychoanalytic resolution of the grandiose self as part of a systematic analysis of narcissistic character resistances regularly brings to the surface (that is, activates in the transference) primitive object relations, conflicts, ego structures, and defensive operations characteristic of developmental stages that predate object constancy. These transferences, however, are always condensed with oedipally derived conflicts, so that they are strikingly similar to those of patients with borderline personality organization.

(c) The resolution by psychoanalytic treatment of these primitive transferences and their related unconscious conflicts and defensive operations permits the gradual integration of contradictory self and object representations containing libidinal and aggressive investments and, in the process, the integration and consolidation of a normal self. Simultaneously, object relations evolve from partial into total ones, object constancy can be achieved, and both pathological self-love and pathological investment of others are resolved.

(d) Pathological narcissism can be understood only in terms of the vicissitudes of libidinal and aggressive drive derivatives; pathological narcissism reflects not only libidinal investment in the self rather than in objects or object representations but also libidinal investment in a pathological self structure. Similarly, the structural characteristics of narcissistic personalities cannot be understood simply in terms of fixation at an early normal level of development or of the failure of certain intrapsychic structures to develop; they must be seen as a consequence of pathological ego and superego development, derived from pathological development of the self, as now defined.

(4) The absence of controversy regarding the concept of the self as it applies to the healthier spectrum of psychopathology reflects the clinical finding of an integrated self and the capacity for object relations in depth as reflecting these patients' achievement of object constancy. Neurotic patients present an integrated, normal self centered upon the conscious and preconscious aspects of the ego, although including unconscious aspects as well. This normal self is the supraordinate organizer of key ego functions such as reality testing, synthesizing, and integrating. The fact that neurotic patients may have severe disturbances in their relations with others and yet are able to maintain an observing function of their ego, to present a "reasonable and cooperative ego" as part of their armamentarium for psychoanalytic treatment, is a reflection of their having available an integrated self.

(5) This brings us, finally, to a concept of the normal self that, in contrast to the pathological grandiose self, emerges naturally as the tripartite intrapsychic structure is constructed and integrated. From both

clinical and theoretical standpoints we can thus define the self as an integrated structure that has affective and cognitive components, a structure embedded in the ego but derived from precursors of the ego: intrapsychic substructures that predate the integration of the tripartite structure. This view represents a gradual shift away from Rapaport's (1960) depersonified concept of the origins and characteristics of the tripartite structure. The repressive barriers that remain in effect and that maintain the dynamic equilibrium of the tripartite structure also maintain the shadow of unconscious influence and control over the self, not in terms of an abstract psychic energy conceived of along hydraulic lines but in terms of repressed internalized object relations, libidinally and aggressively invested, which strive for reactivation through invasion of the self's intrapsychic and interpersonal field.

Clinical Aspects

For practical purposes, we may classify narcissism into normal adult, normal infantile, and pathological narcissism. Normal infantile narcissism, of significance here only because fixation at or regression to infantile narcissistic goals is an important feature of all character pathology, is characterized by a normal though excessively infantile self structure and a normal internalized world of object relations. Normal adult narcissism exists when self-esteem is regulated by means of a normal self structure related to normal integrated or total internalized object representations; by an integrated, largely individualized and abstracted superego; and by the gratification of instinctual needs within the context of stable object relations and value systems.

In contrast, pathological narcissism is characterized by an abnormal self structure that can be of two types. One type was first described by Freud (1914) as an illustration of "narcissistic object choice." Here the patient's self is pathologically identified with an object while the representation of the patient's infantile self is projected onto that object, thus creating a libidinal relation in which the functions of self and object have been interchanged. This is quite frequently found in cases of male and female homosexuality. Again, although narcissistic conflicts are severer in these patients than in those with character pathology of the normal infantile narcissistic type, they present a normally integrated self and a normal internalized world of object relations.

A second and more distorted type of pathological narcissism is the narcissistic personality proper, a specific type of character pathology that centers on the presence of a pathological grandiose self. Patients with narcissistic personality function along a broad range of social effectiveness. Their surface functioning may show very little disturbance. Only on diagnostic exploration do these patients reveal an excessive degree of self-reference in their interactions with others, an excessive need to be loved and admired, and a curious contradiction between a very inflated concept of themselves and occasional feelings of extreme inferiority. In addition, they have an inordinate need for tribute from others, their emotional life is shallow, and, whereas they usually present some integration of their conscious self-experience, which differentiates them from the typical patient with borderline personality organization, they have a remarkable absence of the capacity for an integrated concept of others, feel little empathy for others, and present a predominance of the same primitive defensive operations that characterize borderline personality organization.

People with narcissistic personalities tend to be inordinately envious of other people, to idealize some people, from whom they expect narcissistic supplies, and to depreciate and treat with contempt those from whom they do not expect anything (often their former idols). Their relations with others are frequently exploitative and parasitic. Beneath a surface that is often charming and engaging, one senses coldness and ruthlessness. They typically feel restless and bored when no new sources feed their self-regard. Because of their great need for tribute and adoration from others, they are often considered to be excessively dependent. But they are, in fact, unable to depend on anyone because of a deep underlying distrust and devaluation of others and an unconscious "spoiling" of what they receive related to conflicts about unconscious envy.

In psychoanalytic treatment, if and when their pathological grandiose self is systematically explored and resolved by means of interpretation, they evidence intense conflicts in which condensation of oedipal and preoedipal issues predominates, with an overriding influence of preoedipal sources of aggression linked to their specific conflicts about envy. In other words, beneath the protective structure of the pathological grandiose self, they reveal the typical conflicts of borderline personality organization. Their superficial relative lack of object relations is a defense against underlying, intensely pathological, internalized object relations.

The psychic structure of the narcissistic personality as described has relevance for treatment, explaining both the development of negative therapeutic reactions linked to unconscious sources of envy and the possibility of resolving, simultaneously with the resolution of their pathological grandiose self, the pathology of their internalized object relations. This concept of psychic structure has important theoretical implications as well. In contrast to the traditional psychoanalytic thinking, that severe narcissism reflects a fixation at an early narcissistic stage of development and a failure to develop object love, what obtains in these cases is that an abnormal development of self-love coexists with an abnormal development of love for others: Narcissism and object relations cannot be separated from each other.

At the highest level of functioning of narcissistic personalities, we find patients without neurotic symptoms, with good surface adaptation, and with very little awareness of any emotional illness except for a chronic sense of emptiness or boredom, an inordinate need for tribute from others and for personal success, and a remarkable incapacity for intuitive understanding, empathy, and emotional investment in others. Highly intelligent patients at this level of narcissistic personality functioning may seem quite creative, but careful observation of their productivity over a long period of time will give evidence of superficiality and flightiness. Few of these patients come to treatment unless they are suffering from some complicating neurotic symptom; they tend to develop, over the years, secondary complications to their narcissistic pathology, which worsens their functioning in middle and advanced age but, paradoxically, also improves their prognosis for psychoanalytic treatment in the middle years (Kernberg, 1980; see also chap. 4). At that stage of life, they tend to develop chronic depressive reactions, highly inappropriate use of denial, devaluation, and at times hypomanic personality traits to defend themselves against depression, and an increasing sense of emptiness and of having wasted their life.

The middle range of the spectrum of narcissistic psychopathology corresponds to the typical cases I just described, which ideally have an indication for standard psychoanalysis.

At the severest level of the spectrum of narcissistic pathology we find patients who, despite the defensive functions that the pathological grandiose self provides for some continuity in social interactions, present overt borderline features—that is, lack of impulse control, lack of anxiety tolerance, severe crippling of their sublimatory capacities, and a disposition to explosive or chronic rage reactions or severely paranoid distortions. Many of these patients respond well to modified expressive psychotherapy rather than to psychoanalysis proper. The treatment coincides with that outlined for borderline personality organization (see chaps. 6 and 7), modified in the light of the psychoanalytic technique described below. When expressive psychotherapy is contraindicated, a supportive approach is recommended for these patients.

One prognostically crucial dimension along which one can explore narcissistic personality structures is the extent to which aggression has been integrated into the pathological grandiose self or, to the contrary, remains restricted to the underlying, dissociated, and/or repressed primitive object relations against which the pathological grandiose self represents the main defensive structure. One may describe a developmental sequence of the integration of aggression into the psychic apparatus, from (1) primitive dissociation or splitting of aggressively invested object relations from libidinally invested object relations, to (2) later condensation of such primitive aggressive object relations with sexual drive derivatives in the context of polymorphous perverse sexual strivings, to (3) predominant channeling of aggression into a pathological narcissistic character structure with direct investment of aggression by the pathological grandiose self. All three of these developmental fixations and/or regressions can be found in narcissistic personalities, each leading to different clinical characteristics.

When dissociated, aggressively invested part-object relations are directly manifest, we encounter the overt borderline-functioning narcissistic personality, with general impulsivity and a proneness to paranoid developments and narcissistic rage. When condensation with partial sexual drives has taken place, sadistically infiltrated polymorphous perverse fantasies and activities are highly manifest. When primitive aggression directly infiltrates the pathological grandiose self, a particularly ominous development occurs, perhaps best described as malignant narcissism (see chap. 19).

In this last instance we find narcissistic patients whose grandiosity and pathological self-idealization are reinforced by the sense of triumph over fear and pain through inflicting fear and pain on others, and also cases in which self-esteem is enhanced by the sadistic pleasure of aggression linked with sexual drive derivatives. Narcissistic personalities with joyful types of cruelty; patients who obtain a sense of superiority and triumph over life and death, as well as conscious pleasure, by severe self-mutilation; and narcissistic patients with a combination of paranoid and explosive personality traits, whose impulsive behavior, rage attacks, and blaming are major channels for instinctual gratification, all may reflect the condensation of aggression and a pathological grandiose self and may find the treatment situation a welcome and stable outlet for aggression that militates against structured intrapsychic change.

In other narcissistic personalities, however, the grandiose self is remarkably free from directly expressed aggression. Repressive mechanisms protect the patient against the underlying primitive object relations that condense sexual and aggressive drive derivatives. In these cases "narcissistic rage" or paranoid reactions develop in later stages of the treatment as part of the therapeutic process and have far less ominous implications.

There are still other cases in which some sublimatory integration of aggression has taken place, related to neurotic character structures in which aggression has been integrated with existing superego structures; these patients have a clinically more favorable type of self-directed aggression and capability for depression. Also, some narcissistic personalities functioning at the highest level may have achieved sublimatory integration of aggression into relatively adaptive ego functions, pursuing ambitious goals with an appropriate integration of aggressive drive derivatives.

A relatively infrequent and particularly complicated type of narcissistic personality is the "as if" personality, which differs from the usual type of "as if" personality (with its chameleon-like, ever-shifting, pseudohyperemotional, and pseudoadaptive qualities). The "as if" qualities in the patients I have in mind reflect secondary defenses against a pathological grandiose self. These patients are reminiscent of Marcel Marceau miming the man who takes off one mask after another and finally discovers in despair that he cannot tear the last one off. These patients shift from act to act without knowing who the actor is, other than that he is a sum of impersonations. Usually this character constellation protects the patient from severe paranoid fears; less frequently, against unconscious guilt.

In the light of the integration of or defenses against aggression outlined, the most serious cases prognostically are those with a pathological infiltration of aggression into the grandiose self per se and those in whom secondary, "as if" characteristics represent a defense against strong underlying paranoid traits.

A final factor that also has crucial prognostic significance for the treatment of narcissistic personalities is the extent to which antisocial trends are built into the patient's narcissistic character pathology. The stronger the antisocial tendencies, the poorer the prognosis. Usually, antisocial tendencies go hand in hand with a lack of integration of normal superego functions and also with the failure to develop a modulated capacity for depressive reactions. The quality of object relations is also inversely related to antisocial trends. When antisocial trends are manifested in patients who also present a sadistic infiltration of the pathological grandiose self or direct expression of severely sadistic sexual behavior, the prognosis significantly worsens.

CHAPTER 12: *Technical Strategies in the Treatment of Narcissistic Personalities*

The most important aspect of the psychoanalytic treatment of narcissistic personalities is the systematic analysis of the pathological grandiose self, which presents itself pervasively in the transference.

What is unique about narcissistic character pathology is that the pathological grandiose self is utilized in the transference precisely to avoid the emergence of the dissociated, repressed, or projected aspects of self and object representations of primitive object relations. The effect of the activation of the grandiose self in the psychoanalytic situation is a basic distance, an emotional unavailability, a subtle but chronic absence of the normal or "real" aspects of a human relationship between the patient and analyst in which the patient treats the analyst as a specific individual. In contrast, the activation of a pathological self-idealization on the patient's part, alternating with a projection of such self-idealization onto the analyst, conveys the impression that there is only one ideal, grandiose person in the room and an admiring yet shadowy complement to it. Frequent role reversals between patient and analyst illustrate this basically stable transference pattern.

Elsewhere (1975), I have described the manifestations of this transference constellation in detail, its recruitment, at its service, of primitive defense mechanisms and their functions, and the analysis of its various aspects. Here I would only stress that the analyst has to interpret, among other things, the mechanism of omnipotent control by which the patient characteristically attempts to redesign the analyst to suit his own needs. The analyst must give the impression of being brilliant and knowledgeable so that the patient will feel that he is in the presence of the greatest therapist of all time. Yet the analyst must not be too brilliant lest he evoke the patient's envy and resentment. The analyst has to be as good as the patient; neither better—thus evoking envy—nor worse—thus provoking devaluation and a sense of total loss.

The analyst's systematic efforts to help the patient understand the nature of this transference rather than to fulfill his expectations for admiration and reconfirmation of the grandiose self typically evoke anger, rage, or a sudden devaluation of the analyst and his comments. Similar reactions characteristically follow times when the patient has felt important understanding and help coming from the analyst, understanding and help that painfully bring him to an awareness of the analyst's autonomous, independent functioning. The analyst's tolerance of such periods of rage or devaluation, his interpretation of the reasons for the patient's reactions gradually permit the patient to integrate the positive and negative aspects of the transference: to integrate idealization and trust with rage, contempt, and paranoid distrust.

Behind the apparently simple activation of narcissistic rage lies the activation of specific, primitive, unconscious internalized object relations of the past, typically of split-off self and object representations reflecting condensed oedipal/preoedipal conflicts. In this context, periods of emptiness and the patient's feeling that "nothing is happening" in the treatment situation may often be clarified as an active, unconscious destruction of what the patient is receiving from the analyst, a reflection of the patient's inability to depend on the analyst as a giving maternal figure.

The patient's avid efforts to obtain knowledge and understanding from the analyst in order to incorporate them as something forcefully extracted rather than something received with gratitude contribute to the unconscious spoiling of what is received, a complex emotional reaction first clarified by Rosenfeld (1964) and one that usually takes a long time to resolve. Typically, lengthy periods of intellectual self-analysis, during which the patient treats the analyst as absent (which may elicit negative countertransference in the form of boredom), are followed by or interspersed with periods when the patient eagerly expects and absorbs interpretations, attempts to outguess the analyst, rapidly incorporates what he has received as if he himself knew it all along, only once more to feel strangely empty, dissatisfied, as not having received anything after this new knowledge has been, as it were, metabolized.

By the same token, the patient typically, by projection, assumes that the analyst has no genuine interest in him, is as self-centered and exploitative as the patient experiences himself to be, and has no authentic knowledge or convictions but only a limited number of tricks and magical procedures which the patient needs to learn and incorporate. The more corrupt the patient's superego, and the more he needs to project devalued self and object representations, the more he suspects the analyst of presenting similarly corrupt and devalued characteristics. The gradual emergence or breakthrough of more primitive transferences may shift this overall picture into the expression of paranoid distrust and direct aggression in the transference. The apparent disruption of what may have earlier appeared as an "ideal" relation represents, in a deeper sense, the activation of a more real, though ambivalent and conflictual, relation in the transference, reflecting the activation of primitive object relations in it.

Some common and particularly difficult chronic character defenses that tend to distort the psychoanalytic situation gradually and incrementally are discussed below.

Secondary Character Defenses

As-If Character Resistances

I am referring here not to the "as if" personality as usually described but to the subgroup of narcissistic patients (mentioned in chap. 11) who always seem to be playacting. Patients with such characteristics may learn to imitate the "perfect analysand," apparently conveying significant elements of the past with appropriate thoughtfulness and in dramatic revelations. They learn to "associate perfectly," including appropriate shifts from feeling to thinking, from present to past, from fantasy to reality. Only the fact that their emotional relation to the analyst fails to deepen reveals their as-if quality. The paranoid fears that may emerge when no playacting can be achieved in response to the analyst's interpretation of this very condition reveal the real point of conflict. The activation of authentic anxiety and pain may lead to the beginning of the exploration of the function of this behavior.

Paranoid Micropsychotic Episodes

This term refers here to developments in some narcissistic personalities when narcissistic resistances are worked through and also in other types of character pathology when massive projective mechanisms are analyzed and the patient is attempting to defend himself against what he experiences as unbearable guilt feelings alternating with the sense of being massively attacked by the analyst. (For further details, see chap. 19.) At such points, the patient may, for example, transitorily acquire the conviction that the analyst is lying to him, cheating him, betraying him in some way, artificially attempting to provoke him or make him suffer, or obtaining sadistic pleasure from manipulating him in various ways. The analyst may also be perceived as dishonest or corrupt at such times, especially, of course, by patients who struggle with a sense of corruption or dishonesty in themselves. At other times, the analyst is perceived as attempting sadistically to make the patient feel guilty or trying callously to oblige him to submit to the analyst's rigid, conventional viewpoints.

The problem is that such paranoid episodes may be resolved by a sealing over of the paranoid transference rather than by authentic working through. The patient's profound conviction of the analyst's unworthiness then remains repressed or split off from other transference developments. This compromise solution may temporarily protect the patient's sense of security and self-esteem but it eventually leads to reactivation of such paranoid episodes. The patient's conviction of the analyst's "badness" gradually accumulates from episode to episode, eventually leading to a massive acting out, a sudden disruption of the treatment, or an artificial kind of termination, with the patient's insisting that he could never trust the analyst and that termination is an escape from a dangerous enemy. It was only the painful experience of the failure of some psychoanalytic treatments that seemed on the road to resolution of various types of severe character pathology that permitted me to diagnose this constellation of paranoid episodes. I have learned to work them through in other cases by interpretively linking the episodes, by analyzing the pathogenic "sealing over" process during temporary improvements, and by being generally alert to the continuity masked by apparent discontinuities in the transference. In more general terms, character resistances that bring about a discontinuity in the psychoanalytic process over time are an important cause of analytic stalemates and should alert the analyst to the possibility that the patient may not be analyzable.

The Problem of Secondary—and Primary—Gain

In contrast to the secondary gains derived from certain neurotic symptoms, all pathological character traits provide a "secondary gain" that is very difficult to differentiate from the primary, unconscious motivation of the pathological character constellation. Paradoxically, the adaptive qualities of many types of severe character pathology improve the patient's functioning and diminish his motivation for change. The classical examples are the advantages derived from certain narcissistic traits in adolescence and early adulthood that worsen the prognosis for treatment at that time, whereas such patients have a better prognosis in middle age, or when gains stemming from the narcissistic pathology are reduced. The social effectiveness of some counterphobic characters provides another example.

Characterological Sadism

I am referring here to certain narcissistic patients whose pathological grandiose self is infiltrated with primitive aggression and whose sadism is ego-syntonic (a condition elaborated on in chap. 19).

For these patients, the analytic situation itself is so gratifying that it eliminates the need for change, which leads to therapeutic stalemate. The extent to which the analyst can maintain empathy with his patient without submitting masochistically to him and can provide strict limits in reality without in turn acting out sadistic aspects of the countertransference may have a crucial influence on the outcome of work with these character resistances. These are obviously cases in which analyzability is in question; the conditions under which the analyst may help such patients also hold for cases in which psychoanalysis is contraindicated but expressive psychotherapy is the treatment of choice.

Characterologically Defended Severe Repression: The "Dull" Personality

This subsection discusses patients with at least normal and often superior intelligence whose repressive mechanisms are not only highly effective and rigid but are reinforced by their character pathology. In such patients a complicated system of rationalization and controlled "living out" of reaction formations secondarily protect repression, and/or emotional crises hide, behind their explosiveness, the maintenance of basic underlying repressions. It is difficult to link this pattern to any particular type of character pathology. It can be observed in hysterical, obsessive, and narcissistic personalities and sometimes in patients who, despite their lack of awareness of emotional reality, are very willing to undergo psychoanalysis for many years. These patients, who do not present a narcissistic personality structure, nevertheless convey a resilient, pseudorealistic adaptation to the treatment situation that corresponds to a similarly "solid" adaptation to life outside their particular area of symptomatic disturbance. It is as if they experience psychoanalysis only as an "educational" opportunity that further increases their adaptation without bringing about any authentic experience of the dynamic unconscious.

I have seen a few such cases and have supervised the treatment of others. The earlier literature described cases in which the unconscious did not seem to emerge as prevalent, but out of this general category the more specific constellations of types of negative therapeutic reaction, narcissistic character pathology, and other character resistances have crystallized. I think that there remains a residue of such cases that requires further exploration. Some of these patients escape our present diagnostic capabilities and are diagnosed now only in terms of the stalemates in their analyses.

Advanced Stages of the Treatment

After several years of systematic exploration of the defensive functions of the pathological grandiose self in the transference, a stage may be reached in the psychoanalytic treatment of narcissistic personalities in which the grandiose self disintegrates into its constituents. The patient enacts internalized object relations in a repetitive alternation or interchange with the analyst of representations of the patient's real and ideal self, ideal object, and real object. In other words, the patient may alternately identify with the idealized, grandiose, persecutory, frustrating, manipulative, dishonest, sadistic, or triumphant aspects of the idealized or real aspects of early self and object representations while projecting the complementary roles of persecuted, devalued, frustrated, defeated, or exploited self and object representations onto the analyst. Or the patient may project such component representations of the grandiose self onto the analyst while he identifies with the complementary roles of infantile self and object representations.

This stage in the treatment is rarely reached before the third year of psychoanalysis; if it has not yet become apparent by the fifth year one may have to ask whether resolution of the patient's pathological grandiose self is possible. Most frequently, the working through of this stage extends from the third year to the termination phase of psychoanalysis. In the final stages of resolution of the grandiose self the treatment situation usually resembles that of the ordinary psychoanalytic case in that the patient can now establish a real dependence on the analyst, can explore both his oedipal and preoedipal conflicts in a differentiated fashion, and can simultaneously normalize his pathological object relations and his narcissistic regulatory mechanisms.

Because the pathological grandiose self protects the patient from the intense intrapsychic conflicts so typical of borderline pathology, the unconscious conflicts emerging in the transference at this stage are strikingly similar to those of borderline personality organization in general.

Throughout these years a therapeutic alliance can usually be established, which prevents psychotic regressions in the transference, permits the analyst to control severe acting out without abandoning a position of technical neutrality, and facilitates the development of the patient's observing ego and of a reliable object relation with the analyst. All this permits the psychoanalytic treatment to proceed without setting up parameters of technique, such as are often necessary in the treatment of narcissistic patients with overt borderline functioning.

During advanced stages of the treatment of narcissistic personalities one often observes an oscillation between periods of idealization and overtly negative transference, in the course of which the pathological narcissistic idealization described above is gradually replaced by higher levels of idealization. It is important to explore the changing nature of these periods of renewed idealization. At the higher level—in contrast to narcissistic idealization—the patient no longer views the analyst as a projection of his self idealization (narcissistic idealization) but sees him as an ideal parental (or combined parental) figure who has been able to tolerate the patient's aggression without counterattacking or being destroyed by it. This advanced type of idealization contains elements of guilt, which express the patient's acknowledgment of his aggression; it also contains gratitude, which expresses the patient's understanding of the analyst's confidence and trust in him, reflected in the unwavering though tactful adherence to the truth of what has been going on in their relation.

Periods of predominantly negative transference, characterized by rage, the activation of a relation with a threatening, sadistic, dishonest, and manipulative mother or condensed mother/father figure, may gradually evolve into the patient's alternately identifying with this sadistic parental image or with the complementary image of the persecuted victim of parental aggression, thus identifying himself and the analyst alternately with previously dissociated or split-off self and object representations. The analysis of the alternate activation of these self and object representations of this particular "object relation unit" may then be gradually integrated with the dissociated or split-off idealized part-object relations, so that self representations gradually coalesce into an integrated self and object representations into an integrated concept of the parental objects.

In advanced stages of the treatment, after this systematic interpretation of the positive and negative transferences has permitted the integration of part-object into total-object relations (in other words, after the achievement of object constancy with an integration of good and bad self representations and of good and bad object representations), the dissolution of the pathological grandiose self and of narcissistic resistances in general permits the emergence of normal infantile narcissism in the context of the analysis of condensed oedipal and preoedipal relations.

During advanced stages of the treatment of narcissistic personalities, a normal capacity to depend on the analyst gradually replaces the previous incapacity to depend on him. Now the patient may use interpretations to continue his self-exploration rather than as a starting point for greedy expropriation of hidden knowledge from the analyst. The patient may now talk about himself to the analyst instead of talking to himself alone or to the analyst only as a plea for gratification. The patient may now experience new sources of gratification and security from the certainty that he is able to learn about himself, to deal creatively with his own difficulties, and, above all, to maintain securely inside, in the form of internalized good object representations, what he has received from the analyst.

The sense of internal wealth stemming from the gratitude for what he has received and confidence in his own goodness typically brings about a decrease in the patient's envious reactions and in his need to devalue what otherwise would trigger envy; the patient may observe a parallel increase in his capacity for emotional and intellectual learning. The patient, in short, gradually feels free of his internal sense of emptiness, the pathological, driven quality of his ambitions, and the chronic feeling of boredom and restlessness.

In the area of his sexual conflicts, in addition to the activation and potential resolution of oedipal conflicts condensed with preoedipal issues, the patient may now tolerate and resolve the deepest preoedipal roots of envy of the other sex, which is such a prominent aspect of the sexual difficulties of narcissistic personalities and a basic source of their unconscious rejection of a sexual identity that would have to be limited to "one sex only." Grunberger (1979) described the unconscious narcissistic fantasies of being both sexes simultaneously, which protect some narcissistic patients from envying the other sex. Clinically, change in this unconscious fantasy and the working through of envy influence the narcissistic patient's growing capacity to fall in love and remain in love, and particularly to establish a definite sexual and emotional commitment without chronically feeling that he is missing something (Kernberg, 1976). At this stage, some patients' resolution of their unconscious, inordinate envy of the other sex may bring about the appearance of jealousy as a new emotional capacity, a painful entry into the triangular conflicts of the oedipal stage.

I have stressed the overriding importance of a systematic analysis of narcissistic transference resistances—that is, of the pathological grandiose self in the transference. This does not imply an artificially chartered course of action in the treatment of patients with narcissistic pathology. There are many cases in which, in the initial stages of the treatment, other neurotic conflicts stemming from various sources or linked with reality problems appear to dominate the patient's material. The analyst has to take up what seems emotionally dominant in the analytic situation first and let himself be guided by the patient. Sooner or later, a point is reached in the analysis of these cases where narcissistic transferences become the dominant emotional theme; these must then be taken up, worked through, and resolved.

This task is made more difficult by the fact that narcissistic character pathology, like all character pathology, shows typically in the nonverbal aspects of the patient's behavior. In addition, what the nonverbal behavior of the patient reflects in these cases is not only a specific unconscious object relation of the past reactivated in the transference but a more generalized, subtle, yet overwhelming unconscious effort to eliminate all specific, "real," past and present object relations other than the activation of the pathological grandiose self.

That destruction or deterioration in the analytic situation of all other specific transference relations from the patient's past affects the relation of the patient to the psychoanalytic setting in subtle and chronic ways, not only in specific behaviors and attitudes toward the analyst. It may appear first in the analyst's emotional awareness of the strange absence of any real dyadic relation in the transference, as if he were alone in the office or as if the patient were alone; the analyst may subjectively experience a diffuse, paralyzing transitory loss of his own sense of identity.

It would be dangerous to conclude, however, that the analyst's concentration on his own emotional reaction to the patient is an exclusive guideline to the diagnosis and interpretation of narcissistic resistances. There is always the danger that other sources of countertransference reactions influence the analyst's perception of the patient and that in the presence of any predominant character pathology—including narcissistic pathology—the analyst may focus rigidly or prematurely on the analysis of character or of certain frozen aspects of the transference. The analyst needs to focus simultaneously on the implications of the verbal content of the hours (the analysis of free associations), on the manifestations of nonverbal behavior, on the impact of the patient's personality on the psychoanalytic setting, and on the implicit and underlying constant type of relation with the analyst that is being activated. Observation of the patient's behavior, cognitive analysis of all the data, and empathy both with the patient's subjective experience and with what he has dissociated or projected at that point provide a broad base for interpretation.

I am stressing here the importance of maintaining a broad spectrum of psychoanalytic data rather than overemphasizing any particular aspect of these sources of information. Such multiple perspectives, including a focus on the central subjective experience of the patient, on the patient's dissociated experiences, and on the direct meaning of verbal and nonverbal communications, need to be complemented by the analyst's willingness to explore various hypotheses dealing with the same material over a period of time, deciding on their value, on their appropriateness in the light of the patient's total responses to them. A condition for the application of multiple hypotheses over time, however, is the availability to the psychoanalyst of a coherent integration of such hypotheses, in contrast to the erratic application of different and implicitly contradictory theories or formulations. The developmental frame evolved from contemporary ego psychology in the light of object relations theory should permit the establishment of such an integrative frame for dealing with the broad spectrum of psychopathology that today can be psychoanalytically explored.

Modell (1976) and Volkan (1976), while approaching narcissistic personalities within an ego-psychology object relations model quite closely related to the one underlying my technique, have proposed that, in the initial stage of the analysis of these patients, the narcissistic idealization and the patient's incapacity to absorb interpretations be respected in a "holding" function that corresponds to a "cocoon" phase of the analysis. These authors think, however, that the analyst must gradually interpret the narcissistic grandiose self and thus facilitate the activation of the patient's primitive levels of internalized object relations in the transference. From that point on, I think their approach largely corresponds to the one outlined here.

Supportive Psychotherapy with Narcissistic Personalities

In chapter 11 I classified narcissistic personalities according to the severity of their pathology into overtly borderline cases and nonborderline-functioning cases, and in chapter 10 I recommended psychoanalysis as the treatment of choice for the latter in contrast to expressive psychotherapy for the former. But at times when expressive psychotherapy is contraindicated, it becomes necessary to use supportive psychotherapy for these patients.

In addition to the general considerations given earlier, a dominance of the following negative prognostic features suggests that supportive psychotherapy is preferable. In some patients the pathological grandiose self is infiltrated with aggression, so that the patient presents with conscious ideals of cruelty and destructiveness which may be manifest in sadistic perversions or in conscious enjoyment of other people's suffering, in violence, and in severe forms of physical self-destructiveness. Other factors suggesting that supportive therapy would be more appropriate include severe antisocial features, chronic absence of actual involvements with other human beings (for example, a restriction of all sexual life to masturbation fantasies), characterologically anchored and rationalized chronic rage reactions, and transitory paranoid psychotic episodes. In all these cases it is advisable to carry out an extensive evaluation with a probing, expressive approach and to decide on a supportive modality of treatment only by exclusion. Again, as in all cases of supportive psychotherapy, treatment goals should be set together with the patient, his active cooperation should be expected, and work between psychotherapy sessions should be monitored.

Typical in the supportive psychotherapy of these patients is the activation of certain defense mechanisms that are characteristic of narcissistic psychopathology and that need to be focused on and worked with in noninterpretive ways. The patient's apparent development of intense dependency on the therapist may be a pseudodependency, rapidly punctured by radical devaluations of the therapist. It is important, therefore, to maintain a realistic therapeutic relationship, focusing on the patient's responsibilities in the treatment process, tactfully cautioning him against unrealistic idealizations of and expectations from the therapist rather than directly feeding into his apparently dependent relation to the therapist. It is helpful to evaluate carefully the patient's disappointment reactions to the treatment sessions for their implicit function of devaluing the therapist and their origins in previous developments in the psychotherapy.

For example, after the patient has received significant new understanding from the therapist, paradoxical disappointments (related to acting out unconscious envy) may be expected; these should be pointed out to the patient in terms of an observable sequence of behavior. The primitive pathological idealization typical of the narcissistic personality should be tactfully acknowledged and its potentially negative effects on the patient's independent functioning pointed out. The patient may see godlike qualities in his therapist, but he should be helped to understand that it is difficult to identify oneself with such a figure without running into serious problems in ordinary life or to accept the responsibility for independent living when a godlike therapist seems to be available to solve all problems magically. Naturally, the connection between primitive idealizations and the rapid spoiling of such idealizations by disappointment reactions and the underlying devaluation may also help the patient to acquire some distance from his tendencies to idealize the therapist in unconsciously self-defeating ways.

Patients with intense rage reactions linked to frustration of narcissistic needs, particularly if these rage reactions evolve into paranoid micropsychotic episodes, require a very active, painstaking evaluation of all elements in the reality of the therapeutic interaction that may have triggered the patient's rage and his paranoid distortions of the therapist. Under the effects of projective mechanisms, the patient's distortions of the reality of the therapeutic interaction must be carefully and tactfully clarified in order to reduce them. The problem here is that the patient may experience any effort to clarify the immediate reality as judgmental or sadistically accusatory on the part of the therapist. It is essential for the therapist to clarify again and again that he is not blaming the patient, that, to the contrary, he is trying to help the patient understand the relation between his perceptions and his emotional reaction, regardless of whether these perceptions were realistic.

There are times when the reality of the interaction cannot be clarified immediately. In these circumstances the task is simply to acknowledge that patient and therapist may perceive reality in completely different ways without necessarily having to accept that one or the other of these perceptions is correct. In practice, a statement such as "I think I understand the way you are seeing my behavior, and I am not arguing with it; at the same time, I must tell you that I see it differently, although I acknowledge your perception as well. Do you think you can tolerate our working together while each of us acknowledges to the other that our views are completely different?" is often sufficient to continue work within a temporarily psychotic transference such as a paranoid micropsychotic episode.

In fact, the therapist's tolerance of a patient's narcissistic rage and paranoid distortion in the transference and his expressing acknowledgment of the patient's courage in maintaining their relationship in the light of such a stressful situation may lay the groundwork for later exploration of the patient's rage reactions and pathological character patterns in other interpersonal interactions.

At the same time, the analysis of what may be going on in other people interacting with the patient, the analysis of their hurt feelings or grandiose or derogatory reactions toward the patient as he describes them, may open the way for later exploration of similar reactive patterns in the patient himself. The analysis of the patient's grandiosity and depreciatory behavior projected onto other people warrants much time because of its potential for leading to the study of similar reactions in the transference.

It is important to analyze the patient's sources of conscious and preconscious distrust in sexual relations (derived from unconscious envy of the other sex and the deep preoedipal pathology in relation to mother that contributes to narcissistic distortions of love relations). The careful exploration of conscious and preconscious sources of distrust and abandonment of sexual partners may have preventive value. By the same token, narcissistic patients with sexual promiscuity require a tolerant acceptance of their behavior. They must be helped to become aware (and to remain tolerant of this awareness) of their incapacity to maintain stable sexual relations and of their consequent loneliness and isolation.

This is an area requiring special tact and patience. A grandiose male patient's search for the perfect unavailable woman, for example, and his relentless destruction of valuable relations with women that he is temporarily able to achieve represent, one might say, an existential tragedy. The therapist, by sharing his understanding of both the patient's needs and his external reality, may make it possible for the patient to attempt new solutions to the problem even though the therapist has not offered direct help. Under optimal circumstances, such an approach may lead to a reduction of the patient's conscious expectations in his relations with the other sex, more careful behavior in his relations with partners, tolerance of some frustrations in the light of awareness of the alternative—chronic loneliness. Unfortunately, supportive psychotherapy is usually much more limited than expressive modalities of treatment in bringing about change in the psychosexual area.

A patient's acting out of a need for omnipotent control in the therapy hours may restrict the therapist's independence of action. In subtle but deeply influential ways, the patient forces the therapist to attempt to be as good as the patient expects him to be—without being better than or different from the patient, which would threaten the patient's self-esteem. In practice this requires the therapist to become aware of the patient's use of disappointment reactions to control him. The therapist must diagnose such disappointment reactions, ventilate them fully, and help the patient to tolerate his disappointments in the therapist and, correspondingly, in others. In the context, realistic exploration of such disappointments may lead the patient to an awareness of his excessive demands upon others and the social conflicts these bring about. Nonjudgmental evaluation of these issues may provide great help to patients who are unaware of how actively they themselves are destroying their opportunities in work and social life.

A major problem with some narcissistic patients who are functioning on an overtly borderline level is the discrepancy between their high ambitions and their incapacity to realize these ambitions. Many patients prefer to go on welfare rather than undergo the humiliation of working in what they consider an inferior job. Active exploration of this contradiction and the therapist's emphasis on the negative effects of social ineffectiveness on self-esteem may help the patient to achieve a compromise solution between his level of aspirations and his capacity.

Narcissistic patients' tendency to eagerly "incorporate" what they receive from the therapist and make it theirs—a tendency related to unconscious "stealing" from the therapist in an effort to compensate for envy of him and to reconfirm the patient's pathological grandiose self (Rosenfeld, 1964)—may actually foster psychotherapeutic work in supportive psychotherapy. The patient may adopt the therapist's ideas and attitudes as his own and use them in his daily life, while still reassuring himself that he can do it all alone. If such an identification with the therapist has adaptive functions, even if it is based on pathological types of idealization, it should be tolerated and its strengthening of the patient's autonomy accepted. In fact, this mechanism has potentially positive effects in supportive psychotherapy of narcissistic personalities by counteracting the potentially negative effects of their unconscious envy.

CHAPTER 13: *Character Analysis*

In line with earlier efforts to enrich an ego-psychology approach to psychoanalytic technique with object relations theory (see Kernberg, 1980, chap. 9), my aim here is to integrate my ideas regarding the structural characteristics of severe character pathologies with Fenichel's (1941) theory of technique. Fenichel's proposals for metapsychological criteria for interpretation both incorporated and critically revised Wilhelm Reich's (1933) technical recommendations for analyzing character resistances.

According to my understanding, unconscious intrapsychic conflicts are not simply conflicts between impulse and defense but are between two opposing units or sets of internalized object relations. Each of these units consists of a self and an object representation under the impact of a drive derivative (clinically, an affect disposition). Both impulse and defense find expression through an affectively imbued internalized object relation.

Pathological character traits carry out dominant, chronic defensive functions in the psychic equilibrium of patients with severe character pathology. All character defenses consist of a defensive constellation of self and object representations directed against an opposite and dreaded, repressed self and object constellation. For example, a man who is excessively submissive may be operating under the influence of a unit consisting of a self representation submitting happily to a powerful and protective parental (object) representation. But this set of representations is defending him against a repressed self representation rebelling angrily against a sadistic and castrating parental representation. These conflicting internalized object relations may, under optimal circumstances, become reactivated in the transference, in which case character defenses become transference resistances. Formulating the interpretation of these transference resistances in terms of their hypothesized internalized object relations may facilitate the reactivation of these component self and object representations in the transference, thus transforming the "hardened" character defense into an active intrapsychic and transferential conflict.

The severer the patient's character pathology, the more pathological character traits acquire specific transference functions and become both character resistances and specific transference resistances simultaneously (Fenichel, 1945b, pp. 29, 537). The compromise formation between impulse and defense represented by these pathological character traits also leads to more or less disguised impulse gratification in the transference. The fact that in severe cases pathological character traits prematurely and consistently intrude in the transference situation means that the patient seems to enter prematurely a stage of severe distortion in his relation to the analyst, which resembles the ordinary transference neurosis but also differs from it. The typical transference neurosis in less severe cases takes some time to develop and is usually accompanied by a diminishing of the patient's neurotic manifestations outside the analytic sessions. The transference of the patient suffering from severe character pathology, however, seems to consist of the patient's playing out in the sessions a pattern that simultaneously persists in the rest of his life as well. In addition, the severity of the pathology is reflected in the degree to which pathological character traits are expressed in nonverbal behavior in the treatment situation rather than by means of free association.

To further complicate matters, the severer the character pathology, the more the patient's nonverbal behavior, examined over many weeks or months, also shows a paradoxical development. Chaotic shifts occur from moment to moment in each psychoanalytic session, making it very difficult to select the predominant material for interpretation. And yet, over a period of weeks, months, or even years, a strange stability in that apparent chaos can be detected. An unconscious, highly specific set of distortions emerges in the patient's relation to the analyst which reflects defensively activated, internalized object relations. These have to be resolved as part of the analysis of the transference in order to obtain significant structural intrapsychic change. Frequently, two contradictory sets of primitive object relations are activated alternately, functioning as defenses against each other; sometimes their mutual dissociation is the dominant resistance that must be worked through. Or else one specific primitive object relation acquires a long-term, subtle, but controlling influence over the patient's relationship with the analyst and expresses itself in a distortion of the psychoanalytic setting over time rather than in concrete developments that fluctuate session by session.

Clinical Vignette

Mr. T. A professional in the field of social rehabilitation, an unmarried man in his mid-thirties, consulted because of difficulties in his relations with women and in his work with clients, a severely limited capacity for empathy, and a general sense of dissatisfaction expressed in experiences of boredom, irritability, and uncertainty over the meaning life held for him. He suffered from a narcissistic personality without overt borderline or antisocial features.

His initial attitude toward entering psychoanalysis and the method of free association was marked by strong ambivalence. On the one hand, he considered me one of the more desirable analysts in the relatively small local professional community where I worked; on the other hand, he thought that psychoanalysis was a rather old-fashioned and "passé" technique, and he regarded what he experienced as my rigid maintenance of a psychoanalytic stance as pompous and pedestrian. His own theoretical approach and background were almost diametrically opposed to psychodynamic views. In the early stages of his psychoanalysis, Mr. T was also extremely concerned about my interest in what he was saying; he suspected me of total indifference to him and interpreted any movement I made behind the couch as activity having no relation with him (such as balancing my checkbook). He became very angry when I failed to remember a name or an event he had mentioned in an earlier session.

Mr. T's free associations centered on his relation with his latest woman friend. At first he considered her very attractive and desirable, but he gradually discovered shortcomings in her that made him feel that she was getting much more from him than he was from her and led him to wish to terminate the relationship. In this context, his general suspiciousness of women, his fear that they were exploiting him, emerged as a major theme. This fear could be traced back to the relation with his mother, a locally prominent socialite who dominated his father and whom he had experienced as dominant, intrusive, dishonest, and manipulative. The patient described his father as a hardworking and effective businessman, withdrawn and chronically unavailable during Mr. T's childhood.

During the first two years of his psychoanalysis, the connection between his reactions to his girlfriend, his mother, and me became more and more evident. I was hypocritically pretending that I was interested in him when in reality I was using him for my own financial interest, or pretending to listen to him when I was engaged in my own activities. Similarly, his girl pretended to love him but was interested only in exploiting him socially and financially. Gradually it also became apparent that in his treatment of her he himself was dominant and exploitative, expecting her to guess his moods and respond to his needs without his paying attention to hers. Whenever I tactfully tried to make him aware of his contribution to their difficulties, Mr. T angrily accused me of trying to make him feel guilty and of acting the way his mother did toward him. He saw me as sly, intrusive, dominant, and guilt provoking, just like his mother.

In the transference, my enactment of the replica of his mother now seemed complete: Either I was silent, indifferent, and only pretending to be interested in him or I was actually interested in brainwashing him with my views by making him feel guilty and sadistically enjoying that control. Efforts to convey to him that he was attributing to me aspects of his own behavior toward women that he could not tolerate himself were futile. He broke up with his girlfriend and, several months later, established a new relationship with a woman which soon became a facsimile of the previous one.

Over the next year, the same issues seemed to repeat themselves endlessly in free association and in his relationship to me. I gradually reached the conclusion that the enactment of the relationship with his mother in the transference and with his girlfriends served powerful defensive as well as instinctual purposes. It was as if he managed to obtain some secret (at least partial) satisfaction of his unacknowledged needs for sadistic control from the women he saw. The women also served as receptacles for massive projection of his mother, thus providing rationalizations for his attacks on them.

In the third year of his psychoanalysis, I realized that Mr. T's relation to me in the transference had basically not changed since the beginning of treatment. Nor had his discovery of childhood experiences with his mother (which explained, apparently, his current relations to his girlfriends and to me) resulted in any change of his consciously held convictions about his present or past. I also noticed in his continuing suspicion and anger toward me an easy activation of fantasies of stopping the treatment. Although he never actually stopped, I did not have the feeling of certainty about his engagement in analysis that I had with other patients who might miss occasional sessions when acting out negative transference reactions but without shaking my conviction that they would return. With this man, I sensed both a fragility in our relation and a definite lack of deepening of it.

I also observed, over a period of months, that Mr. T listened to my interpretations eagerly enough, but he then either agreed with them, with the implication that he had earlier reached those very conclusions himself, disagreed with them immediately, or attempted to argue with me about them. Interpretations that he did not accept immediately he simply dismissed. At other times, he appeared very much interested in an interpretation and, in fact, attempted to use it in counseling his own clients, but he never gave any evidence of making use of it to deepen his understanding of himself in his hours with me. In short, his reactions to my interpretations reflected a chronic incapacity to depend upon me for further psychological exploration. Instead, he seemed intent on extracting interpretations from me and appropriating them for his own use. Abraham's (1919), Rosenfeld's (1964), and my own (1975) observations on narcissistic transference resistances clearly applied to this patient.

When I attempted to interpret these dynamics to him and to explore the functions of his attitude, it emerged that Mr. T was protecting himself against intense feelings of envy of me by utilizing for his own purposes whatever he saw as new and good coming from me. These envious feelings and the defenses against them reflected both preoedipal and oedipal conflicts. It gradually became evident to him that, although he could thus protect himself from feeling envious of me, he was precluding using my comments for his own self-exploration. This discovery led us back to his initial derogatory and critical attitude toward psychoanalysis as opposed to his affirmation of his own very different approach to clients.

Over a period of time, Mr. T began to understand that he was torn between his views of me as someone who might be instrumental in helping him to overcome his difficulties with women, someone he would therefore feel extremely envious of, which was intolerable, and someone he did not have to envy at all, which would reconfirm his conviction that nothing was to be expected from psychoanalysis. This analysis of his attitude toward my interpretations and, by implication, of his sharply contradictory and constantly oscillating attitude toward me intensified his sense of restlessness and loneliness in the sessions. He felt that even if what I was pointing out to him was accurate, my doing so implied a grandiose triumph over him and showing off on my part; as a result, he felt powerless, lost, and rejected by me.

In this context, in the fourth year of his psychoanalysis, the following rather protracted episode took place. Mr. T became increasingly alert to whatever he could experience as my shortcomings, both in and outside the sessions. Unbeknown to me, he developed a network of information about me that extended through various related groups in the small town where we both lived and culminated in his establishing contact with a group of disaffected members of the local psychiatric community who deeply resented the institution I was in and my role in it. Mr. T began to extract from one person who felt especially hostile to me information that the patient considered damaging to me, while feeding his contact information about my shortcomings as an analyst. When this information, amplified, came back to my patient through a third person, he became alarmed and "confessed" the whole process to me. That he had for weeks been withholding all these developments from me in itself illustrates the tenuousness of the therapeutic relationship, the limitations in the patient's free associations, and the distortion in the psychoanalytic setting.

My immediate emotional reaction to Mr. T's confession was intense. I felt hurt and angry, controlled by the patient, and helpless. It took several hours before I realized that Mr. T's relationship to his mother had now become activated with reversed roles, that he was now identifying himself with the aggressor, and that I, in the countertransference, was identifying with him as the victim of his mother's manipulations. I also became aware of the patient's intense fear that I might retaliate or abandon him and that this fear was clearly mixed with guilt feelings. After exploring his fantasies about my retaliating and rejecting him—he spontaneously remarked that that is what he would feel like doing in similar circumstances—I said that his description of his own behavior resembled his descriptions of his mother's treatment of him, an interpretation he could now accept. I also told him that his awareness that his curiosity about me contained aggressive elements made it less necessary for him to deny these feelings. Mr. T then said that he had found the exchange of information with the hostile group exciting. He had felt all along that he was transgressing our essential understanding about open communication, risking, as he saw it, the continuation of his relation with me but also experiencing a sense of freedom and power that was exciting, even intoxicating. In fact, he added, now that he was no longer afraid that I would throw him out, he could see something "good" in the entire experience.

Further exploration led to his awareness that his sense of satisfaction, power, and excitement came from his feeling that he could successfully control and manipulate me and I was really quite limited by my analytic attitude; he had never seen our relationship in this context before. This, in turn, led to further exploration of his now activated relationship to me in which he dared to identify with his mother, acknowledging a profound sense of power and satisfaction in expressing aggression that he had never dared to accept in himself, while I appeared in the role of himself, helplessly dominated by him as his own mother. This aggression included elements of orally determined envy and anal-sadistic impulses condensed with castrating impulses (which became dominant at later stages of the analysis).

For the first time, Mr. T was able to experience an identification with the image he had projected of his mother throughout all these years. At the same time, he achieved contact with the aggressive, revengeful components of his envy of me. Over the next few months it became possible to point out to him how his image of himself as helpless, empty, defeated, and lonely vis-à-vis exploitative women was a defense against the opposite self-image, in which he identified with his powerful mother and sadistically enjoyed himself in relating to women and to me as his (her) powerless slaves. The result was an integration of the previously dissociated and repressed sadistic self representation identifying with his mother and the empty, impotent self defensively set up against it. As a consequence, and in the context of the integration of these contradictory affects and self representations, Mr. T became more able to explore his relationship to me in depth and to deepen his understanding of his relationship to women and to his mother as well. Beyond that, a new image of me began to emerge in the transference. I became a tolerant and warm father toward whom the patient experienced dependent and sexual longings, marking, for the first time, a shift in the nature of the predominant transference paradigm and in his experience of the past.

Several technical aspects of this case might be highlighted. First, the early activation of transference resistances (Mr. T's anger and suspicion of my lack of interest in him) repeated aspects of his relations to women. I could therefore immediately integrate the analysis of character resistances with the main themes emerging through free association (his relation to his girlfriends). Next, the partial nature of his self representation, his related incapacity for deepening his emotional relationship to me as well as to his girlfriends, and the corresponding rigidly maintained version of his past gradually emerged as a self-perpetuating, global resistance to further advance in the treatment. Now my focus on the patient's attitude toward my interpretations permitted the interpretation of the most pervasive aspect of his narcissistic personality structure, namely, his identification with a sadistic maternal representation as a core constituent of his pathological grandiose self. The working through of that feature in the transference was necessary for any further move in the psychoanalytic process.

It should be stressed that the excited and sadistic behavior toward me, connected with a dissociated self representation, was available as a conscious experience in Mr. T's relations to various women, where it was expressed only in temper tantrums and protracted emotional storms that were "justified" by his massive projection of mother's image onto the women. Hence, this particular self representation was conscious yet dissociated from self experiences in which Mr. T felt lonely and inferior. He rationalized and protected himself against these feelings by primitive defensive operations, particularly projective identification. The expression of this grandiose and sadistic pattern in the transference and its integration, by means of interpretation, with contradictory self representations of the defeated, exploited child marked the successful completion of a systematic analysis of the corresponding character resistances that had first emerged in relation to my interpretations. In retrospect, the patient could understand that, in rejecting my interpretations as well as in coopting them, he had subtly enacted his mother's role and also his own role as a frustrated child.

This development also illustrates one interesting difference between the narcissistic grandiose self and the dissociated or repressed normal self representations against which the grandiose self is defending. The patient's dominant self-concept was of himself as a mistreated child entitled to compensation. This concept was hidden behind a self-righteous and well-rationalized exploitation of women and a derogatory dismissal of whatever might stir his envy. In contrast, the sadistic, angry, yet excited aspect of the self that emerged in the transference was also part of the normal, aggressively infiltrated self representation, paradoxically closer to authenticity and depth in relation to objects than the defensive surface self representation. At the deepest level, his concept of his sadistic mother included the projection onto her of his own rageful feelings from many sources.

From a still different viewpoint, the sense of stalemate I experienced throughout an important part of the third year of treatment could retrospectively be interpreted as the consequence of the mechanism of omnipotent control. The patient was successfully interfering with my interpretation of the dissociated aggressive aspects of his self, angrily accusing me of trying to make him feel guilty every time I attempted to interpret aggressive aspects of his behavior that he could not accept in himself. It was as if I had to function as a dominant mother or else remain impotently in the background. My hurt and angry reaction after his acting out of the negative transference aspects signaled, in addition to my own countertransference potential, the activation within me of his image of himself as the helpless, attacked, and hurt little boy faced with an overpowering mother. My emotional reaction could thus help me to further analyze an aspect of his experience of himself in relating to his mother, while pointing to his enacting the role of his mother in his relation to me. This formulation makes use of the concepts of concordant and complementary identification in the countertransference proposed by Racker (1957), which emphasized an object relations perspective in the analysis of countertransference.

Strategies of Character Analysis

The severity of character pathology is not in itself sufficient to indicate whether interpretation of character resistances should be given early or later. In this regard, Fenichel's (1941, p. 67) proposal that character defenses be examined in accordance with what is predominant at any point in the analytic situation is a reasonable approach to the practical issue of when to interpret character resistances. He suggests first work-

ing with the patient's habitual and continuous character defenses in order to "release the personality from its rigidity" and working with other
character resistances only when they have become transference resistances (p. 68). But one first has to know whether what one is confronting is character resistance and, if it is, whether it is economically predominant at the time.

Fenichel suggests working "at the point of the *most important* current instinctual conflicts. It is the point of the most important conflicts *at
the moment*" (1941, p. 47). In my view the economic criterion for interpretation is determined by the point of highest affect disposition in the material. Insofar as drives (whether functioning as part of the defense or on
the impulse side of the conflict) are manifest as affectively invested internalized object relations, the affectively predominant object relation in
the analytic situation represents the economically dominant instinctual
conflict as well. But affective dominance is not equivalent to consciousness or surface manifestations. As Fenichel put it: "For we must operate
at that point where the affect is actually situated at the moment; it must
be added that the patient does not know this point and we must first
seek out the places where the affect is situated" (1941, p. 45).

I propose that the evaluation of (1) the content of free associations,
(2) the prevailing nature of the interactions in the patient/analyst relation—including the patient's noverbal behavior during the sessions—and (3) the patient's overall relation to the psychoanalytic setting
over a period of months or even years makes it possible to discern
whether pathological character traits have invaded the transference, resulting in a condensation of transference and character resistances, and
whether these character resistances have become affectively predominant, thus justifying the highest priority as the focus of psychoanalytic
interpretations.

If free association is proceeding satisfactorily, if the resistances
emerging in the context of exploring possible restrictions of free association can be interpreted—regardless of whether these are directly linked
to the transference—and if the patient's awareness of his intrapsychic
life as well as his emotional relationship to the analyst deepens over
time, then the interpretation of nonverbal behavior in the sessions can
wait until it can be incorporated naturally into the themes of the free associations and the transference.

Specific clinical situations are encountered in which nonverbal behavior strongly emerges in the sessions and in which the affect and object relations implied by the patient's nonverbal behavior and verbal
communications are congruent or complementary. When a consonance
exists between the nonverbal and verbal material, understanding the
transference implications of both usually permits a deeper understanding of both. In other words, if both verbal and nonverbal material indi-

cates the nature of the issues that predominate affectively in the content of the hour, the economic principle of interpretation in the sense of working at the point of the most important current instinctual conflict (Fenichel, 1941, p. 47) can be applied. Usually the material can also be understood simultaneously in terms of the dynamic principle—that is, in terms of a conflict between impulse and defense—and the decision can be made which aspect of the defense side of the conflict should be explored before the impulse aspect. Congruence between behavior and content and affective dominance in the hour usually means, by the same token, that the object relations "unit" involved is dominant in the transference as well. Clarification of the dynamic ordering of impulse and defense usually also has topographical aspects, permitting an interpretation from surface to depth, from consciousness to the unconscious. We usually find a consonance of verbal and nonverbal communications in patients with well-consolidated tripartite intrapsychic structure, whose conflicts also tend to be organized intersystemically. It is therefore possible to clarify which system—ego, superego, or id—the predominant defense organization corresponds to and which other system the impulse is stemming from. Thus the structural criteria of interpretation apply as well.

In other clinical situations, however, the conflicts reflected in the verbal content and the interactional material seem dissonant or incongruent. Strong affects in the verbal content and the development of acute or chronic affective interactions reflecting the patient's "frozen" character traits seem strangely unrelated to each other, thus raising the question of what material actually is predominant. Under these circumstances, applying the criteria proposed below usually permits one to arrive at a decision regarding which material should be dealt with first and how to approach it.

It is helpful to consider first whether the patient's free associations are proceeding satisfactorily or whether there is significant conscious suppression of material. Whatever facilitates understanding the motives for conscious suppression and the related transference implications takes precedence here. An understanding of the transference meaning of what is motivating the patient against full compliance with free association usually also provides an answer to what is affectively predominant in the session and whether it relates primarily to the verbal content or to aspects of the patient's nonverbal behavior.

Now, if free association seems to be proceeding satisfactorily, the question of what is predominant in the transference can be examined more easily and helps the analyst to decide whether verbal or attitudinal material predominates. I am suggesting that, with two simultaneous and parallel object-relations "units" revealed in the psychoanalytic situation (one in behavior, the other in the verbal content), the one with both transference dominance and affective dominance takes interpretive precedence. If, however, affective dominance and transference dominance diverge, I think affective dominance (the application of the economic principle) should have priority. I should stress that all defensive and impulsive, verbal and nonverbal, self- and object-related aspects of the material have affective components, so that "affective dominance" does not mean searching for some particular affect or a consciously dominant one, or one linked only with defense or impulse. It is the predominant affect in the total immediate situation that counts, not its access to consciousness. A hysterical temper tantrum, for example, may defend against another dominant affect in the immediate transference situation.

The approach I am suggesting differs from Wilhelm Reich's (1933) insistence that transference resistances anchored in character always be interpreted first. It also differs from Gill's (1980, 1982) insistence that transference always be given the highest priority for interpretation; there are times when affective investment is highest in extratransference issues or in the patient's exploration of aspects of his past. The fact that all analytic material has transference components does not mean that transference material automatically predominates. Sometimes a theme that has strongly dominated the transference for many hours—for example, a patient's chronic dissatisfaction about "not receiving anything from the analyst"—may suddenly shift into a displacement of that complaint onto a third person. Here, affective dominance and transference are still consonant, although the transference is—temporarily—displaced (which may actually facilitate its interpretation).

In addition, at times of rapid shifts in the transference itself, which complicates the task of detecting incongruity between verbal and nonverbal communication, waiting for a crystallization around one of the various affectively important issues present should eventually permit the analyst to decide what is affectively (and, therefore, economically) predominant. Here a "wait and see" attitude is preferable, in my view, to the exclusively topographical standpoint of focusing on what in the material is closest to consciousness. There is never just one "surface" to the material. There are many surface configurations, and the point at which to penetrate from surface to depth (the topographic criterion) depends on what is actually dominant in the total situation. Obviously, when the patient can be helped to acquire awareness of simultaneous, strongly unrelated emotional dispositions in the analytic situation, the exploration of his associations to this observation in itself illuminates the issues involved.

During periods of heightened resistance, the most important material may be relatively distant from consciousness (particularly in personality structures with strong repressive mechanisms). Although I agree that, once one has decided what material is most important, this material should be explored from its defensive side or aspects (which includes consideration of some conscious or preconscious configurations linked to it), access to consciousness does not in itself indicate thematic predominance.

I am here questioning a general tendency for the analyst always to proceed from the surface down, from conscious to unconscious material, disregarding what is economically predominant. However, I also question the tendency to arrive at premature genetic interpretations of the unconscious fantasies reflected in characterologically fixated object relations in the transference. Staying close to the surface manifestations of resistances is as problematic as searching for the "deepest level" of a certain conflict, "deep" usually meaning genetically early. I think the analyst should interpret in depth in the sense of focusing on the unconscious conflicts that predominate in any particular session, the unconscious aspects of the transference in the here-and-now. (But here-and-now must eventually be related to the there-and-then as well!)

Where important discrepancies exist between the verbal and nonverbal communication, when free association seems to be proceeding satisfactorily but without any real deepening of the material, and when, in addition, there are indications of stalemate in transference developments—or a loss of previously gained understanding of the current nature of the transference—I have found it helpful to give clear precedence to the analysis of the object relations aspects of the patient's attitudes over those derived from his verbal communications. The same "rule" applies to situations in which the patient either is repetitively acting out or seems to be developing strong potential for acting out. Giving precedence to nonverbal communication also applies to situations in which general emotional dispersal, an exacerbation of splitting mechanisms, results in affective fragmentation and becomes a major transference resistance, which occurs particularly in strongly schizoid personalities.

I would also give preference to the interpretation of behavior over that of dissonant verbal communications for patients with "living out" lifestyles, those whose free associations remain fixed at a surface level, or those who lack a thoughtful, cooperative attitude. In all these cases, Reich's recommendation that attitudes be interpreted before verbal content and that this be considered a special application of the principle of interpreting "surface" before "depth," "defense before content," still seems valid. Similarly, borderline character pathology, in which severe acting out colors the initial stage of the treatment, also requires rapid interpretation of the transference meanings of pathological character traits.

In other words, when free association "gets stuck" in the context of important activation of pathological behavior patterns in the analytic situation or in the patient's external life, analytic exploration of these behaviors and clarification of their relation to the transference are indicated. To put it still differently: From an economic viewpoint, discrepancies between verbal and nonverbal behavior require an interpretive approach to the total picture generated by these discrepancies. In practice, therefore, character resistances in the transference should be analyzed early on.

In other cases, severe distortions in relation to the psychoanalytic setting become apparent over a period of time. In the vignette presented earlier, after a period of progress in the third year of the analysis, a therapeutic stalemate highlighted the pathology of the patient's relation to interpretations and to the analyst in general (the subtle compromise solutions between envious idealization and devaluation). In still other cases, much like those described by Reich, the patient's free associations apparently flow, with abundant information about present and past and flexible shifts from affects to intellectual thoughts, from fantasy to reality, from the transference to the patient's external life, and so forth (thus imitating Ferenczi's 1919 and Glover's 1955 descriptions of optimal free association), but without any real deepening of the transference relationship or any manifestation of a particular nonverbal behavior in the sessions that would lend itself to exploring the transference.

In these cases, again it is the total relation to the analyst that is usually highly distorted, and it is this distortion that must be diagnosed, particularly as it affects the patient's relation to the analyst's interpretations. Here the interpretation of pathological character traits coincides with the interpretation of the patient's attitude toward the interpreting analyst. Under conditions of such stalemates, this subject matter has high priority. Otherwise, such patients typically acquire a superficial "learning" of the psychoanalyst's theories as a way of defensively resisting full awareness of their unconscious intrapsychic conflicts, with consequent limited therapeutic effects.

Under these circumstances, it is important to clarify the unconscious aspects of the patient/analyst interaction in the here-and-now as a crucial step to full understanding of the object relation that is being played out, without attempting prematurely to achieve genetic reconstructions. Here-and-now interventions should not be conceptualized as artificially cut off, dissociated from their there-and-then aspects. The issue of their relevance to the past should be kept in abeyance, however, until the unconscious aspects of the transference are fully explored. The patient often finds it easier to accept a transference interpretation if a tentative reference to the childhood origin of a certain attitude to the analyst is made; hence, genetic reconstructions should not be reserved for the final stages of analysis. But here I am stressing the need first to clarify the unknown in the present: a step erroneously bypassed in many patients with severe character pathology.

Spelling out a patient's unconscious fantasy on the basis of a specific object relation enacted by his chronic nonverbal behavior in the sessions corresponds to a psychoanalytic construction. But it is necessary to follow this construction with a genetic reconstruction only after the patient's associations gradually transform this fantasy into an antecedent object relation, with the appearance of new information regarding his past and a natural reordering of the new and old information in this area. Establishing the actual genetic sequence of such recovered material requires that the analyst actively order and reorder these genetic units of the patient's unconscious conflicts (Blum, 1980).

The analyst's exploration of his own emotional reactions to the patient under conditions of stalemate may be crucial to the diagnosis of both chronic countertransference distortions (which are more pervasive though less obtrusive than acute countertransference developments) and subtle but powerful transference acting out that might otherwise not have been diagnosed. In this regard the analysis of the analyst's total emotional reaction is a "second line" of approach when the first line of approach—direct transference exploration—proves insufficient (Heimann, 1960; Kernberg, 1975).

The analysis of an implicit and, for the patient, often completely unconscious "interchange" of role relations with the analyst highlights the advantages of studying the analyst's moment-to-moment affective responses to the patient. Such analyses also point the way to differentiating countertransference reactions in a strict sense (the analyst's unconscious conflicts activated in response to the patient's transference) from the analyst's global emotional response to the patient. We know that these two aspects of the analyst's reactions are complementary. For practical purposes, however, the distinction facilitates a more open exploration of the moment-to-moment shift in the analyst's affective responses to and fantasies about the patient's immediate attitudes and chronic attitudinal dispositions, thereby enriching the analyst's understanding of the verbal content of the patient's communication. Need I stress that the analyst's utilization of his own emotional reaction to the patient certainly does not mean sharing that reaction with the patient?

Metapsychological Considerations

I now return to consider Fenichel's economic, dynamic, and structural criteria for interpreting character resistances, combining these with the interpretation of internalized object relations represented in such character resistances. Regarding the economic criterion, I have stressed the need first to interpret the material that is affectively predominant, while simultaneously questioning whether closeness to consciousness is a significant criterion for determining such predominance of affects. This

view underlies everything I have said regarding the difficulty in choos-
ing economically predominant issues when information stemming from
the patient's verbal and nonverbal communications is not congruent.

Regarding the dynamic criteria for interpretation, I reported earlier
(1980, chap. 10) that, when transference regression is severe or in analyzable patients with borderline personality organization, the predominance of splitting over repressive mechanisms permits the alternation in
consciousness of the dynamically opposed components of intrapsychic
conflict so that access to consciousness per se does not serve to indicate
which is the defense and which the impulse aspect of the conflict. Defense and impulse can be rapidly interchanged in the alternating reversals of activated object relations that are typical of part-object relations,
and conflictual impulses are conscious and mutually dissociated or split
off rather than repressed. Here, consciousness and unconsciousness no
longer coincide with what is at the surface and what is deep, what is defense and what is content. But while the topographic approach to interpretation (the ordering of the material from surface to depth) no longer
holds for such borderline structures, the moment-to-moment decision of
which is the defensively activated ego state directed against which other
"impulsive" ego state is very important. Hence, both the economic and
the dynamic criteria of interpretation as spelled out by Fenichel are still
fully relevant. This brings us to the structural aspects of interpretation of
character resistances at various levels of severity of psychopathology.

The structural considerations regarding the interpretation of character resistances refer to the organization of the predominant internalized
object relation activated in the transference in the context of a particular
character trait or pattern. When we diagnose "units" of internalized object relations, we are diagnosing substructures of the tripartite structure.
We are, in fact, applying a structural perspective where the overall tripartite structure may not yet (or may no longer) be operative. The patient's attitude, as mentioned before, reflects the enactment of a self representation relating affectively to an object representation or the
enactment of an object representation (with which the patient appears to
be identified at the moment) relating affectively to a self representation
(now projected onto the analyst). One primary consideration here is the
extent to which both self and object representations are rooted in
broader aspects of the patient's ego or superego, reflecting broadly integrated concepts, values, and emotional dispositions of ego and superego
or, to the contrary, the extent to which they are dissociated or split off
from other self and object representations. Part-object relations are more
disruptive, bizarre, fantastic than the total-object relations. The latter reflect more ordinary childhood experiences which, although repressed,
become integrated with the child's ego and superego.

In the context of these elaborations of the structural aspects of pathological character traits in the transference, one important question arises. Does the object relation activated reflect intersystemic or intrasystemic conflicts? And in the case of intersystemic conflict, to which agency do the self representations and object representations correspond? Or, which object relation corresponds to the defense and which to the impulse side of the conflict, and in which agency is each embedded? In intrasystemic conflicts, split-off internalized object relations may at first appear mutually delimited yet intrinsically undifferentiated, intense yet vague, and always highly fantastic and unrealistic. They should be translated into an intelligible affective experience in the here-and-now, a fantasy enacted by them within which the defensive and impulsive aspects, in turn, have to be clarified in terms of which split-off object relation acquires a momentary defensive function against an opposing (impulsive) one. Attention to the interchange between patient and analyst of self and object representations—the alternation of complementary roles in the transference—should be integrated into the interpretation of these expressions of the conflict. That task often requires relatively rapid, imaginative tracking of what appear to be chaotic interactions. The analyst's systematically pointing out to the patient how he feels under the impact of a self representation and the particular object representation activated at different times may permit the analyzable patient with severe character pathology to achieve a degree of integration and empathy with himself and with his objects which will contribute to transforming part-object into total-object relations. In the clinical vignette presented earlier, Mr. T's gradually growing awareness of his identification with his sadistic-mother image as well as with his mistreated and frustrated self-image led to his awareness and eventual tolerance and integration of contradictory tendencies in himself, of love and hatred, and of his exploitive and devalued self experiences previously projected onto his girlfriends.

As regressive transferences emerge in the treatment, the patient's observing ego may be temporarily swept up by them. It is important for the analyst to maintain a clear image of how a "normal" person would respond, under the circumstances, to the analyst's interpretive comments. This theoretically "normal" person is usually represented by the collaborative work of the patient's observing ego with the analyst, but it may be almost totally missing, temporarily in all patients, and chronically in patients with severe character pathology. With severe cases, therefore, the analyst's evocation of a "normal" counterpart to the patient's actual regressive behavior becomes crucial. This means that the analyst has to "split" himself. One part of him is "experiencing"—accompanying the patient into regression and transforming his behavior into the construction of an enacted unconscious fantasy. Another part of him is "distancing"—maintaining objectivity precisely at times when objectivity is most challenged. The boundary function in the analyst's mind between fantasy and reality requires his tolerance of primitive fantasy and emotions and of internal discrepancies between the understanding of what is going on and the level at which the patient can be approached. The analyst must be able to maintain firm convictions together with flexibility.

In the long run, when character analysis is systematically pursued, a paradoxical situation may emerge. Some patients find it much easier to talk about their past than about the unconscious aspects of their current relationship to the analyst. The analyst himself may begin to wonder whether he is neglecting the exploration of the past in his emphasis on the present. Other patients may "jump" over the real past and link the conscious present with what they assume are the deepest levels of past conflicts: they "easily" connect current conflicts with, for example, "castration anxiety," but no concrete and painful aspects of childhood emerge.

Careful working through of character resistances, maintaining constant alertness to whether the patient is changing not only his current experience of the psychoanalytic situation—thus indicating authentic shifts in transference patterns—but also how he experiences his past—thus expressing the working through of transference patterns—may confirm the authenticity of psychoanalytic work, in contrast to a mechanistic translation of current difficulties into the patient's own rigidly maintained myths regarding his past.

CHAPTER 14: *Self, Ego, Affects, and Drives*

The Ego and the Self

Terminological Issues

A survey of the psychoanalytic literature on theories of the ego and concepts of the self reveals a considerable terminological confusion. That the terms *ego* and *self* are sometimes used interchangeably, sometimes carefully distinguished from each other, and sometimes treated ambiguously probably is due to the way in which Freud used these words, the way Strachey translated them, and the subsequent elaborations others made on them.

Freud preserved throughout his writings the German *Ich*—"I"—for the ego as both a mental structure and psychic agency, and also for the more personal, subjective, experiential self. In other words, Freud never separated what we think of as the agency or system ego from the experiencing self. This use of *Ich* resulted in a sacrifice of clarity and precision, but it kept the meaning of the word open-ended.

The ambiguity resulting from Freud's use of *Ich* has been compounded, it seems to me, by Strachey's decision to translate *Ich* as "ego," a word that has an impersonal quality which seems appropriate enough for Freud's structural theory (1923) but less fitting for the more personal, subjective *self*.

There are innumerable examples of the use of *Ich* before 1923 to designate subjective experience and self-esteem—what Rapaport might have critically designated the "anthropomorphization" of the concept ego. This characteristic of Freud's concept of *Ich*—which I consider a strength, not a weakness—persists throughout his work. The most dramatic example is probably his statement in *Civilization and Its Discontents* (1930a), where the *Standard Edition*, faithful to the German original, reads (p. 65): "Normally, there is nothing of which we are more certain than the feeling of our self, of our own ego." The German version says (1930b, p. 423), "Normalerweise ist uns nichts gesicherter als das Gefühl unseres Selbst, unseres eigenen Ichs." Here self and ego are explicitly equated!

I think that Strachey's translation of Freud's *Ich* as "ego" has had an effect on our understanding of Freud's thinking. I agree with Laplanche and Pontalis in their extensive discussion of this issue (1973, p. 131) that Freud always maintained the ambiguity, the internal tension of his concept of *Ich*—to indicate its system properties as well as the fact that, as part of these system properties, the ego is the seat of consciousness and, with it, the consciousness of one's self or of the self as a person.

A second source of difficulty is the use of *self* to describe the person or individual interacting with other persons or "objects," as Hartmann did in 1950:

But actually, in using the term narcissism, two different sets of opposites often seemed to be fused into one. The one refers to the self (one's own person) in contradistinction to the object, the second to the ego (as a psychic system) in contradistinction to other substructures of personality. However, the opposite of object cathexis is not ego cathexis, but cathexis of one's own person, that is, self-cathexis; in speaking of self-cathexis we do not imply whether this cathexis is situated in the id, ego, or superego. This formulation takes into account that we actually do find "narcissism" in all three psychic systems; but in all of these cases there is opposition to (and reciprocity with) object cathexis. It therefore will be clarifying if we define narcissism as the libidinal cathexis not of the ego but of the self. (It might also be useful to apply the term self-representation as opposed to object representation.) [p. 127]

Hartmann is here making a distinction that, as we shall see, permitted the development of Jacobson's (1964) crucial contributions to ego psychology: the distinction between the self as the person and the intrapsychic representation of the person or self representation, a third term requiring clarification.

Jacobson (1964), referring to these problems of terminological confusion, said, "They refer to the ambiguous use of the term ego; i.e., to the lack of distinction between the ego, which represents a structural mental system, the self, which I defined above, and the self representations. Hartmann (1950) . . . suggested the use of the latter term (analogous to object representations) for the unconscious, preconscious, and conscious endopsychic representations of the bodily and mental self in the system ego. I have worked with this concept for years, because I found it indispensable for the investigation of psychotic disorders" (pp. 18–19). Jacobson, in agreement with Hartmann, defines the self "as referring to the whole person of an individual, including his body and body parts as

well as his psychic organization and its parts. . . . The 'self' is an auxiliary descriptive term, which points to the person as a subject in distinction from the surrounding world of objects" (1964, p. 6).

It seems to me that Hartmann, by attempting to free the term *ego*
from Freud's ambiguity, impoverished it. Like Strachey, he wanted to
give the ego concept consistency. And in placing the "self" in contradistinction to the object, Hartmann in effect removed the "self" from metapsychology. The definition of *self* in the *Glossary of Psychoanalytic Terms
and Concepts* (Moore and Fine, 1968) confirms this idea. It states: "The total person of an individual in reality, including his body and psychic organization; one's 'own person' as contrasted with 'other persons' and
objects outside one's self. The 'self' is a common-sense concept; its clinical and metapsychological aspects are treated under self image, self representation, etc. See ego, identity, narcissism" (p. 88). To call the self a
"common-sense concept" effectively removes it from psychoanalytic
consideration.

In my view, Hartmann's fateful separation of the concept of ego
from self and of self from self representation created a problem in the
historical development of psychoanalytic theory; it artificially separated
the structural, experiential, and descriptive aspects of ego functions.
This separation unnecessarily complicated conceptualizing the relations
among "impersonal" ego functions, subjectivity, and character structure. For example, Jacobson's (1964) effort to develop a metapsychology
of the experiential aspects of the self was made more difficult by what
she felt was a need to differentiate, at every step, ego functions from
self functions, the affective investment of self representations and object
representations from diffuse activation of affects.

I therefore propose eliminating from further consideration, for the
purpose of this discussion, the use of the concept of self as opposed to
object. Such a concept of the self leads to "psychosocial" or interpersonal descriptions and to confusing psychoanalytic with sociological
concepts, a confusion found, for example, in some of Erikson's writings.

The replacement of the topographical by the structural model of the
psychic apparatus led Freud to examine the roots of the ego in the id as
a precipitate of the id, and to pursue the idea that the ego was dependent on the apparatus of perception and consciousness. The ego became
an apparatus of regulation and adaptation to reality simultaneously with
its carrying out of defensive functions and compromise solutions to conflicts among the id, superego, and external reality. Freud's structural
perspective apparently caused him to reduce his emphasis on the functions of self-awareness and self-feeling, on self-esteem regulation within
the ego; or perhaps he was led temporarily to understand some of these
functions mostly in terms of intersystemic conflicts.

However, Freud also maintained an ambiguity in his concept of the origins of the ego, and it is no coincidence that object relations approaches as well as contemporary ego psychology have their origin in his formulation of the structure of the ego. His much-quoted statement in "The Ego and the Id" (1923, p. 29) is still pertinent:

When it happens that a person has to give up a sexual object, there quite often ensues an alteration of his ego which can only be described as a setting up of the object inside the ego, as it occurs in melancholia; the exact nature of the substitution is as yet unknown to us. It may be that by this introjection, which is a kind of regression to the mechanism of the oral phase, the ego makes it easier for the object to be given up or renders that process possible. It may be that this identification is the sole condition under which the id can give up its objects. At any rate the process, especially in the early phases of development, is a very frequent one, and it makes it possible to suppose that the character of the ego is a precipitate of abandoned object-cathexes and that it contains the history of those object-choices.

This is in consonance with Freud's (1914) paper "On Narcissism" and with his understanding of the superego as also derived from the internalization of parental objects.

Jacobson rescued the "self" by elaborating on the concept of self representation. And just as she found this concept indispensable for investigating psychotic disorders, so I have found it indispensable for understanding neurotic, borderline, and narcissistic pathology, as well as normal development.

Insofar as the self as person is a psychosocial, behavioral, and interactional entity, I suggest replacing "self" with "character." Character reflects various configurations of normal or abnormal ego structure expressed in repetitive behavior patterns. It is true that character defenses include the symbolic expression of self and object representations, and have, therefore, a self representational quality as well, but I think the terms *character defense*, *character formation*, and *character structure* are more precise and clinically more useful than that of the *self* when referring to the person.

I propose, instead, to reserve the term *self* for the sum total of self representations in intimate connection with the sum total of object representations. In other words, I propose defining the self as an intrapsychic structure that originates in the ego and is clearly embedded in the ego. To conceptualize the self in this way is to remain close to Freud's implicit insistence that self and ego are indissolubly linked. The libidinal investment of the self thus defined is related to the libidinal investment of the representations of significant others, and the libidinal investment of one's own person corresponds to the libidinal investment of others (external objects). All these investments are related and reinforce each other.

Developmental Issues

It seems to me that the structural theory, particularly as elaborated by Jacobson (1964) and Mahler (1979), contains a rich and sophisticated developmental concept of the self, an elaboration of the dual aspects of Freud's *Ich*.

There are two aspects of Freud's (1923) formulations regarding the origin of the ego that have been elaborated and gradually integrated with contemporary psychoanalytic formulations regarding earliest development. The first is his idea that the ego differentiates from the id, or an original undifferentiated ego–id matrix, by its crystallization around the system perception-consciousness. The second is his suggestion that the ego is a precipitate resulting from the internalization of the representations of instinctually invested objects. That the infant's perception and consciousness should be activated particularly when he or she is actually interacting with mother and that evolving instinctual investments of her should leave traces in the early ego's field of consciousness are probably broad enough statements to cover very contrasting psychoanalytic approaches. The differences between competing psychoanalytic approaches focus, however, on a number of issues that lead us directly to the question of the origin of the self (as I have redefined it).

First, can we conceive that an infant has the capacity to differentiate himself from mother from the beginning of life? Melanie Klein (1946) and her follower Segal (1979), as well as Fairbairn (1954) from the British Middle Group, clearly appear to think so, whereas Jacobson, Mahler, and I and also Winnicott (1958, 1965) question this idea and assume an initially undifferentiated stage.

If an initially undifferentiated state of varying duration is assumed, does it contain a "purely narcissistic," primary, omnipotent self representation, or does it contain undifferentiated self/object representations? This seemingly abstract question is crucial, in my view, to formulating a contemporary metapsychology of narcissism.

Jacobson (1964) proposed restricting the term *primary narcissism* to the undifferentiated stage of development, which she saw as one of undifferentiated drive cathexes of the "primary psychophysiological self," marked only by states of rising and diminishing tensions. At the same time, she considered the psychophysiological self a purely descriptive concept, unrelated to metapsychological considerations.

Jacobson saw the origin of the ego as intimately linked to the originally fused self images and object images—to what I am calling the originally undifferentiated self/object representation in it. She saw this image as invested with what, following Freud's terminology, she called "secondary narcissism." She here gave what I think is the prevalent contemporary ego-psychology answer to this question: that the first instinctual, particularly libidinal, investment is to an undifferentiated self/object representation. Later, the gradual differentiation of self and object representations will result in a differentiated investment of libido (and aggression) as well. As differentiated self representations and object representations are built up, so is libidinal investment in the self representation and in the object representation.

With the differentiation of self and object, the investment of the external object is experienced as a continuation of the investment of its earlier, undifferentiated version. Object representations and external objects are now invested simultaneously and reinforce each other. This view, which contrasts with earlier psychoanalytic assumptions about the infant's prolonged state of psychological isolation from the human environment, is supported by actual infant observation and the impressively early discriminatory reactions to environmental stimuli reflecting mother's interaction with him.

Jacobson's formulation solves, in my view, the issue of the origin of instinctual investment of self and objects—the question of whether narcissism predates object investment or whether they occur simultaneously. Her formulation also links structure formation within the ego to the setting up of internalized representations of self and object as primary organizing substructures. It creates the basis for a description of the vicissitudes of self and object representations—multiple, contradictory, nonintegrated at first, gradually consolidating into integrated self and object concepts.

Jacobson's formulations contribute a theoretical background against which to view Mahler's (1979) research on autistic and symbiotic childhood psychosis and on the stages of normal and abnormal separation-individuation. Mahler provides both direct observational and psychoanalytic data that permit one to trace the stages of development Jacobson postulates.

However, Jacobson's pushing back the stage of "primary narcissism" to an assumed earliest phase of diffuse discharge onto the "psychophysiological self" leaves obscure the issue of the origin and development of drives and their relation to instinctual investment of self and object representations. Jacobson's formulation of self and object investments assumes that libidinal and aggressive drives differ in nature.

Still another question regarding the development of the ego and the self relates to the question: Does the self originate only from blissful states of merger with mother and their corresponding undifferentiated self/object representations, or does it originate from the integration of such states with states of merger of self and object representations under the impact of painful, frightening, frustrating, or even catastrophic experiences? This question is crucial because completely different developmental schemata evolve according to how one responds to it.

Probably all psychoanalysts who have dealt with this question would agree that the gratifying, blissful states constitute the core of the ego's self-feeling or self-experience. Some would go so far as to consider the building up of an integrated concept of the self on the basis of such early merger experiences as constituting the final, integrated, normal self.

In such a view, the normal self would reflect the appropriately toned-down derivative of the originally blissful merged self/object representation. According to this view, frustrating experiences and the aggression these trigger would not be part of the original self but would be part of the "not me" experience, an external threat to the self, not intrinsically linked with it. Although Kohut did not actually formulate a comprehensive model of earliest development, his theory (1971, 1972, 1977) might fit this line of thinking. At a metapsychological level, this thinking permits omitting aggression from the theory of ego and self development.

The alternative concept is that self development also occurs at times of heightened frustration and painful or traumatic experiences. Such experiences determine the building up of merged self/object representations under the aegis of frustration and pain. These mental representations are invested with aggression. They will later evolve into frightening, aggressive, and devalued experiences of the self and into frightening, aggressive, sadistic representations of objects. They eventually lead to the existence of the multiple contradictory self and object representations that are so challenging to the child's development during separation-individuation. These mental representations explain the pathological fixation at the rapprochement subphase of development (Mahler, 1971), when differentiated yet nonintegrated self representations and contradictory representations of significant objects result in the syndrome of identity diffusion. In contrast, the normal integration of contradictory self and object representations marks the transition from separation-individuation "toward object constancy."

This concept of self development under both libidinal and aggressive conditions is common to Jacobson, Mahler, and myself, and also to Fairbairn and Klein; Winnicott's developmental model leaves the impression of a certain ambiguity in this regard. Because in Kleinian thinking the problem of self and object differentiation has hardly been explored (with the exception of a partial examination in one paper by Bick [1968]), the correlation of Jacobson's, Mahler's, and my views with Kleinian developmental schemata cannot really be achieved. Fairbairn's (1954) assumption of an integrated "pristine" ego from birth on raises other problems with regard to developmental timetables.

The concept of the origin of self representations and self experience under the impact of both aggressively and libidinally invested states of merger leads to a concept of the self as the product of the eventual integration of such contradictory self representations and of the corresponding integration of the derivatives of libidinal and aggressive drive investments as well. In fact, the model I am proposing conceives of the self as invested with both libidinal and aggressive drive derivatives integrated in the context of the integration of their component self representations. This model solves the puzzling question of how psychic-structure formation, self development, and instinctual development correlate. It also suggests an explanation for the concept of neutralization of drives (Hartmann, 1955).

The self, then, is an ego structure that originates from self representations first built up in the undifferentiated symbiotic phase in the context of infant–mother interactions under the influence of both gratifying and frustrating experiences. Simultaneously the system perception-consciousness evolves into broader ego functions as well: the developing control over perception, voluntary motility, the setting-up of affective memory traces, and the system preconscious. The self as a psychic structure originates from both libidinally and aggressively invested self representations. It is, in short, an ego function and structure that evolves gradually from the integration of its component self representations into a supraordinate structure that incorporates other ego functions—such as memory and cognitive structures—and leads to the dual characteristics implied in Freud's *Ich*.

Motivational Forces: Drives, Affects, and Object Relations

I think it is no coincidence that the controversies in psychoanalysis about the concept of the self are so closely linked with the controversies over instinct theory, especially over the nature and role of aggression in early development. Analogous to the reaction to Freud's discoveries regarding infantile sexuality which imputed to psychoanalysis a morbid and exaggerated concern with sexuality, Freud's dual instinct theory has continued to arouse strong cultural reactions against the concept of aggression as a basic instinct. "Orthodox" psychoanalysts generally are believed to have a distinct, harsh, aggressive outlook on life as well as on patients' difficulties. Kohut's (1971, 1977) developmental model, emphasizing the central nature of the cohesive self (the motivational force of which is not spelled out and is only implied as a self-generating maturational drive), is but one of many psychological and culturalist psychoanalytic theories that explicitly or implicitly reject instinct theory, particularly aggression, and the biological basis of human development.

Perhaps a failure to reexamine instinct theory, particularly the relation between affects and drives, in the light of new neuropsychological and observational-developmental data has contributed to the uncertainty regarding the motivational forces of earliest development. That this is more than a purely theoretical issue, that it is directly relevant to the question of the origin and development of the self and therefore of narcissism, should be evident from what I have said in the preceding section about the development of earliest self and object representations in the context of the infant/mother interaction. What follows is an effort to integrate findings from contemporary neuropsychological studies of affects and research on infant development with a revised formulation of the dual instinct theory.

Affective behavior strongly influences object relations from birth on (Izard, 1978; Izard and Buechler, 1979). A central biological function of inborn affective patterns—with their behavioral, communicative, and psychophysiological manifestations—is to signal the infant's needs to the environment (the mothering person) and thus to initiate communication between the infant and mother, which marks the beginning of intrapsychic life (Emde et al., 1978). Recent research has surprised us with the description of a high degree of differentiation in infant/mother communications, present from very early on (Hoffman, 1978). Neuropsychological theorizing now assumes the storage of affective memory in the limbic cortex, which, as direct brain-stimulation experiments indicate, permits the reactivation of both the cognitive and the affective aspects of past experience, particularly the subjective, affective coloring of that experience (Arnold, 1970). Affects, operating as the earliest motivational system, are therefore intimately linked with the fixation by memory of an internalized world of object relations (Kernberg, 1976).

If we assume that affective memory structures reflecting pleasurable relations of infant and mother, in which self and object representations are as yet undifferentiated, build up separately from the unpleasurable affective memory structures in which self and object representations are also undifferentiated, it would seem logical to raise the following questions: Is the biologically determined activation of affects a reflection of the activation of libidinal and aggressive (or still undifferentiated) drives, or are affects themselves—rather than drives—the essential motivational forces? Or do these affective structures rather serve to link behavior with intrapsychic registration of the infant's interactions with his mother so that the primary motivational system consists of internalized object relations rather than either affects or drives?

I suggest that affects are the primary motivational system, in the sense that they are at the center of each of the infinite number of gratifying and frustrating concrete events the infant experiences with his environment. Affects link a series of undifferentiated self/object representations so that gradually a complex world of internalized object relations, some pleasurably tinged, others unpleasurably tinged, is constructed.

But even while affects are linking internalized object relations in two parallel series of gratifying and frustrating experiences, "good" and "bad" internalized object relations themselves are being transformed. The predominant affect of love or hate of the two series of internalized object relations becomes enriched, modulated, and increasingly complex.

Eventually, the internal relationship of the infant to the mother under the sign of "love" is more than the sum of a finite number of concrete loving affect states. The same is true for hate. Love and hate thus become stable intrapsychic structures, in genetic continuity through various developmental stages; by that very continuity, they consolidate into libido and aggression. Libido and aggression in turn become hierarchically supraordinate motivational systems which express themselves in a multitude of differentiated affect dispositions under different circumstances. Affects, in short, are the building blocks, or constituents, of drives; affects eventually acquire a signal function for the activation of drives.

At the same time, the relatively crude, undifferentiated early affective responses evolve into differentiated affects with diverging subjective components, cognitive implications, and behavior characteristics. Various authors have classified affects phenomenologically (Plutchik, 1980). The changing nature of affective responses to the same external object and its internal representations does not by itself permit establishing continuity in the development of unconscious intrapsychic conflict by means of "primary" affects.

Libido and aggression, however, manifest themselves clinically in a spectrum of affect dispositions and affect states. We can thus trace clinically the vast array of affect states and their corresponding object relations to aggression, libido, or—at later stages of development—condensations of these two drives. Also, the relation to an object changes under the influence of the biological activation of new affect states, which emerge throughout development and cause the quality of the drives to shift. For example, preoedipal libidinal strivings for mother change under the impact of sexually tinged affect states that emerge during the oedipal stage. These affects organize themselves into genital urges operating in continuity with earlier libidinal strivings. But the subjective quality and motivational implications are different. Similarly, aggression directed toward the same libidinal object, also manifested in various component aggressive affective states, transcends each of these concrete aggressive affects and—particularly after condensation and integration of aggressive and libidinal drives—brings about or contributes to a new complexity of object relations and a new set of higher level or more complex, integrated affect states (such as sadness, tenderness, guilt, or longing).

Should we maintain the term *drive* for these hierarchically supraordinate motivational systems of aggression and libido? This discussion is unfortunately confused by the result of translating into English Freud's terms *Trieb* and *Instinkt*. Freud preferred *Trieb*, best translated as "drive," precisely because he conceived of drives as relatively continuous psychic motivational systems at the border between the physical and the mental, in contrast to instincts, which he viewed as discontinuous, rigid, inborn behavioral dispositions.

Unfortunately, the *Standard Edition* translates *Trieb* mostly, if not consistently, as "instinct." In light of the contemporary prevalent concept of instincts in biology (Tinbergen, 1951; Lorenz, 1963; Wilson, 1975), the term *instinctive components* for inborn perceptive, behavioral, communicative, psychophysiological, and subjective experiential patterns—that is, affects—seems appropriate, in contrast to the use of the term *drives* for the motivational systems libido and aggression. Freud's concept of psychological drives in contrast to biological instincts here fits remarkably well with contemporary biological developments (Kernberg, 1976).

Having explained how I see the relation between drives and affects, I hasten to add that drives are manifest not simply by affects, but by the activation of a specific object relation, which includes an affect and in which the drive is represented by a specific desire or wish. Unconscious fantasy, the most important being oedipal in nature, includes a specific wish directed toward an object. The wish derives from the drive and is more precise than the affect state, an additional reason for rejecting a concept that would make affects rather than drives the hierarchically supraordinate motivational system.

By the same token, if drives are clinically manifested by concrete wishes toward objects, and if drives originate in affect-laden experiences with the earliest object, could not the primary motivational system best be conceptualized as the internalized object relations? Is the search for an object the primary motivational system? Fairbairn clearly thought so, and, in light of Kohut's (1977) rejection of drives as motivational systems for the preoedipal levels of development, it would seem that he also thought so. I have several reasons for disagreeing.

First, the organization of intrapsychic reality in terms of love and hate is more important for our understanding of the continuity in intrapsychic development, unconscious conflict, and object relations themselves than the fact that these contradictory states are originally directed toward the same object—mother—or that, in the oedipal phase, a male and a female object are the recipients of the child's dominant needs and strivings. The relation between libido and aggression, and between pregenital and genital strivings, provides explanatory power for the contradictory relations to the same objects.

Second, the very nature of aggressive strivings results in a struggle against the consolidation of object relations and includes as a major purpose the elimination of the frustrating, dangerous, or competing object. In this regard, it is typical of object relations theories that put object relations as the primary motivational system to neglect the importance of aggression and therefore of unconscious intrapsychic conflict.

Third, the fundamental shift in the quality of libido under the impact of oedipal developments referred to above—in other words, the central importance of genital infantile sexuality—is also typically underestimated in theories that consider the relation to the object as hierarchically supraordinate to drives.

Returning to the issue of the motivational forces determining the origin of ego and self, I think that my proposed reformulation of the dual-instinct theory solves the question regarding the maturation and development of libido and aggression left open by Jacobson. It also provides a psychoanalytic model for earliest development that does justice to the crucial function of affects in activating the earliest infant/mother interactions. Furthermore, it explains the relation of affects to the internalization and development of self and object representations. I think this view is commensurate with Spitz's (1965, 1972) formulations regarding organizers of early ego development and also with Mahler's findings. Finally, it provides a bridge between Freud's theory of the ego as evolving from the system perception-consciousness, on the one hand, and from the precipitate of object relations, on the other, without having to assume a degree of early differentiation incommensurate with our present knowledge of infant development.

PART FOUR: *Severe Regressions:*
  Diagnosis and Treatment

CHAPTER 15: *Stalemates in Treatment*

Many borderline patients do not change significantly over years of treatment despite the efforts of skilled therapists of various orientations. Because of my particular interest in these patients, I have had the opportunity of acting as a consultant in the treatment of many such cases. What follows are some general considerations regarding the issues frequently involved in the patient's failure to change and some suggestions for managing therapeutic stalemates.

Negative therapeutic reactions are a major cause of stalemate. However, I think it preferable to discuss these issues in terms of the lack of significant change and to restrict the meaning of negative therapeutic reaction to the worsening of the patient's condition, particularly as reflected in the transference, at times when he is consciously or unconsciously perceiving the therapist as a good object who is attempting to provide him with significant help. Negative therapeutic reactions derive from (1) an unconscious sense of guilt (as in masochistic character structures); (2) the need to destroy what is received from the therapist because of unconscious envy of him (typical in narcissistic personalities); and (3) the need to destroy the therapist as a good object because of the patient's unconscious identification with a primitive, sadistic object who requires submission and suffering as a minimal condition for maintaining any significant object relation (as in some borderline and many schizophrenic patients who confuse love and sadism [Kernberg, 1975]).

My findings seem consonant with those of others (Olinick, 1964; Rosenfeld, 1971, 1975; Valenstein, 1973; Asch, 1976) who, from varying clinical and theoretical standpoints, stress the importance of preoedipal conflicts, severe aggression, and structural issues involving early self and object representations (rather than later superego/ego conflicts) in negative therapeutic reaction. These dynamics are highly relevant to the

241

issue of why many borderline patients who apparently were appropriately selected for psychotherapeutic treatment—and in whom one expected significant change—fail to change significantly. The persistence of pathological behavior and the failure to respond to intensive psychotherapy often reflect underlying negative therapeutic reactions which may infiltrate the entire treatment situation for months and even years.

Therapeutic stalemate may be manifest from the beginning of treatment or may make its appearance after years of therapy have produced some significant change. Even though the therapist is naturally more optimistic when a therapeutic stalemate develops after years of treatment which has already achieved some significant change, such late stalemates are often so intense as to cause the therapist to doubt his estimation of previous change. The deterioration in the transference and in the patient's entire life may be so severe that all previous change seems to have been annulled.

The features most frequently encountered both in cases where no change occurs from the beginning of the treatment and in those that develop this complication after many months or years are, first, unchanged grandiosity in severe narcissistic structures. These patients may dehumanize the treatment situation. Even narcissistic patients who seem to be functioning at a nonborderline level may completely deny any emotional reality in the transference. Other narcissistic personalities may have to deny retrospectively the help they have received from the analyst, experiencing all improvement as due to their own efforts—often "in spite of" the analyst—and end the treatment with a total devaluation of the analyst while still carrying away their "self-originated" improvement in an unconscious "stealing" of the analyst's work or creativity.

Severe masochistic acting out related to the submission to and triumphant identification with a relentless, sadistic superego formation is also characteristic of stalemates, as is an even more primitive identification with a sadistic "mad" object who provides love only in the context of suffering and hatred. Any satisfactory relation is thus equivalent to killing—and being killed by—the needed parental image and therefore losing it. To triumph over all those who do not suffer from such a horrible human destiny is the only protection against a sense of total psychic disaster.

The need to neutralize or defeat the therapist's efforts may evolve into a vicious cycle. As the therapist persists in helping the patient in the face of obvious lack of response or even worsening of the patient's condition, the patient's envy and resentment of the therapist's commitment and dedication may reinforce his guilt over mistreating the therapist (who, in contrast to the patient's other experiences, does not respond to hatred with hatred) and thus his need to escape from guilt.

Severely regressed patients may feel relieved when the therapist loses patience and "counterattacks." And although the patient may rationalize his relief by the idea that the therapist is "human after all," on a deeper level there is usually an increase in the defenses against guilt feelings; the patient sadistically acts out his triumph over the therapist, with the danger of reconfirming the pathological vicious cycles of interactions he has engaged in with significant others in the past.

Sometimes, under conditions of chronic therapeutic stalemate, one may observe the apparently strange occurrence of some improvement in the patient's functioning outside the sessions. Or the patient may appear increasingly willing to continue an impossible therapeutic situation endlessly. At some point it is as if the treatment had replaced life and the patient were expressing in his behavior an urgent wish and magic command that the treatment continue forever (therefore without any change), that reality be left aside in an unconscious collusion between therapist and patient. The therapist may feel intuitively that the patient will experience any challenge to this stable equilibrium as an unbelievable act of cruelty, as if the therapist were throwing him to the lions.

In the midst of such a stalemate, patients may quite directly demand that the therapist compensate them for their past suffering by dedicating his life totally to them. But, regardless of the extent to which the therapist goes out of his way to accommodate the patient's desires, eventually the following issues tend to become prominent:

First, the patient may destroy time in the sense of losing his perspective on time; that is, he focuses on each session as if time had come to a halt between the sessions and as if both patient and therapist were going to live, and the treatment continue, forever.

Second, this destruction of time may be accompanied by specifically ignoring and rejecting evidence of the therapist's concern and dedication. It is as if the patient's suspiciousness and destructive disqualification of the therapist were geared to destroying love with cruelty, while projecting this cruelty onto the therapist. Relentless accusations implying that the therapist does not love the patient enough are the most frequent but not the severest manifestations of this tendency. Uncannily, at times when the therapist may in fact be so internally exhausted that he withdraws temporarily from active attempts to work with the patient, the patient's accusations often diminish, and an eerie unconscious collusion fostering paralysis and emptiness in the psychotherapeutic situation may ensue.

Third, the patient may attempt to convince the therapist that ordinary psychological understanding and empathy have no place in this situation. If this effort succeeds, the therapist may then think that he should replace his concrete understanding of the dynamics of the transference by more general formulations of ego arrests, lack of capacity for emotional understanding, cognitive deficits, and the like. There are, of course, patients with such limits in their ego functioning, for example, an incapacity for symbolic communication as part of minimal brain dysfunction. However, what is striking in these cases is that a careful initial study or review of the cases under consideration reveals that, in contrast to those with minimal brain dysfunction, they fail to reveal such deficits, and that often, to the contrary, early in the treatment many of the patients had given some evidence of a capacity for psychological understanding. Sometimes even very experienced therapists may have to ask for help at points when ordinary human understanding no longer seems to work, only to find from the observation of others that the patient has given evidence of much more understanding of what has been going on than he has revealed to the therapist. (This phenomenon has occurred with dramatic frequency in consultation work with such cases.)

In short, something very active in the patient attempts to destroy time, love and concern, and cognitive understanding. I think that the therapist is here facing the activation of the deepest levels of aggression. Sometimes it is hopeless to resolve these severe treatment stalemates; however, it is sometimes possible to do so with an essentially analytic approach. To this end, certain therapeutic tactics and attitudes become crucial.

Impatience in the "Here and Now"

First of all, instead of resigning himself to a passive "wait-and-see" attitude in each hour, while actually becoming increasingly discouraged as time passes, it is helpful for the therapist to temper the patience he usually maintains over an extended period of time with impatience, a refusal to accept passively the destruction of concrete psychotherapeutic work in each session. The therapist must actively counter the acting out of severe aggression. This "activity" does not mean that he has abandoned the position of technical neutrality.

There are times when the therapist may feel exhausted, unable to think or say anything. When treatment remains at a stalemate, the therapist may sometimes feel not only that nothing is being accomplished in the session but that he has nothing new to offer. He is, as it were, completely paralyzed in terms of any thought, feeling, or intervention that might influence the situation. For the therapist to be forced into such a subjective sense reflects the destruction or denial of the present interaction's significance. Such a situation can only evoke anxiety in the therapist.

The therapist may feel that he needs a new beginning but does not know where to start; he feels responsible for tasks unfulfilled and a sense of guilt for permitting the patient to continue in a situation that is, as far as the therapist can see, not helpful. Such feelings will also activate whatever countertransference potential exists. The therapist may benefit by exploring this fully within himself, utilizing bad moments in the patient's treatment for learning more about himself.

If and when the therapist can reassure himself that his intervention will be determined not by his own countertransference needs but by the real needs of the patient, he should then confront the patient actively with the fact that nothing is happening and that both patient and therapist have the urgent task of exploring why this is so. Indeed, this may be the major task for both participants. If the patient reacts with anger and suspicion to these efforts to examine and resolve a therapeutic stalemate, his distortion of what the therapist is doing should be interpreted.

One patient in analysis immediately fell asleep whenever the analyst focused on the transference; he never fell asleep at other times. The patient gradually extended this behavior to all situations when the analyst made comments that the patient suspected were indirectly related to an effort to focus on the transference, including all comments related to the patient's falling asleep, to his falling asleep when the analyst commented on the danger of his falling asleep, and so on. Retrospectively, this may seem an extreme, almost amusing case of repression, but while it was going on it reflected the patient's unconscious effort to defeat the analyst, whom he perceived as a sadistic father image. The analyst began to focus more and more on the patient's extraordinary tranquility and lack of concern in the face of this development, which had brought about a therapeutic stalemate lasting for months. In the process, the interpretive focus broadened until the patient's entire life seemed to center on his tendency to fall asleep during the analytic hours. The systematic analysis of this behavior eventually revealed its function as an acting out of negative transference stemming first, from the rebellion against the oedipal father, and later, from conflicts with the preoedipal mother.

It hardly needs to be stressed that the therapist should intervene only when he is not under the sway of negative, hostile affects toward the patient. Such aggression toward the patient may be a "normal" reaction, but it usually becomes condensed with whatever potential for aggressive countertransference reactions exists in the therapist. The therapist should contain this reaction and use it for understanding. The patient may become alarmed at what he perceives as the therapist's aggressive, confronting attitude, and the interpretation of the patient's fears that the therapist is about to stop the treatment as retaliation against the patient's unconscious efforts to undermine it may be an important step in clarifying the nature of this transference situation.

My point is that it is better for the therapist to risk becoming a "bull in a china shop" than to remain paralyzed, lulled into passive collusion with the patient's destruction of time. At the very least, an active approach reconfirms for the patient the therapist's concern, his determined intolerance of impossible situations, and his confidence in the possibility of change. Particularly with patients who have been in treatment for many years, the therapist may find it more and more difficult to face his growing awareness of lack of change. The accumulation of guilt for having tolerated the stalemate over an extended period of time, realistic or unrealistic as it may be, is one more impediment to change, this one stemming from the therapist.

Focus on Time and Treatment Goals

The therapist needs to remind the patient of the lack of progress in treatment, to bring into focus again and again the overall treatment goals established at the initiation of treatment and the patient's apparent neglect of these while assuming an attitude that the treatment should and could go on forever. In this connection, the therapist needs to stress the differences between realistic treatment goals and the patient's life goals, as noted by Ticho (1972).

For example, a 45-year-old woman who had divorced her husband as the latest reenactment of a long series of sadomasochistic relationships with men (all of which concluded in her being frustrated and disappointed by their abandonment of her) developed a prolonged rage reaction to the therapist because he did not respond to her amorous advances toward him. Careful and fairly full interpretation of the meanings of this pattern over an extended period of time had not led to its solution. When the therapist finally realized that the patient had maintained the secret fantasy of marrying him as part of her initial decision to enter treatment, he confronted her with this information. Faced with this unrealistic confusion of her life goals and her treatment goals, the patient angrily terminated the treatment and refused to continue or to initiate treatment with somebody else. The issue of treatment goals should have been explored from the beginning of her treatment.

Focus on Destruction of External Reality

The focus on the broad goals of the treatment should be complemented by a sharp focus on the patient's immediate reality. Usually, in extreme, prolonged stalemate, the patient also neglects the circumstances of his immediate reality and reveals an almost conscious sense of triumph in defeating his own efforts, a triumph over the therapist, whose impotence is reconfirmed every day as impossible situations develop and disaster is courted. It is essential that the therapist interpret the unconscious (and sometimes conscious) rage toward him expressed in the patient's playing Russian roulette in his daily life.

The patient will have to assume responsibility for his immediate life situation as well as for his long-range plans. This is a responsibility that I think we expect of any patient who undergoes psychoanalytic psychotherapy on an outpatient basis, and it constitutes the reality baseline against which transference acting out can be evaluated and interpreted. In extreme stalemate, acting out may take the form of burning all bridges in the present external life and in the future, with the implicit expectation that the therapist will assume full responsibility; this must be interpreted consistently.

All this points to the crucial need for a careful initial evaluation of the indications and contraindications for psychoanalysis or intensive psychoanalytic psychotherapy of borderline (and other) patients. It illustrates what I have suggested earlier (chap. 6) are the three issues that codetermine the priorities for interpretive work in each session with borderline patients: the predominant transference pattern at any particular moment, the patient's immediate life situation, and the overall goals of the treatment.

Interpretations of Dissociated Love and Concern

The therapist can also be helpful under the conditions described by consistently interpreting the splitting between the patient's angry, demanding, and self-defeating attitudes in the transference and his periods of calm, friendly, relaxed, and concerned behavior toward the therapist. There is a need to bring such islands of potentially observing ego, particularly of remaining self-concern, together with the major area of the personality, where aggression dominates unbound and unchecked. Although this tactic may seem obvious in theory, in practice one cannot underestimate the relief a therapist may experience from at least a few quiet, relaxed, "good" moments in his interactions with a patient whose treatment is otherwise becoming a nightmare for him.

The therapist may be tempted to collude with splitting mechanisms in the patient as one way of preserving his own good feelings about the patient in the face of his generally unrelenting aggression. The therapist must make a deliberate effort to keep in mind that the patient has given evidence of a capacity to work on his problems (otherwise he would not be in the kind of treatment he is in), and the therapist must also remember the patient's "good" aspects. It is this confidence in the patient's potential, a basic trust in his capacity to learn, that permits the therapist to confront him actively without colluding in defensive islands of friendliness and without drowning in guilty feelings stemming from the patient's accusations that the therapist is attacking him.

In other words, confidence in what the patient might become is the basis of strength from which confrontation may be carried out so that it is free from punitive implications. Paradoxically, the therapist who can maintain this kind of confidence in the patient's potential without denying the defensive aspect of the patient's temporary "friendliness" in the face of all-encompassing aggression will be freer and more effective in dealing with the negative transference than the therapist who attempts to maintain an image of the patient's "nice qualities" dissociated from the unpleasant or frightening aspects of his behavior.

A corollary of this attitude is to expect nothing in terms of immediate, short-range change in the sessions, to maintain a consistent attitude of concerned challenge from hour to hour, while expecting that any change will take a very long time indeed. The patient may be willing to "improve" for the therapist's sake, thus tempting the therapist to feed into his efforts to replace life with the treatment situation. The therapist has to interpret this aspect as well. In the long run, the combination of sublimated impatience in each session, a questioning and concerned attitude, an expectation of no immediate change, and yet confidence regarding the prospects for long-term change may provide a very strong, supportive effect to the treatment.

The alternative to this optimistic attitude is a quiet, almost masochistic submission to the patient's omnipotent control in the sessions, an effort to maintain a picture of the patient as a "nice person," the gradual development of pity for the patient (a frequent manifestation of the therapist's counteraggression), and the tendency to suddenly give up at some point in what might be called a quiet temper tantrum. A realistic decision to terminate the treatment should be the result of an ongoing process in which patient and therapist share the growing conviction that not much more can be accomplished in a given treatment situation.

Secondary Gain of Treatment

In conditions of chronic stalemate it may help the therapist to reevaluate whether the patient realistically has anything better to look forward to than his present life and treatment situation. Sometimes the patient in chronic therapeutic stalemate or negative therapeutic reaction manages to contaminate the therapist's mind with the growing conviction that the patient cannot expect anything better from life than what he has right now, that the patient really would not be capable of having a more satisfactory life if he were functioning on his own.

This problem becomes particularly important with middle-aged and older patients, with whom the illusion cannot be maintained that if all else fails youth holds its own promises for the future. It is of course important to evaluate at the beginning of treatment whether the patient—if and when his treatment goals are accomplished—will have anything better to look forward to than his present life situation. If the therapist is convinced, for example, that the patient's life has passed by, that the amount of destruction the patient has incurred in terms of the possibility of love, family life, work or creativity, and sources of gratification in general is such that there is really not much to hope for, then perhaps there is no reason to subject the patient to intensive psychoanalytic psychotherapy.

It is true that at times a change in the patient's internal attitude toward life may be what is aimed for, but this should be a clearly understood, shared treatment goal. As an illustration: A patient came to treatment because his wife had abandoned him for another man. His initial treatment goal was to become healthy psychologically so that he could get his wife back. Only after some discussion of treatment and life goals was he able to realize fully that psychological treatment not only would not guarantee his getting his wife back but would not even assure him of the possibility of forming another satisfactory relationship with a woman; the most he could expect was a change in those internal attitudes that interfered with the potential of a good relationship.

The diminishing possibility of finding a satisfactory sexual and particularly a marital partner as life goes on has to be part of the discussion of treatment and life goals. These preconditions permit the therapist, during periods of lengthy stalemate, to reconfirm internally his confidence that the patient has potentially something better to look forward to.

The Therapist's Tolerance for Aggression

It should be kept in mind that borderline patients are struggling against a terrifying past and are incapable of projecting into the future any conception of a better life than they have had. Therefore, the therapist's conviction that the patient *can* live a better life and that loss, severe illness, and failure can be tolerated and worked through, if not fully surmounted, becomes very important. The therapist's belief that it is possible to "start all over again" can become a powerful instrument in the interpretation and working through of the transference.

Realistic treatment goals include the acceptance not only of unresolved shortcomings but of the unavoidability of aggression in ordinary life. It is essential that the therapist come to terms with and tolerate aggression both in himself and in others. The therapist's tolerance of his own aggression and that of the people he loves may make it easier for him to interpret the patient's aggression. To face the existence of aggression squarely and to maintain a realistic attitude about the limitations of the therapeutic relationship is in contradistinction to such antitherapeutic attitudes as obsessive coldness, narcissistic withdrawal, "messianic oneness" with the patient, and above all, a naive, Pollyannaish denial of the ambivalence of all human relations.

The therapist's ability to accept truths about himself and his own life may permit him to express in his behavior the conviction that the patient will also be able to accept truths about himself and his life. Uncompromising honesty in facing the most turbulent and painful of life's prospects may become part of very concrete interventions with patients having long-term stalemates in treatment. The therapist's confidence that the patient can tolerate and accept the truth about himself expresses confidence in his potential resources. For example, the therapist's understanding of his own fantasies about the needs of older patients for sex, companionship, and social effectiveness may help him cut through the patient's defensive use of old age as a device for making the therapist feel guilty or as a rationalization for self-destructive resignation.

The Therapist's Holding Function

In chronic therapeutic stalemate the therapist performs a "holding" function. I have observed periods in the psychoanalysis or psychoanalytic psychotherapy of borderline patients where, as Winnicott suggests (1960a), a silent regression takes place to what amounts to a primitive form of dependency on the analyst, experienced as a "holding mother." At such times, the analyst's intuitive, empathically understanding presence may be preferable to the disturbing, intrusively experienced effects of verbal interpretations. Such periods of quiet togetherness and intimacy, in which the patient's "true self" may emerge beyond his "false self" (his artificial, pseudoadaptive efforts), differ dramatically from the situation in chronic states of stalemate where the patient's sense of not being understood or loved by the therapist and of the therapist's intrusiveness is a product of the patient's defensive negation of his own destructive needs and efforts.

It is true that during chronic periods of acting out of destructiveness in the transference the therapist's remaining silent and sitting back may temporarily relieve the patient's anxiety and rage. But this relief often turns out to reflect the patient's fantasied satisfaction of his aggression—for example, his fantasy that his envious attacks have destroyed the therapist's creative processes, particularly the capacity for independent, creative thinking. Thus the therapist's apparent tolerance for the patient as he is may on a deeper level feed the patient's experience of the therapist as giving in to his demands and destructiveness. This situation is radically different from the moments of silent concern and empathy on the part of the therapist that are met by the patient's awareness of these characteristics of the therapist. There is, however, another "holding" function exercised by the therapist at times of chronic therapeutic stalemate: namely, that provided by his ongoing confidence that the patient can change, his concern for the passage of time, and his intolerance for chronic impossible situations.

I believe that an essentially analytic attitude, reflected in a position of—or ongoing movement toward—technical neutrality, provides the optimal background for an interpretive approach to borderline patients. Such "holding," "mothering," or "emotionally corrective" functions as are implicit in this context (Winnicott, 1960a; Modell, 1976) have an important therapeutic value, but for reasons that are more complex than a simple re-creation or compensating reenactment of a normal mother–child (infant) relation.

Mahler's (1971) proposal that borderline pathology is related specifically to the rapprochement subphase of the separation-individuation process seems to me to coincide with my proposal that the problem with borderline patients is not the lack of differentiation of self from nonself but the lack of integration of "good" and "bad" self and object representations. The principal problem with these patients is their failure to achieve a satisfactory loving relation with an object that can be trusted and relied upon in the face of their aggression toward it, despite their awareness of the shortcomings of and frustrations stemming from that object, and in the context of tolerating painful guilt, concern, and gratitude toward that loved object. For the patient to accept closeness and being understood and to rely on the therapist requires acceptance of his own aggression and trust that it will not destroy the therapist or his love for the therapist. For the therapist to be able to "hold" the patient means accepting the reality of the patient's aggression without being overwhelmed by it, trusting in the patient's potential for loving despite his current difficulties in expressing love, and believing in the possibility that life has something to offer the patient notwithstanding his limitations.

For example, one patient's severe hypochondriacal tendencies diminished when he could experience a capacity to express love and concern for his wife and children. Feeling that he was now able to give made it possible for him to accept the prospect of his future illness and death. Previously he had unconsciously perceived death as the final condemnation, as being swallowed up by his own "evil nature" in a world that was empty and devoid of love. Another patient, a woman with a narcissistic personality whose life centered on keeping up a semblance of youthfulness and carefully disguising all manifestations of the aging process, could accept "letting go" in the sense of looking her age and accepting the aging process when her fear over her terrible envy of the young decreased and when, in spite of this envy, she was able to invest interest in the young people who surrounded her in her daily life and work.

For the patient to be able to accept being "held," to rely on another person, also means accepting the possibility of "letting go," with the knowledge that all relations are limited and uncertain. The essential requirement for accepting this possibility is a toning down of fears about one's own aggression. The achievement of this capacity in treatment is reflected in the patient's becoming able to accept closeness to the therapist even with the time limitations of the treatment hours and to accept that the therapist has a life of his own beyond the patient and the sessions with him.

I have stressed that it is not enough for the therapist to be emotionally available, warm, and sympathetic and to tolerate aggression without responding in counteraggressive ways; he must at all times maintain an intellectual clarity, expressed in good reasons why he does or does not carry out certain interventions. He must also maintain an awareness of the realistic limits of the effectiveness of his interventions.

The treatment of borderline patients is usually a slow, uncertain, and repetitive process of exploration of meanings, confrontation, testing of interpretive hypotheses, and working through of self-defeating character patterns rather than experiences of sudden discovery or cathartic awareness. The first, usually weak signs of change in any rigid character pattern (such as malignant grandiosity, self-defeating narcissism, chronically triumphant masochism, total denial of emotional reality, or the self-perpetuating trickery of antisocial exploitation) may be so brief and transitory that any hope originally triggered by such early changes is soon dashed.

The achievement of change in the predominant constellation of internalized object relations is a long and slow process. This is one more reason why impatience with stalemate in every session should be coupled with great patience for absence of change (while remaining aware of this absence) over a long period of time. Manifestations of growth in the capacity for love, concern, and gratitude are usually complex, turbulent, and unclear at first; in contrast, hatred often has a clarifying, precise, boundary-drawing quality to it. While the patient, in the process of experiencing hatred of the therapist, may become precise, clear, excited, or even elated, the therapist's concern for his patient at that time may have a confusing and even somewhat disorganizing effect on his own thinking. And yet this confusion and turbulence are the raw material for the therapist's growing understanding of the patient. The early stages of "humanization" of the patient may take the form of chaos, depression, and suffering. There is no easy way in the long road toward understanding.

The expectation that our increasing knowledge will shorten the psychological treatment of severe character pathology and the borderline disorders may represent one more illusion about the process, technique, and outcome of psychotherapy. But the possibility of diagnosing the major transference patterns reflecting the predominant conflicts in the area of borderline patients' object relations after a limited period of treatment seems a realistic consequence of our growing knowledge about these patients. Such an early diagnosis should enable us to define more concretely, after an initial period of psychotherapy, what significant changes can be expected in these patterns and their respective sequences: Here may be an area for research on the process and outcome of intensive psychotherapy.

CHAPTER 16: *Diagnosis and Clinical Management of Patients with Suicide Potential*

Diagnosis

To evaluate suicide potential during an initial diagnostic study is obviously more difficult than when the therapist is familiar with the patient. The appraisal of suicide risk in patients who are first seen in a diagnostic evaluation should include consideration of the clinical severity of depression, affective disorders superimposed on borderline personality organization, and chronic self-mutilation and suicide as a "way of life."

The Clinical Severity of Depression

This diagnostic focus includes both the intensity of suicidal ideation and plans for action as well as the extent to which the depression affects behavior, mood, and ideation. The severity of the depression can be gauged by the degree to which behavior is slowed down, ideation is slowed down (and concentration therefore affected), and sadness is replaced by an empty, frozen mood with a subjective sense of depersonalization. In addition, the presence or absence of biological symptoms of depression (reflected in eating patterns, weight, sleep patterns, digestive functions, daily rhythm of depressive affect, menstrual patterns, sexual desire, muscle tone) supplies crucial information regarding the severity of the depression. In general, the severer the clinical depression accompanying suicidal ideation and intention, the acuter the danger. In patients with major depressive episodes who do not suffer from borderline personality organization, the suicide risk is particularly marked during the stage of recovery from paralyzing depression; in borderline patients, by contrast, their chronic impulsivity spreads the suicide risk over the entire depressive episode. The danger is especially urgent in patients who exhibit all three series of indicators (suicidal ideation and intention, depressive retardation of psychic functions, and biological features of depression) simultaneously.

In contrast, the extent to which histrionic behavior is present—the dramatic display of affect in infantile personalities—is less relevant for the evaluation of the severity of depression and suicide risk. There may be acute danger of suicide in patients whose dramatic behavior persuades the therapist to dismiss the severity of the depression or whose momentary histrionic cheerfulness and general lability of affect convey the false impression that the depression is not severe.

What has impressed me in evaluating the suicide potential of borderline patients is the uselessness of the patients' conscious rationalizations, such as the expression of "needs for dependency," of consciously experienced "hopelessness," of loss of the capacity for "trusting," of suicide as a "cry for help," and the various other rationalizations of their depression that these patients often express in the initial interview. In clinical practice, the question is not whether a patient has a general feeling of "hopelessness" but what, concretely, he is hopeless about: receiving love from an ambivalently experienced object? being able to control an object or to carry out an act of revenge? Similarly, the issue is not whether he is able to "trust" the therapist—there is no reason to expect a patient to trust anybody he hardly knows—but whether he is willing to communicate honestly about himself regardless of how he feels about the therapist. A common feature of all these issues is the need to evaluate the secondary gain of suicidal behavior, which leads to the evaluation of suicide as a "way of life."

The misuse of psychoanalytic concepts in constructing dynamic hypotheses to evaluate suicide potential may be a key factor in failing to properly diagnose and treat severely suicidal borderline patients. Psychodynamic factors are indeed important, but they have to be assessed on the basis of the currently enacted object relations with the therapist rather than being evaluated on the basis of the patient's consciously expressed fantasies.

Major Affective Disorder Superimposed on Borderline Personality Organization

Patients with bona fide manic-depressive illness may present a borderline personality organization as the stable characterological background against which cyclical affective episodes develop. Diagnosis and clinical management are more complicated with these patients than with the more frequently encountered type of manic-depressive patients with neurotic or normal personality organization. In my experience, many patients with borderline personality organization respond less satisfactorily than their normal or neurotic counterparts to psychopharmacological treatment for a major affective illness, and the distinction between psychotic episodes and latent periods of the affective illness is less clear. The danger is great, under such circumstances, that the clinician will underestimate the seriousness of suicidal intentions, particularly if the patient's history suggests that such intentions have been chronic and more integrated with his basic personality structure than is actually the case. An acute and severe suicide potential may be underestimated if the patient has a long history of severe personality disturbances with recurrent depressions without suicidal intention. When the presenting affective symptomatology is hypomanic rather than depressive, there is even greater danger of missing suicide potential linked to a sudden shift into a depressive phase.

Chronic Self-Mutilation and Suicide as a "Way of Life"

The DSM-III diagnosis of borderline personality disorder stresses chronically suicidal and self-mutilating tendencies as major characteristics of these patients. Clinically, one finds these tendencies in patients with infantile personality, narcissistic personality functioning on an overt borderline level, "as if" personalities, and other patients with borderline personality organization whose major characteristic is pseudologia fantastica. Finally, some atypical, chronically psychotic patients may mimic this type of borderline patient. For practical purposes, it is helpful to evaluate all these patients both descriptively and psychodynamically (i.e., in terms of the functions of the defensive operations and primitive object relations dominating in the transference). Such a combined evaluation permits the distinction of several subgroups.

(1) One frequent constellation is the presence of chronic self-mutilating behavior in patients with predominantly infantile personality and borderline personality organization, the type that corresponds quite closely to the descriptive diagnosis of borderline personality disorder in DSM-III. Clinically, self-mutilating behavior and/or suicide gestures emerge at times of intense rage attacks or rage mixed with temporary flare-ups of depression. Further exploration frequently shows that these gestures are designed to establish or reestablish control over the environment by evoking guilt feelings in others—when, for example, a relationship with a sexual partner breaks up or when parents strongly oppose the patient's wishes. At other times, suicidal or self-mutilating behavior may be an expression of unconscious guilt over success or over the deepening of a psychotherapeutic relationship—the latter being a relatively benign type of negative therapeutic reaction. Patients with a history of negative therapeutic reaction who have infantile features combined with depressive-masochistic characteristics are particularly at risk for suicide attempts.

(2) A much severer type of chronic self-mutilating behavior, frequently linked with suicidal tendencies, is an expression of what I am calling *malignant narcissism* (see chap. 19). This phenomenon is found in patients with borderline personality organization and a predominantly narcissistic personality structure functioning on an overt borderline level—that is, with a general lack of impulse control, anxiety tolerance, and sublimatory channeling. These patients have lifestyles that are as chaotic as that of the infantile personality, with whom they are frequently confused. However, in contrast to the intense dependency and clinging behavior of infantile personalities (or, more generally speaking, of borderline patients without pathological narcissism), these patients are basically aloof from and uninvolved with others; their attacks of rage and/or depression occur when their pathological grandiosity is challenged and they experience a traumatic sense of humiliation or defeat.

Malignant narcissism refers to patients presenting an infiltration of aggression into the pathological grandiose self that characterizes the narcissistic personality. In contrast to the ordinary type of narcissistic personality, these patients experience increased self-esteem and confirmation of their grandiosity when they can express aggression toward themselves or others. Pleasure in cruelty, sadistic sexual perversions, as well as pleasurably experienced self-mutilation are part of this picture. The sense these patients convey of being capable of calmly damaging or even killing themselves, in contrast to the fear and despair and the "pleading" efforts of their relatives and staff to keep them alive and to maintain their human contacts, illustrates a dramatic distortion of the gratification of self-esteem. The patients' grandiosity is fulfilled by their feeling of triumph over the fear of pain and death and, at an unconscious level, by their sense of being in control over death. Some patients with anorexia nervosa belong to this subtype.

Both types of patients just described may in addition present chronic drug abuse, alcoholism, or both. Under these circumstances, the suicide risks increase and the prognosis is even less favorable, especially for patients with malignant narcissism. If these patients also present antisocial features (typically, dishonesty regarding their use of drugs or alcohol), the risk of suicide is further enhanced. Patients who simultaneously display general impulsivity, dishonesty, chronic self-mutilating tendencies, alcohol and/or drug abuse, and a profound interpersonal aloofness or emotional unavailability may develop suicidal behavior at any time; the risk cannot be accurately assessed at any specific point. This fact has to be accepted as a built-in danger in any treatment endeavor.

In my experience, the two most frequent causes of suicide by hospitalized psychiatric patients are insufficient control over the patient's life during the treatment of patients with this disastrous combination of symptoms and the premature discharge of psychotically depressed patients who are clinically improving.

(3) A third type of chronic self-mutilating and related suicidal behavior is present in certain atypical, chronically psychotic conditions that mimic borderline conditions. Examples are some chronic schizophrenic patients (the truly "pseudoneurotic schizophrenia"), some patients with chronic schizoaffective illness, and some with chronic paranoid psychoses who present a much better integrated personality structure than is true in most cases of paranoid schizophrenia. These patients often do not fulfill the criteria for psychotic illness on a purely descriptive basis. Only a structural diagnosis (see chaps. 1 and 2) reveals loss of reality testing. These are patients with essentially psychotic personality organization whose intermittent depressions may acquire psychotic features with overvalued or even delusional depressive ideas. When these patients are not in a depressive episode they are socially withdrawn and aloof in therapeutic interactions. They frequently reveal a history of bizarre suicide attempts marked by unusual degrees of cruelty or highly idiosyncratic features (corresponding to their autistic fantasies about bodily or psychological transformations). One can also include here those patients who attempt suicide under the effect of persecutory delusions or hallucinatory demands. In fact, I have seen several patients who harbor delusions that they are condemned to die or that they have orders to kill themselves. These delusions may extend over years within a context of depression, schizoid aloofness, or paranoid personality features.

Clinical Management

The first area of concern is the severity of the depression, which, superimposed on a borderline personality organization, may imply an acute suicide risk. In my view, patients with borderline personality organization and a superimposed major affective illness who present suicidal ideation require immediate hospitalization, psychopharmacological treatment for the affective disorder, and, if there is a history of lack of response to psychopharmacological treatment or an extremely acute suicide potential, electroconvulsive treatment. Patients who present a history of bizarre suicide attempts, psychotic personality organization, or a psychotic syndrome at present (whether schizophrenic, schizoaffective, or paranoid) and suicidal ideation warrant at least diagnostic hospitalization and intensive treatment of the psychotic syndrome. Obviously, if such patients also present lack of honesty in their communications with the therapist, they have to be considered high suicide risks. In all cases the treatment of the psychotic syndrome takes precedence over the treatment of the underlying personality disorder. In practice this usually implies psychopharmacological treatment, at least brief hospitalization, possibly electroconvulsive treatment, and careful mapping out of the patient's previous psychiatric history in preparation for evaluation of the long-term suicide risk once the acute psychosis has been resolved.

The combination of chronic impulsivity in a borderline patient with the acute potential for a suicide attempt in a complicating manic and/or depressive episode requires hospitalization, even if the patient's past history is well known and apparently reassuring and he has managed to establish a psychotherapeutic relationship with an evaluating psychiatrist. Perhaps the most dangerous period of the treatment of such patients is when they are recovering from a severe acute psychotic depression. Suicide attempts are more likely to occur at this stage in any event, and, in these cases suicidal intentions are blurred by the reappearance of the patient's usual severe character pathology. The premature discharge of depressed patients because of their apparently dramatic symptomatic improvement and their emphatic denial of suicidal intentions is a major factor encouraging suicide after such discharge. This practice has probably become more frequent, given the combination of financial, bureaucratic, and ideological pressures for more rapid discharge of patients from psychiatric hospitals.

In patients with borderline personality organization who do not present a major affective illness or any other psychotic syndrome and where suicide intention and depressive mood are not accompanied by biological symptoms of depression or the slowing down of behavior, thought content, or mood—in other words, where the depression itself does not appear to be clinically severe—the question of outpatient versus inpatient treatment can be raised. A crucial variable is the presence of antisocial features, particularly any evidence of dishonesty in what the patient says about himself. If the past history shows withholding of information from other psychiatrists or psychotherapists, especially information regarding suicide attempts, alcoholism, or drug abuse, it is preferable to assume that the patient's information cannot be considered reliable in the present either and to hospitalize him for a more careful evaluation of his present suicide potential and behavior.

Patients who show lack of concern about themselves and an indifferent, derogatory, or bland attitude toward the diagnostician while simultaneously presenting evidence of suicidal behavior should be considered potentially dishonest and therefore at high risk of suicide. Tactfully confronting the patient with the discrepancy between his suicidal behavior and his apparent lack of concern about it may clarify the extent to which splitting mechanisms and denial, as against conscious manipulation and dishonesty, are responsible. A patient's rage when confronted with contradictory aspects of his behavior will give the diagnostician some basis for evaluating the suicide potential; a patient who is evasive and aloof does not permit an evaluation in depth of his psychic reality. In all cases, the diagnostician has to evaluate not only the patient's verbal communications but his total behavior. This observation might appear superfluous if one did not so frequently observe a dangerous tendency of diagnosticians to underestimate the many forms human aggression and aggression against the self can take.

Patients with infantile and masochistic features who do not present drug addiction or alcoholism, whose attitude is dependent and clinging rather than aloof or withdrawn, and whose honest communication about themselves is combined with expression of concern over their illness may be tentatively treated on an outpatient basis if they can convince the examining psychiatrist of their commitment not to act on their suicidal impulses or to contact him immediately should they feel they cannot control these wishes so that hospitalization can be initiated. However, with patients whose suicidal intentions or behavior emerges in the course of an adequate, intensive psychotherapeutic treatment and who give evidence of the development of a chronic negative therapeutic reaction, it is unwise to rely on any such contract. It is preferable to start these patients on a new psychotherapeutic relationship with a different therapist in the hospital. Obviously, if past history indicates that the patient has been able to respond positively to psychotherapeutic treatment, the possibility of starting treatment on an outpatient basis is strengthened.

In all cases, if the diagnostician is convinced, on the basis of solid evidence in the patient's past history as well as in their present interaction, that the patient is communicating with him honestly, his day-to-day estimate regarding the patient's suicide potential is likely to be more accurate.

If hospitalization is indicated but the patient refuses to accept it, the psychiatrist's responsibility includes the mobilization of all social and legal resources to permit the initiation of treatment under optimal conditions. Under no circumstances should the psychiatrist carry out treatment under conditions that will increase the danger of suicide. Here the unconscious tendency to "play God" is counterpart to dangerous naiveté in neglecting the severity of destructive tendencies in the patient and his family. One frequent precipitating factor of suicide by borderline cases in outpatient treatment is, unfortunately, the psychotherapist's agreement to treat such patients under less than optimal circumstances—for example, permitting them to refuse certain aspects of the treatment (medication, day care, family involvement, and so on) or accepting their failure to attend sessions regularly or to communicate openly.

Consistent, straightforward discussion of the patient's chronic suicide potential is a key aspect of the hospital treatment of all borderline patients with these chronic suicidal characteristics. I have noted earlier that the premature discharge of patients with major affective illness when their clinical improvement from depression maximizes their suicide risk is a classical mistake. An equally devastating and unfortunately frequent mistake is the effort on the part of hospital staff to engage borderline patients in pleasant and gratifying interactions while ignoring or denying the severity of their malignant, manipulative, dishonest behaviors. The danger of reinforcing splitting mechanisms by treating all these warning signals as isolated episodes and focusing attention on the "positive" aspects of the patients' interactions cannot be overstressed.

Consistent confrontation of the patient's contradictory behavior patterns, a steady focus on his lack of concern about himself, on how he undermines potentially helpful relations with others, on his failure to collaborate with the treatment efforts, all tend to create immediate tension, turmoil, and open expression of aggression in the patient's interpersonal field in the hospital. By the same token, however, the patient's capacity for taking responsibility for himself, for collaborating honestly with psychotherapeutic efforts, can best be diagnosed under circumstances of open and direct—if also defiant and angry—communications, and realistic postdischarge plans can be developed more easily. In contrast, an atmosphere of superficial friendliness and underlying denial of the patient's difficulties often eventuates in renewed self-destructive, self-mutilating, or suicidal behavior once the patient has left the hospital.

In many cases, the severity of the patient's chronic self-destructive potential cannot be reduced significantly even during extended periods of hospitalization. Sometimes acceptance of a chronic risk of suicide is the price of outpatient treatment, which one hopes will challenge the patient with a more productive lifestyle and with a psychotherapeutic relationship in the context of the real world, unlike the artificially protective hospital environment. What can be done to reduce patients' suicide risks under such circumstances?

First of all, the secondary gains of suicidal behavior have to be diagnosed and controlled. Chronic suicide threats and behavior reflecting the acting out of dissociated sadistic tendencies toward the patient's family, which permit him to dominate the family and combine primary and secondary gain of illness, must be interpreted and brought under control. Work with the patient's family may become a crucial part of the treatment. It is important for patients to learn that their threats of suicide have no power over the therapist.

The therapist should convey to the patient that he would feel sad but not responsible if the patient killed himself and that his life would not be significantly affected by such an event. The therapist thus creates a healthy basis for a new object relation, unlike those the patient has had with his family.

Second, the therapist should tell the patient's family that the patient is chronically apt to commit suicide, indicating to them that the patient suffers from what might be described as a psychological cancer from which he might die at any time. The therapist should tell all those concerned that he is willing to engage in a psychotherapeutic effort to help the patient overcome this illness, but he should give no firm assurance that he will be successful or guarantee protection from suicide over the long period of treatment. This realistic definition of the treatment may be a most effective way to protect the psychotherapeutic relationship from the destructive involvement of other family members and from the patient's efforts to control the therapy by inducing in the therapist an "indirect countertransference" (Racker, 1968), characterized by guilt feelings and paranoid fears regarding third parties.

Third, with patients who present chronic suicidal or self-mutilating potential, that potential must be explored consistently and woven into the analysis of all interactions with the therapist. It is difficult to do full justice to this technical recommendation without offering detailed clinical material. For practical purposes, work with such chronic suicide potential becomes an essential aspect of psychotherapeutic technique, an ever-present element in the therapist's interpretations of the material.

Fourth, it is important that the therapist who treats borderline patients with chronic suicide potential in an outpatient setting not accept impossible treatment arrangements that require unusual efforts or heroic measures on his part. In the long run, whenever more is demanded of the therapist than would be reasonable in the average psychotherapeutic treatment, the end result is a reinforcement of the patient's self-destructive potential. At times, even psychotherapists as well as hospital staff may gradually develop the unconscious (and even conscious) wish that an impossible patient would "disappear," thus reenacting in the countertransference the patient's own death wishes, as well as his family's death wishes toward him. In this connection, naiveté regarding a patient's suicide potential is not infrequently matched with naiveté regarding the family's attitude toward the patient—specifically, their death wishes toward what they regard as an impossible member of the family. Hospital staff are often confronted with a family that has made vigorous attempts to obtain the discharge of a patient who is acutely suicidal, often under the promise of transferring the patient to another psychotherapeutic setting, only to then "innocently" give the patient the time and the place to kill himself. The best way to counter the patient's death wishes is to take them very seriously and to consider the "contamination" that they bring to the patient's immediate environment.

As I stress elsewhere (see chap. 19), the therapist's acceptance of the possibility of failing with a patient is a crucial element in the treatment of patients with malignant narcissism and severe suicide potential. The patient's unconscious or conscious fantasy that the therapist desperately wants the patient to stay alive and that the patient therefore has power over the therapist, as well as over life and death, needs to be explored and resolved in the treatment.

Every attempted or completed suicide implies the activation of intense aggression not only within the patient but within his immediate interpersonal field. The psychotherapist who seems to react only with sorrow and concern to the suicidal patient is denying his own counteraggression and playing into the patient's dynamics. The therapist must be able to empathize with the patient's suicide temptations, with his longing for peace, with his excitement of self-directed aggression, with his pleasure in taking revenge against significant others, with his wish to escape from guilt, and with the exhilarating sense of power involved in suicidal urges. Only that kind of empathy on the part of the therapist may permit the patient to explore these issues openly in the treatment.

Any psychotherapeutic relationship that extends over many months under unrealistic conditions, without honest communication and clearly delimited and accepted responsibilities on the part of both participants, may also be playing into the patient's suicide potential. There are times when a psychotherapist, recognizing the impossibility of the treatment situation, has to have the courage to end it, even if the patient uses the threat of suicide to try to keep a sadomasochistic relationship alive. Such a termination of treatment should correspond not to an impulsive acting out of the countertransference but to a well-thought-out plan that may have to include temporary hospitalization while the psychotherapist disengages himself from the treatment, extensive work with the family, and/or extended consultation by the psychotherapist with an experienced colleague. The best way of helping some patients is for the therapist to acknowledge honestly that he may not be able to help them, that they may be helped better by a colleague or that they cannot be helped at all at this stage of our knowledge and therapeutic resources.

CHAPTER 17: *Countertransference, Transference Regression, and the Incapacity to Depend*

Dimensions of Countertransference

The relationship between countertransference and the psychoanalyst's personality may be considered according to at least three conceptual dimensions. The first is what I would call a spatial, or "field," dimension and has to do with what actually is included under the term *countertransference*. I think of this field as a series of concentric circles, the inner ones representing the narrow concepts of countertransference, the outer ones representing the broader concepts. The temporal dimension differentiates acute from long-term "permanent" countertransference reactions. A third dimension is represented by the severity of the patient's illness.

The Countertransference "Field"

Countertransference narrowly defined, as is prevalent within ego psychology, is the analyst's unconscious reaction to the patient (Little, 1951; Reich, 1951). One may restrict the term further to the analyst's unconscious reaction to the patient's transference (Kernberg, 1975). This concept is in line with the original meaning of *countertransference* in psychoanalytic literature and adequately allows for "blind spots" in understanding the patient's material derived from the analyst's unresolved neurotic conflicts.

A second, broader circle encompassing the first one extends the concept to the analyst's total conscious and unconscious reactions to the patient. This concept includes the analyst's appropriate emotional responses to the patient's transferences and to the reality of the patient's life and the emotional effects on the treatment situation determined by the analyst's own reality as it may become affected by the patient. The

264

justification for this broader concept of countertransference derives from the effects on the treatment of the deeply regressive transferences of borderline patients, the acting out that characterizes severe character pathology in general, and the unconscious (and conscious) destructiveness of some narcissistic borderline and paranoid patients, which may threaten not only the treatment but the patient's—and even the analyst's—life.

A still broader circle includes, in addition to the two mentioned above, the habitual specific reaction of any particular analyst to various types of patients, a reaction that includes countertransference dispositions and manifestations as defined and the analyst's general personality traits. Certain personality traits may become activated in certain treatment situations, with both defensive and adaptive functions in response to transference onslaughts.

Much apparent controversy regarding the management of countertransference derives from the different ways in which countertransference has been defined. A comprehensive definition that includes the entire spatial field of countertransference phenomena while still clearly differentiating the components of this field may resolve the problem.

The Temporal Dimension

Three types of countertransference reactions can be distinguished on the basis of time. First are acute or short-lived reactions, which, according to how countertransference is defined, may be determined solely by the patient's transference or by the total patient/analyst interaction.

Next are long-term countertransference distortions: subtle, gradual, and insidiously expanding distortions of the analyst's attitude toward the patient over an extended period of time. As Tower (1956) has pointed out, these are often recognized only retrospectively. They usually occur in working with a particular transference pattern, especially in the early stages of treatment, when resistance intensifies that pattern. The resolution of that transference pattern by interpretation may illuminate the chronic countertransference distortion, which now disappears, together with the shift in the transference. The analyst can alert himself to such long-term countertransference reactions by comparing the "special" reaction a given patient evokes in him with his reactions to other patients.

Finally, a still more extended countertransference reaction is the "permanent countertransference" described by Reich (1951), which she believes (and I agree) reflects the analyst's character pathology. It hardly needs to be said that the analyst's personality plays a role in any analysis. His position of technical neutrality does not mean that the patient cannot distinguish and recognize many aspects of the analyst's actual appearance, behavior, attitudes, and affective reactions. In fact, one might say that patients hang the fabric of their transference onto the protuberances of the analyst's personality.

Whereas these real aspects of the analyst lend themselves to rationalization of transference developments, they do not deny the origin in the past of the patient's transference, and they do not necessarily correspond to the analyst's character pathology. Patients rapidly become expert in detecting the analyst's personality characteristics, and transference reactions often first emerge in this context. But to conclude that all transference reactions are at bottom, at least in part, unconscious or conscious reactions to the reality of the analyst is to misunderstand the nature of the transference. The transference is the inappropriate aspect of the patient's reaction to the analyst. The analysis of the transference may begin by the analyst's "leaving open" the reality of the patient's observations and exploring why particular observations are important at any particular time.

If the analyst is aware of realistic features of his personality and is able to accept them without narcissistic defensiveness or denial, his emotional attitude will permit him to convey to the patient: "So, if you are responding to something in me, how do we understand the intensity of your reaction?" But the analyst's character pathology may be such that the patient's transference reaction to him results in the erosion of technical neutrality. When the analyst is incapable of discriminating between the patient's realistic and unrealistic perceptions of him, countertransference is operating.

Countertransference and the Severity of the Patient's Pathology

I have described in earlier work (1975) a continuum of countertransference reactions, ranging from responses to the typical analytic patient who establishes a well-differentiated transference neurosis to reactions to a psychotic patient with psychotic transference. Countertransference reactions to the borderline conditions and pathological narcissism occupy an intermediate position on this continuum. The more regressed the patient, the more he forces the analyst to reactivate regressive features in himself in order to keep in touch with the patient. This brings the total personality of the analyst into the foreground. The more regressed the patient, the more his characteristic pathogenic conflicts are infiltrated by primitive aggression, expressed in the transference as direct or indirect attacks on the analyst. Such attacks activate an emotional response in the analyst reflecting, as Winnicott (1949) pointed out, his reaction not only to the transference but also to the total patient/analyst relation. Under such circumstances, the broader concept of countertransference becomes operational. The more regressed the patient, the more global will be the analyst's emotional reactions.

The analyst's global reactions, then, include not only countertransference dispositions in a restricted sense but also what Racker (1957) calls "complementary identifications" with the patient's activated and projected object representations. The analyst's understanding of the unconsciously activated internalized object relations in the transference is thus enriched. In contrast to Racker, however, I would stress that in a position of complementary countertransference, the analyst may identify not only with the patient's "internal objects" but with his projected self representations as well, while the patient enacts his identifications with an internalized object representation.

The activation in the psychoanalytic situation of a primitive internalized object relation within which patient and analyst maintain their reciprocity but repeatedly exchange their roles (identifying themselves alternately with self and object representations) has fundamental diagnostic and therapeutic functions. To utilize these developments therapeutically, the analyst must maintain strict analytic boundaries to control acting out and preserve his internal freedom for fantasizing ("reverie") in order to diagnose the projected aspects of the patient's object relations. The analyst must also continually separate out such projected material from his own countertransference dispositions (in a restricted sense) and must transform his introspection into transference interpretations that preserve an atemporal quality until confirmatory material permits genetic placing. In other words, the analyst's tolerance for distortions of his intrapsychic experience under the impact of transference regression in the patient may become empathy with what the patient cannot tolerate within himself. The empathy may eventually generate crucial knowledge for transference interpretations.

Grinberg (1979) has proposed differentiating the analyst's complementary countertransference, derived from the activation in him of past internal object relations under the influence of the patient's transference, from "projective counteridentification," when such activation stems almost entirely from the patient's transference. This proposed distinction enriches the analysis of countertransference reactions. In practice there is always a complementary relationship between the internal world of the patient and that of the analyst activated in countertransference developments.

As the severity of the patient's illness increases, his expression of emotional reality takes nonverbal forms, including behavioral communications that may include subtle or crude efforts to exert control over the analyst. These efforts may be so extreme as to threaten the boundaries of the psychoanalytic situation (a phenomenon examined further in the next section). Such developments, however, should not lead to the frequent mistake of expanding the concept of countertransference to include all the problems the analyst has in handling difficult patients. Errors owing to lack of experience or knowledge are just that, not countertransference.

Countertransference and Transference Regression

In view of the dimensions along which countertransference can be classified and their connections with the analyst's personality, I think there is an advantage in maintaining a comprehensive concept of countertransference. To link the analyst's unconscious reaction to the transference with his total emotional reaction to the patient makes it possible to diagnose how the patient's transference leads to distortions in the psychoanalytic situation and also to evaluate the analyst's realistic emotional reactions and his countertransference in a more restricted sense.

Under ordinary circumstances the analyst's character pathology or personality restrictions should have little or no effect. But with severely pathological patients whose intense primitive aggression infiltrates the transference, the analyst's personality will be subjected to countertransference reactions in a broad sense, which may result in activating his pathological character traits. Especially when treatment is stalemated and in the presence of severe negative therapeutic reactions, the analyst's broader emotional reactions may depend on his personality characteristics.

Perhaps the most vulnerable aspect of the therapist's personality under such extreme conditions is his creativity as a psychoanalyst. By creativity I mean the capacity to transform the patient's material imaginatively into a comprehensive dynamic formulation or into an organizing central fantasy or into a particular experience that vividly and concretely illuminates the entire material in new ways. Psychoanalytic creativity is intimately related to concern for the patient and to maintaining an awareness of the patient's positive qualities in the face of his unremitting aggression. One of the sources of this creativity is the analyst's ability to sublimate his aggression via the "penetrating," clarifying aspects of analytic technique. Concern, as Winnicott (1963) has pointed out, has deep roots in the wish to undo aggression by providing love to a significant object. Obviously, the analyst's creativity also expresses the sublimatory aspects of his libidinal investment in the patient. It is only natural for the patient's aggression to be directed precisely at this creativity. The narcissistic patient in particular focuses his envy on this analytic creativity, the source of what he is receiving from the analyst.

When the analyst is faced with the patient's effort to denigrate, neutralize, and generally destroy his technical equipment, self-respect, and personal security, his confidence in his ability to counteract these tendencies by tolerance, understanding, and creative interpretive work—without denying the severity of the aggression in the transference—permits him to continue working with the patient and thus to continue to be a good object for the patient in spite of the aggression directed toward him.

But concern for the patient, especially at times of violent acting out of the negative transference, also renders the analyst more vulnerable. His attempt to keep in touch with a patient's "good self" while being berated for his comments and silences and to maintain not only respect for the patient but an awareness of the loving and lovable aspects of his personality requires that he be emotionally open to the patient. This, of course, exposes the analyst even further to the onslaught of the patient's aggression. The defensive withdrawal from attack, the sharpened affirmation of social boundaries that protect us from sadistic assaults under ordinary social circumstances, is deliberately reduced in the analytic situation, a circumstance that may tempt the patient to extreme unreasonableness and demandingness.

By the same token, the threat of unbearable guilt forces the patient to resort increasingly to primitive projective mechanisms to justify his aggression; and primitive projection, particularly projective identification, is a powerful interpersonal weapon that "unloads" aggression onto the analyst. The patient may provoke the analyst into counteraggression and then, triumphantly, utilize this development as a rationalization of his own aggression. In treating borderline patients or patients with severe character pathology, there are times when paranoid fantasies regarding these patients may invade the analyst's free time in almost uncanny ways, illustrating the reversal of persecutory fantasies in the transference. Finally, because the analyst stands for the patient's weak, frail, submerged good self, the patient may project his good or idealized self representations onto the analyst, almost "for safekeeping," and yet need to attack them under the effects of aggression and envy, originally self-directed. Racker (1968) has stressed the high risk, in such circumstances, that the patient will successfully reinforce whatever masochistic traits the analyst may still retain.

In the long run, patients with severe chronic regression and primitive aggression prevalent in the transference, or patients with severe negative therapeutic reactions reflected in their consistent "spoiling" of the analyst's work and his positive disposition toward them, necessarily activate the analyst's normal narcissistic defenses, geared to protect his creativity and self-esteem. This may now complicate his acute countertransference reactions. By the same token, the analyst's ability to sublimate, which protects and preserves his creativity and self-esteem in the face of aggression, may become crucial in delimiting, localizing, and keeping within reasonable bounds whatever countertransference reactions he develops.

Countertransference and the Incapacity to Depend on the Analyst

Oddly enough, the clinical situations just described can be produced when there is minimal transference regression and almost total absence of manifest aggression in the transference. I am thinking of certain patients who have a chronic incapacity to depend upon the analyst. These patients present subtle, pervasive, and highly effective transference resistances against being dependent on the analyst and against the related regression in the transference in general.

Clinical Characteristics

On the surface, these patients convey the impression that they are incapable of establishing a transference relationship; they seem to be presenting a "resistance against the transference." However, this resistance is part of a complex transference pattern that reflects a particular subtype of narcissistic character pathology. Because the term *dependence* is vague and ambiguous, this pattern requires further clarification.

I am not referring to patients who present acute or chronic resistance against "depending" on the analyst because they are afraid to submit to a feared parental image or are afraid of heterosexual or homosexual longings or have reaction formations against passive oral needs and against intense ambivalence from many sources. I am referring, rather, to patients who, from the beginning of treatment, establish a remarkably stable relation to the analyst characterized by difficulty in really talking *to* him about *themselves*. They talk to the analyst in order to influence him or talk to themselves about themselves, leaving the analyst with the distinct feeling that he has been eliminated from their awareness.

These patients have great difficulty in listening to the analyst as a stimulus for further self-exploration. They have a constant, unwavering, automatic way of listening as if they were searching for hidden meanings, for the analyst's intentions, for the "mechanisms" operating in his mind, his theories and technique. They cannot permit themselves to be surprised by what emerges in their own minds in response to his comments. They conceive of psychoanalysis as a learning process in which knowledge comes from the analyst, to be carefully screened and evaluated by them and then consciously assimilated or rejected.

These patients cannot conceive of any knowledge about themselves that may emerge from their unconscious, surprising them, and that requires truly collaborative work with the analyst in order to be understood and integrated. They usually have great difficulties in experiencing sadness, depression, and guilt, which would reflect deeper concerns for their internal world; they cannot conceive unconsciously of the mutuality of a good mother/child relation and cannot, in an unconscious sense, "care" for themselves. They dramatically illustrate the narcissistic incapacity to love oneself and to trust one's internal world.

Although what I am describing is a typical transference configuration of narcissistic personalities, not all narcissistic personalities present these characteristics. This particular configuration is not linked to the severity of narcissistic pathology, which is generally expressed in extreme pathology of object relations, antisocial features, and paranoid transference regressions (including paranoid micropsychotic episodes). Hence, one may find the incapacity to depend in narcissistic patients with both favorable and very unfavorable prognoses for treatment. Also, although this transference configuration, once detected, is fairly similar from case to case, the underlying conflicts and repressed transference dispositions vary a great deal. For example, in the course of resolving this transference resistance, one may find depressive reactions related to unconscious guilt, severe paranoid trends reflecting condensed oedipal/preoedipal conflicts, or homosexual conflicts. Some patients present a general incapacity to fully experience emotions and to verbalize them in relation to very early traumatic circumstances. McDougall's (1979) description of countertransference developments under such circumstances corresponds to my own experience.

Impact on the Analyst

The transference picture I am describing has a profound effect on the analyst's countertransference and seriously challenges his creativity.

First of all, insofar as these patients never really form a deep emotional relation to the analyst, they convey the impression that no transference is developing. Particularly for the inexperienced analyst or candidate, patients who can associate freely, who appear to have the freedom to submerge themselves into primitive fantasy, childhood memories, and emotional expression, and yet who develop no transference may be puzzling and disquieting. The situation is very different from that created by the obsessive patient, whose intellectualization and rationalization, isolation, reaction formation, and other high-level defenses convey a difficulty in experiencing emotions although the patient is deeply involved in the transference.

Second, these narcissistic patients' constant scrutiny of the analyst's interpretations, their unrelenting "interpretive" scanning of all his comments, may have a paralyzing effect on the analyst's communications over an extended period of time. This is a more effective effort at control than the usual narcissistic attempt to keep the analyst's interpretations within a certain range, to make sure that he does not say anything unexpected (which would evoke the patient's envy) or anything too easily devalued (which would trigger severe disappointment reactions). In contrast to these "range restrictions" in what the patient can accept from the analyst, the patients under review receive everything in ways that tend to neutralize or eliminate the direct emotional impact of the interpretation. They leave the analyst with the impression that he has been talking to himself or that his communications, once expressed, have evaporated before reaching the patient.

In addition, the consistent screening of the analyst inevitably results in the patients' careful mapping of his "real" features, his peculiarities and idiosyncrasies. The analyst may have the uneasy feeling of being exposed to a somewhat benign, perhaps slightly ironical, amused, or obviously suspicious scrutiny, a more pervasive attempt at control than occurs in any other analytic relation.

Furthermore, these patients "learn" the analyst's language, his theory, his preferred expressions so completely that they can combine descriptions with interpretive considerations so skillfully "spliced" that the analyst can no longer differentiate emotion from intellectualization or regressive fantasy from psychoanalytic theories. In fact, the patient himself cannot differentiate what is authentic, what comes from him, and what he has learned from the analyst. It is all assimilated into a psychological structure that prevents either the patient or the analyst from learning about the unconscious aspects of the patient's pathology. In the end, the patient himself is the victim of his incapacity to depend on the analyst.

The effect of these developments on the analyst may be a loss of spontaneity. Rather than work with evenly suspended attention, he may attempt defensively to control his own communications. The apparent lack of transference involvement and development over a long period of time may induce in the analyst a discouraging sense that nothing is really happening, without his being able to pinpoint where the difficulty lies. He may finally come to feel a sense of paralysis and futility. He may even end up in collusion with the patient, splitting off session from session in a repetitive pattern of giving up and starting all over again.

Therapeutic Approach

It is not very difficult to diagnose a stalemate stemming from a chronic defense against dependence. To resolve it, however, taxes the limits of the analyst's capacity to work with countertransference reactions along the entire spectrum of the dimensions outlined earlier, especially his capacity to maintain his creativity. In particular, this stalemate taxes the analyst's evocative fantasy, his capacity to use his emotional knowledge about how a patient and an analyst relate to each other under ordinary circumstances. I refer to what Loewald (1960) described as the underlying relationship between patient and analyst in the psychoanalytic situation: One person dares to depend on another, and the other in turn accepts that dependence while respecting the first person's autonomy.

It is helpful for the analyst to maintain in fantasy a clear image of how a "normal" analysand might respond to his interventions, exploring his own reactions while experiencing himself in an open and safe relationship with the analyst. These conditions are present when the patient's observing ego is working in collaboration with the analyst. The analyst's capacity to experience himself both as an analyst and as a patient in a dependent position may create a highly subjective and experiential, yet realistic, frame against which the patient's incapacity to depend can be diagnosed and gradually interpreted.

Careful attention to the patient's reactions to interpretations is the best guide to exploring and resolving this complicated transference resistance. The patient may, in his effort to diagnose "how the analyst did it," impute to the analyst intellectualization and extraneous theories or "countertransference" reactions. This may open the road to clarifying with the patient how difficult it is for him to conceive of the possibility that the analyst has responded spontaneously and is interested in helping the patient improve his self-understanding rather than in manipulating him or brainwashing him with theories. In this context, the analyst may suggest that the patient is depreciating his own fantasy life and capacity for emotional experience, although he seems to be questioning the analyst's capacity for spontaneous introspection. The typical paradoxical reactions of narcissistic personalities who, after feeling helped or understood by the analyst, develop an increased need to deny such help or understanding may also be used to clarify this pattern by facilitating the interpretation of spoiling operations (Rosenfeld, 1964).

At times, the "meaninglessness" or the lack of emotional contact between patient and analyst may be repeating a specific pathogenic relation with parental objects. The hopeless, angry, stubborn patient challenges the analyst to demonstrate the difference between the present analytic encounter and the past. Unconscious envy of the analyst, perceived as independent and secure in his creativity, and the corresponding need to spoil his work complicate that challenge. The difficulty is that the interpretation of this pattern may itself be prematurely and intellectually captured by the patient and woven into his associations and his denial of psychic reality. Here, consistent working through and attentiveness to the defensive use of intellectualized insight may prove helpful.

Quite frequently, the focus on the patient's unconscious identification with a frustrating, sadistic, persecutory object from his past, which makes him distrust both the analyst and his own internal world (at bottom, an aggressive and rejecting maternal introject who denies the patient's dependent needs together with his emotional life in general), may clarify and resolve this pattern in the context of the analysis of the component identifications of the grandiose self. Here, the self-idealization of the patient who denies his need of others is condensed with identification with an aggressor (who has not yet become unmasked as an aggressor toward the patient's normal, infantile, dependent self).

An interesting development in patients who are beginning to work through this type of transference is the tendency, whenever some new understanding has been achieved, to revert to denial of any emotional relation to the analyst. Thus the pattern, which had originally been consistent and permanent, now begins to oscillate, reappearing when the transference relationship deepens. Repeated interpretation of this pattern when the analyst recognizes its reemergence may facilitate working through, although the repetition may often evoke in the patient the complaint that the analyst is continuing to focus on the same issues and is thus denying the patient's progress.

In these patients, the development of severely regressive transference dispositions and intense emotional reactions—even if they are strongly paranoid—indicates movement in comparison with the previously stable transference resistance. The prognosis for patients who never become able even to understand the nature of this incapacity to depend on the analyst is much poorer. To differentiate these two kinds of patients takes time. Intellectual acceptance of the analyst's interpretation of the patient's incapacity to depend on him has to be differentiated from emotional understanding, which eventually is translated into shifts in the transference.

CHAPTER 18: *Clinical Aspects of Severe Superego Pathology*

The two dominant prognostic indicators for the psychoanalytic and psychotherapeutic treatment of patients with borderline personality organization and narcissistic personalities are the quality of object relations and the quality of superego functions.

The quality of object relations refers to the patient's internal relations with significant others, not simply to the nature of his interpersonal exchanges. If the patient, in spite of his severe psychopathology, is still able to relate to another person in depth, to preserve a lasting, nonexploitive, nonparasitic relationship with a person who is close to him, he is capable of maintaining object relations. In contrast, the patient who is totally isolated socially, in whom no deep relation with anyone is available at the level of conscious and preconscious awareness, the patient whose only significant involvement with others occurs as part of masturbation fantasies, and the patient who presents only minimal awareness of or interest in the characteristics, concerns, and wishes of others, all reveal severe damage in the realm of object relations.

To maintain ordinary social honesty and to experience an appropriate sense of guilt and moral responsibility in relations with other people, speak for the ability to maintain basic superego functions. In contrast, a pervasive dishonesty in human relations and lack of concern and responsibility in all human interchanges indicate the absence or deterioration of superego functions. Naturally, the severity of the superego pathology is reflected in the degree of antisocial behavior present. It is important to remember, however, that superego pathology should be evaluated on the basis of the person's internal relation to his social environment rather than according to conventional or legal definitions of what is antisocial.

The psychoanalytic treatment of narcissistic personalities reveals interesting and complex relations between superego pathology and the quality of object relations. Narcissistic personalities of all degrees of severity reveal antisocial features with surprising frequency. Even those with relatively adequate social functioning, whose pathological grandiose self provides them with well-compensated gratifications of self-esteem and whose superficial social interactions and capacity for deeper investment in others are still available, may present chronic antisocial behavior in the form of stealing and falsifications in their work or in their sexual activities.

Because such antisocial features are prognostically so important, I investigate them in all patients with narcissistic personality (even those with apparently very good social functioning) and have often found surprising discrepancies between a relatively undamaged quality of object relations and an unsuspected severe superego pathology. In contrast, some narcissistic patients who function on an overt borderline level and show extreme and pervasive pathology of object relations have surprisingly intact superego functions.

It is only in the fortunately small subgroup of narcissistic pathology where aggressive infiltration of the pathological grandiose self gives rise to what I call malignant narcissism (see chaps. 16 and 19)—that is, ego-syntonic grandiosity combined with cruelty or sadism and severe paranoid personality traits—that deterioration of object relations regularly goes hand in hand with deterioration of superego functions. I have found that all patients with antisocial personality structure present severe narcissistic pathology, destruction of their internal world of object relations, and extreme and usually untreatable superego pathology. Such patients are at the limits not only of analyzability but of treatment with any modified psychoanalytic psychotherapies. The evaluation of the quality of object relations, of superego pathology, and of the nature of pathological narcissism tells us whether a patient is treatable.

Theoretical Considerations

I have found Edith Jacobson's ideas on the development of superego structures a most valuable frame of reference for understanding the vicissitudes of normal and pathological early superego formation. I shall therefore summarize Jacobson's pertinent contributions before expanding on her theoretical frame to explain the severe superego pathology under consideration here.

Jacobson (1964) describes three broad stages or layers of normal superego formation. The first and deepest layer is represented by the sadistic superego precursors that reflect the internalization of the fantastic, sadistically prohibitive, and punitive object images or, rather, the "bad" fused self and object representations that the infant projects onto the frustrating mother and other objects as part of an effort to deny its aggression. A second layer is based on the fusion of ideal self representations and ideal object representations; the integration of this layer constitutes the ego ideal and represents a final effort to reconstitute the original libidinally invested symbiotic relation with mother at a higher level of intrapsychic aspirations and demands. Under optimal circumstances, a toning down of both the earliest sadistic and later idealized superego precursors occurs, repeating within the evolving superego the processes of integration of good and bad object relations that previously occurred within the ego. Jacobson has noted how such integration and toning down permit, in turn, the internalization of a third layer of superego determinants, namely, the realistic, demanding, and prohibitive aspects of the parents that characterize the later stages of the oedipal phase and bring about the final consolidation of the superego as an integrated structure.

The next stage of development, latency, processes of depersonification, abstraction, and individualization occur in the superego, bringing about regulation of self-esteem by more focused, delimited, cognitively differentiated affects and demands, in contrast to the earlier, superego-controlled regulations of self-esteem by means of generalized mood swings. Specific guilt feelings and self-criticism reflect a sophisticated developmental elaboration of depressed moods under the influence of superego integration. The mature superego is characterized by control exerted through mild or modulated mood swings, guilt feelings, and a growing sense of autonomy, whereas a pathological, excessively aggressive, and primitive superego is characterized by the predominance of severe depressive moods. In addition, feelings of inferiority and shame reflect the participation of the ego ideal in superego regulation of the ego; the greater the defect in superego integration, the more feelings of inferiority and shame predominate over the capacity for experiencing modulated depressed affects (such as sadness) and differentiated guilt feelings.

The next stage of superego development occurs in adolescence. Jacobson describes the partial repersonification, reprojection, and redissolution of the superego that occur as the adolescent reinforces infantile prohibitions against oedipal strivings. At the same time, the adolescent must identify with an adult model of sexual behavior in order to integrate the tender and erotic aspects of sexual drives. Here, the extent to which such partial redissolution and reprojection of the superego occur and the extent to which normal ego identity is still maintained differentiate normal and neurotic adolescents from their borderline and narcissistic counterparts (Jacobson, 1954, 1961, 1964).

Clinical Considerations

Levels of Superego Pathology

The spectrum of superego pathology presented below illustrates failures at the various levels of superego formation outlined by Jacobson. I describe a continuum of severity of superego pathology ranging from the practically untreatable antisocial personality to patients with neurotic character pathology. My emphasis is on the relations among superego pathology, pathology of object relations, pathological narcissism, and the vicissitudes of the transference of these patients.

The Antisocial Personality

The most extreme superego pathology is found in patients with antisocial personality disorder—the psychopaths in a strict sense. These patients lie to the therapist, fully aware that they are lying. They understand the "moral" requirements of external reality to which they have to pay lip service, but they do not understand that these represent an authentic system of morality that other persons have internalized. Instead they perceive moral demands from the environment as a conventionally accepted "warning" system, to be exploited by the corrupt (like themselves) and submitted to by the naive and the sly.

These patients can lie and cheat effectively. They understand that they may be caught, but they do not understand that their lying and cheating will affect the internal relation of others to them. Because they are unable to experience any authentic investment of love in others, they cannot appreciate the difference between such investments that others may have for them and ruthless exploitation and manipulation. They tend to destroy the possibility of any emotional relationship with the therapist without even understanding that they are doing so.

Their capacity to lie effectively reflects an integration of the self of a sort, but it is one based upon the pathological grandiose self of the narcissistic personality and one totally identified with the pleasure principle. Some of these patients present an infiltration of this grandiose self with aggression and a subsequent ego-syntonic search for the gratification of sadistic urges. There is a continuum from the passive, exploitative, parasitic psychopath to the frankly sadistic criminal. Social conditions facilitating the expression of primitive aggression and cruelty provide a natural accommodation for these personality structures.

Except under unusual circumstances, psychotherapeutic treatment is contraindicated for these patients. The overtly sadistic members of this category may be too dangerous to treat in the ordinary psychotherapeutic setting, and the enactment of an overt sadistic triumph through extreme depreciation of the therapist matched with direct financial or other exploitation of him may become a frightening experience to the therapist. With passive or parasitic psychopaths, it may be only confrontation with their antisocial behavior that triggers violent paranoid regressions in the transference, within which they activate a sadistic grandiosity similar to that of the directly aggressive type (while still projecting this tendency onto the therapist).

One patient, an antisocial personality with predominantly sadistic features, entered psychotherapeutic treatment under pressure from his family and in order to avoid going to jail because of his involvement in break-ins and stealing. He talked openly during his sessions with me about a planned robbery. He made it clear through subtle but unmistakable threats that he would know how to protect himself in case I chose to harm him by reporting him to the law. It is difficult to convey the overpowering sense of superiority and security this man expressed. His relaxed smile suggested that he totally depreciated me, and there were times when he managed to paralyze my thinking so that it was difficult for me to intervene at all. I decided to interrupt the treatment after reaching the conclusion that the combination of legal problems and therapeutic issues was beyond my capacity.

Another patient with antisocial personality and a history of stealing and parasitic exploitation of others, but without any evidence of manifest violence, a man who was generally described as pseudosubmissive and sly, stole things from my office. Although at first I could not be certain that he was responsible for the missing objects, I found myself watching him in the sessions and checking my office when he left. After I finally raised a question regarding one small object that had disappeared from my waiting room after a session with him, the patient "confessed" that he had taken it and brought it back. He gave, however, no evidence of shame or guilt, and the sessions that followed (until the interruption of the treatment a few weeks later) were marked by my uneasy sense that I was unwillingly engaged in a watching game to protect my property. When I tried to explore the psychological implications of this interaction, the patient rejected, with amusement, my insistence on dwelling on an episode that was "a matter of the past."

Narcissistic Personality with Ego-syntonic Antisocial Behavior

The next level on the continuum of superego pathology is represented by narcissistic personalities functioning on an overt borderline level and with antisocial features but not an antisocial personality proper, and patients with malignant forms of pathological narcissism whose aggressive sense of entitlement is expressed in ego-syntonic antisocial behavior. These patients develop severe paranoid features in the transference even if their descriptive personality does not include dominant paranoid traits. They may even develop delusional paranoid regressions in the transference.

The sessions of one patient with a narcissistic personality and severe paranoid features were dominated by his grandiosity and bravado. He filled the hours with complaints about the stupidity, ignorance, and unfairness of various authorities and forced me either to listen to him silently—with the implication that I was agreeing with him—or, if I "dared" to question any of his statements, to become one more example in his world of unfair authorities. Along with his almost inpenetrable grandiosity went a charm that permitted him to make really outrageous statements. As long as I did not contradict him openly, he maintained an amused and friendly manner in the hours. He also lied to me regarding antisocial behavior he was engaged in, particularly involving drugs; on some occasions it was only the communication from the police to his parents, which reached a social worker and finally myself, that permitted me to know what was going on in his life. Once confronted, he readily admitted that he had been lying, defending his behavior as perfectly logical in a world of narrow-minded and restrictive authorities.

This patient, however, in contrast to those mentioned earlier, was also able to subtly express dependent aspects in his relationship with me; he became very upset if I did not see him at his regular time, and he was extremely disturbed by any delay in starting his sessions. Although he finally interrupted the treatment, he maintained occasional contact with me, considered the possibility of resuming treatment in the future, and was subsequently able to engage in limited periods of psychotherapeutic treatment with other therapists. According to reliable follow-up information, at least the antisocial aspects of his functioning gradually diminished.

In these patients the antisocial behavior has an aggressive, enraged, revengeful quality that is the counterpart of their severely paranoid tendency to attribute similar reactions to everyone else. The lying and cheating are ego-syntonic within the context of their picture of the world as a place where one must either cheat and lie or kill in order to survive or must assure his psychological safety by being beyond the fear of death. There is more savage aggression and sadism than callous or gleeful dishonesty in these patients, and very often a remnant of ordinary honesty can be found in their emotionally uninvolved social relations.

Jacobson (1971), in her description of the paranoid urge to betray, points to the childhood history of such patients as characterized by mistreatment, neglect, cruelty, and severe marital discord between the parents. These patients early developed a submissive, masochistic attitude toward the parents, while their underlying hostility found expression in the cruelties they inflicted upon their younger siblings and in attempts to pit other members of the family against each other. Jacobson describes the alternation between overt aggressiveness and paranoid traits, on the one hand, and submissiveness and betrayal together with other antisocial tendencies, on the other.

At the most pathological end of the spectrum, including the antisocial personality proper and the narcissistic personality with strong antisocial features and/or malignant narcissism, there is a clear predominance of the most primitive layer of sadistic superego precursors. These include an expression of aggression that is practically unmitigated by any integration with idealized superego precursors and an urge for power over and destruction of all object relations (other than a complement of totally submissive and exploited "slaves" who permit enactment of the power such sadistic superego precursors aspire to).

In the antisocial personality proper, it is as if the patient identified himself with a primitive, ruthless, totally immoral power that can obtain satisfaction only through the expression of unmitigated aggression and requires no rationalization for its behavior and no adherence to any consistent value other than the exercise of such power.

In the narcissistic personality with antisocial features and in malignant narcissism, however, there is at least some beginning availability of idealized superego precursors in the sense of a condensation of the sadistic superego precursors with some expectation of a primitive idealized kind. The patient's sadistic and exploitive behavior is "morally justified," at least to himself. In the transference, such nonpsychopathic patients react with intense rage if the "justification" for their cruel and exploitive behavior is challenged. It is as if these patients were identifying not simply with a sadistic killer, as in the case of the psychopath, but with an extremely cruel deity, a ruthless and self-centered god.

The activation of paranoid ideas in the transferences of these patients reflects the enactment of the sadistic grandiosity and ruthlessness of this most primitive, unmitigated, or non-neutralized layer of superego formation. The presence of sadistic or violent parental images, as well as constitutional factors interfering with the neutralization or control of primitive aggression, is presumably etiologically dominant here. The patient's unconscious identification of his grandiose self with the characteristics of these primitive, sadistic superego precursors also indicates the frailty or unavailability of any alternative internalized object relations and the destruction of all libidinally invested self and object representations.

The past internalized world of object relations uncovered by genetic reconstruction in patients with the severe levels of superego pathology just described typically includes the image of overpowering parental figures experienced as omnipotent and cruel. These patients invariably felt that any good, loving, mutually gratifying relationship with an object was unavailable or, if available, was frail, easily destroyed, and, even worse, a direct invitation to attack by the overpowering and cruel parent. They typically had a sense that total submission to—in fact, total absorption into—the power of the cruel and omnipotent parent was the only condition for survival and that therefore all ties to alternative good but weak objects had to be severed. Finally, the exhilarating sense of power and enjoyment achieved once the identification with a cruel omnipotent object had been completed provided them with a sense of freedom from fear, pain, and dread and the conviction that gratification of aggression was the only significant mode of relating to others.

Dishonesty in the Transference

The next level of superego pathology is represented by patients who chronically suppress or distort important information regarding their lives or subjective experiences, in other words those who lie by omission as well as commission in the treatment situation. These patients include borderline patients without conspicuous narcissistic psychopathology as well as some narcissistic patients functioning on an overtly borderline level. Here the dishonesty is largely of a "protective" nature, there is little direct or overt antisocial behavior, and the quality of object relations is better maintained. Sometimes the relative severity of the superego pathology may be overlooked for extended periods in treatment.

Typical examples include patients who omit talking about important aspects of their daily life experiences and interactions because they fear the analyst will criticize or try to disrupt such behaviors. Patients sometimes "confess" their behavior to the analyst only to continue it afterward, with the implied assumption that their confession relieves them of responsibility for their acts. The analyst must decide whether he will consent to the continuation of this behavior by receiving the information in silence or take responsibility for disrupting it.

In contrast to the patient with the more restricted symptom of keeping secrets in an area about which he feels extreme shame or guilt but which does not involve major antisocial or self-destructive behavior and to the patient operating under the sway of unconscious denial, who is cognitively fully aware of a certain experience or behavior but unaware of its emotional implication, the patient who chronically lies is fully aware of both the cognitive and the emotional importance of the issues suppressed.

Miss U. A woman with a history of chronic drug abuse and alcoholism was involved with a man who was a drug dealer. For a long period of time she deliberately withheld from me her awareness of her boyfriend's criminal activities. She "confessed" only when the death of a close friend, which she suspected had been caused by the criminal group to which her boyfriend belonged, produced intense anxiety in her.

I explored with her the factors that had prevented her from telling me about the criminal culture surrounding her. It emerged that underneath her fear that I would forbid her to continue the relationship with her boyfriend or would terminate her treatment because of my indignation over her involvement with a shady group of people lay the deeper fear that she would betray to her boyfriend her having talked about his activities to me; this would endanger my life because his group might want to eliminate me once I "knew too much." This revelation led, in turn, to Miss U's expression of her fear concerning her own death wishes toward me and her masochistic submission to a social situation that she perceived as dangerous to her own life.

In the early stages of the treatment, Miss U, a typical infantile personality with borderline personality organization, had freely revealed masturbatory fantasies involving sexual orgies with her parents. I had privately wondered to what extent she had indeed been witness to or participated in incestuous or perverse sexual activities in early childhood. These masturbatory fantasies eventually turned out to have much more complex genetic origins and did not represent direct sexual experiences of that kind in early childhood. However, several months after the disclosure of her habitual lying to me regarding the nature of her boyfriend's activities, new information regarding her unconscious past emerged, suggesting that her mother had been chronically afraid of being poisoned by Miss U's father—so afraid that she used to have the family dog taste her food before she would eat it. The patient had enacted in the transference her identification both with the mother, who was threatened by a murderous husband, and with the murderous father, who was "poisoning" the relationship with me as well as potentially causing my death.

Denial of Moral Responsibility

The next level of superego pathology is characterized by what might be summarized as denial of moral responsibility for one's actions. In contrast to the previous group of patients mentioned, mostly with borderline personality organization but without dominant narcissistic features, this group is represented by patients with typical narcissistic personality but without antisocial behavior in a strict sense or overt lying in the transference. In these cases we find no conscious suppression, systematic omission, or distortion of certain information but, rather, an "innocent" revelation of contradictory experiences and behaviors, separated

by a barrier of mutual denial—a manifestation of the underlying mechanism of splitting—leading to the denial of concern, of a sense of responsibility, and of guilt feelings.

These patients do not lie consciously in the ordinary sense of the
word. Their dishonesty is in refusing to accept responsibility for the reliability of their feelings, intentions, and actions. In fact, it is striking how
easily some of these patients, who usually have a history of manipulative, controlling, and exploitive behavior with others, are able to "brainwash" the therapist with the logic of their bland, cavalier dismissals of
personal responsibility and concern for themselves and for others.
Clearly, these patients show a cognitive continuity of their mental
states, but they maintain an affective discontinuity that protects them
from anxiety or guilt and from any identification with moral values.
They seem to illustrate simultaneously the defensive use of splitting and
the totally self-centered behavior that one may observe in children before superego integration has taken place. In addition, they show significant impoverishment in their capacity for investment in depth in object
relations. Their ability to cause the analyst to doubt his own value judgments and even his ordinary concepts of responsibility and guilt is impressive. These patients, in short, have an uncanny talent for corrupting
the analyst's value systems in relating to them. The following illustration is typical.

Miss V. A young woman with a narcissistic personality and without
overt borderline features one evening told a man that she loved him and
that he was the only man in her life. An intense sexual relationship was
developing between the two. Simultaneously, she was also developing
an intense relationship with another man. A few nights later, she also
told the second man that she loved him and that he was the only man in
her life. Miss V talked about this quite openly in the sessions.

When I raised the question whether this was a source of conflict for
her, she first reassured me that it was not because the two men did not
know each other. After I had ascertained that she meant this in all sincerity, I asked whether it might be a source of conflict for her that she
had told both men, almost at the same time, that she loved them and
that each was her only love. Miss V very matter of factly said that she
had been completely sincere in making these statements to both men,
that her feelings had changed completely from the night on which she
had talked with the first man to the night she had talked with the other.
She felt that her men could always be certain of her being honest with
them. She said she never made any secret of the fact that her feelings
changed and that therefore she could not guarantee anybody "eternal
love." One of her major complaints, in fact, was the lack of appreciation
of her honesty and the contradictory behavior of men with whom she
had been involved. At first, men accepted a relationship in which she

would be very loving and giving, although making it clear that she could not assure them of what her feelings would be in the long run and that she needed to preserve her freedom. Eventually, however, even the men who paid lip service to her statements in the beginning became very angry because she would get involved with other men later on.

Miss V was not jealous when her men became involved in other love affairs; on the contrary, these were a welcome relief. The incapacity to experience jealousy is quite frequent in narcissistic personalities. Obviously, she suffered from severe pathology of object relations, an inability to commit herself in depth to anyone or to permit herself to depend fully on anyone. However, in contrast to the cases mentioned earlier, this patient had a more appropriate and even considerate attitude toward people with whom she was not intensely involved emotionally; she maintained an ordinary sense of honesty in her social relations. In relation to me, she demonstrated over many months a severe lack of apparent involvement but no lying by omission or commission. Miss V eventually learned that a radical abandonment of all hope for love defended her against deep fears of disappointment and rage. The exploration of these features in the transference opened the road to exploring the pathology of her object relations.

These patients' superego pathology is reflected in the absence of concern, the lack of capacity for a sense of moral responsibility and guilt, and the rationalizations of their behavior presented with a disarming logic. The ego-syntonicity of their behavior that is not overtly antisocial makes it very difficult for the therapist to help them become aware that there is a problem behind this apparent lack of "moral" problems. Such a patient may experience any "moral" concern the analyst might express as not only judgmental but persecutory and sadistic as well. In contrast to antisocial personalities who are "honest" about their antisocial activities without any concern or guilt, Miss V and the cases she represents are not openly exploitative of others or antisocial. Their incapacity to establish object relations in depth is at least as self-destructive as it is destructive to their relations with others.

With patients presenting dishonesty in the transference and an inability to assume moral responsibility there is a lack of integration of the normal superego, a relative unavailability of ordinary internalization of the third level of realistic parental prohibitions and demands. These patients present a dissociation between projected sadistic and idealized superego precursors, reflected clinically in antisocial behavior rationalized in the context of paranoid transferences linked with the projection onto the analyst of sadistic superego precursors. The idealized superego precursors may be projected onto the analyst at other times or onto other transference objects toward whom a masochistic submissiveness contrasts with the dishonesty in the paranoid transference. In the case of a consolidation of a pathological grandiose self, that grandiose self incorporates the idealized superego precursors, while the sadistic superego precursors are projected in the form of paranoid trends. Despite the dominance of devaluation and other primitive defensive operations, which damage their internalized world of object relations, all these patients are still able temporarily to maintain idealized object relations, and sometimes the rudiments of higher levels of superego formation are reflected in their capacity for maintaining ordinary conventional honesty.

The dominance of early sadistic superego precursors in all the cases examined so far has devastating effects upon the internalization of object relations. In these patients' internal world, and therefore in their perceptions of their interpersonal reality, one is either extremely powerful and ruthless or one is threatened with being destroyed or exploited. If good object relations are in constant danger of destruction by such malignant forces, they may be devalued because of their implicit weakness. In this way primitive superego pathology and pathology of internalized object relations reinforce each other.

Some patients on this intermediate level develop a completely false, cynical, and hypocritical mode of communication, an erasing of all judgments that imply a comparison of good and bad objects. They negate the importance of any investment in objects as a condition for successful maneuvering in the chaos of human relations. What might be called the dishonesty of the "innocent bystander" replaces the dangerous identification with the cruel tyrant.

When major and chronic dishonesty pervades the treatment situation, a defensive dehumanization of object relations may have been achieved, so that there is no longer a danger that love will be destroyed by hatred or that hatred will evoke devastating retaliation. These characteristics are found to a lesser degree but, by the same token, can be studied more easily in patients with milder superego pathology, those presenting a lack of a sense of responsibility for their own actions.

Here there have been sufficiently idealized superego precursors available to permit at least the self idealization of a grandiose self and a minimal integration of sadistic and idealized superego precursors, to the extent that an ordinary sense of conventional morality can be maintained. These patients, however, by fragmenting all intense emotional involvements with significant others, make their human relationships shadowy or unreal, and they are protected from paranoid developments by eliminating altogether the "threat" of their needs for dependency on others and, with that dependency, for demands and prohibitions, expectations and longings, gratification and frustration. They thereby eliminate all human intimacy.

Paradoxically, then, patients with narcissistic personality, an incapacity to accept a sense of continuity in their responsibility and concern for others, but without manifest dishonesty, combine a relative absence of antisocial features with a remarkable absence of the capacity for object relations in depth.

Contradictory Ego and Superego Features as Part of General Borderline Pathology

The next level of superego pathology is to be found in the majority of patients with borderline personality organization but without the antisocial and/or narcissistic features mentioned earlier. These patients are aware of strong and contradictory urges that they cannot control. They spontaneously express concern that in mental states contradictory to the current acceptable one they may feel or act in ways that would be unacceptable to them now. Clinically, this condition may be illustrated by patients with dissociated, severe suicidal tendencies who are nevertheless concerned over their suicidal potential and willing to ask for help when they feel threatened by such powerful impulses.

These patients' capacity to experience concern for themselves and others and to tolerate guilt feelings when they act aggressively toward those they love indicates both a beginning stage of internalization of superego functions and a much stronger capacity for emotional investment in others, both prognostically favorable signs. Superego pathology here is really part of the general pathology of borderline personality organization and reflects the predominance of primitive defensive operations, a tendency to defensively dissociate and project superego pressures as part of the activation of general splitting mechanisms.

Such patients may present a surface functioning that seems more chaotic, contradictory, and immature (in the sense of being perpetually in emotional turmoil in their object relations) than that of the preceding level of narcissistic pathology. Their clinging attachments to others, however, their intense if contradictory involvements, signal that they have preserved a capacity for object relations. At this level, both sadistic and idealized superego precursors are available, and, although superego functioning may still be largely dissociated, there are already available more advanced superego features relating to the internalization of more realistic parental images at the time of later stages of oedipal development.

Antisocial Behavior Expressing Unconscious Guilt

Finally, with the achievement of a developmental level at which the integration of contradictory sadistic and idealized superego precursors becomes possible and with the consequent decrease of reprojection of primitive superego precursors onto the parental oedipal images, the internalization of the third layer of superego formation becomes possible. The internalization and supraordinate integration of the oedipal level of superego functions permit the development of ordinary superego pathology in the neurotic patient or of normal superego development in general. Here the quality of object relations reflects the integration of the normal self concept and of internalized object representations. The absence of antisocial features, the maintenance of an individualized sense of morality, the capacity for object relations in depth, and the absence of pathological narcissism are accompanied by and reflect the presence of a solid, at least partially abstracted, individualized, and depersonified superego structure. Under these conditions, the enactment of antisocial behavior reflects specific unconscious fantasies related to an essentially masochistic submission to a sadistic but well-integrated superego, the need for expiation of unrealistic unconscious guilt.

The corresponding final level of superego pathology is that of patients with neurotic personality organization and a well-integrated but excessively severe, sadistic superego. Here, unconscious superego-determined guilt is usually reflected in various types of ego inhibitions and symptom formations and repression of aggressive and/or sexual instinctual needs in the context of predominantly oedipal conflicts relatively undistorted by condensation with preoedipal features. Most of these patients present no specific superego pathology other than an unconscious dominance of an infantile morality linked with a fixation on oedipal prohibitions and demands. These patients usually do not present antisocial features; they are honest and have a sense of moral values; they have a full range of normal, integrated internalized object relations as well. A normal integration of the self concept replaces the pathological integration of a grandiose self of narcissistic character pathology.

In some cases, however, selected antisocial behavior may reflect the acting out of unconscious guilt. These are "criminals from a sense of guilt" (Freud, 1916), who represent only a small proportion of patients with antisocial behavior. Characteristically, patients with superego pathology at this level do not present the severely regressive paranoid reactions in the transference that one finds in patients with antisocial behavior of the levels of superego pathology mentioned earlier.

A patient in charge of a research laboratory in the physical sciences had a compulsive need to falsify his research data so that they would be in accordance with the results he desired. Then, because he felt so guilty, he repeated the same experiments several times to assure himself that his falsified data were unreliable! On one occasion, when his real findings seemed to support his manipulated findings, he did not trust them and had to repeat the experiments over and over again over an extended period of time. The net results were the risk of being found out and having his professional career destroyed and a damaging reduction of his productivity. The unconscious submission to a sadistic and envious father image, who, in the patient's mind, could not tolerate the patient's professional success, and the acting out of both success as rebellion and dishonesty as a search for punishment could be worked through over an extended period of analysis. This patient presented no other antisocial features. He suffered a form of circumscribed superego pathology at a level of development of an integrated superego in the context of neurotic character pathology.

The sequence I have described suggests the relations between superego development and narcissistic pathology, paranoid tendencies, destruction of internalized object relations, and antisocial behavior.

At the lowest levels of our spectrum, the quality of object relations and that of superego functioning practically coincide; at intermediate levels of pathology the relations between superego development and the quality of object relations become more complex and varied. Finally, in focusing upon the vicissitudes of psychopathology at the severe end of the spectrum of superego distortions, this formulation should strengthen the view that the processes by which the superego is developed and integrated extend over a much longer period of time than was originally assumed. Significant normal or pathological superego developments take place from the second and third year of life on, preceding and crucially influencing the integration of the oedipal and postoedipal superego. Further superego developments occur in adolescence as well as, presumably, in adult life.

CHAPTER 19: *Paranoid Regression and Malignant Narcissism*

As I have already mentioned (see especially chap. 12), patients with narcissistic personalities who are undergoing resolution of the pathological grandiose self frequently present complications so severe that the treatment may be stalemated or prematurely disrupted. Because the clinical picture is of a condensation of grandiose and sadistic strivings (a reflection of a pathological grandiose self that has been infiltrated with aggression), I call this phenomenon *malignant narcissism*. Malignant narcissism becomes manifest in the form of particular distortions in the transference, sometimes from the beginning of treatment, sometimes after a certain degree of regression in the transference has taken place.

In either case, malignant narcissism is characterized by any or all of the following: (1) paranoid regressions in the transference, including "paranoid micropsychotic episodes"; (2) chronic self-destructiveness or suicide as a triumph over the analyst; (3) major and minor dishonesty in the transference; and (4) overt sadistic triumph over the analyst, or malignant grandiosity.

Clinical Descriptions

Paranoid Regression

These paranoid developments in the transference are characterized by the appearance in the patient of intense suspiciousness of the analyst, which may take on delusional qualities and characteristics and may last for a segment of a single hour to several weeks or (rarely) months. Outside the transference, the patient does not appear to suffer from psychotic regression. To the contrary, his object relations with significant others very often seem to clear up or acquire split-off idealizing qualities.

290

In the midst of such episodes it is difficult for many patients to continue to lie on the couch. They have to sit up and watch the analyst in order not to be surprised by him, to avoid sudden attacks, and to exercise what often amounts to sadistic control of him as part of the dominance of projective mechanisms. I have observed, in this context, the development of hallucinatory phenomena in the transference, such as the perception of fecal smells, distortions in how the patient perceives the analyst or objects in the office, and distortions of what the analyst says.

The paranoid episodes may disappear as suddenly as they began, without any appreciable working through in the transference and with a concomitant reactivation of the pathological grandiose self in the patient. In fact, the failure to work through and resolve such paranoid episodes may bring about a temporary reorganization of the pathological grandiose self and, at the same time, an undercurrent of a transfer of split-off or dissociated paranoid convictions about the analyst from one episode to the next. Grievances thus gradually accumulate and periodically explode and may eventually lead to disruption of the treatment.

Characteristically, these paranoid episodes begin suddenly around an ambiguity in the treatment situation or in the analyst's attitude, which the patient interprets in a paranoid way. By means of projective identification, the patient unconsciously attempts to induce in the analyst the animosity, hatred, dishonesty, or manipulation of which the patient now accuses him.

These paranoid regressions have to be distinguished from intense rage attacks (narcissistic rage), which narcissistic patients commonly experience when frustrated in their narcissistic needs, and from the strongly negative transference reactions with paranoid features that may evolve in late stages of the analysis of patients with all kinds of character pathology when deep levels of superego formations emerge in the transference. Unlike ordinary neurotic patients, malignant narcissists suffering such paranoid regressions lack the capacity to continue relying on the analyst in the midst of paranoid fears in the transference.

Self-destructiveness as Triumph over the Analyst

This clinical constellation is characterized by physically or emotionally self-destructive behavior when the patient, in the transference, experiences himself as threatened in his present "balance of power" with the therapist. In contrast to self-mutilating or suicidal behavior when the patient has experienced actual rejection—a symptom presented by many borderline patients, including those with narcissistic personality—here the self-destructiveness is triggered by a challenge to the patient's conscious or unconscious fantasies of grandiosity or power. The patient's determination to take self-destructive action reflects not simply "rage turned against the self" but, typically, a calm, determined, even elated attitude. Sometimes there is conscious enjoyment of the idea of "fooling" the therapist, an almost sadistic pleasure in hidden preparations for self-destructive acts. For instance, a patient seriously burned her arms, and, while attending psychotherapy sessions wearing clothes with long sleeves to cover her deep and festering wounds, she gleefully told the therapist how well she was feeling. Often the patient looks forward to the therapist's consternation, sense of impotence, worry, and fear for the patient's life as the strongest confirmation of his triumph over the therapist. The most prominent feature of these self-destructive tendencies is the sense of power the patient experiences in relation to the analyst. The patient becomes victim and victimizer in one; he may acquire a sense of freedom from fear as well as a sense of triumph over the analyst (whom he perceives as concerned about but impotent in the face of the patient's self-destructive behavior).

This self-destructive constellation raises the question of the differential diagnosis of various types and degrees of masochism. In a clinical sense, masochistic character pathology and the corresponding masochistic transference developments may be classified into a spectrum of constellations, from the most benign to the most malignant. At one extreme we find the cases of moral masochism corresponding to unconscious guilt feelings, and the development of negative therapeutic reactions reflecting such unconscious guilt in the transference. These patients usually have depressive-masochistic personality features and a well-integrated tripartite intrapsychic structure; even during masochistic acting-out, self-destructive tendencies are at least partly ego dystonic.

A second level of masochistic character pathology and the corresponding developments in the transference are reflected in sadomasochistic personality structure and transferences in which there are alternations between sadistic and masochistic behavior and contradictory character traits, sometimes reflecting identification with the aggressor and sometimes ego-syntonic self-punishment as an expression of unconscious guilt-raising attacks on the now-projected sadistic attacker. Masochistic sexual deviations usually correspond to one of these two levels of masochistic personality structure, as do many sadomasochistic perversions.

At a third level of severity of self-destructive tendencies we find negative therapeutic reactions as an expression of unconscious envy of the analyst, a prevalent development within the transferences of narcissistic patients which requires long-term attention and working through but is essentially not an aspect of malignant narcissism. Here, however, the term *masochism* no longer applies as an intended, wished-for self-punishment. To the contrary, the self-defeating behavior is a by-product of the patient's need to avoid envy of the helpful therapist.

At the severest level of self-destructiveness we find the tendency toward unconscious identification with a primitive, sadistic parental image, in which suicide or self-mutilation acquires the function of free expression of aggression, a sense of total control over one's destiny, and the revengeful punishment of an object (the analyst) who differs from or would threaten the primitive sadistic object with whom the patient is identified. In addition, at this level the fantasied destruction or disappearance of the self becomes equivalent to power over the persistence or disappearance of the entire world. Here the pathological grandiose self, identified with a sadistic, cruel, triumphant aggressive object, reflects the condensation of libido and aggression at its most malignant, severely regressed level. Any perceived threat to the omnipotent control of the grandiose sadistic self has to be answered with the destruction of that threat: basically, the therapist's life-preserving and life-enhancing function. Finally, in connection with these truly malignant features of self-destructiveness as a character trait activated in the transference, there may also be a glimmer of hope that the analyst will rescue the patient from death and self-mutilation. It is this deepest level of self-destructiveness, the enactment of an identification with a primitive, sadistic object representation, that becomes predominant in the transference of some patients with malignant narcissism.

Miss W. A narcissistic personality and chronic alcoholic continually expressed rage against those who were not brought up as she was in what she experienced as the icy world of extremely wealthy, emotionally unavailable, unwaveringly polite yet aloof parents, interested only in the surface behavior of the patient and her siblings, not in their feelings or emotional well-being. Miss W, of high intelligence and striking physical attractiveness, treated men cruelly and drowned herself in alcohol whenever her intolerable longings for love came to the surface.

In the transference, she sometimes perceived me as one more edition of a powerful and indifferent, unavailable parental image combining features of both parents and against whom she felt intense rage. Sometimes she regarded me as an authentically friendly and nice but fumbling and incompetent therapist, unable to empathize fully with her suffering or to withstand her destructive powers. At a deeper level, she was extremely resentful of the possibility that I might live in a world not contaminated by the terrible experiences of her own world.

From the beginning Miss W triumphantly warned me that the treatment was bound to fail. My willingness to continue despite episodes of severe acting out involving alcohol abuse as well as other self-destructive behavior only reinforced her views of me. Notwithstanding her chronically frozen, haughty, and aloof attitude, she conveyed to me a subtle yet pressing hope that I would not give up on her, that I would rescue her in spite of herself. The manifest grandiosity and derogatory attitude toward me, however, were highly effective in distorting the nature of our relationship, so that much time had to be taken up with clarifying the complex nature of her self-destructive ploys and dealing with her endless efforts to undermine the treatment by mobilizing relatives and other professionals to question me. Miss W finally transferred to another psychiatrist directly after a suicide attempt which she barely managed to survive. That treatment, in turn, was disrupted a few months later, and the patient left town.

Another patient, the son of a prominent surgeon, suffered from a recurring form of skin cancer and felt a gloating triumph over me because of my unawareness, for a period of several weeks, that the cancerous growth had reappeared on his skin and that he had managed to hide this from an examining physician.

Still another patient, a typical illustration of chronic suicide attempts as a "way of life," had the following dream shortly before a major suicide attempt. She dreamed that she was the assistant to the director of a nursing home who had invited all the relatives of his elderly clients to a party to be held in another place. After getting them away with extreme friendliness and tactfulness, the director, with the patient's assistance, gathered all the inmates in a closed and walled-off area and proceeded to gas them to death. In the associations to this dream, it became apparent that the patient identified herself simultaneously with the murderous director of the nursing home and with the victimized inmates.

Dishonesty in the Transference

I am referring here to the patient who at a certain stage of treatment, withholds important information from the therapist so that his understanding of the transference situation and of the patient's life must necessarily be affected.

I referred to these cases in chapter 18 when describing major and minor dishonesty in the transference, including the relatively less severe cases of denial of responsibility for one's actions. Major and chronic dishonesty in particular raises the question of whether malignant narcissism is present. But some patients combine "minor" aspects of chronic suicide wishes with a failure to assume responsibility for their actions and subtle forms of dishonesty; the result amounts to malignant narcissism in the transference.

A patient with chronic suicide tendencies had been musing aloud about her recent freedom from suicidal wishes. This made me wonder whether those casual references might be heralding a new suicide attempt. I asked whether she was certain that she did not have suicidal wishes at this point and whether we should consider once more the possibility that she might need additional help to prevent herself from acting on such wishes.

The patient stated categorically that she was not in a suicidal mood and assured me that there was no risk that she might attempt suicide. I said that her mood had shifted quickly at other times; was she certain that she would not act on suicide wishes if her mood shifted again? Once again she assured me that she would not carry out any suicidal gesture in her present mood. But, she added, of course her mood might change, in which case her assurance to me naturally would no longer be valid. Here the lack of a sense of concern and responsibility for herself and the underlying conflicts involving dissociated aggression emerged directly in the transference. It was very difficult to point to the implicit aggression toward me as well as toward herself in this instance. I had first to free myself from being impressed by the unassailable logic of her statement. In this case a lengthy analysis of her devaluation of my concern for her had to precede exploration of her devaluation of herself, which reflected at the deepest level her identification with a "superior" and indifferent maternal image.

Direct Expression of Sadistic Triumph over the Analyst

This behavior includes conscious, ego-syntonic rage and devaluation of the therapist accompanied by a sense of triumph over him as his response is experienced as less sadistic than the patient's. The patient may insult the therapist over many sessions, and the ego-syntonic sense of certainty and security with which he treats the therapist as an incompetent idiot may become very taxing. The sadistic aspects of this devaluation may include threats of violence or other forms of psychological aggression.

This constellation may also be designated malignant grandiosity: An omnipotent triumph over the analyst for an extended period of time reconfirms the security of the patient's pathological grandiose self, expresses the devaluation of and revenge against the threatening world of internal object relations successfully externalized onto the analyst, and is often accompanied by extreme dehumanization in the transference. This characteristic is found in a spectrum of patients, from the antisocial personality proper to certain narcissistic personalities with paranoid and antisocial features. These patients present very strong, ego-syntonic derogatory tendencies and a well-rationalized sadism in their relationships with others. Lying is usually less of a problem; in fact, these patients exhibit either an arrogant or a sadistic self-righteous affirmation of their antisocial behavior. Drug addicts with this personality characteristic experience a feeling of superiority as soon as the drug frees them from dependency on others or from "externally" controlled gratifications.

As I stated at the beginning of this chapter, malignant narcissism may become manifest in the transference either from the beginning of treatment or after a certain period of time, reflecting a regression in the transference. This observation can be related to the differential diagnosis of the severest constellations of the aggressive infiltration of the grandiose self, namely: (1) the antisocial personality proper; (2) patients with sexual deviations or perversions that include overt and life-threatening sadistic behavior; (3) narcissistic personalities with ego-syntonic rage attacks, antisocial features, or paranoid trends; and (4) narcissistic personalities with overtly borderline characteristics. This differential diagnosis is important because the first two categories are usually untreatable by expressive psychotherapy and present the syndrome of malignant narcissism early on. All other narcissistic personalities, who may develop malignant narcissism at later stages of their treatment, have a much more favorable prognosis.

The antisocial personality presents, in addition to a typical narcissistic personality disorder, chronic antisocial behavior, incapacity to experience guilt or concern, ruthless exploitation of others by parasitic or violent means, intolerance of anxiety, and lack of a realistic sense of time.

The sadistic pervert presents overt sadistic behavior—whether linked to other sexual activities or not—which is intensely exciting and gratifying and overtly violent and dangerous to other people's physical integrity. Such cases do not experience guilt or remorse for their behavior outside the sadistic episodes, as was true of one young man who beat women and threw bricks at them from rooftops when he was sexually excited.

Categories (3) and (4), in addition to not fulfilling the criteria for categories (1) and (2), present at first grandiose and derogatory features. These features, however, on exploration and confrontation, turn out to be ego-dystonic and conflictual. The emergence in these patients of more malignant types of grandiosity later in the treatment reflects a transference regression that is prognostically grave, yet less so than totally ego-syntonic, sadistic grandiosity that is evident from the beginning of treatment. The patient's capacity to establish some dependent relationship with other people improves the prognostic implication of this syndrome. I have already described cases with these characteristics, ranging from the untreatable antisocial personality to the narcissistic personality with ego-syntonic antisocial behavior (see chap. 18); malignant narcissism and severe superego pathology go hand in hand.

Theoretical Considerations

Under optimal circumstances, in advanced stages of the treatment of narcissistic personalities, one observes an oscillation between periods of idealization and overtly negative transferences, in the context of which mutually dissociated, idealized, and persecutory object relations are gradually integrated. Primitive forms of idealizations based upon self-idealization and the splitting off of idealization from aggression shift into more mature idealizations that are reaction formations against aggression and contain elements of guilt. The predominantly negative transferences now reflect condensed oedipal and preoedipal conflicts with early parental images. The gradual integration of these hostile and idealized transferences permits the integration of a normal self and a consolidation of ego identity, and enlarges the capacity for maintaining object relations in depth, thus reestablishing the capacity for normal dependency as well.

In the majority of patients with narcissistic personality, despite the prevailing absorption of idealized superego precursors into the pathological grandiose self, a remnant of idealized superego precursors remains outside the pathological grandiose self. This remnant is condensed with earlier sadistic superego precursors, leading to their mutual neutralization. The integration of these precursors facilitates the internalization and some degree of integration of more realistic parental images linked with later oedipal stages, thus laying the basis for superego functions that remain available even though the pathological grandiose self predominates as the major regulator of self-esteem. These patients as a rule do not develop the syndrome of malignant narcissism at stages of transference regression.

Comparing these relatively benign developments in the advanced stages of the treatment of narcissistic personalities with the malignant developments detailed in the preceding section, one is struck by the central nature of superego pathology in the malignant cases. All the patients with the malignant regressions in the transference described typically present superego lacunae (Johnson, 1949), or the absence of an ordinary sense of morality. In contrast, narcissistic personalities in more benign advanced phases show some capacity for idealization not linked to self-idealization, for investment in and concern about their relations with objects, and for maintenance of an ordinary sense of morality.

I propose that malignant narcissism illustrates a deep level of superego pathology characterized by (1) the absence of idealized superego precursors (idealized self and idealized object representations which would ordinarily constitute the primitive ego ideal) other than those integrated into the pathological grandiose self; (2) the predominance of the earliest level of sadistic superego precursors, which represent, because of their inordinate power, the only reliable internalized object representations available; and (3) the intrapsychic consolidation of a status quo in fantasy that permits survival when the only reliable object representations available would seem to be of sadistic enemies.

If this formulation is accurate, cases of narcissistic personality with malignant narcissism in the transference would illuminate the very core of the complex edifice constituted by the successive layers of superego integration originally described by Jacobson (1964). In all these cases, the psychoanalytic resolution of the pathological grandiose self lays bare the absence of underlying idealized superego precursors (except those that were absorbed into the pathological grandiose self) and the unopposed predominance of non-neutralized, sadistic superego precursors, expressing a condensation of preoedipal and oedipal aggression in unmitigated ways.

At that point, it is as if both libidinally invested and aggressively invested self-representations were reinforcing the predominance of these sadistic superego precursors. The very frailty of the libidinally invested self representations in the presence of the overriding and dominating aggressive superego precursors indicates the danger of destruction of whatever is not adjusted to or incorporated by the dominant intrapsychic sadism. This is, we might say, a version of what a normal person would experience in the nightmare world of Orwell's *1984*. The aggressive self-representations confirm, in the presence of these sadistic superego precursors, that all significant, reliable human interactions are of an aggressive nature.

The question of the etiology of these transference regressions and of malignant narcissism in general is more easily answered in a clinical context than in a theoretical frame. The analyst's efforts to resolve narcissistic transferences in the here-and-now, to explore the unconscious meanings of the patient's transference as a first step before the question "Where does all this come from?" can be raised, represent a safe gateway for the beginning of constructive and reconstructive work. The patient, as I have stressed in chapter 12, has to modify his rigid views about the present before he is ready to reexamine his rigidly held myths regarding his past in the light of new material emerging in free association.

Theoretically, these transferences reflect the vicissitudes of both faulty early superego formation and the lack of consolidation of total-object relations in the context of integration of ego identity. The question, then, may be formulated as follows: What actual and/or fantasied experiences and/or what defenses against both are responsible for a malignant transformation of the world of object relations that leads to the devaluation and sadistic enslavement of potentially good internalized object relations on the part of an integrated, yet cruel, omnipotent, and "mad" (Rosenfeld, 1971) self? The pathological grandiose and sadistic self replaces the sadistic precursors of the superego, absorbs all aggression, and transforms what would otherwise be sadistic superego components into an abnormal self structure that then militates against the internalization of later, more realistic superego components.

I suggest very tentatively that some or all aspects of the following scenario of the patient's past are involved here: (1) the experience of external objects as omnipotent and cruel; (2) a sense that any good, loving, mutually gratifying relationship with an object is frail, easily destroyed, and, even worse, contains the seeds for attack by the overpowering and cruel object; (3) a sense that total submission to that object is the only condition for survival and that, therefore, all ties to a good and weak object have to be severed; (4) once identification with the cruel and omnipotent object is achieved, an exhilarating sense of power and enjoyment, of freedom from fear, pain, and dread, and the feeling that the gratification of aggression is the only significant mode of relating to others; and (5) as an alternative, the discovery of an escape route by the adoption of a completely false, cynical, or hypocritical mode of communication, an erasing of all judgment that implies a comparison between good and bad objects, and negation of the importance of any object relation or successful maneuvering in the chaos of all human relations. In this last instance the dishonest position of the innocent bystander replaces dangerous identification with the cruel tyrant or masochistic submission to him. All these dangers, escape routes, and terrifying conceptions of human reality represent a dramatic, extreme deterioration in internalized object relations.

The condensation of sexual and aggressive drive derivatives of these patients is similar to that of the borderline spectrum. The sexual fantasies of these patients are strikingly similar to those of patients with sexual perversions. There is a consistent aggressivization of all sexual desires. Genital penetration becomes equivalent to destroying the genitals or to filling body cavities with excrement. The penis as a source of poison invading the body is the counterpart to teasingly unavailable breasts that can be incorporated only by cannibalistic destruction. The lack of differentiation of sexual aims, so that oral, anal, and genital fantasies are condensed and simultaneously express impulses and threats from all levels of psychosexual development, corresponds to a parallel dedifferentiation of the sexual characteristics of male and female, so that homosexual and heterosexual impulses mingle chaotically. These patients present what Meltzer (1973) has called "zonal confusions" and "perverse transference" features. Sexual promiscuity may defend them from deep involvement with a sexual partner who would threaten them with the irruption of uncontrollable violence. These patients also present "analization," the sadistic regression of all object relations tending to deny sexual and generational differentiation (described by Chasseguet-Smirgel, 1978), in which object relations are "digested" to the status of undifferentiated "feces."

In this formulation the syndromes of malignant narcissism can be understood as alternative compromise solutions to this assumed dramatic intrapsychic state.

Paranoid regressions can be seen as the patient's attempts to identify with his own sadistic superego precursors as an alternative to being attacked, humiliated, destroyed, and exploited by these same precursors projected onto the analyst. By the same token, his desperate plea that the analyst not fall prey to such sadistic distortions, that he demonstrate goodness and reliability, in spite of or in the face of the patient's aggression, reflects a search for a remnant of a good object relation.

When the patient is chronically self-destructive and suicidal in an unconscious attempt to triumph over the analyst, a more malignant process has taken place. The patient has internalized the paranoid conflict (externalized under paranoid regression) and, by means of a regressive refusion in fantasy, has obtained a primitive identification with the aggressor simultaneously with the enactment of the role of a victim. The patient's self-mutilations and desperate suicidal attacks not only are a triumph over his needs but also represent freedom from fear by identification with the aggressor and yield a deeply gratifying feeling of closeness and belonging by joining the aggressor as victim. This primitive type of masochism is seen at the end of Orwell's *1984* in the tortured victim's love for the sadistic "big brother" who will finally destroy his life. The patient's self-destructiveness is an act of defiance and challenge to the analyst's capacity to stand up to such massive aggression. The analyst may have to prove his power of survival before his capacity for love and his reliability can be trusted. It is typical of these transference developments that the interpretation of suicide wishes as an attack on the analyst diminishes the suicidal pressures and unmasks intense rage toward him.

With major and chronic dishonesty in the transference, a defensive dehumanization of all object relations has taken place, so that there is no longer a danger of love being destroyed by hatred or of hatred evoking devastating retaliation. The mechanization of all object relations, the withdrawal from deep emotional investments into purely erotic and aggressive excitement, eliminates the dangers fully experienced in the other modes of defense. The power of the sadistic superego precursors has been dismantled by eliminating dependency altogether, eliminating expectations and longings, gratification and frustration, and, in fact, intimacy. Jacobson (1971) has pointed to the paranoid patient's urge to betray, which reflects a sudden reversal to aggressive rebellion from masochistic submission to a dreaded enemy. These reversals appear in the history of some paranoid patients and are repeated in the transference.

Finally, the conscious identification with a self-righteous sadistic aggressor denies the existence of all needs for dependency and object relations, of all responsibility and concern for self or others, and reflects both a corruption of all object relations and a primitive type of identification with the aggressor. In extreme cases, this transforms the purely narcissistic into the antisocial personality. Clinically, I have observed

(Kernberg, 1975) that while many narcissistic personalities present anti-social features (and this worsens their prognosis), all antisocial personalities present the characteristics of narcissistic personality structure plus particularly severe destruction of their superego functions.

In summary, then, I am proposing that the development of a pathological grandiose self significantly impoverishes normal superego functioning because the idealized superego precursors are incorporated into this pathological grandiose self. This development leaves the sadistic superego precursors unneutralized and clearly predominant and fosters their projection in the form of paranoid personality traits as an alternative to a superego consolidation with excessive self-directed sadism. Under optimal circumstances, certain idealized superego precursors remain available for neutralization of sadistic superego precursors and permit internalization of the later levels of superego introjects, thus determining the capacity for ordinary morality and protecting the capacity for some degree of ordinary object relations, dependence, and concern, together with a sense of personal responsibility.

When, in narcissistic personalities, severe conflicts around early aggression result in overwhelmingly sadistic superego precursors, these remnants of neutralized superego functions fail; ordinary morality and, with it, the capacity for concern, responsibility, and guilt feelings suffer. At the same time, given the overwhelming power of sadistic internalized object relations, the condensation of the grandiose self with aggression compensates for the potential weakness and frailty of all idealized object relations, and the pathological grandiose self becomes powerful and sadistic and consolidates the general corruption of internalized value systems. There is a parallel between the availability of some investment in object relations, at least the hope for the possibility of love, and the absence of the more malignant aspects of superego deterioration reflected in antisocial features. Severe deterioration and corruption of primitive object relations and of the remnants of a capacity for superego functions go hand in hand; in fact, these conditions are intimately related in their origins.

Accordingly, the search on the part of some patients for a primitive sense of goodness, happiness, fulfillment, and well-being via alcohol, drugs, or fragmented types of sexuality may be considered to contain the seed of what might become a search for love, in contrast to the cold, dehumanized, revengeful, destructive quality of the psychopath. At the same time, however, for some patients the pathological grandiose self may provide a more adaptive intrapsychic structure than the severely paranoid or primitively masochistic tendencies from which such structure protects them. There are some narcissistic personalities whose pathological grandiose self should not be analyzed; rather, a supportive type of psychotherapy geared to improve the adaptation to themselves and to their psychosocial reality should be attempted.

Technical Considerations

Many of the technical considerations that follow may be incorporated
into both psychoanalysis and psychoanalytic psychotherapy; others require the introduction of parameters of technique that makes questionable the possibility of maintaining a psychoanalytic frame.

Cutting across all the types of malignant narcissism in the transference regressions described above, basic issues regarding the probability
of therapeutic resolution of these regressions include the following: (1)
the patient's remaining capacity to maintain a dependent relation to the
psychoanalyst, (2) the patient's capacity to tolerate maintaining a psychotherapeutic or psychoanalytic situation when strong negative transferences predominate, and (3) the availability of treatment arrangements
that realistically protect the patient from severely destructive or self-
destructive acting out which might jeopardize not only the continuation of the treatment but the very life of the patient (or even the
psychoanalyst).

From a practical viewpoint, the most urgent task in dealing with
malignant regressions in the transference is to limit the patient's destructive or self-destructive actions. It is important that the analyst be
able to work without fear of physical assaults. As in the office treatment
of psychotic patients, the analyst's first task is to assure a realistic degree of security for the patient and himself rather than assume omnipotently that he can handle whatever situation might emerge. Acute physical self-destructiveness needs to be sufficiently under control for the
analyst to have a free field for interpretive intervention. The same holds
true for patients whose aggressive behavior may threaten the life or
well-being of others.

A patient whose behavior includes, for example, control of his immediate environment by repetitive physical threats at gunpoint must re-
nounce this behavior before its meaning can be understood and worked
through. This does not mean that the analyst should start by giving orders to the patient but that he does discuss with the patient the reasons
for the need to control this behavior. The therapist must make it clear
that such behavior must be firmly under control as a condition for continuing the treatment. The analysis of this dramatic deviation from technical neutrality may and should follow later. With patients suffering
from anorexia nervosa, for example, it is indispensable that an optimal
weight be achieved and maintained before psychoanalytic exploration of
the underlying conflicts is undertaken.

A second level of priority is the analysis of chronic lying. As long as
verbal communication is used primarily to destroy an honest relationship between patient and therapist, everything else has to wait. Such lying has to be clarified, confronted, and resolved, analytically if possible,

or by means of external social control and consistent confrontation (which usually indicates the need for supportive psychotherapy). The consistent analysis of dishonesty as a major issue in the transference frequently leads to its gradual resolution in the context of the reactivation of the underlying paranoid, primitively masochistic, or corrupt object relations involved.

A third level of priority is analysis of the patient's chronic incapacity to really depend on the analyst. This is the most typical transference resistance in the case of narcissistic personalities, to which I have referred more extensively earlier (chaps. 12 and 17).

The most salient characteristic of the activation of the aggressively infiltrated grandiose self is the need to destroy the analyst psychologically: his interpretations, his creativity, his values as an autonomous good object, and his possessions. The unconscious motivations for such relentlessly destructive needs include envy of the analyst as a nurturing object—typical of narcissistic personalities in general—and, beyond that, envy of the analyst for not being the victim of the same pathology as the patient. The acute awareness that the analyst may be able to enjoy his own life becomes intolerable to the patient imprisoned by his sadistic, grandiose self.

In addition to acting out unconscious and conscious envy, these patients, while enacting their grandiose and sadistic self in the transference, may unconsciously project onto the analyst the remnants of their good, infantile, potentially dependent self, as if for safekeeping. This is a repetition in the transference of the intrapsychic imprisonment of and sadistic attack on the healthy part of their infantile self by the pathologically grandiose, sadistic part. The same projection for unconscious safekeeping may also involve remnants of their good object representations.

One patient described a new girlfriend to me. In contrast to several women he had mentioned previously, this girl sounded more real, and I could visualize her more clearly; I also experienced her, through his narrative, as very decent and likable. When I pointed out this change in the nature of his description the patient immediately and ironically disqualified what I said, adding triumphantly that he was already losing interest in the girl. Over the next few weeks I experienced a sense of mourning for the loss of his relationship with this woman. I raised the question with the patient whether he might be trying to induce in me a sense of mourning for a relationship that he did not dare experience himself. This interpretation was met first with derogatory smiles and eventually with the angry accusation that, in my devious way, I was trying to make him feel guilty. Several weeks later, however, the patient was able to acknowledge his own regret and guilt over his treatment of this woman, whom he now recognized as very valuable.

The most frequent type of effort to destroy the analyst's interpretations, his internal security, and his creativity as a therapist is expressed by the patient's relentlessly devaluing the analytic process, chronic complaints that the treatment is not helping, that the analyst is not saying anything new, and so on, while simultaneously devaluing quickly and peremptorily any subsequent interpretations the analyst might offer. The patient may suddenly dismiss careful interpretive work carried out over a period of many sessions. What is most characteristic and striking is that at such moments of dismissal—which to the patient are apparently glaring illustrations of the analyst's failure—the patient appears happy and triumphant. In fact, it is this expression of triumph after demolishing the analyst's interpretations, in sharp contrast to the chronic complaints that no new interventions from the analyst are forthcoming, that provides the clue to the unconscious function of the patient's sense that he is not being helped.

If the analyst now attempts to interpret the patient's devaluation of his interpretations, the patient's most characteristic response is rage at being "brainwashed" and subjected to what he considers attempts at sadistic and omnipotent control. In fact, a frequent development in these cases is the enactment of power struggles in the transference and the projection of dishonesty and sadistic control onto the analyst. The following case illustrates these features.

Mr. X. A man with narcissistic personality and paranoid regression in the transference pointed out to me on one occasion that I had charged him for a session that we had agreed to cancel. He said this with such an air of naturalness and certainty that, in spite of the fact that I had no written indication or recollection of the agreement, I acknowledged that I might have made a mistake and did not charge him for that session. When the same situation was repeated a few months later, I felt quite certain that I was unlikely to have made such a mistake twice. I asked Mr. X whether he might be in error. He reacted with intense rage, vehemently accusing me of lying. My efforts to explore with him the nature of these fantasies only increased his rage, his feeling that I was accusing him of being a liar, and his unshakable perception of what he described as my ruthlessness and callousness in being willing to lie in order to protect my infallibility. When I tried to link his perception of me with his strikingly similar perception of his mother, whom he consciously experienced as highly manipulative, self-righteous, and dishonest, he furiously protested against my efforts to whitewash his mother as well as myself.

This development in the transference gradually disappeared without being resolved. After a few weeks, Mr. X's attitude became that of a generous victim willing to forgive and forget. He had apparently resolved the stark contradiction between his trust in me as his analyst and his conviction that I had lied to him by attributing my "mistake" to an unconscious process in me, reflecting negative feelings against him that I was not aware of, and to my basically proud and stubborn nature, which he was willing to tolerate because of my redeeming features as his analyst.

A few months later, a serious illness of a member of his family required that Mr. X absent himself from town, and I changed a number of his appointments to make it possible to maintain the continuity of his treatment. At that point, I was hyperalert to any possible misunderstanding regarding our schedule and became fully aware of how extremely controlled I felt by him regarding our arrangements, particularly regarding his monthly fees. Sure enough, the same situation repeated itself, and Mr. X again accused me of having overcharged him.

I now stood firmly by my assertion that the mistake was his, and that this mistake must reflect the activation of an important issue in his intrapsychic life in the relation with me. Mr. X was astonished that, after having lied to him twice (as he now asserted again with total conviction), I would dare not only to play the same trick again but to accuse him of my own behavior. It became quite obvious to me that there was not only an immediate resurgence of his previous paranoid outbreaks in the transference but also an intensification of them, reflecting an accumulation of previously unresolved episodes of this kind. His paranoid regression had clearly assumed delusional proportions.

I pointed out to Mr. X that I believed the sincerity of his assertions, that I had no doubt of his conviction that he was right, and that, painful as this must be to him, I had to tell him of my equally strong conviction that I had not lied to him; in fact I had taken so many precautions regarding his bill that I was absolutely sure I had not overcharged him. I added that he would have to consider whether I too was absolutely convinced of what I was saying—although in his view totally wrong—or was indeed lying. If he believed I was lying, he might have to conclude that I was not to be trusted as his analyst, because the least one could expect from one's analyst was that he be absolutely honest with his patients.

Mr. X was taken aback by what I said and asked whether I was telling him that I was throwing him out. I assured him that I did not want to throw him out but saw no alternative other than these two conclusions for him: Either the two of us lived, at this moment, in two incompatible realities, as if one of us were crazy, or else he was in treatment with a callous, chronic, and ruthless liar. The patient then angrily accused me of accusing him of being crazy. I told him that if it were true that we were living in mutually irreconcilable realities, both of us must be having an experience similar to that of a normal person faced with madness, and I wondered whether he could tolerate such an experience.

The patient now became more thoughtful. He said he really did not

believe that I was lying or that he was crazy. I said I realized how painful it was to be faced with a world of madness, whether in himself or in
a person who is extremely important to him. This statement marked the
beginning of the resumption of psychoanalytic work, with the establishment of a parameter of technique: our mutual acknowledgment of the
total incompatibility of our understandings of reality as a basic subject to
be explored in the treatment. I should add that, in the face of the (at
least temporary) impossibility of resolving Mr. X's projective identification by interpretation, a firm stand on a minimal boundary of reality in
the treatment situation facilitated continuation of the treatment.

Once the patient is aware that the analyst can tolerate their mutually incompatible conceptions of reality, he himself may be able to tolerate such a state of affairs, a first step toward his acknowledgment of his
loss of reality testing. The patient may now develop a tolerance of experiencing a psychotic state: a delusional conviction regarding the analyst. In essence, the analyst's ability to tolerate the patient's psychotic
reality may lead to the patient's tolerating a psychotic nucleus in himself, an acknowledgment that fosters the reestablishment of reality testing in the transference. The same technical approach may be helpful in
the case of hallucinatory, pseudohallucinatory, and illusory developments in the treatment situation. The patient's attribution to the analyst
of grandiose, sadistic, dishonest, even delusional traits may often reflect
characteristics similar to those the patient had described in his parental
figures. Both paternal and maternal qualities, real and fantastic, may
combine in consolidating the sadistic grandiose self. Important genetic
antecedents of the consolidation of the grandiose self may thus be activated directly and by projective identification in the transference. It is
characteristic of such transference developments, however, that attempts at interpretation, tracing their links with their genetic antecedents, usually fail. The principal reason is that it is generally impossible
to interpret transference distortions in terms of the past before the transference has become ego-dystonic.

The analyst may be tempted to agree with the patient that his parents must indeed have been as terrible as he now perceives the analyst
to be. But such an acknowledgment is highly questionable from a theoretical and clinical viewpoint. First, the analyst is in no position to know
whether the patient's parents were in fact as described or whether the
description corresponds to an old or retrospective intrapsychic distortion; second, his acknowledgment of the reality of the patient's perceptions regarding the parents may temporarily soothe the patient but is
usually followed by reinforced efforts to convince the analyst that his behavior is impossible as well.

If the analyst attempts to submit to the patient's grandiose and sadistic control, the result may be to displace the negative transference

back onto the parental and other objects, but the price paid is the impossibility of fully elaborating and working through this central transference paradigm.

In the short run, the analyst's firm stand on reality may increase the patient's rage and tempt him to leave the session, sometimes even the treatment, or, most frequently, to continue his attacks on the analyst. In the long run, and under optimal circumstances, the patient may eventually be able to accept the reality of his distortions of the analyst's behavior and to experience guilt and concern over his unreasonable attacks on the analyst but also relief because the analyst has survived the attacks and is still there, emotionally available to him.

Such positive developments over an extended period of time have a crucial therapeutic function. They signal the beginning of the freeing of the patient's dependent, normal self from its imprisonment by the pathological, sadistic, grandiose one. The patient's acknowledgment of his own inappropriate aggression and his subsequent development of the capacity for experiencing guilt and concern may signal the beginning of the internalization of normal superego precursors and of an object relation in depth that tolerates ambivalence and implies the beginning integration of total-object relations, in contrast to part-object relations.

The risk of premature disruption of the treatment and of chronic, vicious cycles of attack and experienced counterattack on the part of the patient is the negative counterpart of such successful resolution of the activation of this extremely regressive transference.

To resolve long-term paranoid developments in the transference requires that the analyst be patient, alert, and firm. It is important to stress, early on, the risk that the patient may disrupt the treatment and interpret this as a triumph of his grandiose self over his normal, health-seeking self. It is equally important that the patient become aware that the analyst can survive without him and that, in contrast to the patient's illusion (or delusion) that his pathological grandiose self controls the world, the analyst will continue perfectly well and on his own even if the patient ends the treatment. It is also important to interpret the patient's efforts to distort the analyst's not feeling threatened by potential discontinuation of the treatment as meaning that the analyst is rejecting or is indifferent toward him.

In the treatment of patients with malignant narcissism, I have found it helpful to keep in mind that the objectives of the interpretive work are, first, to maintain a consistent affirmation of the reality in the treatment situation by interpreting all its distortions and, second, to help the patient reach the point where he can resume exploring his own unconscious by means of free association, in contrast to focusing all his energies on exploring and controlling the analyst's mind and communications. In other words, the frame of reference within which the regressive transferences of malignant narcissism have to be worked through is the goal of reinstatement or initiation of an ordinary analytic relationship, in which the patient may let himself truly depend on the analyst by exploring his unconscious in the acknowledged presence of the analyst, no longer experienced as malignant.

The pathological, sadistic, grandiose self unerringly attacks whatever the patient experiences as most helpful. The malignancy of this destruction of what is helpful particularly exploits the fact that all interpretations are hypotheses, to be confirmed or rejected by the patient's unconscious reactions to them. If the patient's reactions are highly negative toward interpretive hypotheses that strike him as correct, a very difficult situation emerges. The analyst must diagnose and interpret such immediate striking down of what is helpful. This often means that he has to think about the patient between sessions. To put it differently, these transferences tend to occupy the analyst's mind beyond the sessions, and such preoccupation should be understood not as a pathological countertransference reaction but as a normal reaction to very destructive transferences.

The acting out of the aggression toward the analyst may take the form of missing sessions, not paying bills, slandering the analyst, and even stealing objects from him or destroying objects in his office, engaging in actual hostile behavior outside the sessions against the analyst or persons related to him, or carrying out suicidal gestures as an unconscious expression of triumph over the failing analyst. In addition to consistent interpretation—particularly of the contradictory attitude of a patient who clings to the treatment while seemingly totally engaged in efforts to destroy it—such developments may require the analyst to set limits beyond which he will not continue the treatment. Pointing out the patient's glee during sadistic, devaluating behavior in the sessions may help to make him aware of the destructive aspects of what he rationalizes as "justifiable indignation."

When a patient threatened to throw a heavy ashtray at me, I discussed with him whether he could assure me that he was able to control such impulses; otherwise, I said, I would not be able to continue the session with him. Another patient would leave the couch to sit on a chair at the far end of the room and read to me, in an enraged voice, from a book on psychoanalytic technique offering recommendations that he felt were totally opposed to mine. Here, there was no threat of physical violence, and I did not feel that any action on my part was required to maintain the boundaries of an analytic situation. A third patient once stormed out of my office and yelled back at me from the corridor, where other patients and staff were circulating, that he thought my medical license should be revoked immediately. In this case I firmly told the patient that I would continue his treatment only if he talked to me in ways that would preserve the privacy of our interchange.

To discuss issues openly with the patient before they get out of hand may prevent sudden disruptions of the treatment—initiated not only by the patient but also by the analyst. I am familiar with several cases of malignant narcissism in which the analyst attempted to maintain a semblance of an analytic relationship by not interpreting the patient's aggressive behavior and shortly afterward made a relatively sudden decision to terminate the treatment.

The patient may attempt to destroy what he receives from the analyst and to intimidate him in various subtle ways. He may use language that seemingly indicates insight or expresses fantasies or curiosity about the analyst. Statements such as "I missed you since last session" or "I feel good about what you are saying," or a patient's asking for clarification of an interpretation may appear to bring temporary relief from almost unbearable tensions in the treatment situation. Only in retrospect are such statements recognized as empty of meaning. Over a period of time, however, the analyst learns to recognize by their tone or temporal placement in the hours such misuses of verbal communications. Other patients may attempt to "brainwash" the analyst with idiosyncratic theories about human behavior and effectively occupy much time with these theories while acting out the principal aspects of the transference in a different area. Patients who chronically lie to the analyst may convey an artificiality in the analytic situation that the analyst first attributes to his own difficulty in experiencing empathy with the patient. The analyst may search for deeper countertransference reasons for this failure in empathy, only to discover many months after full communication in the treatment has been restored that he had been accurately registering the "as if" quality of the transference, what Bion (1970) might have designated a "-K" or a "parasitic" transference relationship.

Mr. Y. A prominent politician with a narcissistic personality and a dissociated type of homosexual activity (homosexual episodes were highly ego-syntonic during their development but completely repudiated by him at other times) was concealing the nature of his homosexual escapades, only hinting indirectly at the fact that he was picking up men in public restrooms in areas of town where, because of his public prominence, he could be recognized and easily blackmailed. His vague references to several episodes in which he thought he was recognized finally alerted me to the acute danger in which he was placing himself. My insistent efforts to clarify this issue led him to accuse me angrily of a conventional puritanical and antihomosexual bias. But he also saw me as a fool because I was so slow to realize the danger his behavior was provoking, a danger that he also experienced as highly thrilling. It also became clear that, as long as he was communicating to me his dangerous behavior, he felt it was my responsibility to be concerned about it and he had no need to feel guilty about it. All in all, I was either a sadistic enemy trying to clamp down on him and destroy his only pleasure in life, an indifferent, aloof, totally self-centered therapist, or else a naive fool.

Mr. Y, it is of interest to note, described at great length occasional complex triangularized affairs, such as his search for men who were willing to let him go to bed with their wives in return for homosexual submission to them, the oedipal implications of which were reflected in abundant associations linking such experiences with his childhood. The urgency of exploring his current acting out, the extreme danger of his ongoing, daredevil homosexual activities thus faded into the background, until I woke up to the real urgencies in his total life situation. Here, severe self-destructiveness and lack of honesty in his communications jointly constituted a major transference resistance that required working through before further aspects of the total material could be elaborated. The consistent analysis of these various alternatives, and of his playing Russian roulette while externalizing with me his conflicts related to a minimum concern for himself, finally transformed that repetitive acting out into an intrapsychic conflict.

The therapist's consistent confrontation of the patient who chronically lies may be experienced as a sadistic attack. In fact, patients who present severe superego pathology because of their intolerance of sadistic superego precursors and their projection of such precursors onto others—typically the analyst—will experience any comment that points to their problems in ethical behavior, concern, responsibility, or guilt as a sadistic attack. It is possible that the analyst, in the countertransference, may experience himself as a sadistic persecutor.

The analyst has to be firmly moral, even if the patient accuses him of being judgmental. Sometimes the analyst's need to reassure himself and the patient that, in spite of the patient's behavior, the analyst still accepts and "empathizes" with him may be misused by the patient. The patient interprets the analyst's understanding and tolerance as subtle collusion with antisocial behavior. In this way the analyst may unwillingly and unwittingly foster a corruption in the transference which, while it may reduce the intensity of paranoid regression, actually replaces it with the more malignant problem of further deterioration of the patient's superego functioning.

It is unavoidable to first transform dishonesty in the transference into acutely paranoid transferences, in the course of which the primitive conflicts with sadistic superego precursors are brought into the transference situation and may later on be worked through there. The dangers, then, are: first, an "innocent," playful, or seductive bypassing of the dishonesty in the therapeutic relation, which fosters further corruption of the patient's superego potential; and, second, if paranoid regression develops but is not worked through fully, a rigidification in the transference at a point of such paranoid regression.

Once the patient has been able to acknowledge the fantastic nature of his paranoid distortions of the psychoanalyst and, in this context, the inappropriate nature of his violent attacks on the analyst, periods of severe guilt and depressive reactions may signal his tolerance of internalized superego functions—in other words, the reinternalization of his aggressive superego precursors and self-direction of their aggression.

The capacity for an object relation in depth that the analyst brings to the treatment of these severely ill patients, his absolute honesty and incorruptibility, provide an implicit frame of a potential normal object relation that is unavailable to the patient for long periods of the treatment but optimally will be within his emotional reach in the end. The lack of capacity for normal dependent object relations, a capacity that we take for granted in the ordinary patient who enters psychoanalysis, becomes the main obstacle in the treatment of patients with severe narcissistic psychopathology but also part of the analyst's frame of reference that permits him to clarify the nature of this difficulty and to resolve it analytically. In this regard, the treatable patient with malignant narcissism represents an extreme expression of the challenge and attack on such a basic object relation, and the analyst's capacity to withstand such an attack is one more condition for the treatability of such patients.

In all the types of malignant narcissism I have described, the object relations lying behind conscious and preconscious fantasies about the analyst must be fully explored. The patient's image of the analyst as sadistic, dishonest, indifferent, overpowering, corrupt, and stupid, his unconscious perception of the analyst as a killer, a psychopath, or a bungling fool, needs to be brought fully into the open so that he can discover the source of these distortions.

What actual or fantasied experiences in early childhood, what interplay between unconscious fantasy and actual experiences were responsible for such a state of affairs is another matter, less important as a theory for dealing with malignant narcissism than the expectation that, in the process of resolving this pattern in the transference, the road leading back to this disaster in early development will become clarified.

PART FIVE: *Hospital Treatment*

 Contrasting Philosophies of Hospital Treatment for Severe Psychopathology

Psychoanalytic Contributions to Hospital Treatment

During the first half of this century the large state hospitals, housing from hundreds to thousands of patients, had as their essential tasks to protect the community from mental patients and to provide for these patients over a long period of time a supportive environment within which medical treatment could be applied. It was in the small private psychiatric hospitals, housing between 50 or fewer and 300 patients, that the high staff/patient ratio allowed for the development of a new philosophy of hospital treatment based on psychoanalytic principles.

This new current was expressed through three parallel approaches: the interpersonal, culturalist approach of Harry Stack Sullivan (and the related "psychobiological" approach of Adolf Meyer); the ego-psychology approach, applied by William Menninger, Robert Knight, and Paul Federn; and the British object relations approach, first applied by Thomas Main to "special cases" (most of them patients with borderline personality organization) in the hospital and gradually integrated with the sociological approach of Alfred Stanton and Morris Schwartz (Kernberg, 1976, 1980).

The Sullivanian Approach

Sullivan's work at Sheppard and Enoch Pratt Hospital, in Towson, Maryland, from 1923 to 1930 and subsequently at the Chestnut Lodge Sanitarium in Rockville, Maryland, is summarized in several theoretical and clinical writings by Sullivan himself (1953a, 1953b, 1954, 1956, 1962) and by his leading disciples, particularly Frieda Fromm-Reichmann (1950), Harold Searles (1965), and Otto Will (1967). These views were reinforced by Adolf Meyer's (1957) formulations on hospital treatment, ar-

315

rived at independently at Johns Hopkins Hospital, and by Lewis Hill's (1955) work at Sheppard-Pratt.

Sullivan stressed that psychological investigation can be applied only to interpersonal situations, which may be real or fantasied intrapsychic experiences. He stressed that instinctual bodily needs are normally condensed with the need for other human beings and proposed that the dissociation between strivings to gratify basic bodily needs and strivings for feelings of security derived from appreciation by others (which determines self-esteem) is a basic cause of psychopathology. At a certain level of severity, dissociation of need satisfaction from security satisfaction produces severe anxiety dissociation of a good self from a bad self, and a related malevolent transformation of the normal capacity for tenderness into paranoid suspicion and self-hatred.

The essential task of hospital treatment is to overcome this dissociation by means of intense psychotherapeutic interpersonal interactions with the therapist, which bring the dissociated needs into focus and permit resolution of the transference ("parataxic") distortions. The resolution of severe anxiety linked to such dissociative conflicts fosters growth in the interpersonal relation the patient establishes with the therapist.

The social structure of the hospital is aimed at facilitating the gathering of information about all the patient's interactions. The patient is allowed to express his pathological, regressive needs without being rejected or abandoned. Hospital staff should interact with the patient in terms of their availability as persons rather than as a function of specific skills. All the information gathered from the patient's interactions within the hospital setting should be channeled to the therapist, so that he can integrate it and use it in his psychotherapeutic work.

The psychotherapist, with his interpretive interventions, is the principal therapeutic instrument. The patient's negative transference is interpreted in the light of the meaning of the parataxic distortions that are enacted. Positive transference is utilized mostly for facilitating the patient's growth through resumption of the normal development of interpersonal gratifications in the therapeutic situation and secondarily in growth-promoting relations with other members of the staff as well. According to Searles (1965), establishing a "symbiotic" relationship in the therapy of schizophrenic patients and gradually sorting out the patient's ego boundaries and the reality of the situation permit the patient to separate his self from the therapist and to consolidate his ego boundaries.

In short, the Sullivanian orientation focuses on the dynamics of the current interaction in the hospital, on the alert participation of all personnel in gathering information, and on the interpretation of all interactions by the psychotherapist. The hospital milieu program should facilitate the psychotherapy, but it is not so essential as the patient's interactions with the therapist and the provision within the hospital of individual models for the patient to identify with.

The Ego-Psychology Approach

From 1927 to 1931, Ernst Simmel (1929), in the Tegel Sanitarium near Berlin, attempted to develop new methods of hospital treatment based on psychoanalytic principles. After the Nazis closed the sanitarium, Simmel's ideas inspired William Menninger (1936, 1943) and, later, Robert Knight (1953a, 1953b).

The ego-psychology orientation of these authors, gradually enriched by the theories of Paul Federn (1952), Heinz Hartmann (1964), and David Rapaport (1967), focused on the hospital treatment, not of schizophrenic patients (Sullivan's major interest), but of patients with severe neuroses and character pathology. It was in studying this group of patients that Knight developed his pioneering understanding regarding borderline conditions, first at the C. F. Menninger Memorial Hospital in Topeka, Kansas (between 1937 and 1951), then at Austin Riggs Sanitarium in Stockbridge, Massachusetts.

In this ego-psychology concept the hospital constitutes a protective environment which permits the diagnosis of patients' transferences while protecting them against the consequences of destructive or self-destructive acting out. The patient's transference may be to other staff members or to the entire institution as well as to the therapist, so that his total behavior must be explored. Hospital treatment should include psychoanalytic psychotherapy or psychoanalysis as well as selective restriction of inappropriate behaviors, the analysis of these behaviors, and explanation of the need for this restriction.

At the same time, the hospital should provide socially acceptable outlets for instinctual needs. The therapeutic activities program should foster sublimated expression of aggressive needs. The experiences of work, recreation, study, and artistic expression (the four principal areas of therapeutic activities in the hospital) offer opportunities for adaptive compromises between impulse and defense and therefore have direct ego-strengthening functions. The availability of an optimal hospital structure, neither too rigidly nor too loosely organized, also has ego-building functions. Daily life in the hospital provides experiences of growth and learning by directly raising the patient's self-esteem as a consequence of his more effective functioning in the hospital, decreasing the patient's fears of unconscious impulses by providing external controls, and offering new models for identification.

This concept of hospital milieu treatment encourages the patient's active involvement in therapeutic activities throughout the hospital stay.

This approach was in line with the supportive psychotherapy that Knight (1953b) systematized for borderline patients, a treatment strategy that stressed the search for a more adaptive expression of impulse and defense by means of selectively interpreting some areas while leaving others untouched and by directly strengthening adaptive and sublimatory ego functions in the therapy hours as well.

Federn's (1952) work with psychotic patients focused on the loss of ego boundaries, which Federn believed was experienced by the patients as the loss of a sense organ (which helps the ego to distinguish reality from fantasy). This loss was determined, in his view, by a withdrawal of libidinal cathexes from ego boundaries. In the psychotherapeutic treatment of schizophrenic patients, Federn suggested, it was important to foster the recathexis of ego boundaries by stressing the delimitation between the patient's self and others, by focusing the patient's interest and libidinal investment on a positive transference relation with the therapist and avoiding negative transference developments, and by providing a clear structure around him to facilitate his redifferentiating from his environment. The hospital structure lent itself to this psychotherapeutic approach. The hospital clearly limits space, time, roles, and activities, thereby facilitating reconsolidation of ego boundaries through all the patient's daily activities and interactions.

Hartmann's (1964) concept of the conflict-free sphere of the ego also influenced the ego-psychology approach to hospital treatment. Hospital milieu therapy could tap the patient's ego resources by building on whatever residual strength the patient had and by avoiding regressive experiences that would encourage the expression of primitive, un-neutralized aggression and thereby lead to further loss of ego boundaries. The ego-psychology approach, in short, stressed the importance of a structured environment focused on the confluence of ego-strengthening features in the environment and in the patient's psychotherapy, and deemphasized exploration of the negative transference in patients with ego weakness, particularly in psychotic patients (where most of the burden of the treatment was placed on the hospital milieu program).

Ego-Psychology Object Relations Approaches

The ego-psychology object relations approach derives from a variety of sources, some of them British, some American. Under this heading fall my own ideas on hospital treatment.

Thomas Main (1957) described the group reactions of nurses treating borderline (and some psychotic) patients who had become "special cases" in the Castle Hospital near London. Main found that these patients activated group phenomena in the nursing staff similar to those of the "basic assumptions groups" described by Wilfred Bion in 1952.

Bion later (1961) elaborated on his theory of the regressive phenomena that occur in small groups when their task structure (work group) fails. Bion described the development of certain basic emotional reactions within such a group ("basic assumptions group"), reactions that exist potentially at all times but are activated especially at times of breakdown of the task group. His descriptions of the "fight–flight" assumption, the "dependent" assumption, and the "pairing" assumption are sufficiently well known to require no further elaboration here. What is relevant here is Main's conclusion that regressed (particularly borderline) patients may, under certain conditions, activate their intrapsychic object relations in interpersonal relations with the hospital staff, eliciting in their social field a reenactment of the conflicts within their intrapsychic world. The activation of massive projection, the need for omnipotent control, denial, primitive idealization, and, above all, splitting in the nursing staff reflects both the patient's intrapsychic mechanisms and the behavioral means by which staff relationships are distorted by the patient's intrapsychic world.

In 1954 Alfred Stanton and Morris Schwartz, in a classical study based on their research at Chestnut Lodge, proposed that the social and administrative structure of the psychiatric hospital has a significant impact on the individual patient's functioning and that social pathology reinforces individual psychopathology. Stanton and Schwartz studied the effects of breakdown in staff morale and of covert disagreement among staff on patients' pathological excitement, particularly the activation of the "special case" syndrome. They illustrated how "splits" and covert conflict in the interpersonal and social fields of the hospital may intensify intrapsychic conflicts and disorganization in borderline and in some psychotic patients.

Stanton and Schwartz and Main thus provided a complementary set of formulations that illuminated the relation between social conflict in the hospital and intrapsychic conflicts in patients with severe regression. The finding that the patient's intrapsychic conflicts and the potential cleavages and stresses within the hospital's social system reinforce each other constitutes a most important bridge between the understanding of the hospital as a social system and the understanding of the activation of pathology of internalized object relations of patients in that social system.

These findings and theoretical considerations led me to investigate the general theoretical formulations of the British object relations school, especially the description by Fairbairn (1954) and Melanie Klein (1940, 1945, 1946) of primitive defensive operations, primitive object relations, primitive aggression, and the primitive transferences reflecting all these factors.

The ideas in Main's pioneering paper of 1957, in Bion (1952, 1961), and in Stanton and Schwartz (1954) were first integrated into a philosophy of hospital treatment and applied at the Menninger Hospital in the early 1970s (Kernberg, 1976). These concepts also influenced the American counterpart of the Tavistock Institute for Human Relations in London, the A. K. Rice Institute of the Washington School of Psychiatry, which applied Kenneth Rice's contributions to group psychology (1965) in conferences for mental health professionals throughout the United States from the late 1960s on. The diagnosis of primitive defensive operations, particularly splitting mechanisms, in the patient and in the social group under the effects of the patient's pathological interactions in the hospital resulted in a related emphasis on the interpretation of primitive transferences in the psychotherapy of hospitalized borderline and psychotic patients and a stress on primitive aggression as a fundamental source of intrapsychic conflicts.

This interpretive work with the transference differed from the approaches of both Federn (who had recommended building on the positive transference and avoiding the negative transference) and the Sullivanian school (which focused on the growth potential of current developments in contrast to the analysis of intrapsychic, genetic issues in the transference). At the same time, the theoretical link between Stanton and Schwartz's ideas about the hospital milieu and Main's findings regarding the patient's intrapsychic functions suggested that the hospital milieu had a therapeutic use in addition to serving as an ego-strengthening device. It could serve as a setting within which the patient's intrapsychic conflicts could be played out in the context of group processes, diagnosed in the social field by hospital staff, and brought back into the individual psychotherapeutic work with the patient.

Thus, the effects of the ego-psychology object relations approach included a renewed focus on psychoanalytic psychotherapy—especially with patients presenting severe character pathology and borderline personality organization—a psychoanalytic exploration of group processes, and a reorganization of hospital treatment to permit a combination of these individual and group methods. In contrast to supportive psychotherapy with borderline conditions and the corresponding supportive functions of the hospital milieu developed by Knight, this newer approach emphasized interpreting both the patient's transference in individual psychotherapy and the regressive group processes in the hospital.

Sociological Approaches

Stanton and Schwartz's (1954) finding that covert disagreements among staff could cause regressive behavior in individual patients, pointed to the potentially antitherapeutic effects of hospital treatment. William

Caudill (1958) at the Yale Psychiatric Institute (another small, psychoan-alytically oriented psychiatric hospital) studied the effects of the rela-tions between staff and patients on the development of individual pa-tients in the hospital setting. He found that the isolation of patients from staff, encouraged by a hierarchical hospital structure, negatively af-fected the treatment of individual patients as well as the functioning of the patients as a group. Caudill described how imposing a "patient role" on the patient, through peer pressures for socialization and for accept-ing the doctors' value system, together with the patients' opposition to authority (particularly to nursing staff), foster mutual ignorance of pa-tients and staff, stereotyping, and alternations between permissiveness and restriction in the form of cultural "groundswells," which strongly influence all treatment carried out in the hospital.

Ivan Belknap (1956) and Erving Goffman (1961) studied the effects of the social structure of the hospital on the treatment of psychiatric pa-tients in large public institutions. Their conclusions stressed even more sharply than the investigators previously mentioned the regressive and degrading effects of the traditional hierarchical system in large hospitals, where the deterioration of the patient's self-respect and the general pris-on atmosphere complemented the arbitrary and authoritarian control exerted by the lowest echelons of the hierarchically organized staff. Goffman compared life in the large psychiatric hospital to his studies of other "total institutions," such as armies, prisons, labor camps, ships at sea, and monasteries. He pointed to the dramatic discrepancies between the ideal aims of institutions and their actual functioning as determined by expediency and tradition. Goffman described the "dehumanizing" of the patient so that he could be more easily dealt with as just another unit in a "batch," the regulating of all activities by the "privilege sys-tem," which consists essentially of measuring a patient's health in terms of his obedience, and the process by which the patient accommodates himself to the actual conditions of institutional life.

As a result of these studies and reports in the 1950s, a strong con-sensus developed in the 1960s that the traditional large public psychiat-ric hospital included important antitherapeutic features and that long-term hospitalization itself could adversely affect the treatment of many patients. This conviction gradually merged with the political ideas prev-alent in the 1960s, when traditional authority in general was being in-creasingly questioned. The opposition to the war in Vietnam, the aspira-tions of the counterculture, and the influence in the United States of the antipsychiatry movement that was then evolving in Europe resulted in a strong swing of the pendulum. Hospital treatment in general was ques-tioned, and alternatives to long-term hospitalization (in some instances to all hospital treatment for psychiatric patients) were sought.

Paradoxically, however, while the conclusions of these sociological studies questioned psychiatric hospital treatment in general, a contrary trend evolved from the study of authoritarian features in small psychiatric hospitals. This contrary trend was the effort to transform the traditional psychiatric hospital into a nonauthoritarian, democratically inspired social system. The aim was to provide patients with new sources of emotional growth and self-esteem through their participation in determining the nature and activities of their daily life in a protected environment. Here, the sociological studies of Stanton and Schwartz and of Caudill and the various psychoanalytic approaches converged.

The concept of the therapeutic community emerged as a direct challenge to the regressive and antitherapeutic effects of the traditional hierarchical medical model of the psychiatric hospital. Main (1946) and Maxwell Jones (1953) originally developed the concept of the therapeutic community as a treatment modality; their aims included democratization of the treatment process. The therapeutic community treatment modality is an elaboration of the "team approach" to diagnosis and treatment that has gradually emerged in contemporary psychiatry. Traditionally the decision-making authority is distributed among various disciplines according to the tasks each performs. In the typical therapeutic community, the aim is to minimize hierarchical levels stemming from professional expertise, degrees, and titles and to maximize democracy in the decision-making process.

Therapeutic community models were developed in various hospitals in the United States in the 1960s, especially at Fort Logan in Colorado, at Austin Riggs, and at the Yale Psychiatric Institute. These early experiments were followed by applications at the Menninger Hospital, at the New York State Psychiatric Institute, and at the Westchester Division of the New York Hospital.

Thus, while the antiauthoritarian and prodemocratic groundswell of the 1960s fostered criticism of psychiatric hospitals, it simultaneously resulted in the development of new experimental models of hospital administration which linked the administrative structure with the use of group processes. It also facilitated the examination of the total social system in which the patient developed his life in the hospital. Therapeutic community approaches strengthened the new psychoanalytically derived concepts of hospital treatment and dramatically enriched the armamentarium of treatment modalities and techniques within the psychiatric hospital. From a historical perspective, these two contradictory trends of the 1960s, one toward the elimination of psychiatric hospitals—particularly of long-term hospital treatment—and the other toward the enrichment of psychiatric hospital treatment with new therapeutic modalities, reflected a new phase in the dialectic between the large public institutions and the small psychiatric hospitals.

In the short run, in the early 1970s, the first trend—toward significant restriction and elimination of hospital treatment—prevailed. But in the second half of the 1970s the results of emptying out the large state hospitals generated a sobering awareness of the differences between ideologically determined concepts of eliminating institutional treatment, on the one hand, and the reality of how patients fared in outpatient alternatives to hospital treatment, on the other.

Community Psychiatry, Deinstitutionalization, and Transinstitutionalization

The introduction of the neuroleptics in the 1950s, gradually expanding into a broad armamentarium of psychopharmacological treatment in the 1960s, contributed to a dramatic decrease in the resident patient population of the large state and county mental hospitals in the United States. From a high of 559,000 in 1955, the number of resident patients in state mental hospitals decreased to 200,000 in 1970 and 193,000 in 1976. This trend was reinforced by the rise of community mental health centers throughout the country in the late 1960s and early 1970s.

Strong ideological currents incorporating the social criticism of the negative effects of institutionalization, the "antipsychiatry" philosophy (which considered all treatment based upon traditional hierarchical medical models suspect and wanted to promote the autonomy, self-respect, and self-determination of psychiatric patients), the democratic aspirations of the therapeutic community, the optimism generated by the effects of psychopharmacological treatment and the community mental health movement—all these combined in promoting deinstitutionalization of mental patients as a primary aspiration of the psychiatric profession. Several research findings, highly publicized because they fit into this social atmosphere, indicated the effectiveness of alternatives to hospitalization.

Pasamanick et al. (1967) compared a population of hospitalized patients with an experimental population of patients receiving specially designed home care. Significantly fewer of the hospitalized patients were able to remain in the community after completion of their treatment than patients from the home-care population. A five-year follow-up report, however, presented a more pessimistic outlook, suggesting that there was little difference between patients who were placed in home care and those who were hospitalized; the follow-up showed that the results were uniformly poor. Herz (1971; Herz et al., 1975), comparing day hospital treatment with inpatient treatment of a population selected because both treatment modalities were deemed appropriate to all of them, concluded that the inpatients had a higher readmission rate than the day hospital patients and that after four weeks a small but statistically significant improvement of day hospital patients over inpatients had occurred. In a critical review of recent research and literature on the advantages and disadvantages of hospitalization, Herz (1980) concludes that the day hospital is not only a feasible alternative to inpatient care but may be generally preferable except for severely disturbed, acutely psychotic patients and seriously impaired, acute and chronic patients who do not have adequate social support systems in the community.

In looking back over the research efforts that supported the assumption that alternatives to hospitalization may be preferable in the treatment of many psychiatric patients, one cannot help notice the difference between the quality of the alternative care provided in the experimental studies and the actual alternatives to hospital care available to the large majority of psychiatric patients. The "antihospitalization" ideology inhibited a full evaluation of the social and financial costs of alternative treatment arrangements in comparison to those of hospital treatment for mental patients.

In many cases, state legislatures and commissioners of mental health enthusiastically adopted the philosophy of dehospitalization because it meant a significant decrease in their system's inpatient population and, therefore, in the financial burden for state governments. The result was a strange alliance between economy-minded legislatures and psychiatric administrators, on the one hand, and idealistic community mental health psychiatrists, on the other. And when tens of thousands of patients were literally dumped from large institutions into the local communities without adequate support systems, the communities protested. From 1975 to 1980 a number of inquiries and reports revealed the dismal living conditions of the deinstitutionalized former mental patients. It became evident that one effect of the deinstitutionalization movement had been a "trans-institutionalization" (Robert Michels, personal communication); the chronically ill had simply been dumped from the frying pan into the fire. They were now living in poorly designed, inadequately supervised, substandard nursing homes and other undesirable places.

Another negative consequence of allowing ideological considerations to take precedence over patients' needs was evident in the functioning of many community health centers. In order to democratize treatment, efforts were made to involve the local community in leadership functions in these centers. Community "participation" (interpreted as community control by many), guaranteed by mandated advisory groups that would represent consumers' and citizens' interests, in practice fostered a political organization of certain community groups that utilized participation in community mental health centers for purposes only indirectly related to the treatment of the mentally ill. In some instances mental health professionals, in an effort to involve the local community in the treatment of mental patients, trained nonprofessionals to take over professional functions, relinquished quality control, and permitted a deterioration of the quality of services that led, in some circumstances, to severe political conflicts between community groups and mental health officials.

Perhaps the most serious problem that significantly discouraged the community mental health movement and brought widespread disappointment in the second half of the 1970s was the discrepancy between the many functions they were expected to perform and the inadequacy of their staffing. Again, the clash between ideology and good intentions, on one side, and fiscal realities and technical requirements, on the other, was dramatic. In an effort to control the cost of operating community mental health centers, consistent efforts were made to replace the most expensive professionals (psychiatrists) by less expensive and less well-trained professionals, leading to a significant decrease in the level of professional functioning, disappointments on the part of the most highly trained (and, by the same token, overworked) professional staff, dissatisfaction with the quality of medical care provided, burnout symptoms, and finally, the psychiatrists' abandonment of the community mental health system. In retrospect the polarization between hospital treatment and community treatment seems ideologically motivated and technically absurd. On the basis of clinical and research evidence, a broad spectrum of psychiatric modalities of treatment, which include the availability of short-term and long-term hospital treatment in conjunction with partial hospitalization and all other outpatient modalities, seems to be the optimal model of care.

A Contemporary Outlook on Psychiatric Hospital Treatment

Perhaps the most important trend to emerge in recent years is recognition of the need to develop particular services for particular patient populations, in contrast to the traditional tendency to treat all mental patients as a homogeneous group.

Within the psychiatric hospital itself, specific services are needed to serve different populations. For example, a large psychiatric state hospital should ideally be subdivided so as to provide both acute and long-term treatment services. Within the long-term service, some facilities should be geared to intensive treatment of character pathology, others to the treatment of severely deteriorated, chronic psychotic patients, others to the custodial support of severely ill organic patients (each of these with different staffing and programs). Small psychiatric hospitals would necessarily have to specialize in only some areas, except where staff/patient ratio is very high; the variety of treatments offered could then be augmented but the treatment costs would be very high as well.

Hospital services for acute, short-term treatment would expect the average length of stay to fluctuate from 30 to 90 days. Such services would be ideal to treat acute psychotic illness and to provide a full range of medical and psychiatric diagnoses and treatment, as well as a sophisticated use of the armamentarium of psychopharmacology, psychosocial rehabilitation, and the initiation of aftercare. Such acute services may specialize further in the treatment of alcoholism and drug addiction, affective illness, schizophrenia, or transitory reactive psychosis reflecting acute organic brain syndrome or the temporary regression of borderline conditions. Specialized child and adolescent inpatient services represent one more highly differentiated modality of hospital treatment. Some crisis intervention may be carried out concomitantly with brief hospitalization, although most crisis intervention would be carried out in a day-hospital or outpatient setting.

Long-term hospitalization is indicated for patients with chronic regression who have not responded to treatment and are unable to function in anything but a well-structured hospital and for patients with frequent and prolonged psychotic episodes, where both psychotherapeutic and psychopharmacological modalities of treatment seem indicated. Long-term hospitalization is strongly indicated for patients with severe character pathology and borderline conditions who are extremely self-destructive or present such disorganized functioning that they need the protection of the hospital in order to participate in a therapeutic program.

Patients with borderline personality organization and low impulse control, severe acting out, negative therapeutic reaction, low motivation for treatment, and antisocial features are prevalent in this group. Their program, however, may be different from that required for a subgroup of schizophrenic patients who do not respond to psychopharmacological treatment and seem potentially responsive to intensive psychotherapy. This subgroup also requires long-term hospitalization but with a different structure of hospital treatment. Therapeutic community models are particularly indicated in the long-term treatment of character pathology and borderline conditions, while modified versions of the therapeutic community may have some value in the long-term hospital treatment of schizophrenic patients as well.

Long-term hospitalization geared largely to custodial functions is indicated for patients whose active treatment has convincingly proved to be ineffective and who are unable to live in an environment less structured than a psychiatric hospital. In sum, awareness seems to be growing that a relatively small but significant patient population of chronic, severely ill, psychotic and organic patients requires custodial support, and that an optimally functioning contemporary hospital setting may be far preferable for them to a vegetative existence at the periphery of the local community.

Clinical experience and research regarding the effectiveness of day hospitals has established the importance of this therapeutic modality. Day hospitals may be a viable alternative for acute crisis intervention on a short-term basis and for all cases that would require long-term hospitalization but where a more restricted structure, such as the day hospital can provide, is sufficient. For example, many borderline patients might be treated in a day hospital as an alternative to long-term hospitalization, while the severe destructiveness and self-destructiveness of other borderline patients would contraindicate anything but full hospitalization. Other day-hospital programs should focus on the transitional needs of patients who are moving from hospital treatment, especially long-term hospital treatment, into outpatient treatment and the community.

The treatment objectives and techniques should vary markedly for each of these groups of patients. Psychiatric inpatient treatment, for example, geared to bringing about significant structural intrapsychic change in borderline personality organization so that the patient can move into an outpatient treatment setting not possible before, requires intensive psychotherapy in the hospital and the diagnostic and therapeutic utilization of group processes and therapeutic community models. Such a hospital treatment program is very different from what is required for the ongoing social support and gradual rehabilitation of severely regressed, chronic schizophrenic patients.

A functional distribution of human and financial resources within the large psychiatric hospital might enable it to provide to some extent the intensive treatment given by the small hospital. Modifying the large public hospital in this way would eliminate some of its significant differences from the small private psychiatric hospital.

The development of special geriatric services is a new trend that may dramatically change the hospital milieu for older patients who were previously mixed indiscriminately with the chronic schizophrenic population. Special short-term and long-term geriatric services may contribute significantly to a reduced hospital stay for some geriatric patients, particularly for those with affective disorders.

The function of the day hospital as a transitional setting for former inpatients is complemented by the development of halfway houses, apartment-living programs (where former hospital patients share responsibility and life in an apartment setting), foster home care, and outpatient clubs and social organizations that may be organized around outpatient clinics.

The concept of continuity of care has been critically revised in recent times. It is expensive and usually nonfunctional to have the same staff throughout a patient's progress from inpatient to day-hospital to outpatient treatment. The inpatient staff gradually become overloaded with a growing aftercare and outpatient population, which leads to burnout and inefficiency in utilizing treatment resources. Ideally, continuity of care should be provided by a primary therapist who starts out with the patient in the hospital and maintains a psychotherapeutic relationship with the patient outside the hospital. In this regard, an integrated inpatient hospital program with a staff of psychiatrists fully committed to that program seems more important than the maintenance of contact between the patient and his previous psychotherapist throughout hospital treatment, particularly when long-term inpatient treatment is involved; here it is usually preferable to change therapists.

Currently, in the leading private institutions at the forefront of psychiatric hospital care, treatment modalities include a broad range of group methods, various applications of hospital milieu treatment, therapeutic community approaches, psychopharmacological treatment, psychosocial rehabilitation, and psychotherapy. The team approach to psychiatric patients developed in the past 20 years conceives of nursing, psychiatric social work, therapeutic activities, and psychology as integrated parts of the medical and psychiatric treatment. Each professional in these various disciplines contributes both special skills and a personal interaction with the patient, in which transference and countertransference developments are used as part of the diagnosis of the total social environment surrounding the patient. This immediate social environment is affected by the patient's intrapsychic conflicts and in turn influences the patient. The network of formal and informal, individual, small-group, and large-group experiences in the hospital is the background against which the multiple transferences and countertransferences played out in individual and group situations can be diagnosed and therapeutically utilized.

It seems to me that the hospital is best conceived of as an experimental social setting within which the patient can display his predominant constellations of pathogenic internalized object relations, and in which these activated object relations can be diagnosed and therapeutically modified in the context of individual and group psychotherapeutic interactions. The contributions of psychoanalysis to hospital treatment and the contributions of therapeutic community approaches have facilitated a concept of hospital administration and structure that minimizes the dangers of the hospital as a "total institution" and maximizes the opportunity for new learning experiences.

A major task facing American psychiatry today is to disentangle the new technical knowledge obtained in the past 50 years from the ideological distortions and social extrapolations of that knowledge. In practice, optimal utilization of this knowledge requires that the psychiatric hospital permit the use of staff's emotional reactions to patients for therapeutic purposes and promote an atmosphere of openness and a functional—in contrast to an authoritarian—administrative structure. A functional administrative structure is not a democratic one. The distinction between functional administration and democratic political organization is one aspect of the new learning that is being integrated at this time. By the same token, modern concepts of organizational management may be among the knowledge and skills that the contemporary hospital psychiatrist has to acquire. In addition, the hospital psychiatrist needs to combine knowledge of the full range of psychopharmacological and psychosocial treatments now available, including expertise in the diagnosis and therapeutic utilization of group processes.

CHAPTER 21: *The Therapeutic Community Model of Hospital Treatment for Severe Psychopathology*

Underlying Assumptions

For more than a decade I have been observing the effectiveness and limitations of therapeutic community modalities of treatment. The therapeutic community has transformed the more traditional types of hospital milieu treatment, opened new roads to the inpatient treatment of severe character pathology, and shed new light on the optimal administrative requirements for psychiatric hospitals. Some of these new insights were not only unforeseen but revealed unintended consequences of this treatment modality.

Whiteley and Gordon (1979, pp. 105–27), after pointing out that the term *therapeutic community* is one of the most misused and misunderstood in modern psychiatry, define it as "a specific, specialized treatment process utilizing the psychological and sociological phenomena inherent in the large, circumscribed and residential group. In this respect it is an intensified extension of milieu therapy which has more general implications and applications for patients of all categories in the mental hospital community." In the course of their excellent review of the history and recent developments of therapeutic community models, Whiteley and Gordon introduce an additional dimension to their concept: an ideology. In fact, both Main and Jones—key originators of therapeutic community models—stressed their conviction of the value of democratizing treatment processes and of providing a "therapeutic setting with a spontaneous and emotionally structured (rather than medically dictated) organization in which all staff and patients engage" (Main, 1946, pp. 66–70). Jones (1953) pointed to the flattening of the hierarchical pyramid, role blurring, and open communication as an expression of a democratic therapeutic environment.

I believe that it is from this attempt to combine technical and ideo-

330

logical concepts—that is, the notion of the therapeutic community as a treatment modality and as a democratization of the treatment process —that the new findings and therapeutic advantages, as well as the shortcomings and problems, of this approach emerge.

Although various authors might describe the essential aspects of this approach in somewhat different ways, the basic orientation stemming from Jones and Main emphasized the following features:

(1) *Community treatment.* Staff and patients, functioning jointly as an organized community, carry out the treatment of the patient population; patients actively participate in and are co-responsible agents in their own treatment, not passive recipients.

(2) *Therapeutic culture.* All activities and interactions relate to the goal of reeducating and socially rehabilitating patients. The optimal functioning of patients in the therapeutic community is the first phase in promoting their optimal functioning in the external community.

(3) *Living-learning-confrontation.* An open flow of communication between patients and staff provides immediate feedback regarding observed behaviors and reactions to them. An exploration of the functions of these behaviors in the here-and-now and of alternative new, experimental behaviors will help the patients to cope in the therapeutic community and in the external community.

The methods used to carry out these aims include group meetings (small group, large group, and task group) to facilitate open communication, to generate pressures for socialization and rehabilitation, and to foster a democratic process of decision making.

Three types of meetings are common to therapeutic community models, apart from the category of small-, large,- and task-group meetings:

(1) *The community meeting.* This includes all patients and all staff, and aims to examine the total social environment in which staff and patients participate, the distortions and interferences with a free flow of communication from whatever source, and the development and possible resolution of antidemocratic and authoritarian processes.

(2) *Patient government.* Regardless of the specific form such government takes, therapeutic community models tend to foster patients' organization for the purpose of participating in the social and decision-making processes.

(3) *Staff meeting.* This meeting complements patient government, expresses the concept of democratic decision making among staff, and allows staff to study how they are influenced by pressures from administrative and other sources as well as by their interaction with patients. The staff meeting allows for democratic distribution of authority regarding tasks to be done, in contrast to hierarchical decisions from above.

A number of assumptions regarding therapeutic change are implied in therapeutic community concepts. First, it is assumed—correctly, I think—that patients as individuals and as a group are able to help one another. Second, patients functioning in a group setting may react in "normal," appropriate, and responsible ways as a group, in contrast to individual patients' pathological interactions outside the group setting. Third, by the same token, staff as a group may function pathologically and antitherapeutically although as individuals they may be mature and skillful. In fact, clinical experience has confirmed that the pathology and social effectiveness of groups do not coincide with the pathology and social effectiveness of their individual members.

Fourth, it is assumed that authoritarianism is antitherapeutic and that decisions made on the basis of "power" rather than "reason" militate against patients' best interests. I believe that this assumption is correct if one defines authoritarianism as taking responsibility for making decisions beyond what is functionally warranted. I am suggesting that the antinomy is not of authoritarian versus democratic decision making but of authoritarian versus functional decision making. With this qualification, I agree with the general assumption, abundantly documented in the literature, of the negative, sometimes devastating effects of authoritarian treatment systems on patients' welfare and improvement. Even an authoritarian organizational structure that apparently affects only the upper echelons of staff cannot help affecting all participants in the therapeutic community. Authoritarianism is transmitted by complex psychological mechanisms along the hierarchical ladder, particularly by means of submission to and identification with the aggressor, and it tends to erode the authenticity of patient/therapist relationships throughout the entire hospital system. An authoritarian hospital administration may transform treatment arrangements, distorting them so that they will utterly confound the therapeutic team trying to apply them. Such distortions in treatment arrangement can promote a pseudoadaptation of the patient to the hospital system and interfere with his development of autonomy and growth. An authoritarian hospital structure, almost by definition, interferes with an open, ongoing evaluation of the hospital as a social system.

A fifth assumption is that, in contrast to authoritarian treatment systems, therapeutic community concepts imply that democratization of the treatment process is in itself therapeutic. Democratization increases the patient's self-esteem, the effectiveness of his functioning, and the honesty of his communications and is directly growth promoting. My experience leads me to challenge this assumption. The results of democratizing of the decision-making processes in hospitals have often been a mixture of therapeutic and antitherapeutic. More about this later.

Sixth, collective decision making in an open setting at public meet-

ings is assumed to be therapeutic because it nurtures democratic in contrast to authoritarian processes. Later, I examine the illusions implied in
this assumption.

Seventh, patients are assumed to be able to help one another as individuals and, in the process, to develop interpersonal skills and creativity as well as ego strength. On the basis of my experience, I think this is
remarkably true. However, patients can also have very destructive effects upon one another; for every David and Lisa who help each other,
one can find a psychopath potentially driving another patient to suicide.

The Therapeutic Community and Its Parent Structure

The problem is how to preserve the eminent advantages of the therapeutic community—its therapeutic utilization of the hospital as a social
system, the activation of patients' potentials for contributing to their
own treatment, the development of skills and responsibilities of staff at
lower echelons, the increasing knowledge about the interaction between
the internal world of patients and the structured conflicts in the environment, the corrective emotional experiences provided by the therapeutic
community, and the increase in staff morale—without falling prey to
the serious, sometimes devastating disadvantages, which I am about to
describe, of this otherwise effective therapeutic tool.

The most important prerequisite for the development of a therapeutic community is that it be functionally integrated with the administrative structure of the psychiatric or general hospital within which it oper-
ates. This requirement might seem trivial were it not that, in practice,
leaders of therapeutic communities are so often innocent regarding the
administrative structures, boundaries, and constraints of their institution. Some of them are equally innocent regarding a general theory of
administration or institutional management that would permit a full
analysis of administrative feasibilities and constraints for a therapeutic
community within that particular setting. Unfortunately, even the literature on the therapeutic community does not sufficiently consider the relationship between the therapeutic community structure and the organization into which it must fit.

For example, Marshal Edelson (1970), one of the most sophisticated
theoreticians in this field, is not prone to replace a study of administrative constraints with a declaration of ideological convictions. Yet, while
explicitly describing the administrative and professional implications of
the relation between hospital administration and the director of sociotherapy, he in fact presents models of organizational functioning in
which there is no clear administrative structure linking, for one, the authority vested in the therapeutic community with that of overall hospital

administration. Although he acknowledges the potential for strain and conflicts in his model, his proposed solution is a consultative one, not organizational/administrative.

If the therapeutic community is to explore openly the social system actualized by the patient/staff community, it cannot avoid activating the stress and latent conflicts in the system as well, with consequent influences on the political dimension of the decision-making process in the institution. The assumption that a purely observational, clarifying, and informative approach to conflicts in the social system can be carried out and couched in technical and neutral interpretive terms is an illusion. As evidence, I offer this frequently encountered scenario: An enthusiastic group establishes a therapeutic community model in a sector of the hospital; an "ideal society" is formed which generates gratification, excitement, hope, and perhaps a messianic spirit in both staff and patients, to be followed later by bitter disappointment because of the "lack of understanding" and apparent rejection of this ideal society by the hospital within which it has developed. The final result is that the task is abandoned, the therapeutic community collapses, and the leaders emigrate either into a different system to start the cycle all over again—or into private practice in a mental health profession.

A therapeutic community must be limited in size; the patient/staff community should number between 80 and 100 participants at the most. This means that therapeutic communities can be established only in very small psychiatric hospitals or on relatively small services within a larger hospital. It is no coincidence that some of the most successful models have operated within small psychiatric hospitals, where the complexities of relating to larger administrative structures are less evident.

When the leader of the therapeutic community is fully aware of the organizational structure of the institution, of the degree and stability of the authority delegated to him (and therefore to the therapeutic system he is in charge of), then the limits of the authority vested in the entire community as well as in its individual members can be defined and considered when activated conflicts within the therapeutic system and across the boundaries of the therapeutic community are studied. The leader of the therapeutic community requires clear administrative arrangements linking the community to its environment, and the community leadership should have the capacity to spell these out.

In the last resort, the ideological—in contrast to the technical—convictions about democratic political organization often influence leaders of therapeutic communities and the staff members who share these convictions to operate as if they constituted a minority party in a state governed by authoritarian leadership. Unconsciously or unwittingly, they confuse exploration of the social system with a political means for changing it. The therapeutic aim of the therapeutic community becomes confused with the political aim of democratizing a health-care institution. Eventually, both staff and patients pay the price for this confusion.

The parent structure's support for the therapeutic community system requires constant redefinition and renegotiation. Hence, the leader must have the ability to carry out a political function, not in terms of democratic concepts, but in terms of effective ways of influencing individuals and groups across task-determined boundaries in the institution. The basic skills required for leadership of the therapeutic community also include a solid knowledge of small-group, large-group, and task-group functioning and management; a solid knowledge of individual psychopathology and of its potential influence in distorting small-group processes in the environment; and a solid grasp of psychotherapeutic principles. These requirements determine the problems involved in training appropriately skilled leadership.

Still another requirement for the development of a therapeutic community is a clear definition of the authority, roles, and functions of all individual staff members as well as of formally organized interlocking groups carrying out its functions. The authority delegated to the therapeutic community must in turn be functionally distributed within it. The danger is that group processes that are designed to encourage shared decision making may also blur the issue of whose responsibility it is to carry out those decisions, as well as the nature of the system of inspection, control, and monitoring of the community functions. Another danger is that traditional roles and expertise that have been "imported" into the therapeutic community may be underutilized or that authority may be delegated on political grounds to those who do not have appropriate technical skills. An egalitarian approach that neglects individual differences in capacity, skills, and training may prevail, resulting in inefficiency and waste in using available human resources. The erosion of skills that occurs in small and large groups under the effect of regression into basic-assumptions-group functioning is greatly amplified by the failure to use available skills caused by administrative ambiguity within the therapeutic community.

Therapeutic communities have often been perceived as a threat by the traditional administrative and professional leadership of psychiatric hospitals. Insofar as the authority vested in the medical profession was being challenged in the name of egalitarianism, the threat was real enough. Beyond that, the leaders of the parent structure felt threatened by scrutiny of the distribution of authority, functions, and the like. An open examination of the hospital as a social system inevitably becomes a monitoring of the administrative process, with all the political challenges that implies. It may be argued, of course, that this is a very healthy development for some petrified hospital systems. But proponents of thera-

peutic communities should not be surprised by the active or subtle opposition it evokes in the hospital administration.

The therapeutic community is also a threat to the traditional pa-
tient/doctor relation and to the traditional relations among interdisciplinary staff. In terms of democratizing life in a psychiatric hospital this is
of course an advantage; but in terms of the optimal utilization of all therapeutic resources, it has had unforeseen and partly negative consequences. Relatively uneducated staff in the lower echelons may find
themselves invested with more authority but at the same time with
more direct scrutiny of their functioning. Consequently, their relations
with their administrative and professional supervisors will be strained.
The contradictions among social inequality, inequality in salaries, and
work expectations, dictated by the environment within which the hospital functions, and the development of an egalitarian atmosphere in the
therapeutic community sharpen the awareness of real social conflicts
and contradictions that are beyond the therapeutic community's ability
to resolve satisfactorily. Simmering resentment and unresolved guilt
feelings at various hierarchical levels may increase tensions among staff
and further complicate the analysis, let alone resolution, of tensions in
the social system of the therapeutic community. All of this increases the
danger of diminishing professional efficiency.

Activation of Regressive Group Processes

Therapeutic communities can also become a real or an experienced
threat to the patients' treatment. Because of the number of individuals
involved and the effort to maintain a relatively open flow of communication, patient meetings, staff meetings, and the community meeting itself
easily acquire characteristics of large-group processes; the regressive effects of these processes may affect individual patients' developments in
the community in antitherapeutic ways. Elsewhere (Kernberg, 1976,
chap. 9; 1980, chap. 11) I have stressed the danger that patients as a
group may regress to basic-assumptions-group functioning when functional, task-centered leadership is not available, when the tasks carried
out by patients are not meaningful but trivial, when the delegation of
authority from staff to patient is ambiguous, and when staff's leadership is ineffective. Under such regressive circumstances, patient groups
may become intolerant of individuals, establish a dictatorship of the
group that acquires characteristics of a primitive morality, and foster the
ascendence of personalities with narcissistic and antisocial features to
leadership positions. Staff may contribute to this regression by an ideologically determined denial of differences among individual patients, by
an implicit belief that all patients have the same needs and should be expected to react or participate in similar ways. Patient and staff groups

may enter into unconscious collusion in interfering with the autonomous development of individual patients and in allowing an uncontrolled invasion of privacy that corresponds to the total group's acting out of aggression against individual members.

The understanding that regressive group processes may produce a worsening of symptoms in individual patients may, however, also give rise to the mistaken assumption that all patient pathology corresponds to group processes, thus denying that psychopathology can be individual in nature. Such an attitude promotes a defensive idealization of group processes which feeds into patients' magical expectations of treatment ("If the group functions well, patients will get better").

In addition, groups may develop an exaggerated need for formalities and rituals as a defense against violence (which large groups in particular tend to generate), a defense that may function well for the group but restricts the individual patient's needs. The control of unstructured group processes by the most regressed patients, the chronic monopolizers, highly effective manipulators, or simply the most violent patients may significantly distort the content of meetings and the allocation of resources, thus reducing many patients' treatment time.

Unacknowledged and dissociated sadistic tendencies of individuals may infiltrate the group process in the form of accentuation of bureaucratic rigidities, which serve to control violence while yet expressing it in subtle ways. This excessive formalization of group processes, combined with rigid conventionality (especially regarding sexual issues), may result in throwing the therapeutic community back to restrictive group processes of latency and early adolescence.

Under the conditions of Bion's (1961) basic-assumptions-group developments, all the negative effects of group processes increase. The very concepts of egalitarianism, democracy, and trust in the beneficial effects of open communication may feed into the messianic expectations inherent in the "dependent" or "pairing" basic-assumptions group's development, thus fostering an unrealistic hospital environment which deters the functional reentry of patients into the external world. Under regression into fight–flight conditions, the exacerbation of social struggles within the hospital derived from intrastaff tensions may naturally blend with patients' search for ad hoc "parties" and militant ideologies that rationalize violence.

Proponents of therapeutic communities are often unaware that building up an "ideal society" within a hospital can easily merge with patients' needs to deny their own conflicts—both intrapsychic and interpersonal—and the real contradictions in the external world to which they must eventually return. Hence, the patients adapt to hospital life but are not prepared for reentry into the external environment. Or there may be a subtle assumption that all people are essentially good and that

open communication permits the elimination of distortions in perceptions of self and others that are the ultimate cause of pathological conflict and pathological psychic structure. This philosophical position
denies the existence of unconscious intrapsychic sources of aggression,
in striking contradiction to what staff and patients themselves can observe in patients in a psychiatric hospital.

Intrapsychic versus Interpersonal Factors

Jones (1953, 1956) recommends therapeutic communities for patients
with severe character pathology who require hospitalization; he conceives of the reeducation and resocialization effected by the therapeutic
community as the main if not the exclusive treatment modality for such
patients. He conveys the impression that he sees these patients as social
casualties who require educational support and pressures to provide
them with new social and vocational roles. This view neglects the importance of intrapsychic determinants for psychopathology and supports the illusion that a healthy social atmosphere in the hospital can replace psychotherapy and produce fundamental personality change. I
believe that this concept confuses a psychotherapeutic atmosphere
geared to developing intensive individual and group treatments with
the treatments themselves. To assume that patients are victims of irrational social forces and are in fact expressing them and that a rational society (one without obvious intrinsic contradictions) will permit their full
restoration to health is appealing but naive. It is probably not a coincidence that the idea of the therapeutic community had particular appeal
for the counterculture of the 1960s. By the 1980s the utopian quality
of the ideas and assumptions of many of the models has become more
transparent.

The failure to differentiate the social from the intrapsychic factors
influencing psychopathology may promote a faulty application of systems theory to the psychotherapeutic situation. The assumption that patients' psychopathology directly reflects contradictions in the environment can result in locating the etiology exclusively in the social system.
Here Main's approach and Bion's description of group processes diverge
sharply from Jones's.

This failure to differentiate the intrapsychic from the interpersonal—while continuing to study the relations between the two—
results in a failure to define clearly the indications and limitations of
group-treatment modalities and techniques and to evaluate critically the
effects of combining and overlapping various treatments. It is easy, for
example, for group methods to proliferate in a psychotherapeutic community, so that eventually the same issues and problems are discussed
from different perspectives at different places without regard for the

economy of human resources being consumed. Moreover, there is the ubiquitous possibility that splitting mechanisms will be activated by the simultaneous discussion of the same issues in different settings. In theory, of course, all information flows together in the community, staff, and patient meetings; in practice, however, overflowing agendas and increasing diffusion of information militate against integration of information. In the long run, the loss of privacy may be a lesser evil than the waste of time and human resources brought about when treatment modalities and techniques are not differentiated from one another.

Edelson (1970) attempted to solve the problem of the relation between sociotherapy and psychotherapy by keeping them completely separate. In my view, that solution artificially isolates the patient's dynamics as manifest in his psychotherapy from the patient's dynamics in the therapeutic community. The result is to impoverish both psychotherapy and social modalities of treatment.

My own experiences in leading several different therapeutic communities over a period of more than a decade has led me to the following conclusions.

To begin, the time element is of crucial importance in determining the success or failure of therapeutic community settings. In units for acutely regressed patients, with a rapid turnover related to a short length of stay and acute medical problems constantly requiring urgent attention, therapeutic community approaches seem to work least well. But for patients with chronic character difficulties, in units with slow turnover and extended stays, the benefits of the therapeutic community become greater. This seems to confirm Jones's idea that therapeutic community approaches are indicated for these patients.

In addition, again related to the dimension of time, the short-term (one to six months) effects of therapeutic communities may be strikingly different from the long-term effects. The advantages of therapeutic communities strongly predominate over a shorter period of time, while the problems they generate predominate in the long run. In the short term the activation of patients' potential for helping one another, the highlighting of internal contradictions of the social treatment system, which can often be resolved as they are diagnosed, and the exciting and exhilarating effects of group processes strengthen the bonds among patients, among staff, and between patients and staff and rapidly lead to increases in knowledge about patients that can be used for therapeutic purposes.

In the long-term treatment setting (six months to years), however, the results differ. The agendas of community meetings and all decision-making groups tend to become overloaded. Efforts to stimulate patients and staff to participate freely typically result in the emergence of group resistances and basic-assumptions groups, in the development of passivity among patients and staff alike, in long silences, which waste time, or in the eruption of such an abundance of primitive material that sorting it out in terms of priorities for the community takes up inordinate time. Efforts to solve these problems by making the meetings more formal create the danger of bureaucratization, of slowing down the decision-making process—and once more the agenda becomes overloaded. Gradually, the very need for administrative decision making and the negotiations between the therapeutic community and the external environment that give rise to reality pressures foster a new informal network of decision making. This ad hoc administrative structure may, paradoxically, be optimally functional, but it may also be perceived as running counter to the idea of shared decision making and thus will require further analysis and lengthy negotiations of otherwise obvious community needs.

Patients who tend to be manipulative and/or violent, who are impelled to test the limits of their power and control, frequently present another problem. For example, patients with anorexia nervosa and those who use suicide attempts to control the environment create agonizing conflicts for the nursing staff between their wish to protect the idea of permissiveness on the service and the need to maintain control over life-threatening acting out.

That some of the most violent and manipulative patients manage dramatically to draw attention to themselves and absorb inordinate treatment resources is one of the most consistent features of therapeutic community functioning. In theory, all patients are presented with the same model of social treatment; in practice, violent and manipulative patients may be rewarded by increased attention while other patients fade into the background.

The messianic spirit, excitement, and high morale that therapeutic communities inspire in the short run can obscure the dangerous overstretching of staff derived from lack of a rational distribution of resources and ignoring of time constraints. Eventually, staff exhaustion, particularly among the nursing staff, may bring requests for increased staffing and the need for senior medical personnel to spend more time with nursing. Passivity develops among staff—who continue to attend all meetings but participate less and less—and staff and patients with narcissistic personality features tend to ascend to leading positions. Because narcissistic personalities do not have any real commitment to group goals, they will not be sensitive to intrapsychic stress and conflicts under such trying circumstances. But the ease with which they superficially adapt to group processes—especially when they are the focus of a group's interest and admiration—propels them to leadership functions. This promotes a thrilling pseudo intimacy and tends to erode deep feelings as well as quality control on the service (Kernberg, 1980, chap. 11).

One other manifestation of staff exhaustion and regression is the growth in staff's self-absorption. An outside observer of the development of therapeutic communities over a period of time is always surprised to find that the proportion of time directly spent with patients diminishes and that the number of group meetings involving staff only increases. At the same time, burnout frequently occurs among the leadership of therapeutic communities, so that after three to five years there is a strong tendency for service chiefs who are interested in and committed to therapeutic communities to abandon their positions.

A frequently avoided question is the cost/benefit ratio of the therapeutic community in comparison with traditional psychiatric hospital treatment. Earlier findings indicated that when insufficient staff is available to treat patients in the first place—such as in large state institutions (where the damaging social effects of traditional mental hospitals were first studied)—the use of group methods permits an increase in patient/staff contacts and a humanization of hierarchically rigidified channels of communication between patients and staff. However, the need for individual treatment of patients is not resolved by such an organizational shift, and a natural selection takes place in which only some patients can be helped.

In a modern psychiatric hospital setting, with adequate patient/staff ratios, multidisciplinary approaches, and an adequate complement of senior psychiatric staff, therapeutic communities permit intensifying the individual treatment of patients and enormously enrich the understanding of patients gained on the unit and the treatment modalities and techniques geared to helping them. This positive effect, however, tends to be neutralized in the long run because the time of the most experienced staff members is taken up in group meetings, reducing their availability for individual contacts with patients. Furthermore, the least skilled members of staff are passive at group meetings, neither participating nor necessarily learning much, while their skills in relating to individual patients are underutilized. In short, an irrational and uneconomical distribution of resources develops.

This drawback is worsened by the tendency of the therapeutic community staff to withdraw from the parent hospital unit. Work in the therapeutic community generates an emotionally intense yet protected atmosphere. Staff want to stay together with the patients and resist an open flow of other staff and trainees through the unit for limited periods of learning and eventual export of knowledge of the new treatment modality. Therapeutic community settings are sometimes most reluctant to tolerate students and trainees who have to leave after a limited period of time.

There is a danger that individual staff members may fail to be accountable for what happens to patients between group meetings. A patient's family is often perceived as an intrusive outside force, and communications with family members may decrease while staff is totally engaged in the internal world of the therapeutic community. Thus, patients' reentry into society may suffer.

The treatment of families is usually managed by psychiatric social workers, who may compensate for the inward stance of the therapeutic community by intense family treatment. The problem is that most families may end up in intensive family therapy rather than in reality-oriented psychiatric casework. The social worker can rationalize this result in terms of the psychosocial conception of emotional illness implied in therapeutic community models ("the patient is a product of his family circumstances"), but the number of social workers required to carry out this boundary function also increases.

Quality control tends to suffer when staff members are so intimately involved with one another that senior staff find it awkward to make decisions regarding promotions, firing, and the like and to evaluate whether sufficient learning is occurring. Over a period of time, one would expect that relatively junior or inexperienced staff should be able to take over the therapeutic community functions, thus permitting senior staff to dedicate their time to individual work with patients and/or research and educational activities. This optimal redistribution of time and functions tends to be neglected.

In the initial enthusiasm and excitement of staff and patients working together, personality conflicts among staff tend to be submerged in the strivings for common goals. Over time, however, such personality issues reassert themselves and often cannot be included in the analysis of conflicts among staff—because the theory of the therapeutic community and of democratic decision making has no room for unsolvable personality clashes. In the interest of peace, distortions in the administrative process may evolve. Paradoxically, personality issues now may become more important than in the hierarchical model of hospital administration, where strict rules, regulations, and bureaucratic hierarchical expectations tend to decrease the direct impact of personality functioning.

CHAPTER 22: *Long-Term Hospital Treatment of Severe Borderline and Narcissistic Pathology*

In treating patients with severe psychopathology, especially those with borderline and narcissistic character pathology, I have found a modification of the therapeutic community model integrated with intensive individual psychotherapy effective. The model I am proposing has in common with other therapeutic community approaches the effort to openly examine the total social system within which patients and staff interact on a unit; recognition of the need to establish a functional, nonauthoritarian administrative structure that truly permits the examination of decision-making processes and of failures in the assumption of responsibility and in task performance by both patients and staff; and the high priority given to examining the reality of the patient's life on the unit and its relation to the task of the patient's social rehabilitation.

The approach described here differs from other therapeutic community models, however, in that it is not based on an egalitarian ideology regarding the functions of patients and staff; it does not aspire to democratize treatment processes; it strictly limits the authority vested in the patient/staff community in contrast to that delegated specifically to staff; it is not intent upon creating an atmosphere of permissiveness for its own sake; and in that it is strongly concerned with preventing and correcting role diffusion of staff as part of a constant focus on optimal utilization of human resources and on cost effectiveness.

If channels of communication among staff and between patients as a group and staff as a group are kept open enough to explore the interpersonal conflicts generated around each patient, immediate knowledge of each patient's psychopathology may be gained. In fact, more immediate knowledge may become available—particularly regarding patients with severe acting out—than would be possible by means of psychoanalytic exploration in individual psychotherapy sessions during the same time span. The integration of the knowledge thus acquired with the understanding gained from individual and group psychotherapy powerfully reinforces the utilization of the total social milieu of the hospital for therapeutic purposes.

The development of such a treatment approach requires that all members of the staff carry out two sets of functions simultaneously. The first is related to their special training and professional background: They must interact with patients by means of specific tasks that differentiate their professions or disciplines from others and that correspond to different aspects of the patient's adaptation to reality. The second function is more personal: Each staff member must utilize his natural emotional reactions to the individual patient's interactions with him in order to diagnose a particular human relation thus enacted and the fantasies implied in the emotional constellation generated in the social field. The emotional reactions of staff members to individual patients have to be diagnosed and brought together into a picture that eventually permits them to map the patient's major, activated, conflictual internal object relations in the entire hospital environment.

The specific functions of nursing staff relate to creating and re-creating a home atmosphere on the unit. The specific functions of therapeutic activities (occupational, vocational, artistic, and recreational) relate to reproducing the major areas of normal active work and leisure time outside the home. The specific functions of psychiatric social work relate to the patient's interactions with his immediate social—particularly familial—environment and with the building of bridges between hospital life and that external social environment. The specific functions of the individual and group psychotherapist (most frequently but not always a psychiatrist or psychologist) relate to the exploration of the patient's psychopathology by means of the developments of the transference and the analysis of the total transference/countertransference constellation expressed in the psychotherapy situation as well as in the surrounding social field. Finally, the function of the patient's hospital or unit manager or primary therapist (usually though not always a psychiatrist/administrator) is to coordinate the efforts of the entire staff of the various disciplines mentioned—in other words, to head the interdisciplinary task system in charge of ongoing diagnosis and monitoring of the patient's interactions in his social field, with the double purpose of adjusting the social/rehabilitative program as necessary and providing information to the individual psychotherapist.

A practical problem immediately warranting attention is the question of whether the psychotherapy function and the hospital-management function ("hospital therapy") should or can be carried out by the same person or whether a dual system is preferable. Ideally, these two functions should be separate; however, there are ways of condensing them, during the initial stage of hospital treatment or even for extended periods of time. The technical requirements for adequate handling of the psychotherapeutic relationship (particularly efforts to avoid acting out of the countertransference) and for avoiding authoritarian distortions in the decision-making process regarding individual patients add important complications to such condensed psychotherapist/administrator roles.

The proposed model of hospital treatment has certain practical requirements that lead us to the underlying theory of organization of the service or unit. First, the utilization of staff's emotional reactions to patients for therapeutic purposes requires that staff be selected not only on the basis of professional background and skills but also for certain personality characteristics: openness, willingness and interest in exploring their emotional reactions to others, and freedom from severe psychopathology that would unduly distort their interactions under nonstructured social conditions. Personalities with excessively paranoid, hysteroid-infantile, or narcissistically aloof features are poor candidates for such work.

Second, it is important that an administrative structure be provided that facilitates open exploration of human reactions; that is, a nonauthoritarian structure which requires a nonpunitive, open-minded, respectful attitude. Of course a noncritical, nonjudgmental acceptance of all staff performance may be very detrimental to learning, to staff selection, and to optimal use of staff time. Here, I think, is an unavoidable internal contradiction of the proposed model.

Third, in order for staff members to explore openly their reactions to patients, they must consistently preserve socially appropriate behavior toward patients and clearly delimit their personal boundaries from their professional functions. To be spontaneous and open in their interactions with patients does not mean that members of staff should talk about their personal lives. To maintain staff privacy also means that interpretations of staff's emotional reactions and behavior toward patients that include anything but here-and-now observations should be avoided. The analysis of the meaning of countertransference reactions has to remain at a level of its immediate contextual significance. It is important to avoid exploration of staff's personal past and any emotional "stripping" of staff as a "model" to be imitated by patients. Emotional stripping of staff is a disastrous technique which compounds the regression of patients and of group with that of staff and usually has very negative consequences for everyone involved. A firm self-discipline of staff acting in role and firm, self-imposed control of the expression of sexual, aggressive, and dependent needs on the part of staff are counterparts to the encouragement, otherwise, of natural and spontaneous responses to patients, including a direct reflection of the effects of their communication and behavior on staff. This staff attitude corresponds to the individual psychotherapist's technical neutrality as a baseline for exploring the transference.

The open exploration of the meanings of the patient's behavior through the analysis of all staff interactions with him also requires a definite separation on the part of all staff of the functions of the patient's behavior in the here-and-now from its assumed past, genetic motivations. Otherwise, undisciplined speculations regarding the assumed origins of patients' current behaviors may contribute to creating a pseudo-psychoanalytic ideology and language that tend to confuse concrete, painfully acquired understanding with some generally accepted theories of development. Such speculations make a mockery of understanding patients.

By the same token, although the patient's behavior on the unit or service is public and open to exploration in all its facets, his communications to the individual psychotherapist are private and need to be respected—except when the psychotherapist's use of such communications corresponds to an explicitly agreed-upon contract set up with the patient at the beginning of psychotherapy. For example, the psychotherapist may say to the patient: "Everything we are discussing here will be absolutely private, except that, should I consider you to be in danger of harming yourself or others, I would feel free to take whatever action I have available to communicate these concerns to other members of staff and to protect you from such consequences of your behavior. Should that become necessary, I would of course first let you know."

Communication between the individual psychotherapist and the rest of the hospital staff in this model is therefore asymmetric, which protects the patient's privacy—increasingly so, in fact, as acting out decreases, as the influence of the patient's intrapsychic world upon the immediate social environment becomes less relevant, and as the patient prepares to leave the hospital setting. In contrast, all the patient's interactions within the therapeutic milieu should become available to the individual psychotherapist, usually by means of communication with the unit manager, hospital therapist, or administrator, and should be integrated with the interpretive approach to the patient's total material in the psychotherapy sessions.

Still another requirement of this model is that the authority delegated to all unit staff and to the psychotherapist be kept separate, thus avoiding the possibility that the psychotherapist (usually the senior member of the team), the administrative psychiatrist, or the case manager will control the team. Confusion in the decision-making process facilitates patients' indirectly controlling their social environment through their hospital psychiatrist or their psychotherapist and may become a major channel for acting out. This danger points to the need for clear

delimitation of authority delegated to the various staff members involved in the patient's treatment, in the leadership of groups, and in the
administration of the service.

Miss Z. A patient in her early twenties had what she considered a
wonderful relationship with her hospital psychotherapist, with whom
she discussed her childhood experiences. There was little if any relation
between the contents of the sessions and the patient's current experiences, interactions, and behavior on the service. Simultaneously, Miss Z
was using her relatively inexperienced social worker as her personal
messenger and aide. She successfully manipulated the social worker
into getting material for her from a local college. Miss Z's nurse, the key
member of the team, was aware of how Miss Z manipulated people and
confronted her with this fact. The nurse was therefore Miss Z's enemy,
and much of Miss Z's energy went into mobilizing several of the other
nurses against her. The patient was succeeding in splitting staff and was
expressing her own needs in a split-off way. An empathic, understanding (psychotherapist) mother, an enemy (nurse) mother, and a slave (social worker) mother were permitting Miss Z to maintain her equilibrium.

These events took place when the director of the service was away
for an extended period of time and the usual staff meetings were therefore shifting in their focus onto other, more administrative issues. When
the director of the service returned, a consultant surveyed the situation,
and a special staff meeting was held to discuss Miss Z's treatment. As a
result, the subject under discussion in the psychotherapy shifted from
what happened 15 years ago to what was happening now. The interaction between Miss Z and her therapist became intense, angry, chaotic.
Miss Z's encounters with the nurse became less abrasive as the nurse,
now supported by the other nurses, continued to assert her authority.
The social worker, once she realized that she had been maneuvered into
an inappropriate position, tried to help Miss Z to assume responsibility
for herself. Miss Z reacted by attempting to get rid of the social worker,
but her efforts were fruitless because other members of staff made it
clear that they thought her dealings with the social worker were
problematic.

When the various forces at work were analyzed and understood in
the psychotherapy and her interactions with staff and their relationship
to the transference became the central focus of the sessions, Miss Z's
part-object relations could be integrated and her defenses against ambivalence toward her mother could be worked out. What is of special interest is the awareness on the part of Miss Z's nurse that she was firmer
with this patient than she was with other patients, and the social worker's comment at the staff meeting: "You know, usually I'm very firm
with patients and I don't let myself be handled this way. Here, for reasons that are not clear to me, I've gotten myself into this role." The anal-

ysis of the activation of the patient's intrapsychic life in the interpersonal field of the service and of the particular countertransference reactions and complementary roles in the staff was of crucial importance in getting the psychotherapy under way.

Modes, Objectives, and Techniques of Group Treatments

Before I examine the principal group methods that are part of this approach, the therapeutic functions of these methods should be spelled out. Each patient, according to this concept, requires, above all, one staff member with ultimate responsibility for his treatment in the service and ultimate accountability for therapeutic, administrative, and legal purposes for the duration of the patient's stay. This case manager, hospital therapist, administrative psychiatrist, or administrator/psychotherapist should ideally be a physician in hospital settings, where medical authority is legally required to justify hospitalization and psychiatric treatment. Delegation of such authority to nonphysicians is possible but requires additional modifications in the complex net of delegation of authority on the service.

Each patient also requires an individual psychotherapist who may, under certain arrangements, also act as the unit manager. Although intensive individual psychotherapy is an integral part of the treatment—in fact, the ultimate therapeutic mode that integrates all the information stemming from the patient's environment—this does not mean that direct, planned, and organized interventions on the part of the hospital staff outside the psychotherapeutic sessions are not a crucial aspect of the treatment.

In addition to a managerial authority and an individual psychotherapist, each patient requires the availability of various task groups centered on the specific functions of nursing, therapeutic activities, and social work. These task groups permit the patient to re-create, within the hospital setting, activities linked to living at home, dealing with the social network, and being productively engaged in study, work, recreational, and creative endeavors. Task groups usually are small but they may involve a large number of patients—ideally without ever activating large-group processes (see Kernberg, 1980, chap. 11). Task groups should be highly structured and task oriented to minimize the development of basic-assumptions groups and of large-group processes, and they should require only one or very few staff members.

Each patient also requires some arrangement by means of which the leaders of these task groups can communicate with one another, with the patient's manager, and with his psychotherapist regarding their observations and the patient's interactions with them. These are the functions of team meetings, both intra- and interdisciplinary.

Another highly desirable type of meeting is one that channels the informal interactions of staff and individual patient, the groundswell around any one patient on the unit and in the shops, into a discussion of the learning/living problems on the service, which ideally should include free-floating discussion of concrete tasks involving both patients and staff. These are patient/staff meetings that have a high staff-to-patient ratio and, to be appropriately productive, call for careful delegation on the part of staff to avoid having all members engaged with all patients simultaneously. In other therapeutic community models, this task is often absorbed by the community meeting; in fact it may become an essential aspect of the community meeting, a solution I reject in order to clear the agenda of the community meeting for other purposes. In more traditional psychiatric settings, which do not use therapeutic community models, the daily rounds usually explore the functions I have delineated under team meetings and living/learning meetings.

The proposed model also includes group psychotherapy for most patients and thereby raises the complex issue about the relation between individual and group psychotherapy (to which I shall shortly return).

Although all or most patients require some exploration of their relations with their family, family therapy is one mode that, because of the interest it has evoked, tends to be applied excessively in some settings. I am here distinguishing between the sophisticated social casework needed in most or all cases and the psychotherapeutic treatment of the entire family. Some cases require family therapy, but when the patient is simultaneously in group psychotherapy and individual psychotherapy, there is the danger of overlap, which weakens or dilutes the impact of each and promotes splitting and acting out.

The proposed model does include a community meeting which all staff and patients attend, a meeting carried out with sufficient frequency to capture significant shifts in the social and emotional climates on the unit, but not more often than that. It is important to limit the frequency of community meetings to avoid freezing staff resources in too many large meetings, which may absorb an inordinate amount of time, energy, and attention with a corresponding reduction in staff productivity.

The two major tasks of the community meeting are to explore social processes that affect the total patient/staff community and to explore the process of the community meeting itself, that is, the large-group processes activated therein. Exploration of the social system should include clarification of real interpersonal conflicts that require action by the administrative leadership of the service; yet informality and spontaneity of communications should be maintained (in contrast to bureaucratic, formal processing of information and a set agenda) in order to permit the development and exploration of large-group processes.

The community meeting, then, should explore issues affecting the community and channel them for appropriate decision making. But at the same time, the activation of primitive object relations characteristic of the large group should be tolerated sufficiently to diagnose regressive group processes in the entire service, particularly as expressed in shifts in morale, in the emergence of specific primitive themes, and in the distortion of the social system by specific issues stemming from individual patients, group processes on the service, and the hospital or unit administration.

Such a community meeting requires highly skilled leadership and should be followed by a meeting of staff alone in order to analyze what took place at the meeting and to define and organize the administrative tasks derived from it. An organization of patients parallel to that of the administrative staff group of the service, with an administrative link that permits negotiation among patients as a group, staff, and the administrative leadership of the service, completes the list of group structures included in the proposed model. Let us now examine the objectives and technique of each of these groups.

Task Groups

By definition, the focus is on tasks and not on individual patients. The tasks should be meaningful and related to the patient's life outside the hospital; a cooking class, for example, may be more relevant than the traditional weaving of baskets. The organization of areas, within therapeutic activities, regarding work, study, creative arts, recreation, and vocational rehabilitation (which is actually a condensation of study and work) should permit activities to be tied more closely to interests that patients will return to after leaving the hospital. Task groups permit the provision of opportunities for leadership, for followership, for collaboration within a group, and for testing ego functions as well as mobilizing ego resources. Activities also facilitate the sublimated expression of aggressive, dependent, and sexual strivings. The psychoanalytic study of patients' functioning in such task groups will depend upon the sophistication of staff's observations while conducting these groups. For example, a narcissistic personality's flourishing when he is triumphant in a competitive activity or his enjoyment of something that comes absolutely naturally to him—in contrast to his categorical refusal to engage in any operation that requires a "humiliating" learning process—should be very important material for exploration, tactful confrontation, and further examination in the course of his individual psychotherapy.

Task groups may also include work in the social and political realm of the service, such as patients' government, committees evaluating rules and regulations and making proposals to the unit administration, the organization of weekend activities, and patients' mutual-help groups. Administrative links provided between special patient groups and the unit administration may give meaning and impact to otherwise empty gestures of "democracy." The principal danger in task groups is that, paradoxically, because of a psychoanalytic orientation to the exploration of the meaning of all behavior and ego functioning in them, they may gradually become transformed into ad hoc psychotherapy groups, with the exploration of feelings and conflicts invading the time allotted for consideration of objective tasks.

Team Meetings

Ideally, in a service that has approximately 20 to 30 patients, two parallel staff teams may discuss 10 to 15 patients each, with all the task-group leaders meeting with sufficient frequency to discuss briefly all the patients in their team over a determined time span, say, one week. The case manager or hospital therapist should attend this meeting. His task is to use the information to shape and monitor each patient's therapeutic program and, in addition, to discuss this with the patient and to provide full information to the patient's individual psychotherapist about what he has done. With intelligent delegation of authority within each discipline, it should be possible for, say, a small group of nurses to communicate the information from nursing service to the respective team so that not all members of nursing must attend each team meeting.

This is a crucial meeting, in which patterns of patients' interactions on the service can be detected, their understanding integrated, and dynamic hypotheses formulated in terms both useful for staff orientation and meaningful for the individual psychotherapist. These meetings also permit decision making regarding how the feedback of staff's reactions to individual patients should be constructed, particularly the communication to patients of staff's perception of them in the living/learning meetings.

Living/Learning Meetings

These meetings, consisting of team-meeting staff and all the patients under discussion, focus in turn on each patient's development throughout the service. Ideally, leadership of these meetings should coincide with leadership of the team meeting, usually carried out by a senior member of the staff. These meetings focus on factual discussion of observations of the patient's interaction in the here-and-now of the service. The participation of an entire patient group in this discussion requires once again that strict privacy be maintained regarding the patient's subjective experience in contrast to his behavior; it also permits patients as a group to participate in the discussion regarding each of them. Again, it is important that these meetings be protected from becoming one more edition of group psychotherapy; they should be task groups, without examination of their internal group processes. These groups have a strong supportive and reeducational potential, which should be fully exploited; by the same token, they make it extremely desirable that group psychotherapy carried out within the proposed model maintain an expressive rather than a supportive mode.

The groups described so far should be highly structured, a point that has been made in stressing their specific tasks and their clear differentiation from one another. Regressive processes tend to decrease or go underground in such groups, which permits highlighting the exploration of ego resources and examining patients' functioning at their best but obscures the activation of primitive object relations in the interpersonal field. The following group modes, to the contrary, are geared to activating regressive group processes and primitive object relations in the social field.

Group Psychotherapy

For the reasons mentioned earlier, and especially because supportive elements are so strongly present in the living/learning and team meetings, there is an advantage in keeping group psychotherapy as psychoanalytic as possible. The possibility of exploring primitive defensive operations and object relations in group psychotherapy conducted along the Bion (1961) or the Ezriel (1950)/Sutherland (1952) model (that is, with a focus on group transferences prevailing over the examination of more differentiated levels of individual transferences of the triadic, familial kind) may reinforce and complement the individual psychoanalytic psychotherapy of severe types of character pathology carried out in a hospital setting.

Patients with borderline personality organization who require hospitalization usually present regressive ego functioning. They usually express crucial aspects of their psychopathology by nonverbal means, so that the verbal communication in individual psychotherapy sessions permits the expression of only a limited part of their total transferential field of primitive object relations. A typical development in the hospital treatment of borderline patients who are in individual psychotherapy at the same time is a tendency toward superficiality in the content of the psychotherapy hours or a veering of that content toward the patient's past, while the major transference dispositions are split off and expressed in the social environment. The development of a structured social environment as part of the proposed model both facilitates the diagnosis of such transference potential and permits the control of its acting out, at least in its more dramatic manifestations. It is essential to control the patient's expression of extreme manifestations of his pathology to avoid vicious cycles derived from the direct gratification of primitive needs, the self-rewarding expression of omnipotent control, and projective identification within the social environment. But this control also limits the observation of these extreme manifestations of the patient's psychopathology.

Psychoanalytic group psychotherapy is a controlled outlet for the expression of primitive psychopathology in a social setting that permits its immediate interpretation. In addition, if the individual psychotherapist receives full feedback from the group psychotherapist regarding the patient's development in the group—so that splitting of transferences between individual and group therapy can be monitored and interpreted—group psychotherapy may actually intensify the individual psychotherapeutic experience. In contrast, when group psychotherapy becomes supportive in nature, it becomes more difficult to maintain an interpretive approach in the individual sessions. The group may foster individual patients' resistances, and a tendency develops for such supportive group psychotherapy to duplicate other group processes on the service.

The Community Meeting

The community meeting, as a large group, permits the application of large-group techniques, which examine, by analyzing the primitive contents that emerge in it, the origin of the conflicts that influence the social system of the service. Simultaneously, given that the total decision-making, administrative authority of the service participates in this meeting, the community meeting permits the negotiation of real conflicts within the service. Also, all the dramatis personae involved in the conflicts on the service are present. All this makes it tempting to extend the agenda for this meeting. But this results in an overflow of communication and thus a loss of focus on the task, a diffusion of priorities, and a waste of the resources invested in it. The principal requirement for successful utilization of the community meeting is to set its priorities clearly, a practical issue that the leadership of the therapeutic community has to deal with repeatedly at each meeting.

In the model I am proposing, the task of the community meeting of diagnosing the groundswell of the total social and cultural atmosphere of the service at any particular time takes priority. This includes diagnosis of distortions and conflicts introduced into the service by the administration of the hospital, conflicts within staff, the staff/patient boundary on the service itself, or very severe distortions in the social life of the service evoked by the psychopathology of individual patients. To diagnose such a groundswell in the form of a dominant, widely shared set of experiences, fantasies, and emotions requires using large-group processes in the community meeting. This means an open agenda, free participation of all patients and staff in expressing what is on their minds at the time of the meeting, and the invitation for everyone to bring up anything that might be helpful in clarifying issues affecting all present. This invitation for unstructured communication in the large-group setting activates not only the conflicts enumerated before but also their expression at primitive levels of fantasy formation, which may at times reach quasi-psychotic proportions. The leader of the community meeting as well as the other participants are also invited to explore freely their understanding of what is currently going on, and the meeting is conducted with a focus that shifts from clarification of its own process to specific contents. A tolerance of full expression of regressive primitive fantasies without premature reassurance or clarification may have an important psychotherapeutic impact on the discussion of individual psychopathology in individual psychotherapy and group psychotherapy sessions and may illuminate by implication the fantasies that organize the individual patient's conflicts vis-à-vis the social environment of the service.

In the proposed model of community meetings, the initial focus on the large-group process is matched by a second priority, namely, the task of sorting out the here-and-now problems affecting patient/staff interaction, with the purpose of opening the channels of communication and decision making available for resolution of such conflicts.

I am suggesting that decisions are not made in the community meeting itself. Channels and structures of communication and decision making are identified, however, which makes it possible to proceed toward such decisions, or past decisions and realities are clarified after full ventilation of the fantasies surrounding them. The analysis of unforeseen consequences of decisions made in the past reflects the staff's commitment to reexamine such decisions within the appropriate administrative structures. In addition to emotional processes affecting all staff and patients, the actual functioning of the social system, the relation between intended and actual social structures, and the use and misuse of authority and power in the transactions on the service are examined in the community meeting.

The major advantage of this kind of agenda is that the potentially antitherapeutic effects of large-group processes affecting the entire community can be explored, diagnosed, and resolved. Furthermore, the open examination of administrative issues as they affect everyone's functioning and feelings is an excellent educational tool, which combines teaching the dynamics of the unconscious with analysis of the impact of administration and social structures on the lives of individuals. I have also found this to be one of the most helpful tools in the training of psychiatric residents, nursing staff, and mental health professionals in general. Another advantage is the possibility of integrating the impact of all the various group processes and task systems on the service, diagnosing by means of the overall morale of the service—the quality of which immediately surfaces in such a large-group situation—the functional adequacy of administrative arrangements.

Breakdown in morale as diagnosed in the large-group process may be traced back, as I have suggested elsewhere (1980, chaps. 11–13), to failures in the administrative structure, in leadership, or in task performance. Tracing the source of the breakdown may highlight conflicts of boundary control affecting the total system or any of its subsystems. Although the large-group process as technically conducted here avoids discussion of any individual patient's dynamics or treatment, it generates themes particularly relevant for patients whose psychopathology constitutes a major source of conflict in the service. In short, the exploration of large-group processes in the community meeting has great therapeutic, educational, and administrative value and can be timesaving in all these areas. Elsewhere (1980, chap. 11) I have spelled out the discovery of hidden agendas of the institution in such community meetings and the highlighting of major themes of primitive psychological conflicts.

The chief disadvantages of this proposed model include, first of all, the danger, mentioned earlier, of crowding the agenda; this demands that the leader be intensely alert and self-disciplined. Both leadership and staff must refrain from attempts to solve problems of individual patients, ward management, and general decision making in the community meeting, lest administrative boundaries become blurred. In addition the danger exists that a combination of interpretation of emotional themes and clarification of administrative processes may be misused by staff to "interpret away" a patient's reasons for requesting certain changes. The tool of psychodynamic understanding would thus be corrupted, for it would be used for manipulating power relations between patients and staff. By the same token, however, the availability of clearly defined, alternative channels of communication that permit actual decision making on the basis of the discussions in the community meeting tends to prevent the uncontrolled acting out of primitive levels of aggression by unrelenting passivity and silence extending throughout many meetings.

In contrast, when large-group processes are analyzed in the community meeting without relating them to actual decision-making processes, it is easy for the meeting to regress into overwhelming chaos and destructiveness, so much so that active and constructive functions involving patients and staff may continue elsewhere on the service while all the aggression (of both patients and staff) is dissociated and expressed in this particular meeting and freezes all staff in a position of impotence that affects everybody.

The proposed model for examining large-group processes in the community meeting requires clear administrative arrangements affecting staff and patient/staff boundaries, my next point.

Administrative Requirements

A functional administrative structure in the unit or service or in the entire hospital within which this therapeutic community model evolves is an indispensable requirement. This implies, first of all, that the director of the unit or service must have full authority and boundary control over all transactions between the external environment and the unit and, naturally, across boundaries of task systems within the service itself. Second, the director's authority must be stable, publicly known, and delegated in ways that are, in turn, stable, unambiguous, and publicly known. Third, the model proposed implies a parallel but not overlapping delegation of authority to the hospital therapist or case manager—the "administrative physician"—who has the final medical and general psychiatric responsibility for each patient and, by virtue of this authority, becomes the leader of the immediate interdisciplinary team involved in each patient's treatment.

The administrative psychiatrist's decision, for example, that a patient is suicidal and needs to be on a "close observation" routine can be questioned only by his administrative superior. In a parallel way, all the authority for the organization of resources within each discipline has to be delegated to the director of that discipline, so that the way nursing service, for example, organizes its functions on the service, including the development of task groups involving patients and staff, is totally within the realm of authority decision making of the head nurse or his/her delegate.

Again, in a parallel and still nonoverlapping fashion, the director of the service delegates certain authority to the community meeting regarding its participation in decision making on issues affecting the social life of patients on the service, particularly the boundaries of staff and patients as groups. For example, the extent to which rules and regulations governing the daily life of the service can be altered by a combination of patient and staff committees needs to be clearly defined and spelled out, first by the director of the service and later by the leader of the community meeting. Naturally, if the director of the service himself conducted the community meeting, it would simplify this process. Should he do so, however, he might be tempted to invest the community meeting with so much authority that it would interfere with the authority vested in the hospital therapist and the chiefs of disciplines.

The proposed model allows for an alternative distribution of authority, in which the community meeting has authority only for full exploration of the administrative processes and conflicts on the service. All decision-making authority regarding patients, either as individuals or in groups, is delegated to the hospital therapists, the discipline leaders, and special staff and patient committees. This variation in the model avoids conflicts regarding the decision-making authority of the community meeting and that of all other derived group structures in the service, but the clout of the community meeting as an effective decision-making body is weakened, and its priorities will naturally shift in the direction of the study of its own large-group processes. Or it may become a public-opinion-poll type of assembly characterized by chronic passivity and a sense of futility. Therefore, I think it preferable that significant authority be delegated to the community meeting—although certainly not total authority, for this would result in role diffusion and would be a misapplication of a democratic political structure.

One practical way to facilitate negotiations between patients as a group and staff as a group within the proposed model is to organize a patient government and a corresponding staff committee, which obtains its authority either from that originally invested in the community meeting or directly from the executive, administrative group of the service. Staff "consultants" to patients' government structures may help patients deal more effectively with the administrative structures of the service but must be alert to the potential ambiguity of the nature of the authority delegated to them.

A major problem with this proposed model, and probably with all "participatory management" models, is the tendency of the decision-making processes in groups to expand in proportion to the degree of freedom and openness with which groups work. The result is a gradual overloading of the agenda of all decision-making groups. The sense of priorities is lost, and what follows is management by crises. This can be avoided by a clearly defined leadership of each group structure and by a clear definition of time limits within which certain decisions must be made. If a group cannot make up its mind within the time limit, the leader of the group will make that decision, and if uncertainty in the leader forces the decision-making process up the administrative hierarchy, the decision will be made by the service director himself. The obsessive self-involvement of groups can generally be controlled by reverting to centralization of decision making when the group procrastinates. It helps to keep in mind that the ultimate purpose of the therapeutic community is to treat patients and not to carry out an exercise in government. The ultimate constraint in treating patients is the limitation in staff resources, particularly the time of the most expert members of the staff, and these resources need to be protected.

Under optimal circumstances, long-term hospitalization may be considered completed when the patient's insight or introspection and concern for himself are sufficiently reestablished to strengthen realistic motivations for treatment, when the motivation for treatment itself is reflected in the patient's willingness and demonstrated capacity to assume an increasing degree of responsibility for himself, when a psychotherapeutic relationship has consolidated to the extent that the likelihood of its continuation on an outpatient basis seems a reasonable assumption, and when the patient has regained capacities for carrying out an ordinary social life outside the hospital setting. Significant decrease or resolution of secondary gains of illness is an additional, important indication that the goals of long-term hospitalization have been achieved.

References

Abraham, K. (1919). A particular form of neurotic resistance against the psycho-analytic method. In *Selected Papers on Psycho-Analysis*. New York: Brunner/Mazel, 1979, pp. 303–311.

Abraham, K. (1920). Manifestations of the female castration complex. In *Selected Papers on Psycho-Analysis*. New York: Brunner/Mazel, 1979, pp. 338–369.

Adler, G., and Buie, D. H. (1979). The psychotherapeutic approach to aloneness in the borderline patient. In *Advances in Psychotherapy of the Borderline Patient*, ed. J. LeBoit and A. Capponi. New York: Jason Aronson, pp. 433–448.

Alexander, F., et al. (1946). *Psychoanalytic Therapy*. New York: Ronald Press.

American Psychiatric Association (1952). *Diagnostic and Statistical Manual of Mental Disorders: DSM-I*. Washington, D.C.

American Psychiatric Association (1968). *Diagnostic and Statistical Manual of Mental Disorders: DSM-II*. Washington, D.C.

American Psychiatric Association (1980). *Diagnostic and Statistical Manual of Mental Disorders: DSM-III*. Washington, D.C.

American Psychiatric Association (1981). *Diagnostic and Statistical Manual of Mental Disorders: DSM-III Casebook*. Washington, D.C.

Arnold, M. B. (1970). Brain function in emotion: A phenomenological analysis. In *Physiological Correlates of Emotion*, ed. P. Black. New York: Academic Press, pp. 261–285.

Asch, S. S. (1976). Varieties of negative therapeutic reaction and problems of technique. *J. American Psychoanalytic Association*, 24:383–407.

Balint, M. (1968). *The Basic Fault: Therapeutic Aspects of Regression*. London: Tavistock Publications.

Bauer, S., Hunt, H., Gould, M., and Goldstein, E. (1980). Personality organization, structural diagnosis and the structural interview. *Psychiatry*, 43:224–233.

Beauvoir, S. de (1972). *The Coming of Age*. New York: Putnam.

Belknap, I. (1956). *Human Problems of a State Mental Hospital.* New York: McGraw-Hill.

Bellak, L., Hurvich, M., and Gediman, H. (1973). *Ego Functions in Schizophrenics, Neurotics, and Normals.* New York: Wiley-Interscience.

Berezin, M. (1977). Normal psychology of the aging process revisited. II: The fate of narcissism in old age: Clinical case reports. *J. Geriatric Psychiatry,* 1:9–26.

Berezin, M., and Fern, D. (1967). Persistence of early emotional problems in a seventy-year-old woman. *J. Geriatric Psychiatry,* 1:45–60.

Bergeret, J. (1970). Les États limités. *Revue Française de Psychanalyse,* 34:605–633.

Bergmann, K. (1978). Neurosis and personality disorders in old age. In *Studies in Geriatric Psychiatry,* ed. A. D. Isaacs and F. Post. New York: Wiley, pp. 41–75.

Bibring, E. (1954). Psychoanalysis and the dynamic psychotherapies. *J. American Psychoanalytic Association,* 2:745–770.

Bick, E. (1968). The experience of the skin in early object-relations. *International J. Psycho-Analysis,* 49:484–486.

Bion, W. R. (1952). Group dynamics: A re-view. *International J. Psycho-Analysis,* 33:235–247.

Bion, W. R. (1961). *Experiences in Groups.* New York: Basic Books.

Bion, W. R. (1965). *Transformations.* New York: Basic Books.

Bion, W. R. (1967). *Second Thoughts: Selected Papers on Psychoanalysis.* New York: Basic Books.

Bion, W. R. (1970). *Attention and Interpretation.* London: Heinemann.

Blacker, K., and Tupin, J. (1977). Hysteria and hysterical structure: Developmental and social theories. In *Hysterical Personality,* ed. M. Horowitz. New York: Jason Aronson, pp. 95–142.

Blinder, M. (1966). The hysterical personality. *Psychiatry,* 29:227–235.

Bloch, S., ed. (1979). *An Introduction to the Psychotherapies.* New York: Oxford University Press, pp. 196–220.

Blum, H. (1980). The value of reconstruction in adult psychoanalysis. *International J. Psycho-Analysis,* 61:39–54.

Bromley, D. (1978). Approaches to the study of personality changes in adult life and old age. In *Studies in Geriatric Psychiatry,* ed. A. D. Isaacs and F. Post. New York: Wiley, pp. 17–40.

Carr, A., Goldstein, E., Hunt, H., and Kernberg, O. (1979). Psychological tests and borderline patients. *J. Personality Assessment,* 43:582–590.

Caudill, W. (1958). *The Psychiatric Hospital as a Small Society.* Cambridge: Harvard University Press.

Chasseguet-Smirgel, J. (1978). Reflexions on the connexions between perversion and sadism. *International J. Psycho-Analysis,* 59:27–35.

Chodoff, P., and Lyons, H. (1958). Hysteria, the hysterical personality and "hysterical" conversion. *American J. Psychiatry,* 114:734–740.

Davanloo, H., ed. (1980). *Short-Term Dynamic Psychotherapy.* New York: Jason Aronson.

Deutsch, F. (1949). *Applied Psychoanalysis.* New York: Grune & Stratton.

Dewald, P. (1971). *Psychotherapy: A Dynamic Approach.* New York: Basic Books.

Easser, B. (1966). Transference resistance in hysterical character neurosis: Technical considerations. In *Developments in Psychoanalysis at Columbia University,* ed. G. Goldman and D. Shapiro. New York: Hafner, pp. 69–80.

Easser, B., and Lesser, S. (1965). Hysterical personality: A re-evaluation. *Psychoanalytic Quarterly,* 34:390–405.

Edelson, M. (1970). *Sociotherapy and Psychotherapy.* Chicago: University of Chicago Press.

Eissler, K. (1950). The Chicago Institute of Psychoanalysis and the sixth period of the development of psychoanalytic technique. *J. General Psychology,* 42:103–157.

Eissler, K. (1953). The effects of the structure of the ego on psychoanalytic technique. *J. American Psychoanalytic Association,* 1:104–143.

Emde, R., Kligman, D. H., Reich, J. H., and Wade, T. D. (1978). Emotional expression in infancy. I: Initial studies of social signaling and an emergent model. In *The Development of Affect,* ed. M. Lewis and L. Rosenblum. New York: Plenum Press, pp. 125–148.

Ezriel, H. (1950). A psychoanalytic approach to the treatment of patients in groups. *J. Mental Science,* 96:774–779.

Fairbairn, W. (1954). *An Object-Relations Theory of the Personality.* New York: Basic Books.

Federn, P. (1952). *Ego Psychology and the Psychoses.* New York: Basic Books.

Fenichel, O. (1941). *Problems of Psychoanalytic Technique.* Albany: Psychoanalytic Quarterly, Inc.

Fenichel, O. (1945a). Neurotic acting out. *Psychoanalytic Review,* 39:197–206.

Fenichel, O. (1945b). *The Psychoanalytic Theory of Neurosis.* New York: Norton.

Ferenczi, S. (1919). On the technique of psycho-analysis. In *Further Contributions to the Theory and Technique of Psycho-Analysis.* New York: Basic Books, 1952.

Frances, A. (1980). The DSM-III personality disorders section: A commentary. *American J. Psychiatry,* 137:1050–1054.

Frances, A., and Cooper, A. (1980). The DSM-III controversy: Psychoanalytic perspectives. *Bulletin of the Association for Psychoanalytic Medicine,* 19:37–43.

Frances, A., and Cooper, A. (1981). Descriptive and dynamic psychiatry: A perspective on DSM-III. *American J. Psychiatry,* 138:1198–1202.

Freud, A. (1936). *The Ego and the Mechanisms of Defense. The Writings of Anna Freud,* 2. New York: International Universities Press, 1966.

Freud, A. (1968). Acting out. *International J. Psycho-Analysis,* 49:165–170.

Freud, E., and Meng, H., eds. (1963). *Psychoanalysis and Faith.* New York: Basic Books.

Freud, S. (1914). On narcissism. *Standard Edition,* 14:69–102. London: Hogarth Press, 1957.

Freud, S. (1916). Some character-types met with in psycho-analytic work. *Standard Edition*, 14:309–333. London: Hogarth Press, 1957.

Freud, S. (1923). The ego and the id. *Standard Edition*, 19:3–66. London: Hogarth Press, 1961.

Freud, S. (1930a). Civilization and its discontents. *Standard Edition*, 21:59–145. London: Hogarth Press, 1930.

Freud, S. (1930b). Das Unbehagen in der Kultur. *Gesammelte Werke*, 14:421–506. London: Imago, 1948.

Fromm-Reichmann, F. (1950). *Principles of Intensive Psychotherapy*. Chicago: University of Chicago Press.

Fromm-Reichmann, F. (1959). *Psychoanalysis and Psychotherapy: Selected Papers*. Chicago: University of Chicago Press.

Frosch, J. (1964). The psychotic character: Clinical psychiatric considerations. *Psychiatric Quarterly*, 38:91–96.

Frosch, J. (1970). Psychoanalytic considerations of the psychotic character. *J. American Psychoanalytic Association*, 18:24–50.

Frosch, J. (1971). Technique in regard to some specific ego defects in the treatment of borderline patients. *Psychiatric Quarterly*, 45:216–220.

Furer, M. (1977). Personality organization during the recovery of a severely disturbed young child. In *Borderline Personality Disorders*, ed. P. Hartocollis. New York: International Universities Press, pp. 457–473.

Galenson, E., and Roiphe, H. (1977). Some suggested revisions concerning early female development. In *Female Psychology*, ed. H. P. Blum. New York: International Universities Press, pp. 29–57.

Gedo, J. (1964). Concepts for a classification of the psychotherapies. *International J. Psycho-Analysis*, 45:530–539.

Geleerd, E. R. (1958). Borderline states in childhood and adolescence. *Psychoanalytic Study of the Child*, 13:279–285. New York: International Universities Press.

Gianturco, D., and Busse, E. (1978). Psychiatric problems encountered during a long-term study of normal aging volunteers. In *Studies in Geriatric Psychiatry*, ed. A. D. Isaacs and F. Post. New York: Wiley, pp. 1–16.

Gill, M. (1951). Ego psychology and psychotherapy. *Psychoanalytic Quarterly*, 20:62–71.

Gill, M. (1954). Psychoanalysis and exploratory psychotherapy. *J. American Psychoanalytic Association*, 2:771–797.

Gill, M. (1980). The analysis of transference: A critique of Fenichel's *Problems of Psychoanalytic Technique*. *International J. Psychoanalytic Psychotherapy*, 8:45–55.

Gill, M. (1982). *Analysis of Transference*, vol. 1. New York: International Universities Press.

Gill, M., Newman, R., and Redlich, F. (1954). *The Initial Interview in Psychiatric Practice*. New York: International Universities Press.

Giovacchini, P. (1975). *Psychoanalysis of Character Disorders*. New York: Jason Aronson.

Giovacchini, P. (1978). The psychoanalytic treatment of the alienated patient. In *New Perspectives on Psychotherapy of the Borderline Adult*, ed. J. F. Masterson. New York: Brunner/Mazel, pp. 3–19.

Giovacchini, P. (1979). The many sides of helplessness: The borderline patient. In *Advances in Psychotherapy of the Borderline Patient*, ed. J. LeBoit and A. Capponi. New York: Jason Aronson, pp. 227–267.

Glover, E. (1955). *The Technique of Psycho-Analysis*. New York: International Universities Press.

Goffman, E. (1961). *Asylums*. New York: Anchor, Doubleday.

Goldberg, A., ed. (1978). *The Psychology of the Self: A Casebook*. New York: International Universities Press.

Goldstein, M., and Jones, J. (1977). Adolescent and familial precursors of borderline and schizophrenic conditions. In *Borderline Personality Disorders*, ed. P. Hartocollis. New York: International Universities Press, pp. 213–229.

Green, A. (1977). The borderline concept. In *Borderline Personality Disorders*, ed. P. Hartocollis. New York: International Universities Press, pp. 15–44.

Greenacre, P. (1950). General problems of acting out. *Psychoanalytic Quarterly*, 19:455–467.

Greenacre, P. (1963). Problems of acting out in the transference relationship. *J. American Academy Child Psychiatry*, 2:144–175.

Greenacre, P. (1968). The psychoanalytic process, transference, and acting out. *International J. Psycho-Analysis*, 49:211–218.

Greenson, R. (1954). The struggle against identification. *J. American Psychoanalytic Association*, 2:200–217.

Greenson, R. (1958). On screen defenses, screen hunger, and screen identity. *J. American Psychoanalytic Association*, 6:242–262.

Greenson, R. (1965). The working alliance and the transference neurosis. *Psychoanalytic Quarterly*, 34:155–181.

Greenson, R. (1970). The unique patient–therapist relationship in borderline patients. Presented at the Annual Meeting of the American Psychiatric Association. Unpublished.

Grinberg, L. (1968). On acting out and its role in the psychoanalytic process. *International J. Psycho-Analysis*, 49:171–178.

Grinberg, L. (1979). Projective counteridentification and countertransference. In *Countertransference*, ed. L. Epstein and A. Feiner. New York: Jason Aronson, pp. 169–192.

Grinker, R. (1975). Neurosis, psychosis, and the borderline states. In *Comprehensive Textbook of Psychiatry, II*, ed. H. I. Kaplan, A. M. Freedman, and B. J. Sadock. Baltimore: Williams & Wilkins, pp. 845–850.

Grinker, R., et al. (1961). *Psychiatric Social Work*. New York: Basic Books.

Grinker, R., Werble, B., and Drye, R., eds. (1968). *The Borderline Syndrome*. New York: Basic Books.

Gross, H. (1974). Depression and sadomasochistic personalities. In *Personality Disorders*, ed. J. R. Lion. Baltimore: Williams & Wilkins, pp. 178–192.

Grunberger, B. (1979). *Narcissism: Psychoanalytic Essays.* New York: International Universities Press.

Gunderson, J. (1977). Characteristics of borderlines. In *Borderline Personality Disorders,* ed. P. Hartocollis. New York: International Universities Press, pp. 173–192.

Gunderson, J. (1982). Empirical studies of the borderline diagnosis. In *Psychiatry 1982: The American Psychiatric Association Annual Review.* Washington, D.C.: American Psychiatric Press, pp. 415–436.

Gunderson, J., and Kolb, J. (1978). Discriminating features of borderline patients. *American J. Psychiatry,* 135:792–796.

Gunderson, J., Kolb, J., and Austin, V. (1981). The diagnostic interview for borderlines (DIB). *American J. Psychiatry,* 138:896–903.

Gunderson, J., and Singer, M. (1975). Defining borderline patients: An overview. *American J. Psychiatry,* 133:1–10.

Guntrip, H. (1968). *Schizoid Phenomena, Object Relations, and the Self.* New York: International Universities Press.

Hartmann, H. (1950). Comments on the psychoanalytic theory of the ego. In *Essays on Ego Psychology.* New York: International Universities Press, 1964, pp. 113–141.

Hartmann, H. (1955). Notes on the theory of sublimation. In *Essays on Ego Psychology.* New York: International Universities Press, 1964, pp. 227–240.

Hartmann, H. (1964). *Essays on Ego Psychology.* New York: International Universities Press.

Hartmann, H., Kris, E., and Lowenstein, R. (1946). Comments on the formation of psychic structure. *Psychoanalytic Study of the Child,* 2:11–38. New York: International Universities Press.

Hartocollis, P. (1977). Affects in borderline disorders. In *Borderline Personality Disorders,* ed. P. Hartocollis. New York: International Universities Press, pp. 495–507.

Heimann, P. (1955a). A combination of defense mechanisms in paranoid states. In *New Directions in Psycho-Analysis,* ed. M. Klein, P. Heimann, and R. Money-Kyrle. London: Tavistock Publications, pp. 240–265.

Heimann, P. (1955b). A contribution to the re-evaluation of the oedipus-complex: The early states. In *New Directions in Psycho-Analysis,* ed. M. Klein, P. Heimann, and R. Money-Kyrle. New York: Basic Books, pp. 23–38.

Heimann, P. (1956). Dynamics of transference interpretations. *International J. Psycho-Analysis,* 37:303–310.

Heimann, P. (1960). Countertransference. *British J. Medical Psychology,* 33:9–15.

Herz, M. (1971). Day versus inpatient hospitalization: A controlled study. *American J. Psychiatry,* 127:1371–1382.

Herz, M. (1980). Partial hospitalization, brief hospitalization and aftercare. In *Comprehensive Textbook of Psychiatry, III,* ed. H. I. Kaplan, A. M. Freedman, and B. J. Sadock. Baltimore: Williams & Wilkins, pp. 2368–2381.

Herz, M., Endicott, J., and Spitzer, R. (1975). Brief hospitalization of patients with families: Initial results. *American J. Psychiatry*, 132:413–418.

Hill, L. (1955). *Psychotherapeutic Intervention in Schizophrenia*. Chicago: University of Chicago Press.

Hoch, P., and Polatin, P. (1949). Pseudoneurotic forms of schizophrenia. *Psychiatric Quarterly*, 23:248–276.

Hoffman, M. (1978). Toward a theory of empathic arousal and development. In *The Development of Affect*, ed. M. Lewis and L. Rosenblum. New York: Plenum Press, pp. 227–256.

Hollon, T. (1962). A rationale for supportive psychotherapy of depressed patients. *American J. Psychiatry*, 16:655–664.

Holzman, P., and Ekstein, R. (1959). Repetition-functions of transitory regressive thinking. *Psychoanalytic Quarterly*, 28:228–235.

Izard, C. (1978). On the ontogenesis of emotions and emotion–cognition relationships in infancy. In *The Development of Affect*, ed. M. Lewis and L. Rosenblum. New York: Plenum Press, pp. 389–413.

Izard, E., and Buechler, S. (1979). Emotion expressions and personality integration in infancy. In *Emotions in Personality and Psychopathology*, ed. C. Izard. New York: Plenum Press, pp. 447–472.

Jacobson, E. (1954). Contribution to the metapsychology of psychotic identifications. *J. American Psychoanalytic Association*, 2:239–262.

Jacobson, E. (1961). Adolescent moods and the remodeling of psychic structures in adolescence. *Psychoanalytic Study of the Child*, 16:164–183. New York: International Universities Press.

Jacobson, E. (1964). *The Self and the Object World*. New York: International Universities Press.

Jacobson, E. (1971). *Depression*. New York: International Universities Press.

Johnson, A. (1949). Sanctions for superego lacunae of adolescents. In *Searchlights on Delinquency*, ed. K. R. Eissler. New York: International Universities Press, pp. 225–245.

Jones, M. (1953). *The Therapeutic Community: A New Treatment Method in Psychiatry*. New York: Basic Books.

Jones, M. (1956). The concept of the therapeutic community. *American J. Psychiatry*, 112:647–650.

Kanzer, M. (1968). Ego alteration and acting out. *International J. Psycho-Analysis*, 49: 431–435.

Kernberg, O. (1975). *Borderline Conditions and Pathological Narcissism*. New York: Jason Aronson.

Kernberg, O. (1976). *Object Relations Theory and Clinical Psychoanalysis*. New York: Jason Aronson.

Kernberg, O. (1977). Normal psychology of the aging process revisited—II. *J. Geriatric Psychiatry*, 10:27–45.

Kernberg, O. (1980). *Internal World and External Reality*. New York: Jason Aronson.

Kernberg, O., Burstein, E., Coyne, L., Appelbaum, A., Horwitz, L., and Voth, H. (1972). Psychotherapy and psychoanalysis: Final report of the Menninger Foundation's Psychotherapy Research Project. *Bulletin of the Menninger Clinic,* 36:1–275.

Kernberg, O., Goldstein, E., Carr, A., Hunt, H., Bauer, S., and Blumenthal, R. (1981). Diagnosing borderline personality organization. *J. Nervous and Mental Disease,* 169:225–231.

Kernberg, P. (1982). Borderline conditions: Childhood and adolescent aspects. In *The Borderline Child: Approaches to Etiology, Diagnosis and Treatment,* ed. K. S. Robson. New York: McGraw-Hill, pp. 101–119.

Khan, M. (1974). *The Privacy of the Self: Papers on Psychoanalytic Theory and Technique.* New York: International Universities Press.

Kleeman, J. (1977). Freud's views on early female sexuality in the light of direct child observation. In *Female Psychology,* ed. H. P. Blum. New York: International Universities Press, pp. 3–27.

Klein, D. (1975). Psychopharmacology and the borderline patient. In *Borderline States in Psychiatry,* ed. J. E. Mack. New York: Grune & Stratton, pp. 75–92.

Klein, D. (1977). Psychopharmacological treatment and delineation of borderline disorders. In *Borderline Personality Disorders,* ed. P. Hartocollis. New York: International Universities Press, pp. 365–383.

Klein, M. (1940). Mourning and its relation to manic-depressive states. In *Contributions to Psycho-Analysis, 1921–1945.* London: Hogarth Press, 1948, pp. 311–338.

Klein, M. (1945). The oedipus complex in the light of early anxieties. In *Contributions to Psycho-Analysis, 1921–1945.* London: Hogarth Press, 1948, pp. 311–338.

Klein, M. (1946). Notes on some schizoid mechanisms. In *Developments in Psycho-Analysis,* ed. J. Riviere. London: Hogarth Press, 1952, pp. 292–320.

Klein, M. (1957). *Envy and Gratitude.* New York: Basic Books.

Klein, M. (1963). *Our Adult World.* New York: Basic Books.

Knight, R. (1952). An evaluation of psychotherapeutic techniques. In *Psychoanalytic Psychiatry and Psychology,* ed. R. P. Knight and C. R. Friedman. New York: International Universities Press, 1954, pp. 65–76.

Knight, R. (1953a). Borderline states. In *Psychoanalytic Psychiatry and Psychology,* ed. R. P. Knight and C. R. Friedman. New York: International Universities Press, 1954, pp. 97–109.

Knight, R. (1953b). Management and psychotherapy of the borderline schizophrenic patient. In *Psychoanalytic Psychiatry and Psychology,* ed. R. P. Knight and C. R. Friedman. New York: International Universities Press, 1945, pp. 110–122.

Kohut, H. (1971). *The Analysis of the Self.* New York: International Universities Press.

Kohut, H. (1972). Thoughts on narcissism and narcissistic rage. *Psychoanalytic Study of the Child,* 27:360–400. New York/Chicago: Quadrangle Books.

Kohut, H. (1977). *The Restoration of the Self.* New York: International Universities Press.

Kraepelin, E. (1904). *Lectures on Clinical Psychiatry.* New York: Wood.

Krohn, A. (1978). *Hysteria: The Elusive Neurosis.* New York: International Universities Press.

Kroll, J., Sives, L., Martin, K., Lari, S., Pyle, R., and Zanoler, J. (1981). Borderline personality disorder: Construct validity of the concept. *Archives General Psychiatry*, 38:1021–1026.

Langs, R. (1973). *The Technique of Psychoanalytic Psychotherapy*, vol. 1. New York: Jason Aronson, pp. 538–598.

Laplanche, J., and Pontalis, J.-B. (1973). *The Language of Psychoanalysis.* New York: Norton.

Laughlin, H. (1967). *The Neuroses.* New York: Appleton-Century-Crofts.

Lazare, A. (1971). The hysterical character in psychoanalytic theory. *Archives General Psychiatry*, 25:131–137.

Levine, M. (1942). *Psychotherapy in Medical Practice.* New York: Macmillan.

Limentani, A. (1966). A re-evaluation of acting out in relation to working through. *International J. Psycho-Analysis*, 47:274–282.

Little, M. I. (1951). Countertransference and the patient's response to it. *International J. Psycho-Analysis*, 32:32–40.

Little, M. I. (1957). "R": The analyst's total response to his patient's needs. *International J. Psycho-Analysis*, 38:240–254.

Little, M. I. (1958). On delusional transference (transference psychosis). *International J. Psycho-Analysis*, 39:134–138.

Little, M. I. (1960). On basic unity. *International J. Psycho-Analysis*, 41:377–384, 637.

Little, M. I. (1966). Transference in borderline states. *International J. Psycho-Analysis*, 47:476–485.

Little, M. I. (1981). *Transference Neurosis and Transference Psychosis.* New York: Jason Aronson.

Loewald, H. (1960). On the therapeutic action of psychoanalysis. *International J. Psycho-Analysis*, 41:16–33.

Lorenz, K. (1963). *On Aggression.* New York: Bantam Books.

Luborsky, L., et al. (1958). Treatment variables. The Psychotherapy Research Project of the Menninger Foundation, 2d report. *Bulletin of the Menninger Clinic*, 22:126–147.

McDougall, J. (1979). Primitive communication in the use of countertransference. In *Countertransference*, ed. L. Epstein and A. Feiner. New York: Jason Aronson, pp. 267–304.

MacKinnon, R., and Michels, R. (1971). *The Psychiatric Interview in Clinical Practice.* Philadelphia: Saunders.

MacLeod, J., and Middelman, F. (1962). Wednesday afternoon clinic: A supportive care program. *Archives General Psychiatry*, 6:56–65.

Mahler, M. (1971). A study of the separation-individuation process and its possible application to borderline phenomena in the psychoanalytic situation. *Psychoanalytic Study of the Child*, 26:403–424. New York/Chicago: Quadrangle Books.

Mahler, M. (1972). Rapprochement subphase of the separation-individuation process. *Psychoanalytic Quarterly*, 41:487–506.

Mahler, M. (1979). *Selected Papers of Margaret S. Mahler*. New York: Jason Aronson.

Mahler, M., and Furer, M. (1968). *On Human Symbiosis and the Vicissitudes of Individuation*. New York: International Universities Press.

Mahler, M., and Kaplan, L. (1977). Developmental aspects in the assessment of narcissistic and so-called borderline personalities. In *Borderline Personality Disorders*, ed. P. Hartocollis. New York: International Universities Press, pp. 71–85.

Mahler, M., Pine, F., and Bergman, A. (1975). *The Psychological Birth of the Human Infant*. New York: Basic Books.

Main, T. (1946). The hospital as a therapeutic institution. *Bulletin of the Menninger Clinic*, 10:66–70.

Main, T. (1957). The ailment. *British J. Medical Psychology*, 30:129–145.

Masterson, J. F. (1967). *The Psychiatric Dilemma of Adolescence*. Boston: Little, Brown.

Masterson, J. F. (1972). *Treatment of the Borderline Adolescent: A Developmental Approach*. New York: Wiley-Interscience.

Masterson, J. F. (1976). *Psychotherapy of the Borderline Adult: A Developmental Approach*. New York: Brunner/Mazel.

Masterson, J. F. (1978). The borderline adult: Transference acting-out and working-through. In *New Perspectives on Psychotherapy of the Borderline Adult*, ed. J. F. Masterson. New York: Brunner/Mazel, pp. 121–147.

Masterson, J. F. (1980). *From Borderline Adolescent to Functioning Adult*. New York: Brunner/Mazel.

Meltzer, D. (1973). *Sexual States of Mind*. Perthshire, Scotland: Clunie.

Menninger, K. (1952). *A Manual for Psychiatric Case Study*. New York: Grune & Stratton.

Menninger, W. (1936). Psychiatric hospital therapy designed to meet unconscious needs. In *Psychiatrist for a Troubled World*, vol. 1. Kansas City, Mo.: Hallmark, 1967, pp. 375–385.

Menninger, W. (1943). *Fundamentals of Psychiatry*. Topeka: Capper.

Meyer, A. (1957). *Psychobiology: A Science of Man*. Springfield, Ill.: Charles C Thomas.

Miller, I. (1969). Interpretation as a supportive technique in psychotherapy. *Bulletin of the Menninger Clinic*, 33:154–164.

Millon, T. (1981). *Disorders of Personality: DSM-III: Axis II*. New York: Wiley.

Modell, A. (1976). "The holding environment" and the therapeutic action of psychoanalysis. *J. American Psychoanalytic Association*, 24:285–307.

Money, J., and Ehrhardt, A. (1972). *Man & Woman, Boy & Girl*. Baltimore: Johns Hopkins University Press.

Money-Kyrle, R. (1956). Normal countertransference and some of its deviations. *International J. Psycho-Analysis*, 37:360–366.

Moore, B. (1968). Contribution to symposium on acting out. *International J. Psycho-Analysis*, 49:182–184.

Moore, B., and Fine, B. (1968). *A Glossary of Psychoanalytic Terms and Concepts*. New York: American Psychoanalytic Association.

Novey, S. (1959). The technique of supportive therapy in psychiatry and psychoanalysis. *Psychiatry*, 22:179–187.

Olinick, S. (1964). The negative therapeutic reaction. *International J. Psycho-Analysis*, 45:540–548.

Orwell, G. (1949). *1984*. New York: Harcourt.

Panel (1957). Acting out and its relation to impulse disorders, M. Kanzer, reporter. *J. American Psychoanalytic Association*, 5:136–145.

Panel (1970). Action, acting out and the symptomatic act, N. Atkins, reporter. *J. American Psychoanalytic Association*, 18:631–643.

Panel (1977). Varieties of oedipal distortions in severe character pathologies, W. S. Robbins, reporter. *J. American Psychoanalytic Association*, 25:201–218.

Pasamanick, B., Scarpitti, F., and Dinitz, S. (1967). *Schizophrenia in the Community: An Experimental Study in the Prevention of Hospitalization*. New York: Appleton-Century-Crofts.

Paz, C. (1976). *Estructuras y estados fronterizos en niños, adolescentes y adultos*. Buenos Aires: Grafica Santo Domingo.

Perry, J., and Klerman, G. (1980). Clinical features of the borderline personality disorder. *American J. Psychiatry*, 137:165–173.

Plutchik, R. (1980). *Emotions: A Psychoevolutionary Synthesis*. New York: Harper & Row.

Pope, H., Jones, J., Hindson, J., Cohen, B., and Gunderson, J. (1983). The validity of DSM-III borderline personality disorder. *Archives General Psychiatry*, 40:23–30.

Powdermaker, F. (1948). The techniques of the initial interview and methods of teaching them. *American J. Psychiatry*, 104:642–646.

Rabkin, L. (1965). The passive aggressiveness and learning. *Exceptional Child*, 32:1–3.

Racker, H. (1957). The meaning and uses of countertransference. *Psychoanalytic Quarterly*, 26:303–357.

Racker, H. (1968). *Transference and Countertransference*. New York: International Universities Press.

Rangell, L. (1968). A point of view on acting out. *International J. Psycho-Analysis*, 49:195–201.

Rapaport, D. (1960). *The Structure of Psychoanalytic Theory. Psychological Issues, Monograph 6*. New York: International Universities Press.

Rapaport, D. (1967). *Collected Papers of David Rapaport*, ed. M. M. Gill. New York: Basic Books.

Rapaport, D., and Gill, M. M. (1959). The points of view and assumptions of metapsychology. *International J. Psycho-Analysis*, 40:153–162.

Reich, A. (1951). On countertransference. *Psychoanalytic Contributions*. New York: International Universities Press, 1973, pp. 136–154.

Reich, W. (1933). *Character Analysis*. New York: Farrar, Straus, & Giroux, 1972.

Reider, N. (1957). Transference psychosis. *J. Hillside Hospital*, 6:131–149.

Rexford, E., ed. (1978). *A Developmental Approach to Problems of Acting Out*, revised edition. New York: International Universities Press.

Rey, J. (1979). Schizoid phenomena in the borderline. In *Advances in Psychotherapy of the Borderline Patient*, ed. J. LeBoit and A. Capponi. New York: Jason Aronson, pp. 449–484.

Rice, A. K. (1965). *Learning for Leadership*. London: Tavistock Publications.

Rinsley, D. (1977). An object-relations view of borderline personality. In *Borderline Personality Disorders*, ed. P. Hartocollis. New York: International Universities Press, pp. 47–70.

Rinsley, D. (1980). *Treatment of the Severely Disturbed Adolescent*. New York: Jason Aronson.

Riviere, J. (1936). A contribution to the analysis of the negative therapeutic reaction. *International J. Psycho-Analysis*, 17:304–320.

Robins, L. (1966). *Deviant Children Grown Up*. Baltimore: Williams & Wilkins.

Rogers, C. (1951). *Client-Centered Therapy*. Boston: Houghton Mifflin.

Romm, M. (1957). Transient psychotic episodes during psychoanalysis. *J. American Psychoanalytic Association*, 5:325–341.

Rosenfeld, H. (1963). Notes on psychopathology and psychoanalytic treatment of schizophrenia. In *Psychotherapy of Schizophrenia and Manic-Depressive States* (Psychiatric Research Report No. 17), ed. H. Azima and B. C. Glueck, Jr. Washington, D.C.: American Psychiatric Association, pp. 61–72.

Rosenfeld, H. (1964). On the psychopathology of narcissism: A clinical approach. *International J. Psycho-Analysis*, 45:332–337.

Rosenfeld, H. (1966). The need of patients to act out during analysis. *Psychoanalytic Forum*, 1:19–29.

Rosenfeld, H. (1971). A clinical approach to the psychoanalytic theory of the life and death instincts: An investigation into the aggressive aspects of narcissism. *International J. Psycho-Analysis*, 52:169–178.

Rosenfeld, H. (1975). Negative therapeutic reaction. In *Tactics and Techniques in Psychoanalytic Therapy*, vol. II, *Countertransference*, ed. P. L. Giovacchini. New York: Jason Aronson, pp. 217–228.

Rosenfeld, H. (1978). Notes on the psychopathology and psychoanalytic treatment of some borderline patients. *International J. Psycho-Analysis*, 59:215–221.

Rosenfeld, H. (1979a). Difficulties in the psychoanalytic treatment of borderline patients. In *Advances in Psychotherapy of the Borderline Patient*, ed. J. LeBoit and A. Capponi. New York: Jason Aronson, pp. 187–206.

Rosenfeld, H. (1979b). Transference psychosis in the borderline patient. In *Advances in Psychotherapy of the Borderline Patient*, ed. J. LeBoit and A. Capponi. New York: Jason Aronson, pp. 485–510.

Schilder, P. (1938). *Psychotherapy*. New York: Norton, 1951.

Schlesinger, H. (1969). Diagnosis and prescription for psychotherapy. *Bulletin of the Menninger Clinic*, 33:269–278.

Schneider, K. (1950). Psychoanalytic therapy with the borderline adult: Some principles concerning technique. In *New Perspectives on Psychotherapy of the Borderline Adult*, ed. J. Masterson. New York: Brunner/Mazel, pp. 41–65.

Searles, H. (1965). *Collected Papers on Schizophrenia and Related Subjects*. New York: International Universities Press.

Searles, H. (1977). Dual- and multiple-identity processes in borderline ego functioning. In *Borderline Personality Disorders*, ed. P. Hartocollis. New York: International Universities Press, pp. 441–455.

Searles, H. (1978). Psychoanalytic therapy with the borderline adult: Some principles concerning technique. In *New Perspectives on Psychotherapy of the Borderline Adult*, ed. J. Masterson. New York: Brunner/Mazel, pp. 41–65.

Searles, H. (1979). The countertransference with the borderline patient. In *Advances in Psychotherapy of the Borderline Patient*, ed. J. LeBoit and A. Capponi. New York: Jason Aronson, pp. 309–346.

Segal, H. (1964). *Introduction to the Work of Melanie Klein*. New York: Basic Books.

Segal, H. (1967). Melanie Klein's technique. In *Psychoanalytic Techniques: A Handbook for the Practicing Psychoanalyst*, ed. B. Wolman. New York/London: Basic Books, pp. 168–190.

Segal, H. (1979). *Klein*. Glasgow: Collins.

Selzer, M. (1981). The consultant interview. Unpublished.

Shapiro, D. (1965). *Neurotic Styles*. New York: Basic Books.

Shapiro, E., Zinner, J., Shapiro, R., and Berkovitz, D. (1975). The influence of family experience on borderline personality development. *International Review Psycho-Analysis*, 2:399–412.

Sharpe, E. (1931). Anxiety: Outbreak and resolution. In *Collected Papers on Psycho-Analysis*, ed. M. Brierly. New York: Brunner/Mazel, 1978, pp. 67–80.

Simmel, E. (1929). Psychoanalytic treatment in a sanatorium. *International J. Psycho-Analysis*, 10:70–89.

Small, T., Small, J., Alig, V., and Moore, D. (1970). Passive-aggressive personality disorder: A search for a syndrome. *American J. Psychiatry*, 126:973–983.

Spitz, R. (1965). *The First Year of Life*. New York: International Universities Press.

Spitz, R. (1972). Bridges: On anticipation, duration, and meaning. *J. American Psychoanalytic Association*, 20:721–735.

Spitzer, R., and Williams, J. (1980). Classification of mental disorder and DSM-III. In *Comprehensive Textbook of Psychiatry, III*, ed. H. I. Kaplan, A. M. Freedman, and B. J. Sadock. Baltimore: Williams & Wilkins, pp. 1035–1072.

Stafford-Clark, D. (1970). Supportive psychotherapy. In *Modern Trends in Psycho-*

logical Medicine, vol. 2, ed. D. J. Price. New York: Appleton-Century-Crofts, pp. 277–295.

Stanton, A., and Schwartz, M. (1954). *The Mental Hospital*. New York: Basic Books.

Stern, A. (1938). Psychoanalytic investigation of and therapy in the borderline group of neuroses. *Psychoanalytic Quarterly*, 7:467–489.

Stoller, R. (1977). Primary femininity. In *Female Psychology*, ed. H. P. Blum. New York: International Universities Press, pp. 59–78.

Stone, L. (1954). The widening scope of indications for psychoanalysis. *J. American Psychoanalytic Association*, 2:567–594.

Stone, M. (1980). *The Borderline Syndromes*. New York: McGraw-Hill.

Stone, M. (1981). Borderline syndromes: A consideration of subtypes and an overview, directions for research. In *The Psychiatric Clinics of North America*, vol. 4. Philadelphia: Saunders, pp. 3–24.

Strachey, J. (1934). The nature of the therapeutic action for psycho-analysis. *International J. Psycho-Analysis*, 15:127–159.

Sullivan, H. (1953a). *Conceptions of Modern Psychiatry*. New York: Norton.

Sullivan, H. (1953b). *The Interpersonal Theory of Psychiatry*. New York: Norton.

Sullivan, H. (1954). *The Psychiatric Interview*. New York: Norton.

Sullivan, H. (1956). *Clinical Studies in Psychiatry*. New York: Norton.

Sullivan, H. (1962). *Schizophrenia as a Human Process*. New York: Norton.

Sutherland, J. (1952). Notes on psychoanalytic group therapy. I: Therapy and training. *Psychiatry*, 15:111–117.

Tarachow, S. (1963). *An Introduction to Psychotherapy*. New York: International Universities Press.

Ticho, E. (1972). Termination of psychoanalysis: Treatment goals, life goals. *Psychoanalytic Quarterly*, 41:315–333.

Tinbergen, N. (1951). An attempt at synthesis. In *The Study of Instinct*. New York: Oxford University Press, pp. 101–127.

Tower, L. (1956). Countertransference. *J. American Psychoanalytic Association*, 4:224–255.

Tramer, M. (1931). Psychopathic personalities. *Schweizer Medizinische Wochenschrift*, 217:271–322.

Valenstein, A. F. (1973). On attachment to painful feelings and the negative therapeutic reaction. *Psychoanalytic Study of the Child*, 28:365–392. New Haven: Yale University Press.

Volkan, V. D. (1976). *Primitive Internalized Object Relations*. New York: International Universities Press.

Volkan, V. D. (1979). The "glass bubble" of the narcissistic patient. In *Advances in Psychotherapy of the Borderline Patient*, ed. J. LeBoit and A. Capponi. New York: Jason Aronson, pp. 405–431.

Wallerstein, R. (1965). The goals of psychoanalysis: A survey of analytic viewpoints. *J. American Psychoanalytic Association*, 3:748–770.

Wallerstein, R. (1966). The current state of psychotherapy: Theory, practice, research. In *Psychotherapy and Psychoanalysis: Theory, Practice, Research.* New York: International Universities Press, 1975, pp. 135–186.

Wallerstein, R. (1967). Reconstruction and mastery in the transference psychosis. *J. American Psychoanalytic Association,* 15:551–583.

Wallerstein, R. (1969). Introduction to panel: Psychoanalysis and psychotherapy. *International J. Psycho-Analysis,* 50:117–126.

Wallerstein, R., and Robbins, L. (1956). The psychotherapy research project of the Menninger Foundation (Part IV: Concepts). *Bulletin of the Menninger Clinic,* 20:239–262.

Whitehorn, J. (1944). Guide to interviewing and clinical personality study. *Archives Neurology and Psychiatry,* 52:197–216.

Whiteley, J., and Gordon, J. (1979). *Group Approaches in Psychiatry.* London: Routledge & Kegan Paul.

Whitman, R., Trosman, H., and Koenig, R. (1954). Clinical assessment of passive-aggressive personality. *Archives Neurology and Psychiatry,* 72:540–549.

Will, O. (1967). Schizophrenia: The problem of origin. In *The Origins of Schizophrenia,* ed. J. Romano. Amsterdam/New York: Excerpta Medica Foundation, pp. 214–227.

Wilson, E. O. (1975). *Sociobiology: The New Synthesis.* Cambridge: Harvard University Press.

Winnicott, D. (1949). Hate in the counter-transference. In *Collected Papers.* New York: Basic Books, 1958, pp. 194–203.

Winnicott , D. (1958). *Collected Papers: Through Paediatrics to Psycho-Analysis.* New York: Basic Books.

Winnicott, D. (1960a). Ego distortion in terms of true and fasle self. In *The Maturational Processes and the Facilitating Environment.* New York: International Universities Press, 1965, pp. 140–152.

Winnicott, D. (1960b). The theory of the parent–infant relationship. In *The Maturational Processes and the Facilitating Environment.* New York: International Universities Press, 1965, pp. 37–55.

Winnicott, D. (1963). The development of the capacity for concern. In *The Maturational Processes and the Facilitating Environment.* New York: International Universities Press, 1965, pp. 73–82.

Winnicott, D. (1965). *The Maturational Processes and the Facilitating Environment.* New York: International Universities Press.

Zetzel, E. R. (1956). The concept of transference. In *The Capacity for Emotional Growth.* New York: International Universities Press, 1970, pp. 168–181.

Zetzel, E. R. (1968). The so-called good hysteric. In *The Capacity for Emotional Growth.* New York: International Universities Press, 1970, pp. 229–245.

Zetzel, E. R. (1971). A developmental approach to the borderline patient. *American J. Psychiatry,* 127:867–871.

Index